PERFECT WORLD

5 Rie Aruga

Research Help /
Kazuo Abe (Abe Kensetsu Inc.)

contents

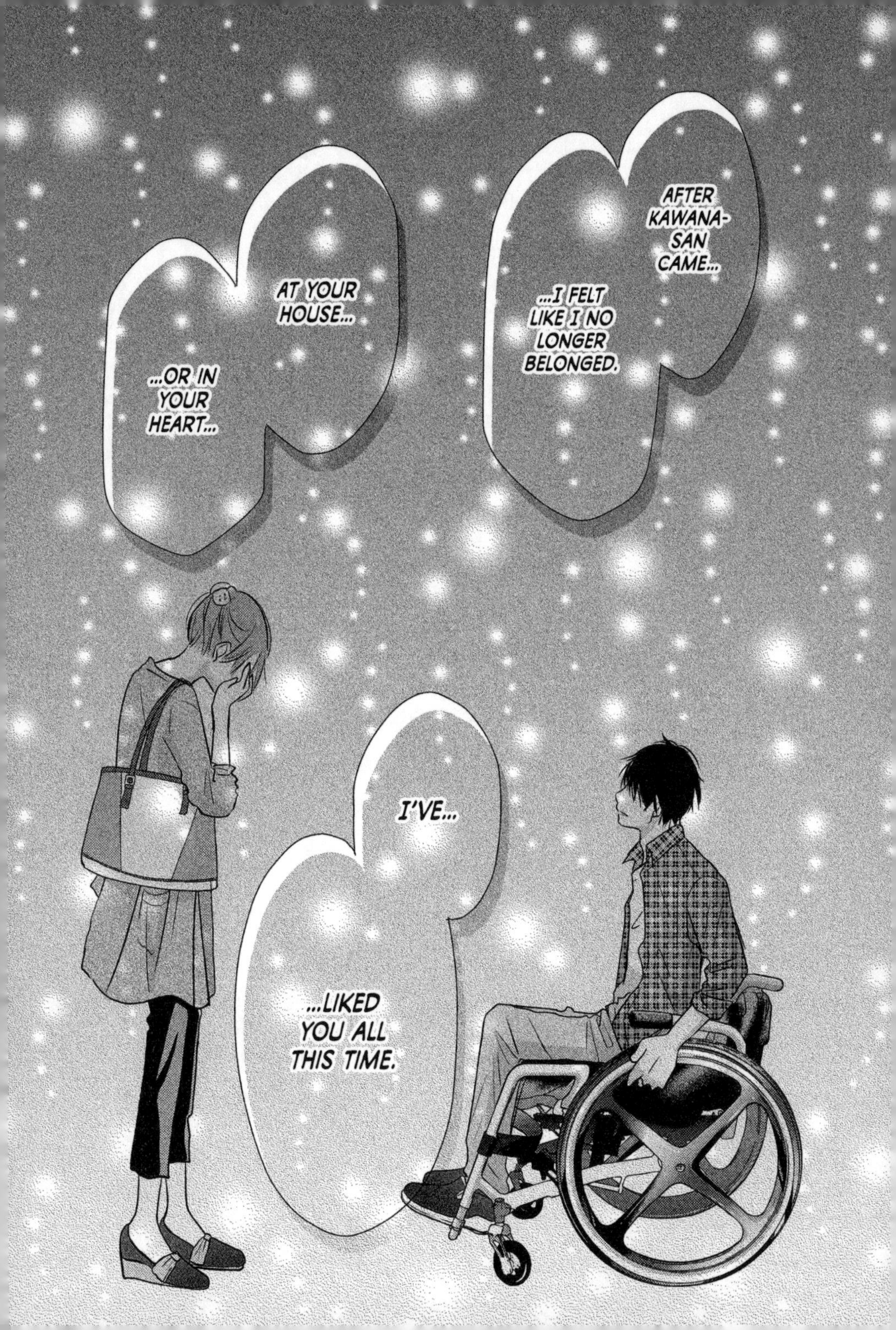
AFTER KAWANA-SAN CAME...
...I FELT LIKE I NO LONGER BELONGED.
AT YOUR HOUSE...
...OR IN YOUR HEART...
I'VE...
...LIKED YOU ALL THIS TIME.

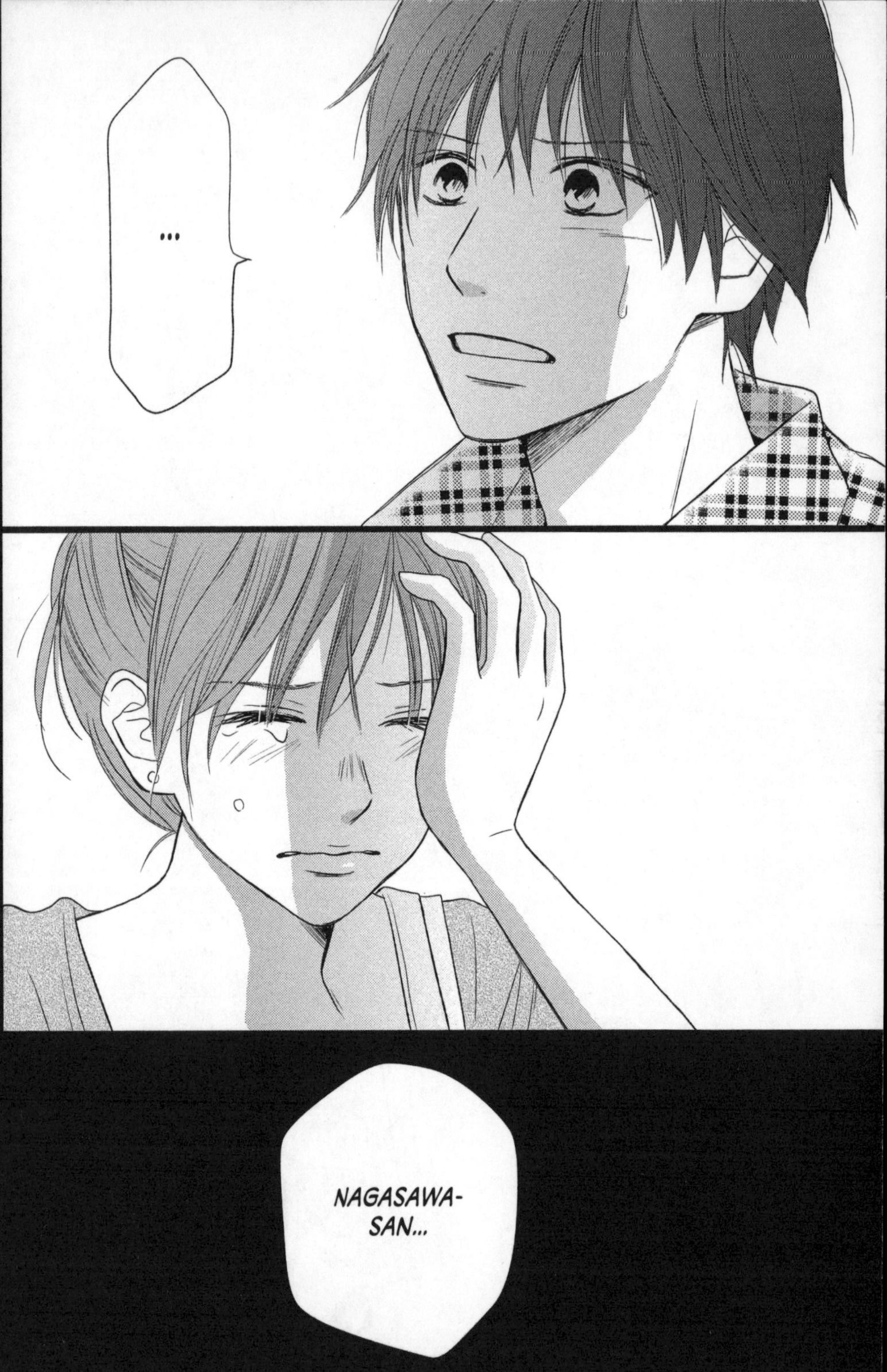
...
NAGASAWA-SAN...

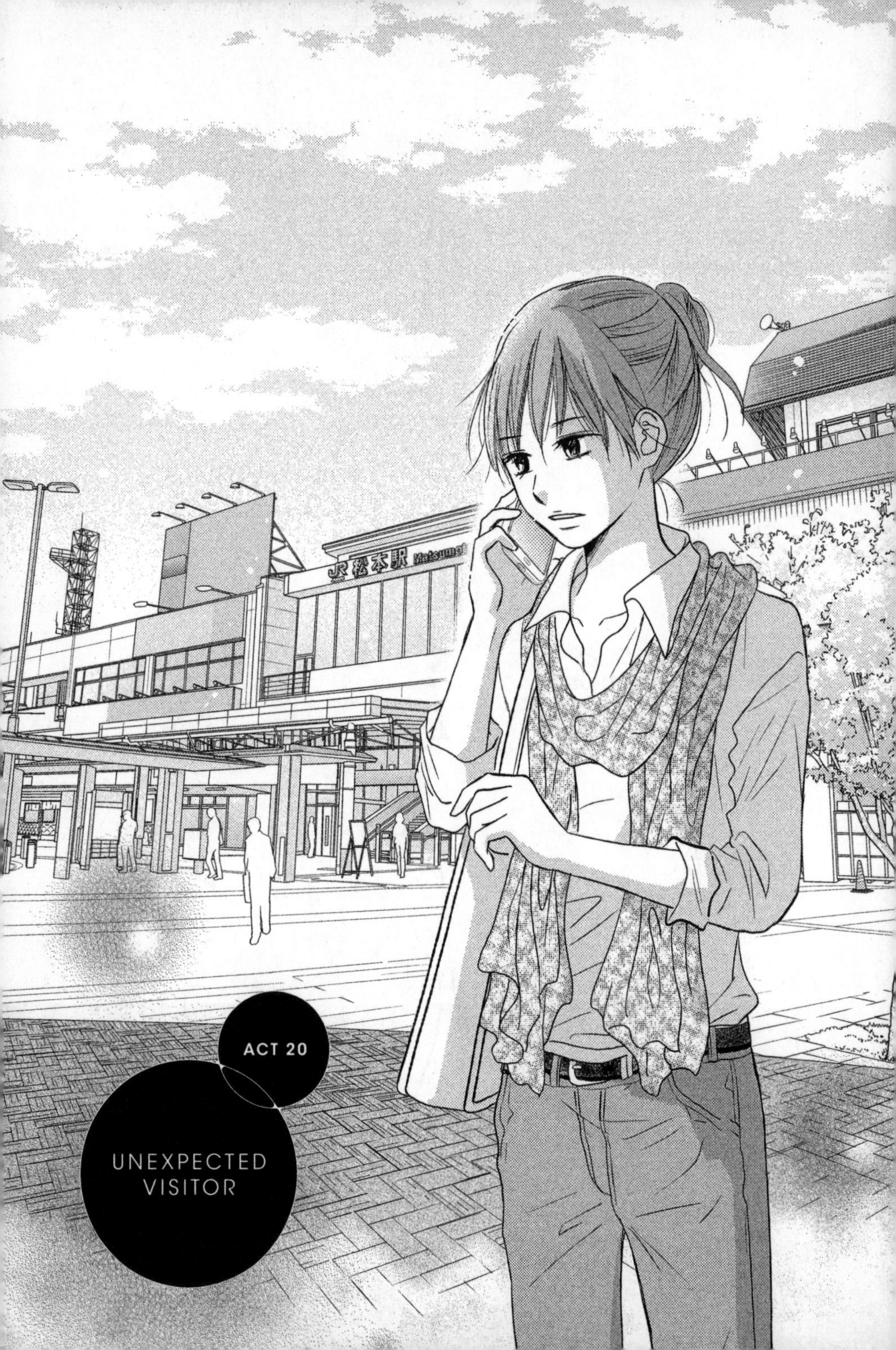
JR 松本駅
ACT 20
UNEXPECTED VISITOR

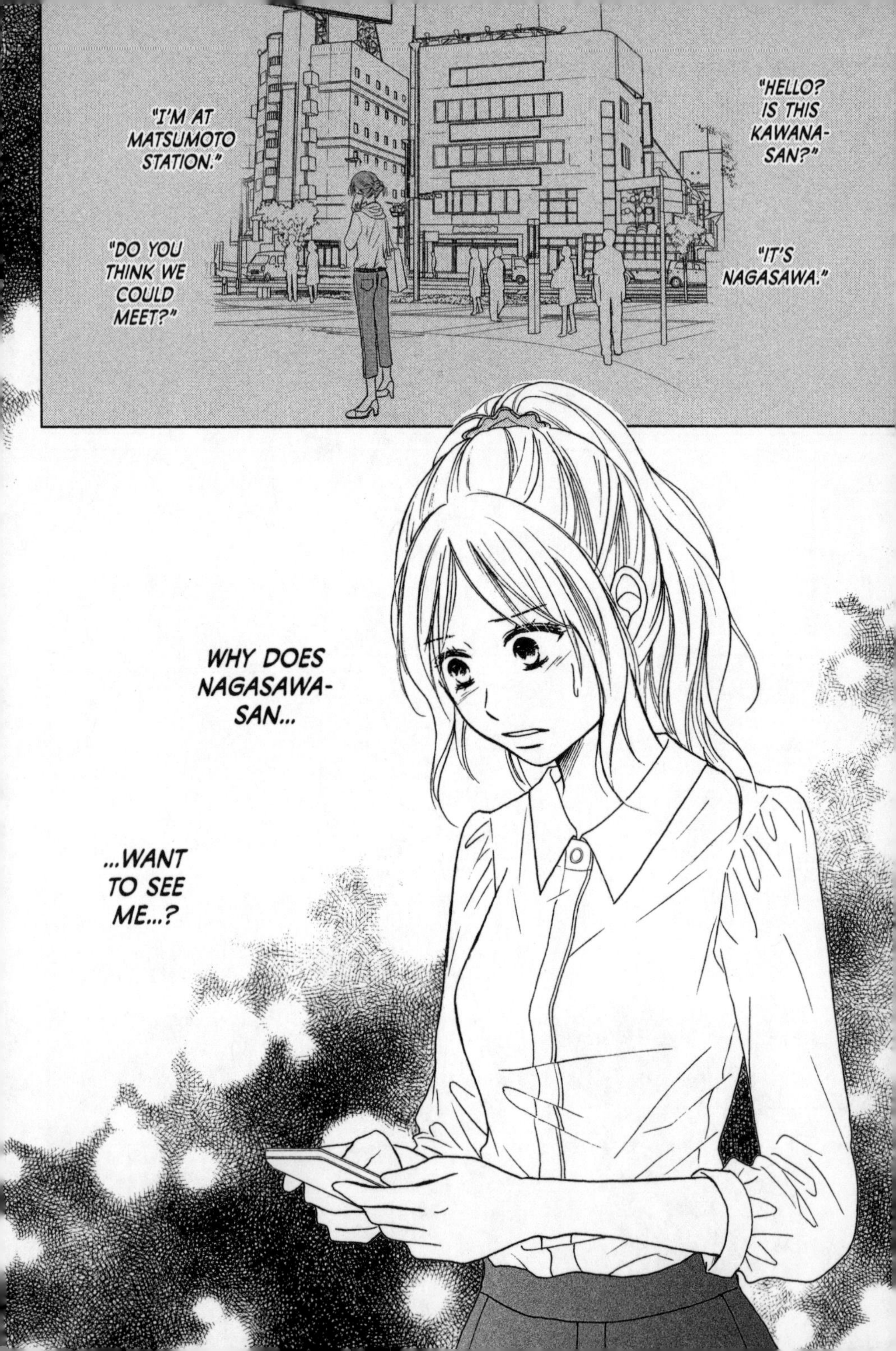
"HELLO? IS THIS KAWANA-SAN?"
"IT'S NAGASAWA."
"I'M AT MATSUMOTO STATION."
"DO YOU THINK WE COULD MEET?"
WHY DOES NAGASAWA-SAN...
...WANT TO SEE ME...?

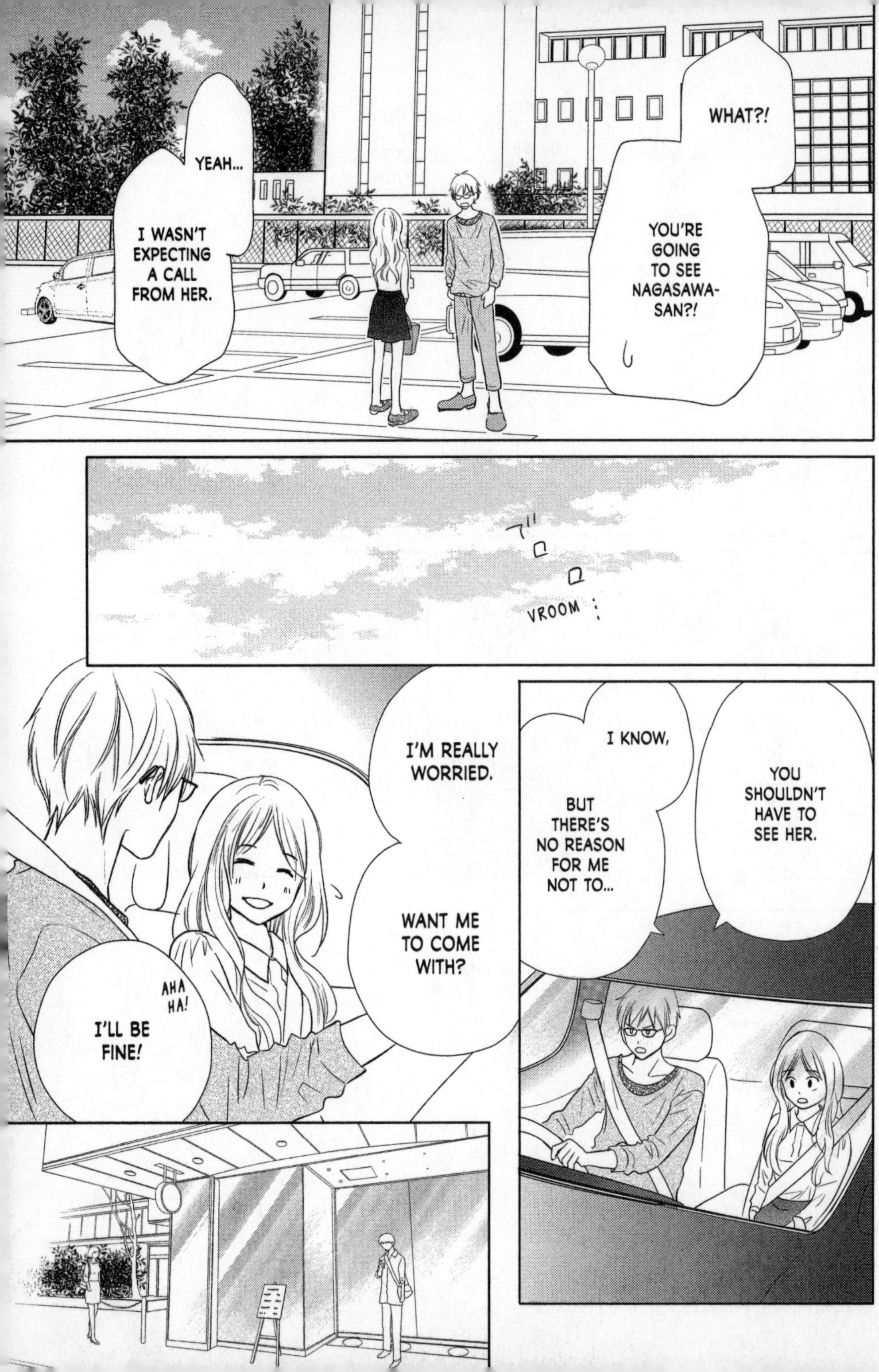
WHAT?!
YOU'RE GOING TO SEE NAGASAWA-SAN?!
YEAH...
I WASN'T EXPECTING A CALL FROM HER.
ブロロ
VROOM
YOU SHOULDN'T HAVE TO SEE HER.
I KNOW,
BUT THERE'S NO REASON FOR ME NOT TO...
I'M REALLY WORRIED.
WANT ME TO COME WITH?
AHA HA!
I'LL BE FINE!

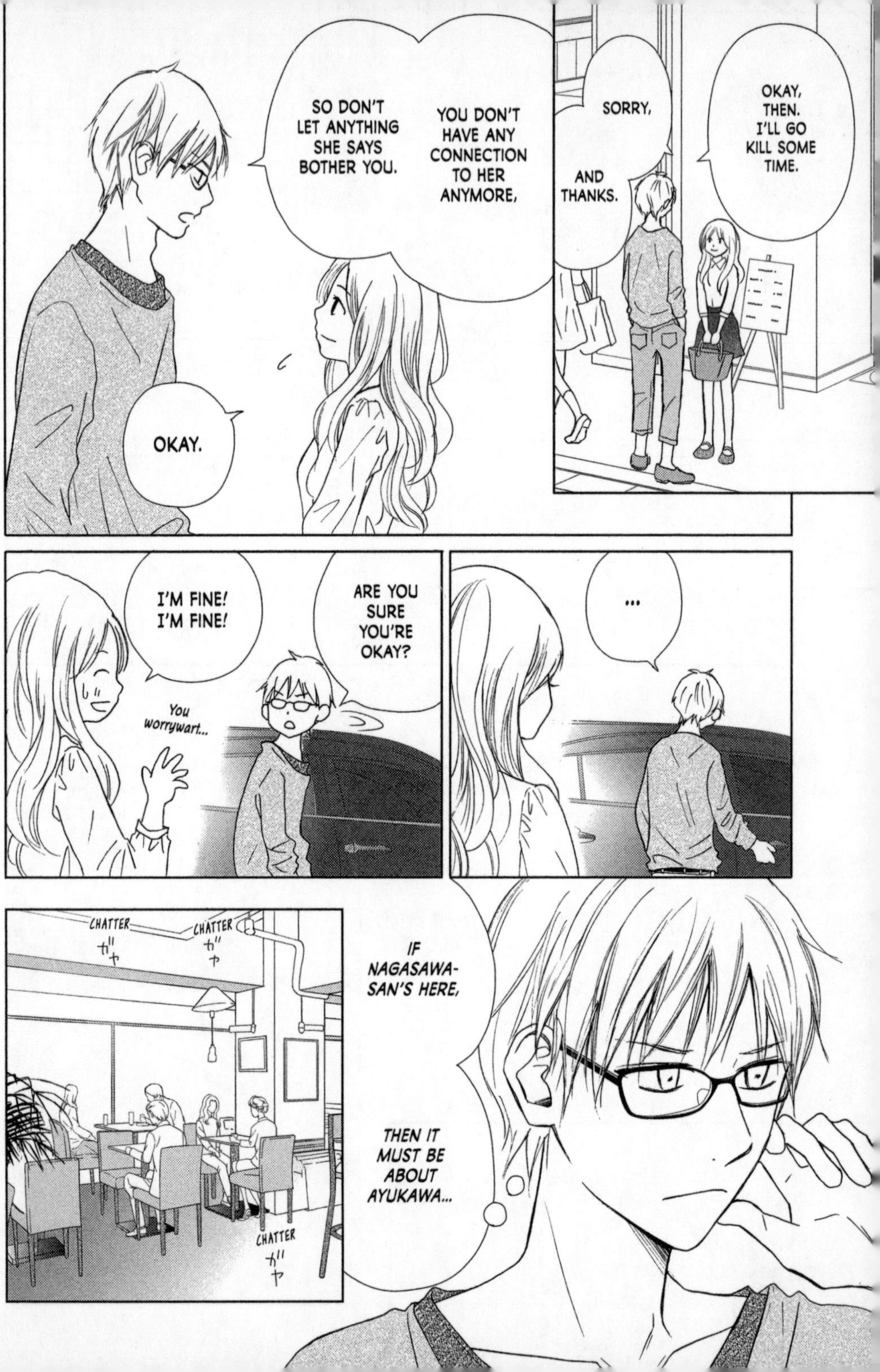
OKAY, THEN. I'LL GO KILL SOME TIME.
SORRY,
AND THANKS.
YOU DON'T HAVE ANY CONNECTION TO HER ANYMORE,
SO DON'T LET ANYTHING SHE SAYS BOTHER YOU.
OKAY.
...
ARE YOU SURE YOU'RE OKAY?
I'M FINE! I'M FINE!
You worrywart...
IF NAGASAWA-SAN'S HERE,
THEN IT MUST BE ABOUT AYUKAWA...
CHATTER
ガヤ
CHATTER
ガヤ
CHATTER
ガヤ

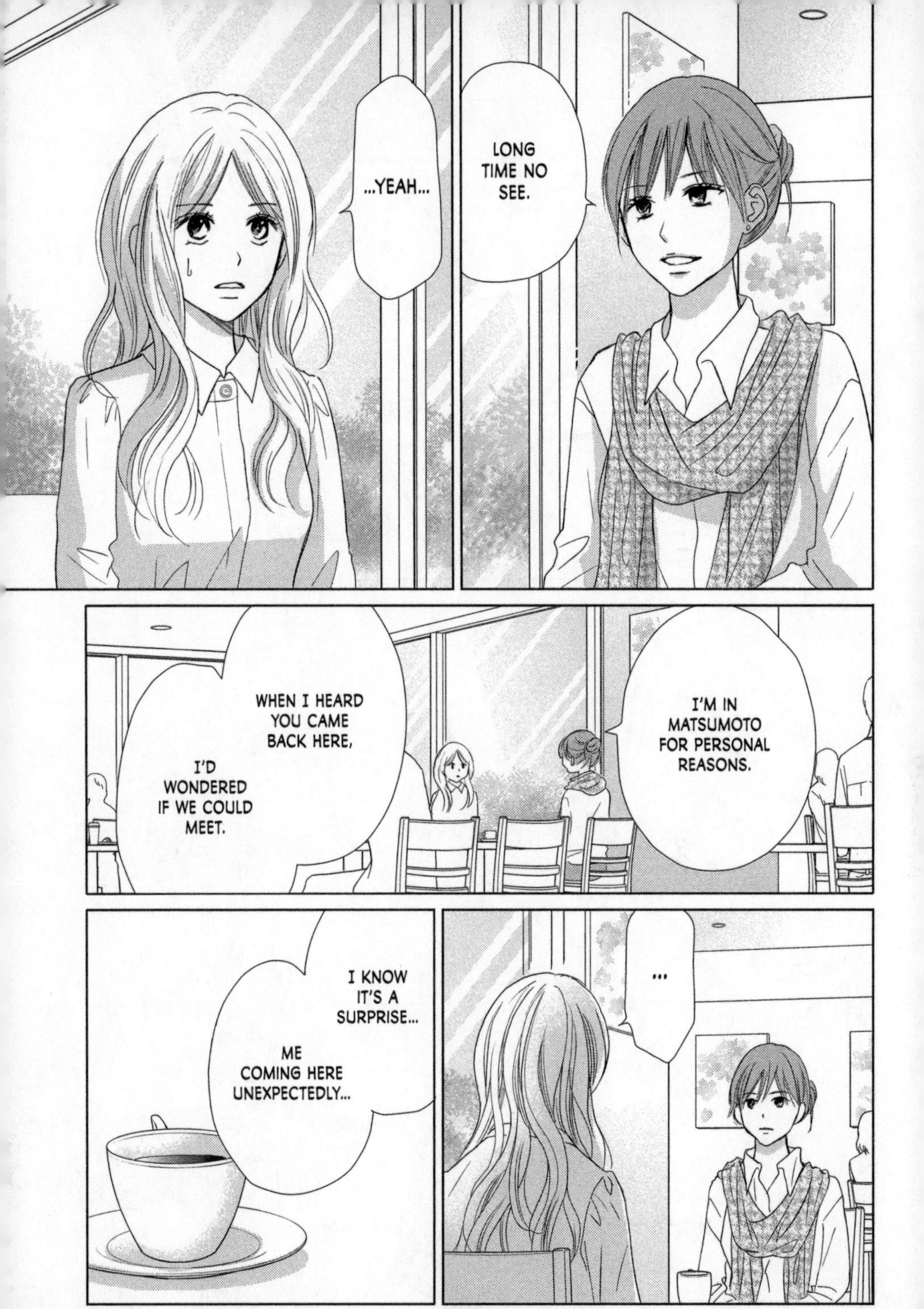
LONG TIME NO SEE.
...YEAH...
I'M IN MATSUMOTO FOR PERSONAL REASONS.
WHEN I HEARD YOU CAME BACK HERE,
I'D WONDERED IF WE COULD MEET.
...
I KNOW IT'S A SURPRISE...
ME COMING HERE UNEXPECTEDLY...

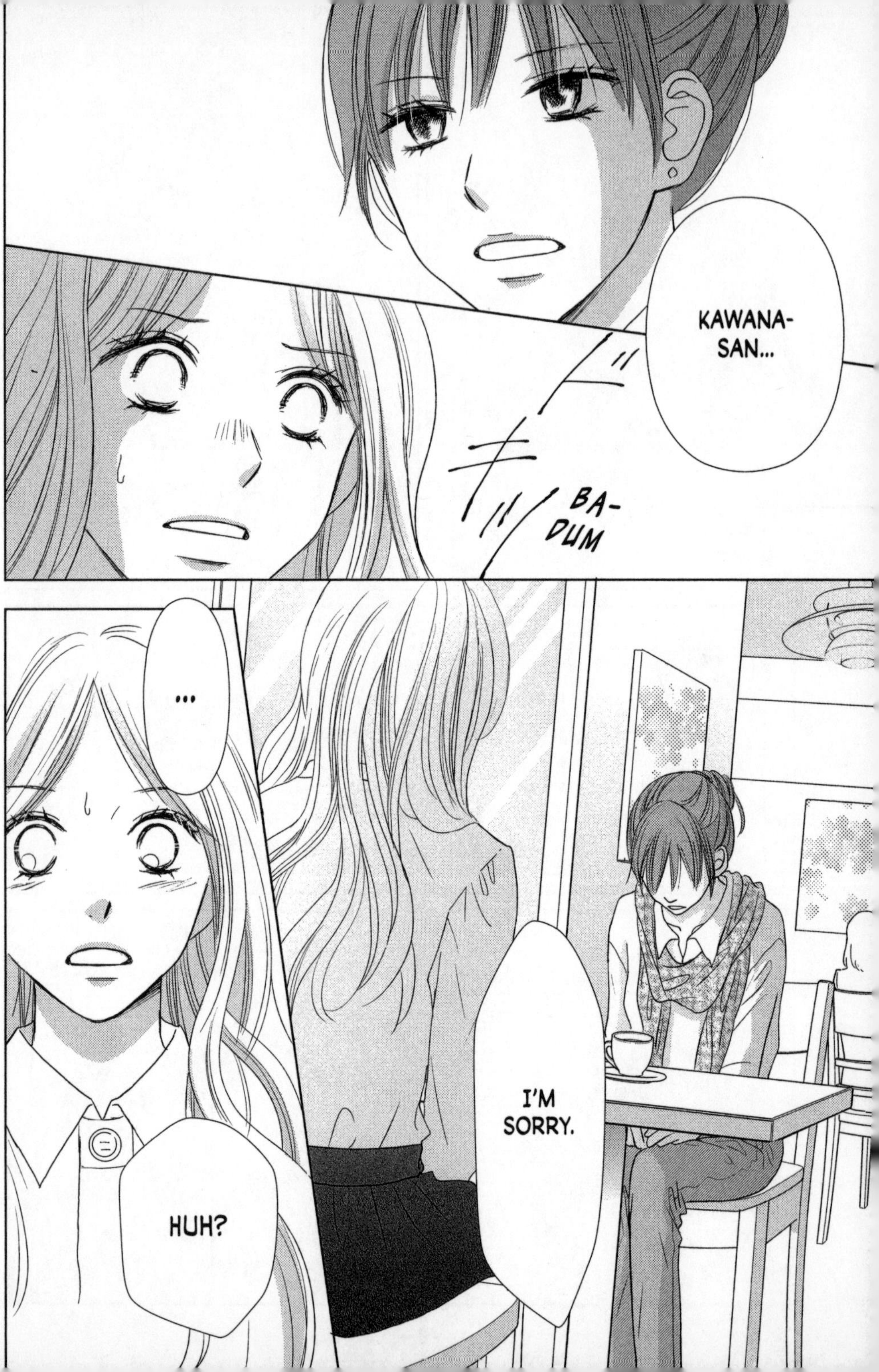
KAWANA-SAN...
BA-DUM
I'M SORRY.
...
HUH?

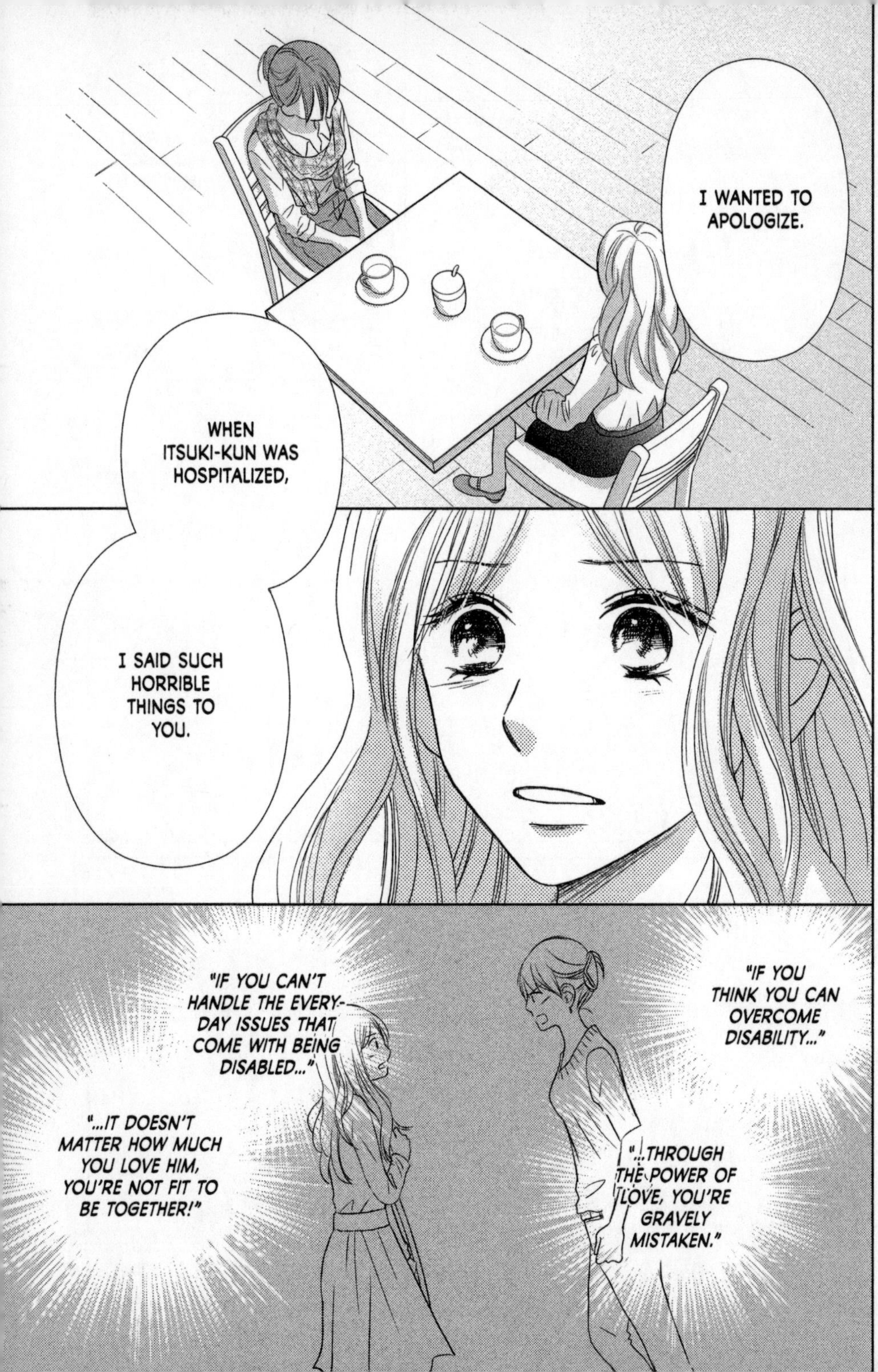
I WANTED TO APOLOGIZE.
WHEN ITSUKI-KUN WAS HOSPITALIZED,
I SAID SUCH HORRIBLE THINGS TO YOU.
"IF YOU THINK YOU CAN OVERCOME DISABILITY..."
"...THROUGH THE POWER OF LOVE, YOU'RE GRAVELY MISTAKEN."
"IF YOU CAN'T HANDLE THE EVERY-DAY ISSUES THAT COME WITH BEING DISABLED..."
"...IT DOESN'T MATTER HOW MUCH YOU LOVE HIM, YOU'RE NOT FIT TO BE TOGETHER!"

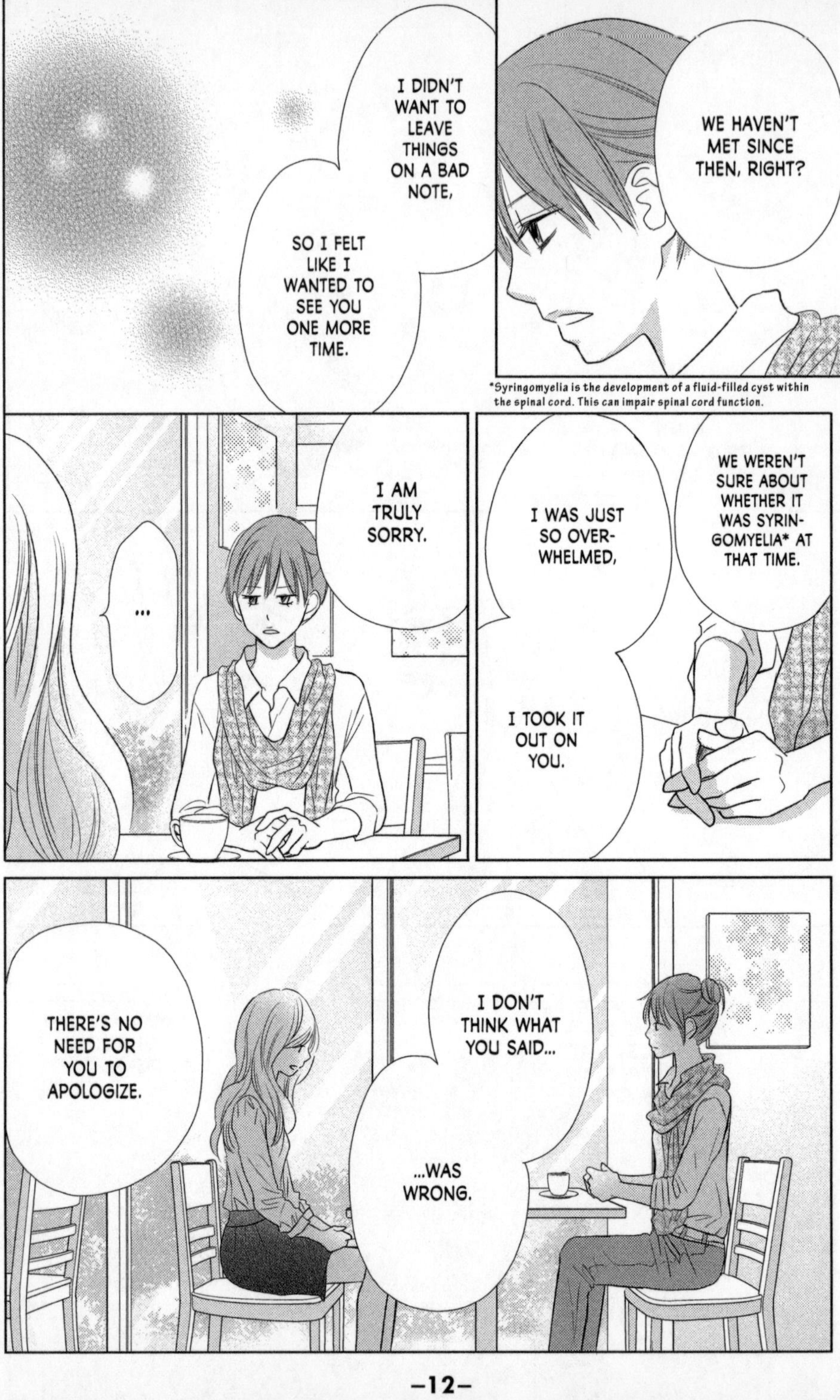
WE HAVEN'T MET SINCE THEN, RIGHT?
I DIDN'T WANT TO LEAVE THINGS ON A BAD NOTE,
SO I FELT LIKE I WANTED TO SEE YOU ONE MORE TIME.
WE WEREN'T SURE ABOUT WHETHER IT WAS SYRIN-GOMYELIA* AT THAT TIME.
I WAS JUST SO OVER-WHELMED,
I TOOK IT OUT ON YOU.
I AM TRULY SORRY.
...
I DON'T THINK WHAT YOU SAID...
...WAS WRONG.
THERE'S NO NEED FOR YOU TO APOLOGIZE.

*Syringomyelia is the development of a fluid-filled cyst within the spinal cord. This can impair spinal cord function.

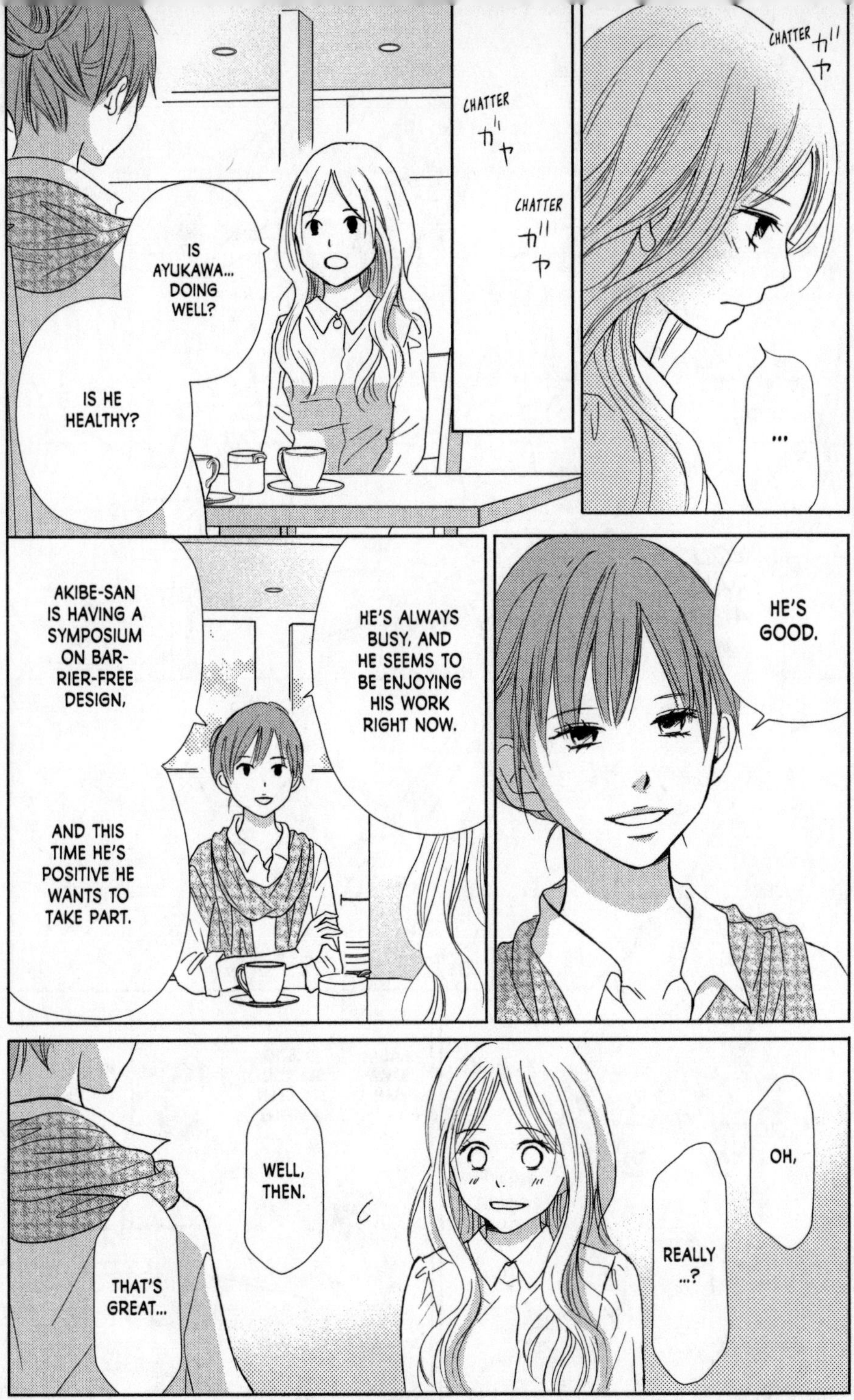
CHATTER ガヤ
...
CHATTER ガヤ
CHATTER ガヤ
IS AYUKAWA... DOING WELL?
IS HE HEALTHY?
HE'S GOOD.
HE'S ALWAYS BUSY, AND HE SEEMS TO BE ENJOYING HIS WORK RIGHT NOW.
AKIBE-SAN IS HAVING A SYMPOSIUM ON BAR-RIER-FREE DESIGN,
AND THIS TIME HE'S POSITIVE HE WANTS TO TAKE PART.
OH,
REALLY ...?
WELL, THEN.
THAT'S GREAT...

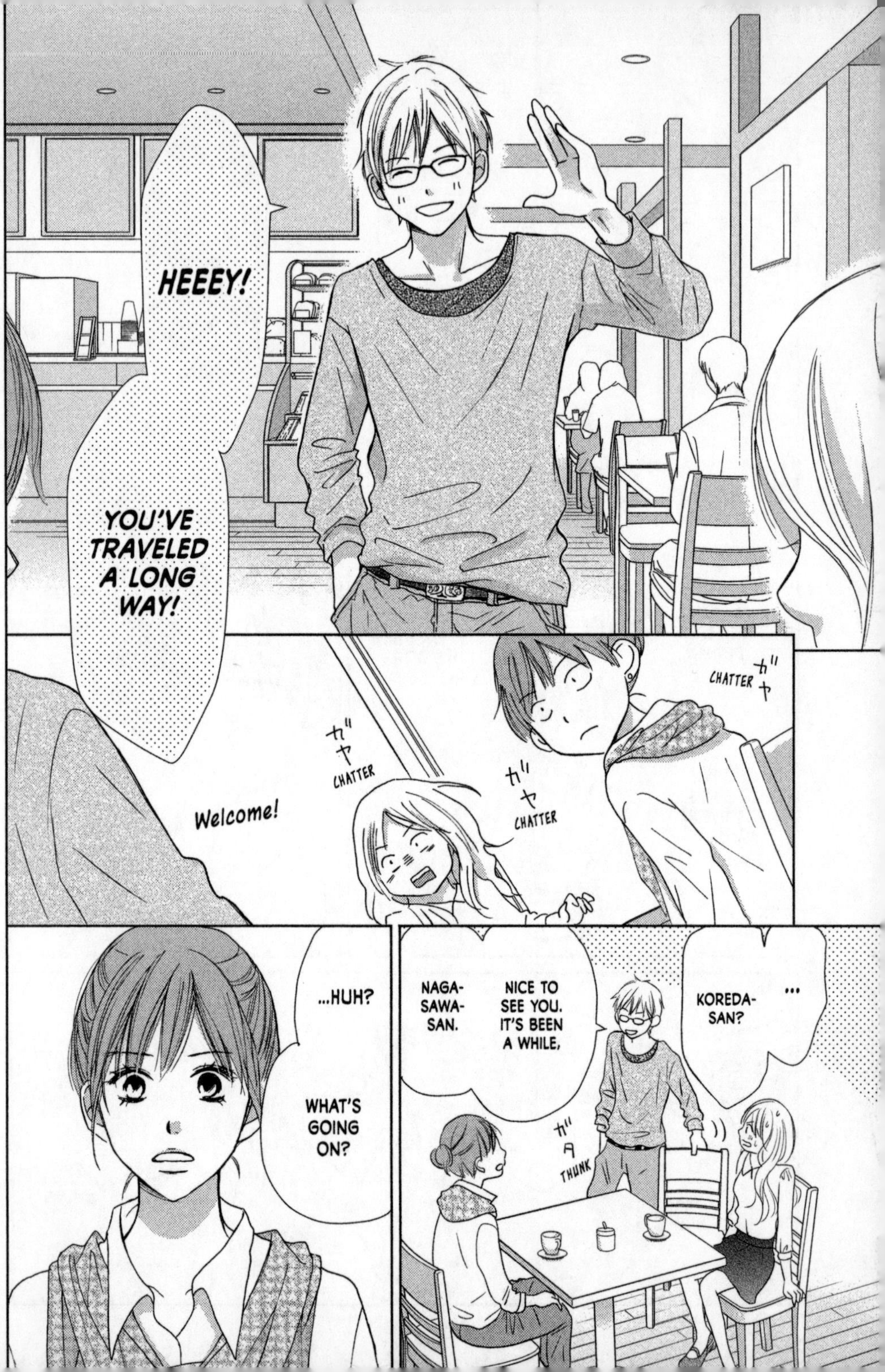
HEEEY!
YOU'VE TRAVELED A LONG WAY!
ガヤ CHATTER
ガヤ CHATTER
ガヤ CHATTER
Welcome!
...
KOREDA-SAN?
NICE TO SEE YOU. IT'S BEEN A WHILE,
NAGA-SAWA-SAN.
ガタ THUNK
...HUH?
WHAT'S GOING ON?

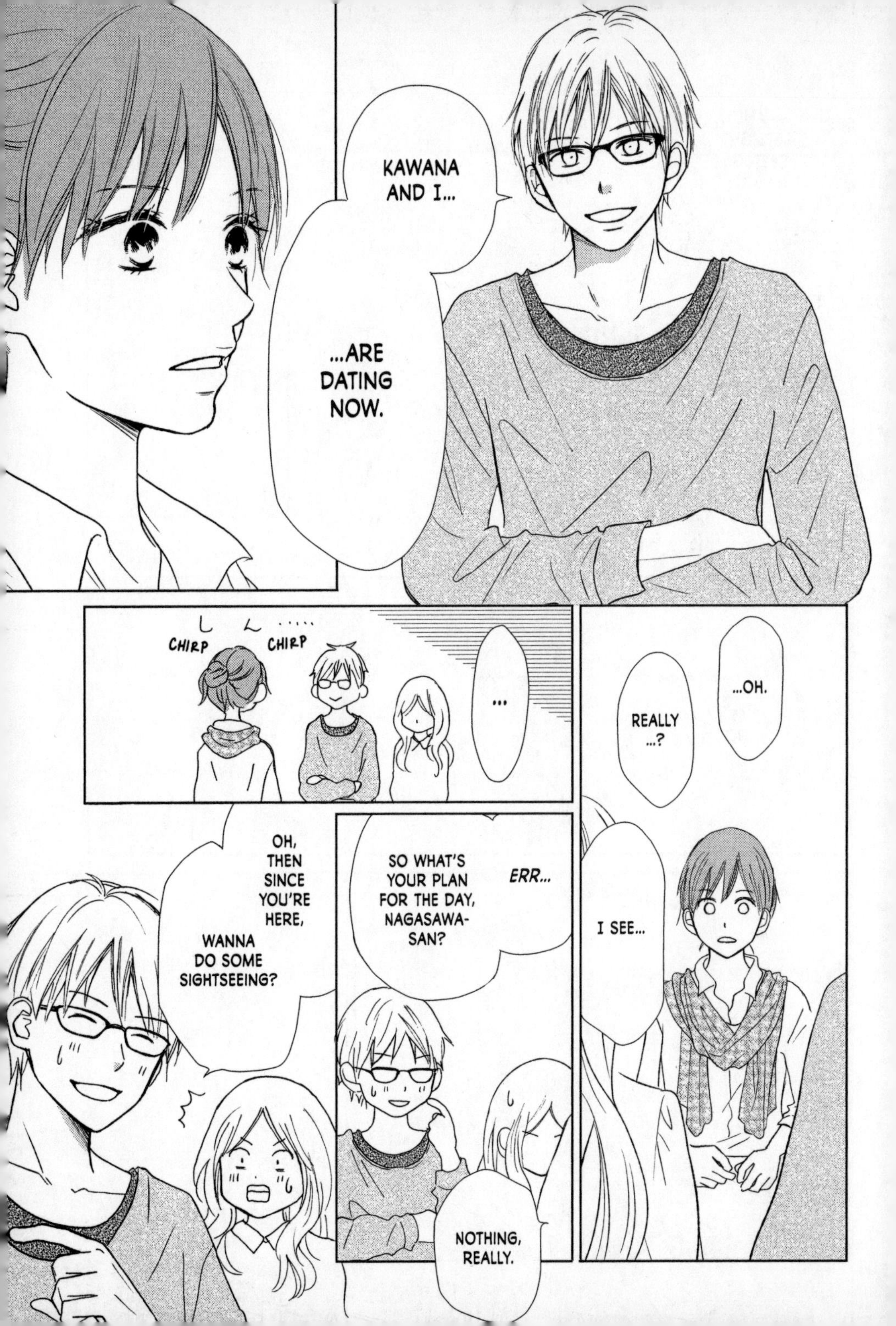
KAWANA AND I...
...ARE DATING NOW.
...OH.
REALLY ...?
I SEE...
...
しん.....
CHIRP
CHIRP
SO WHAT'S YOUR PLAN FOR THE DAY, NAGASAWA-SAN?
ERR...
NOTHING, REALLY.
OH, THEN SINCE YOU'RE HERE,
WANNA DO SOME SIGHTSEEING?

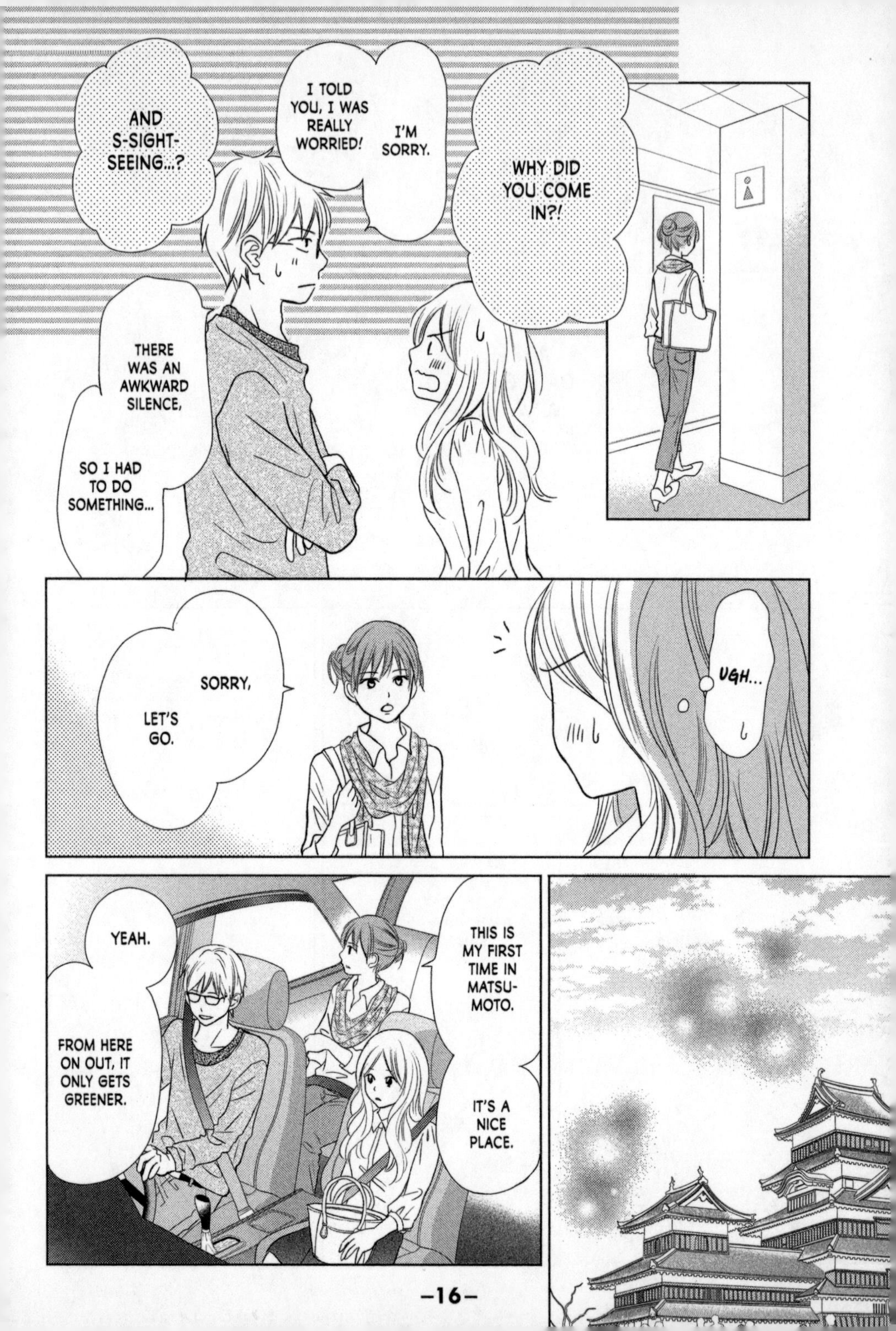
WHY DID YOU COME IN?!
I'M SORRY.
I TOLD YOU, I WAS REALLY WORRIED!
AND S-SIGHT-SEEING...?
THERE WAS AN AWKWARD SILENCE,
SO I HAD TO DO SOMETHING...
UGH...
SORRY,
LET'S GO.
THIS IS MY FIRST TIME IN MATSU-MOTO.
IT'S A NICE PLACE.
YEAH.
FROM HERE ON OUT, IT ONLY GETS GREENER.

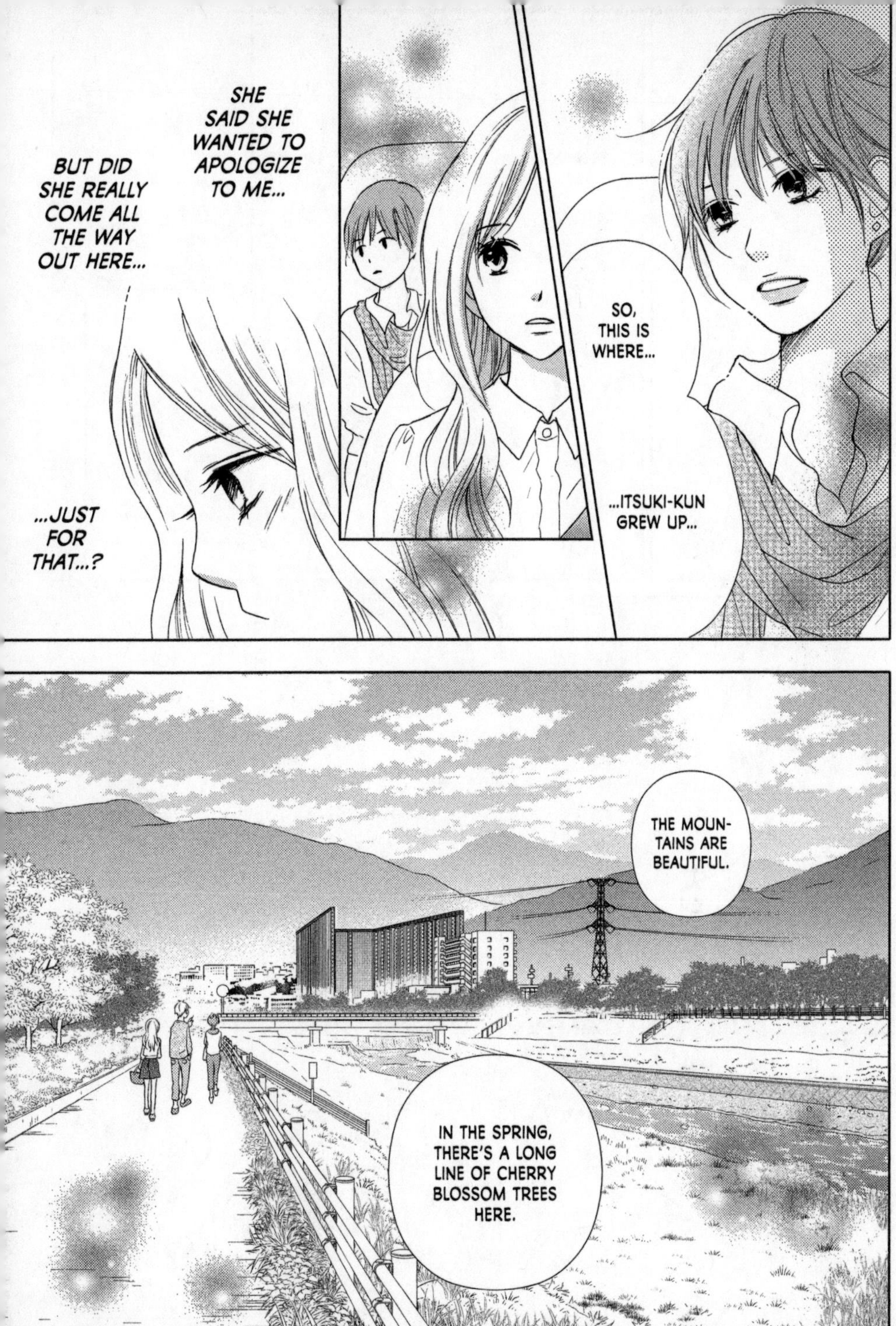
SO, THIS IS WHERE...
...ITSUKI-KUN GREW UP...
SHE SAID SHE WANTED TO APOLOGIZE TO ME...
BUT DID SHE REALLY COME ALL THE WAY OUT HERE...
...JUST FOR THAT...?
THE MOUN-TAINS ARE BEAUTIFUL.
IN THE SPRING, THERE'S A LONG LINE OF CHERRY BLOSSOM TREES HERE.

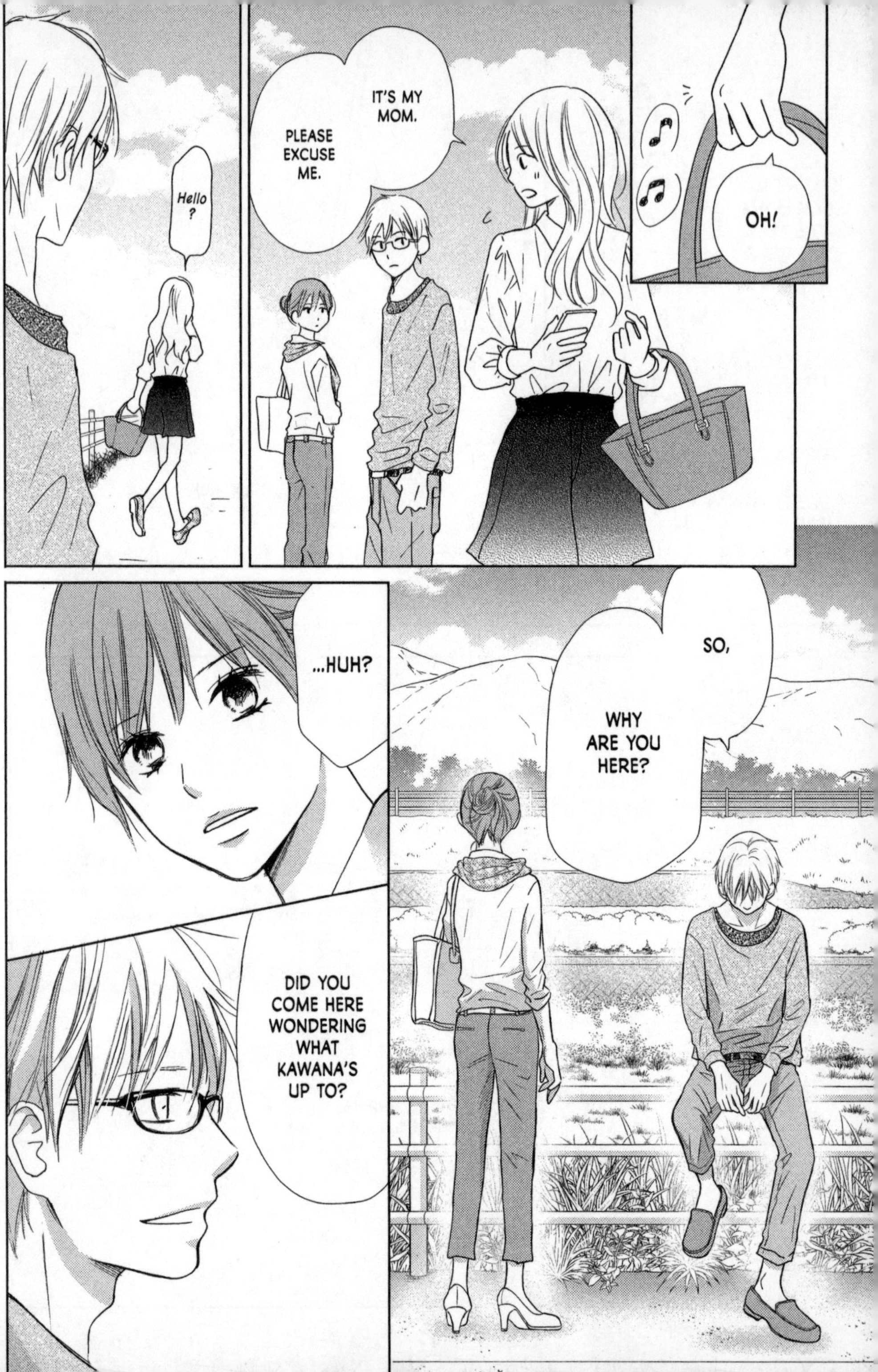
OH!
IT'S MY MOM.
PLEASE EXCUSE ME.
Hello?
SO,
WHY ARE YOU HERE?
...HUH?
DID YOU COME HERE WONDERING WHAT KAWANA'S UP TO?

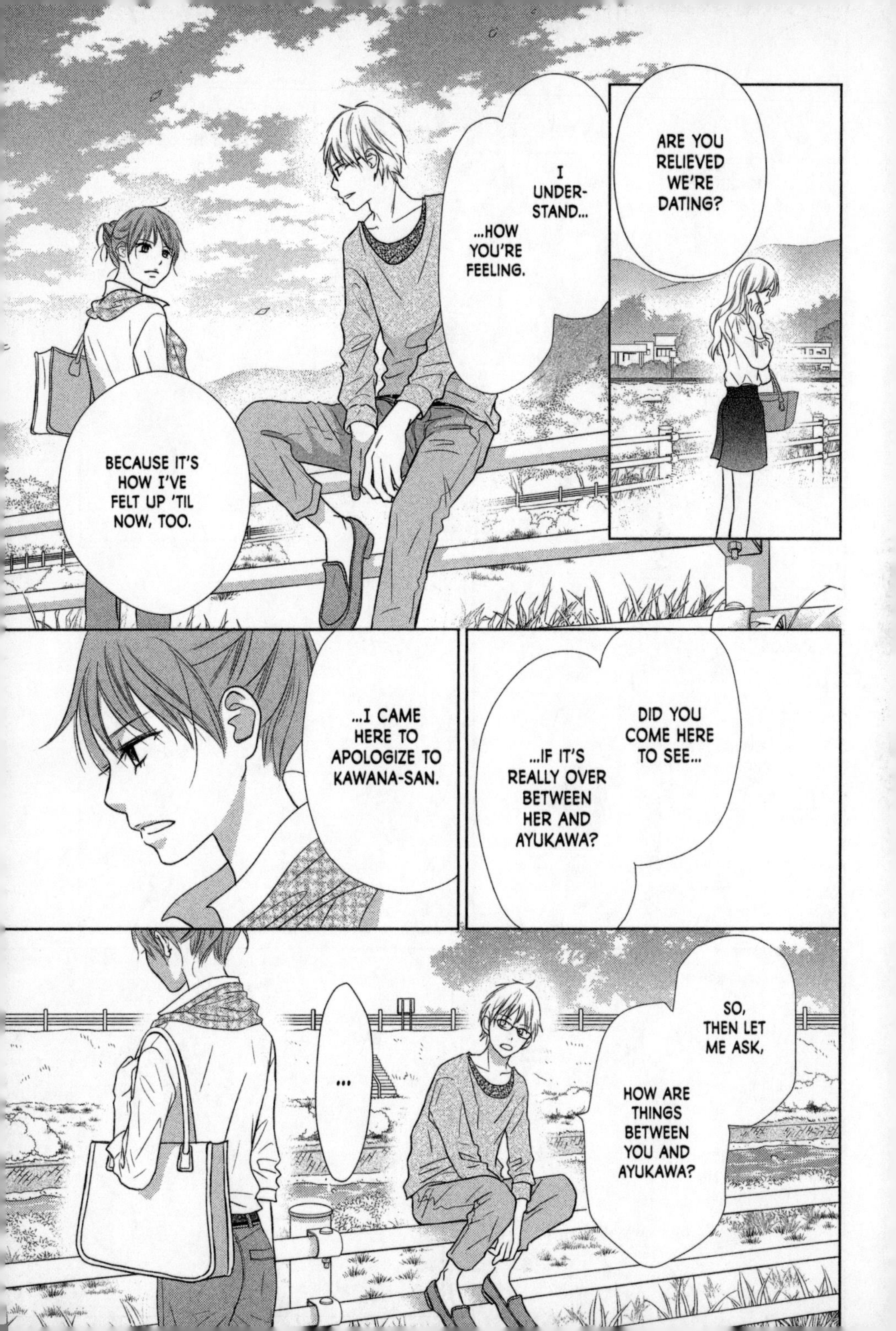
ARE YOU RELIEVED WE'RE DATING?
I UNDERSTAND...
...HOW YOU'RE FEELING.
BECAUSE IT'S HOW I'VE FELT UP 'TIL NOW, TOO.
DID YOU COME HERE TO SEE...
...IF IT'S REALLY OVER BETWEEN HER AND AYUKAWA?
...I CAME HERE TO APOLOGIZE TO KAWANA-SAN.
SO, THEN LET ME ASK,
HOW ARE THINGS BETWEEN YOU AND AYUKAWA?
...

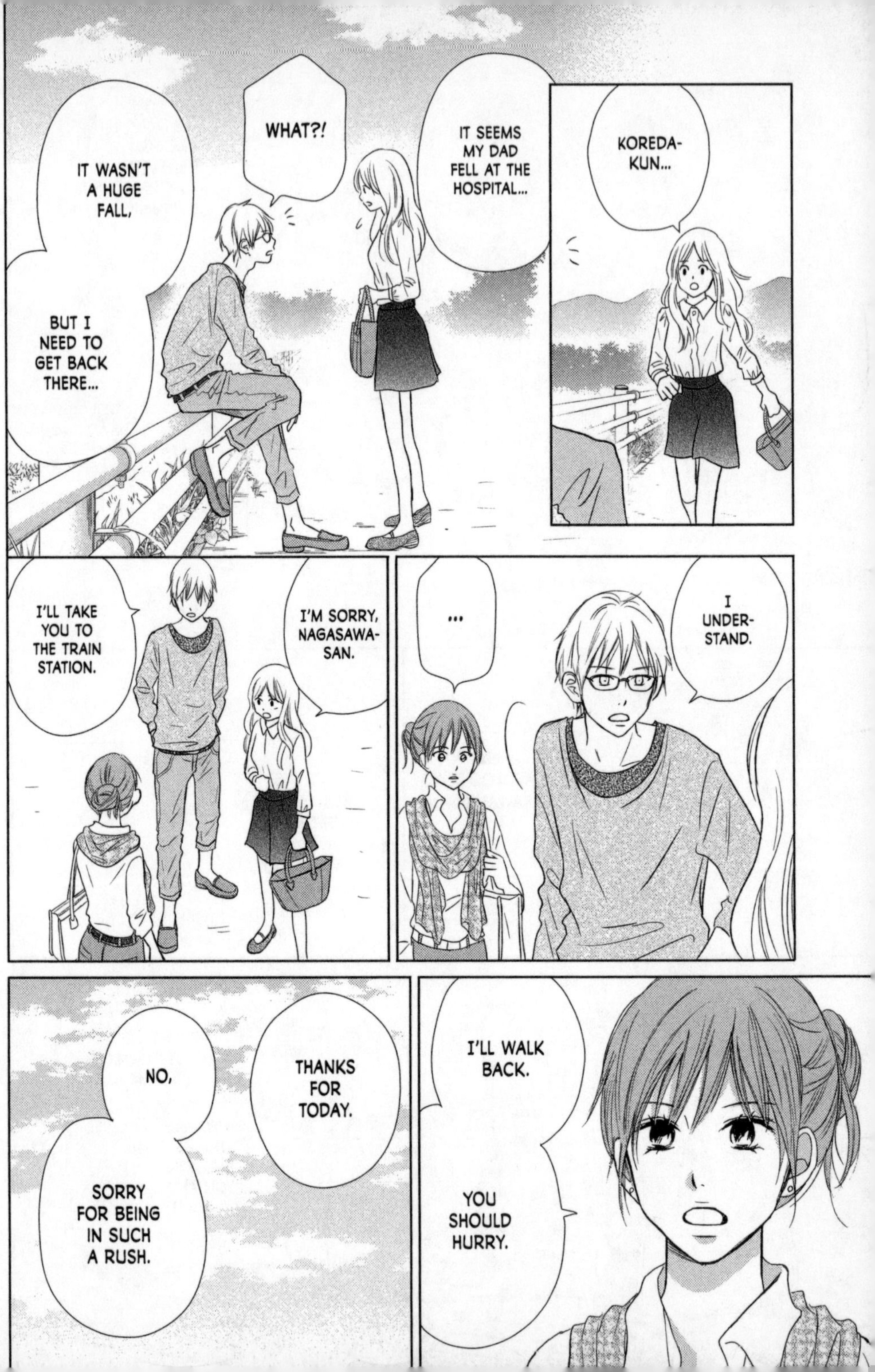
KOREDA-KUN...
IT SEEMS MY DAD FELL AT THE HOSPITAL...
WHAT?!
IT WASN'T A HUGE FALL,
BUT I NEED TO GET BACK THERE...
I UNDERSTAND.
...
I'M SORRY, NAGASAWA-SAN.
I'LL TAKE YOU TO THE TRAIN STATION.
I'LL WALK BACK.
YOU SHOULD HURRY.
THANKS FOR TODAY.
NO,
SORRY FOR BEING IN SUCH A RUSH.

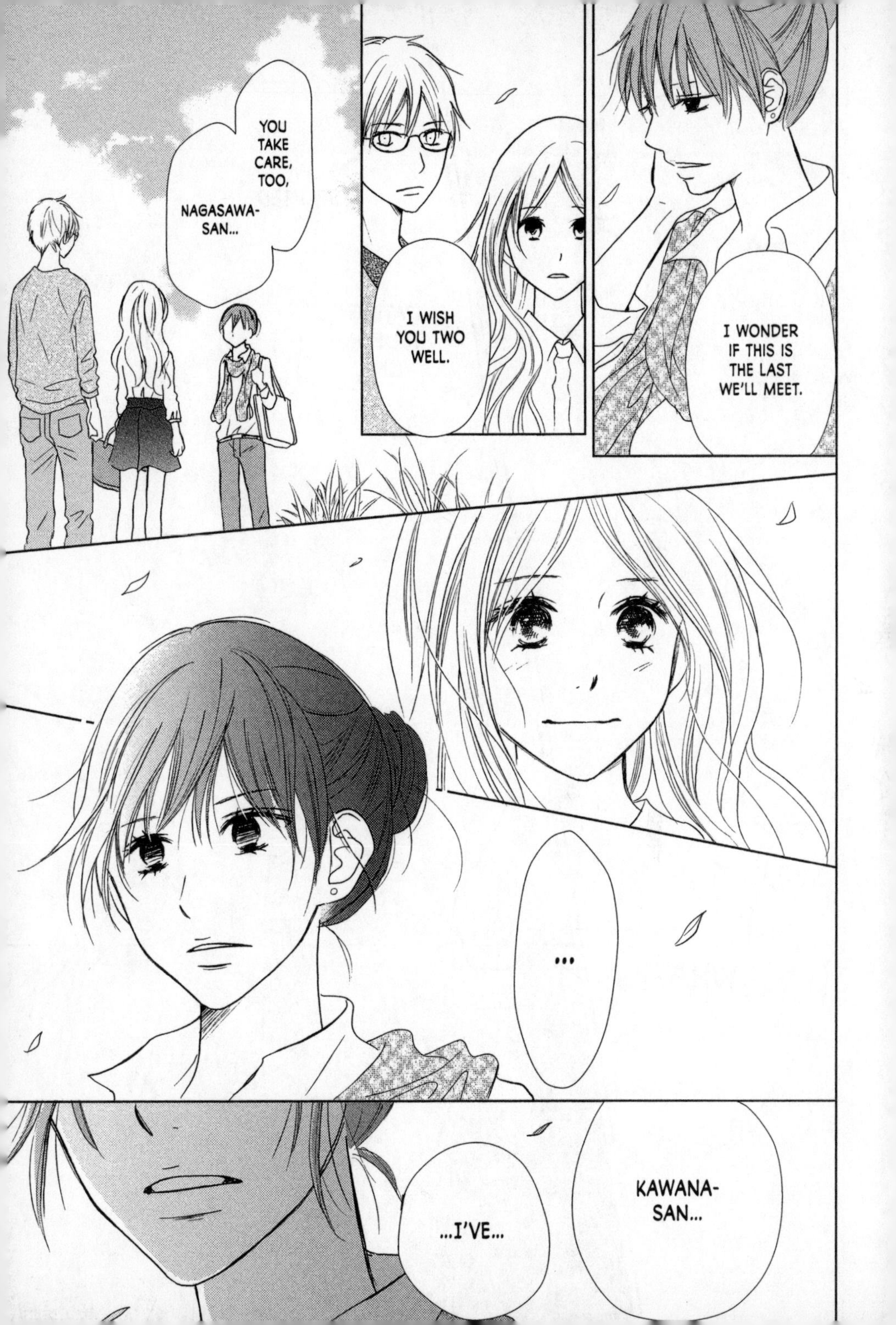
I WONDER IF THIS IS THE LAST WE'LL MEET.
I WISH YOU TWO WELL.
YOU TAKE CARE, TOO, NAGASAWA-SAN...
...
KAWANA-SAN...
...I'VE...

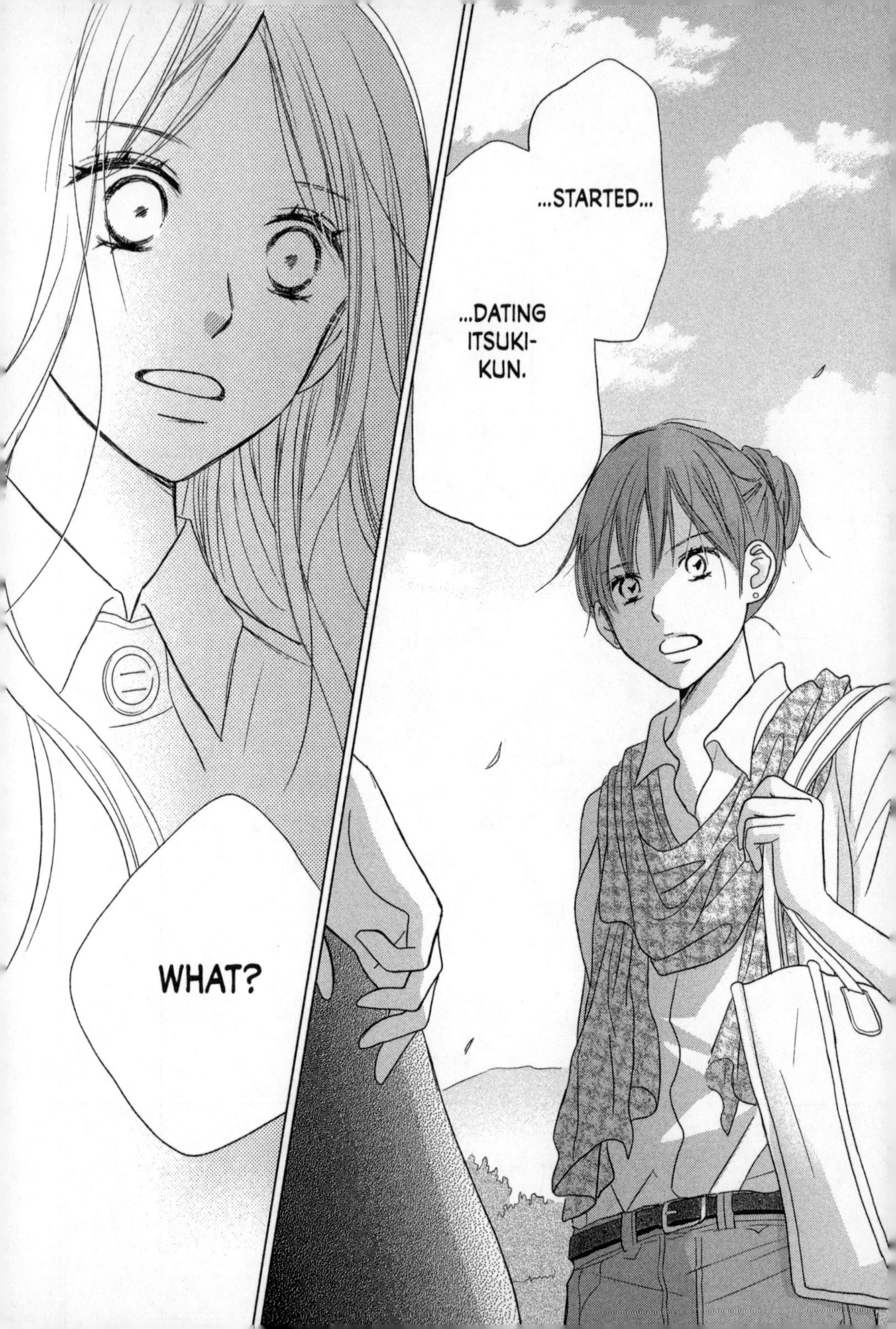
...STARTED...
...DATING ITSUKI-KUN.
WHAT?

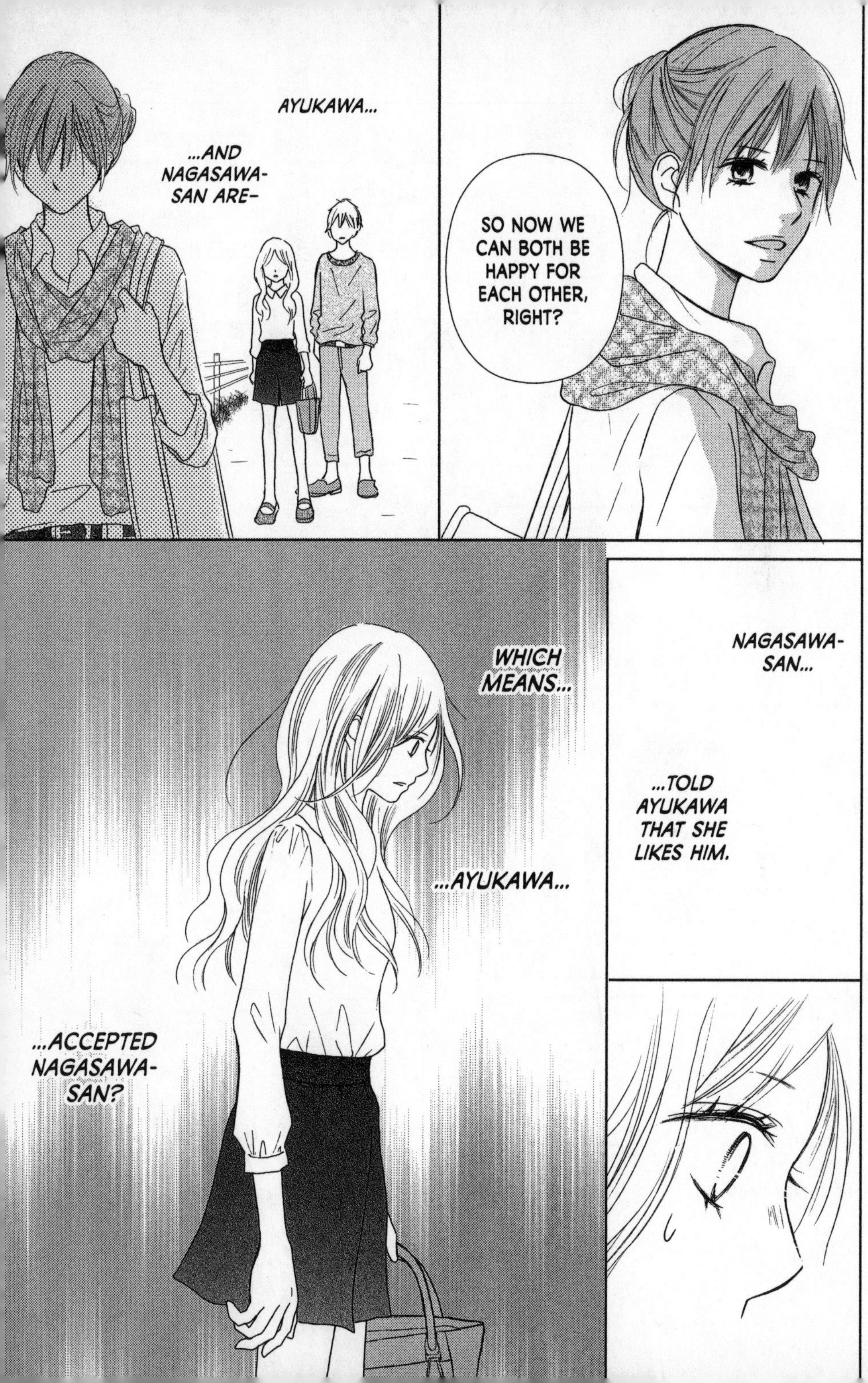
SO NOW WE CAN BOTH BE HAPPY FOR EACH OTHER, RIGHT?
AYUKAWA...
...AND NAGASAWA-SAN ARE-
NAGASAWA-SAN...
...TOLD AYUKAWA THAT SHE LIKES HIM.
WHICH MEANS...
...AYUKAWA...
...ACCEPTED NAGASAWA-SAN?

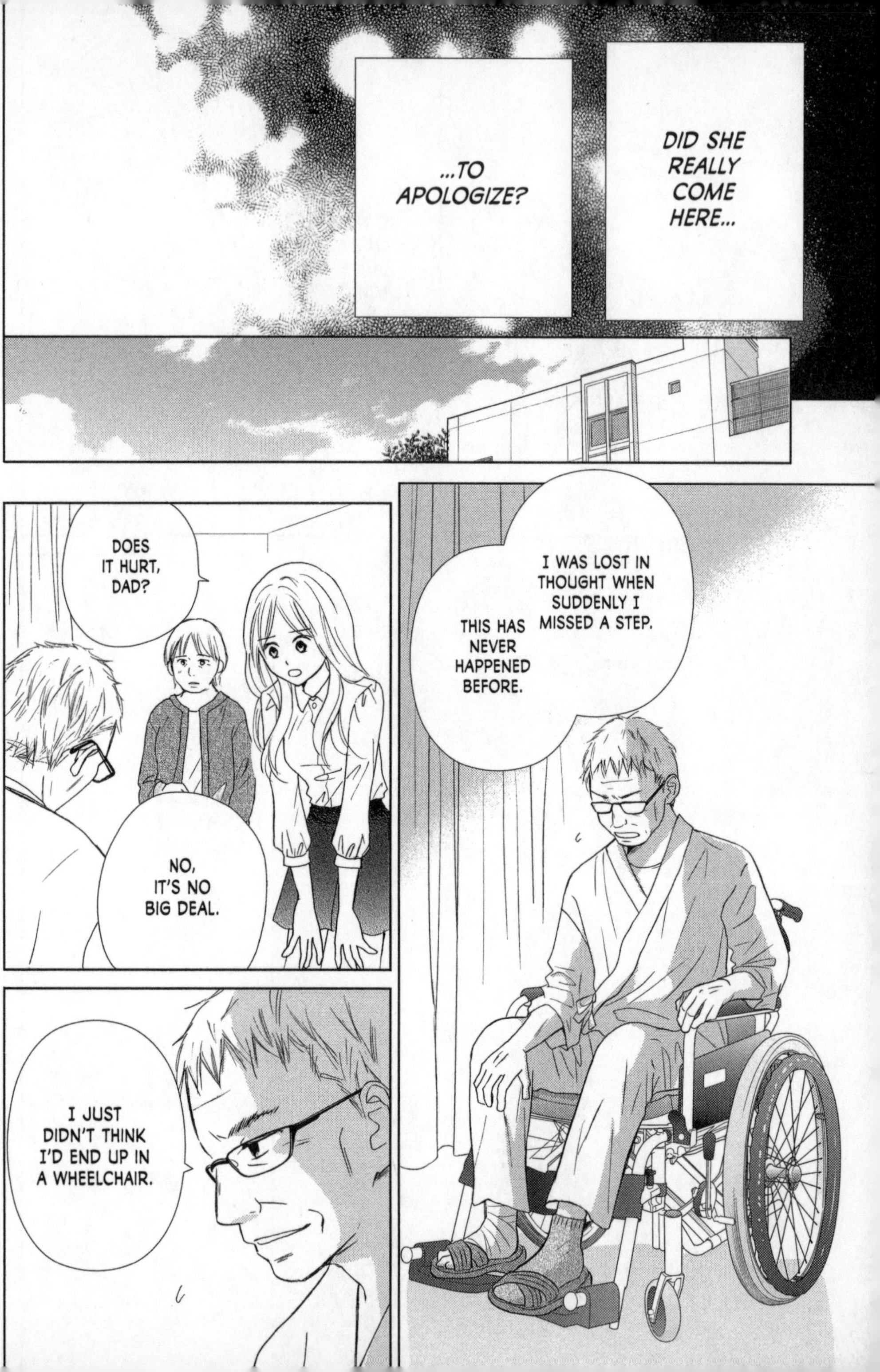
DID SHE REALLY COME HERE...
...TO APOLOGIZE?
I WAS LOST IN THOUGHT WHEN SUDDENLY I MISSED A STEP.
THIS HAS NEVER HAPPENED BEFORE.
DOES IT HURT, DAD?
NO, IT'S NO BIG DEAL.
I JUST DIDN'T THINK I'D END UP IN A WHEELCHAIR.

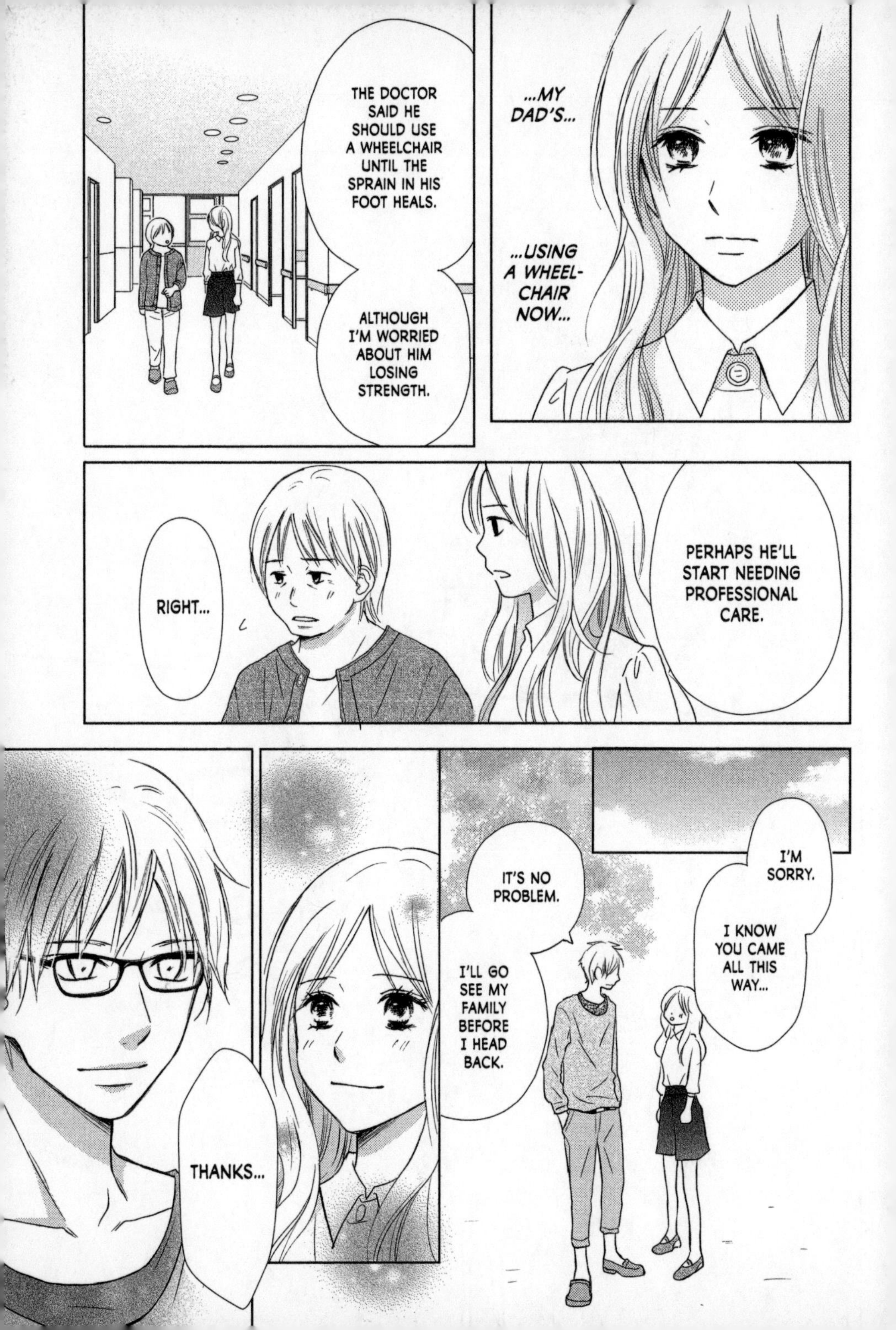
...MY DAD'S...
...USING A WHEEL-CHAIR NOW...
THE DOCTOR SAID HE SHOULD USE A WHEELCHAIR UNTIL THE SPRAIN IN HIS FOOT HEALS.
ALTHOUGH I'M WORRIED ABOUT HIM LOSING STRENGTH.
PERHAPS HE'LL START NEEDING PROFESSIONAL CARE.
RIGHT...
I'M SORRY.
I KNOW YOU CAME ALL THIS WAY...
IT'S NO PROBLEM.
I'LL GO SEE MY FAMILY BEFORE I HEAD BACK.
THANKS...

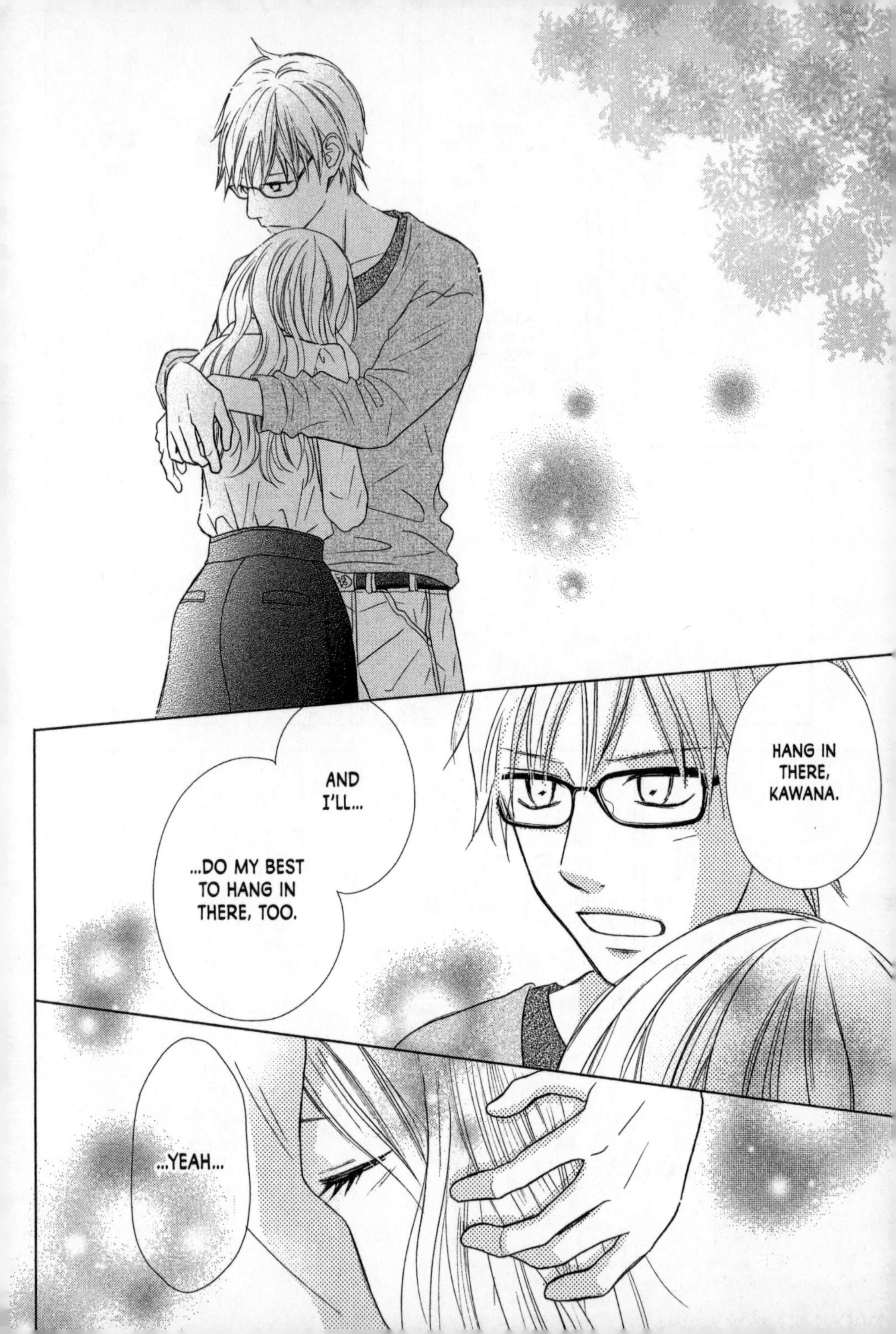
HANG IN THERE, KAWANA.
AND I'LL...
...DO MY BEST TO HANG IN THERE, TOO.
...YEAH...

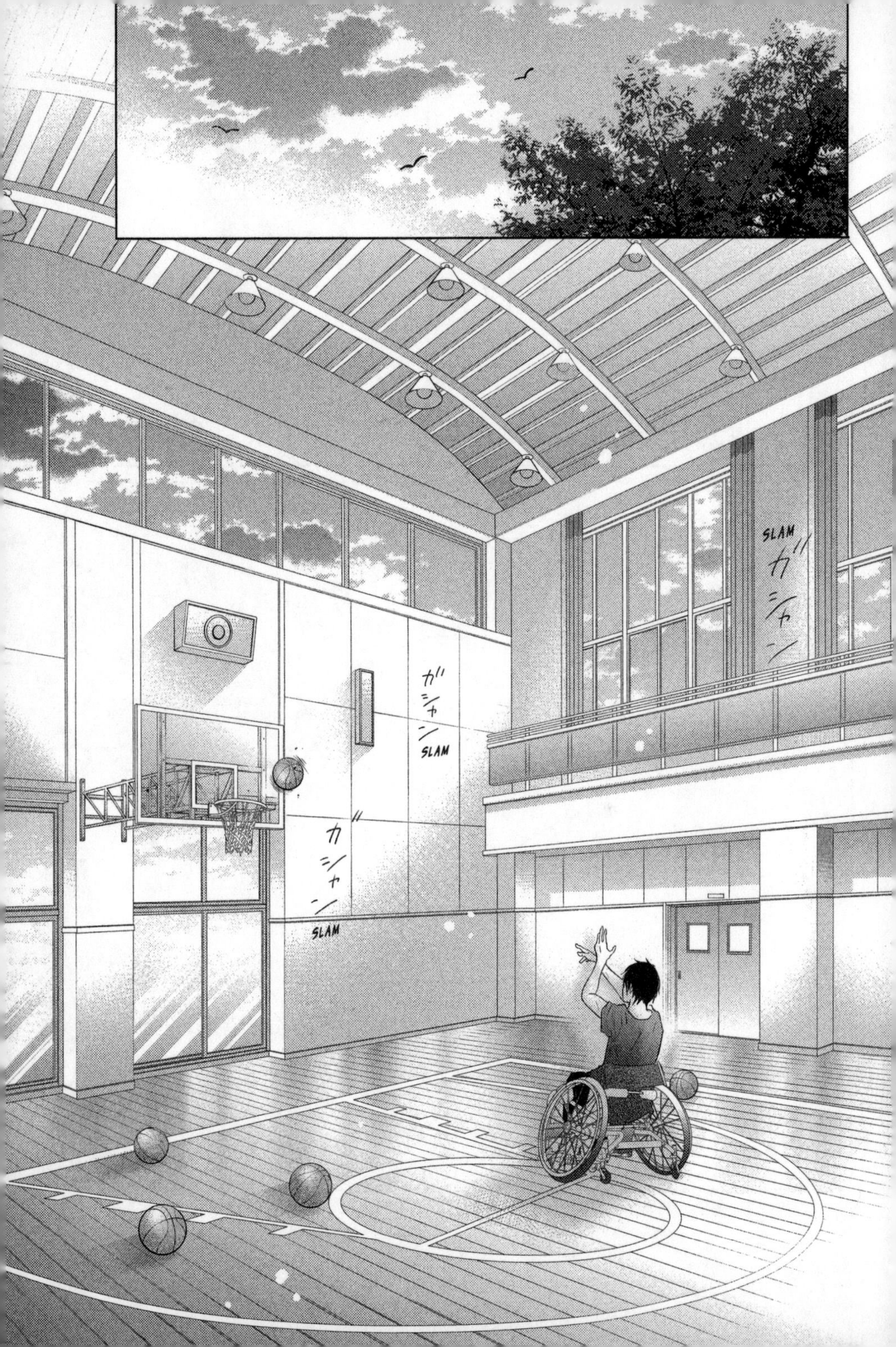
SLAM
ガシャン
ガシャン
SLAM
ガシャン
SLAM

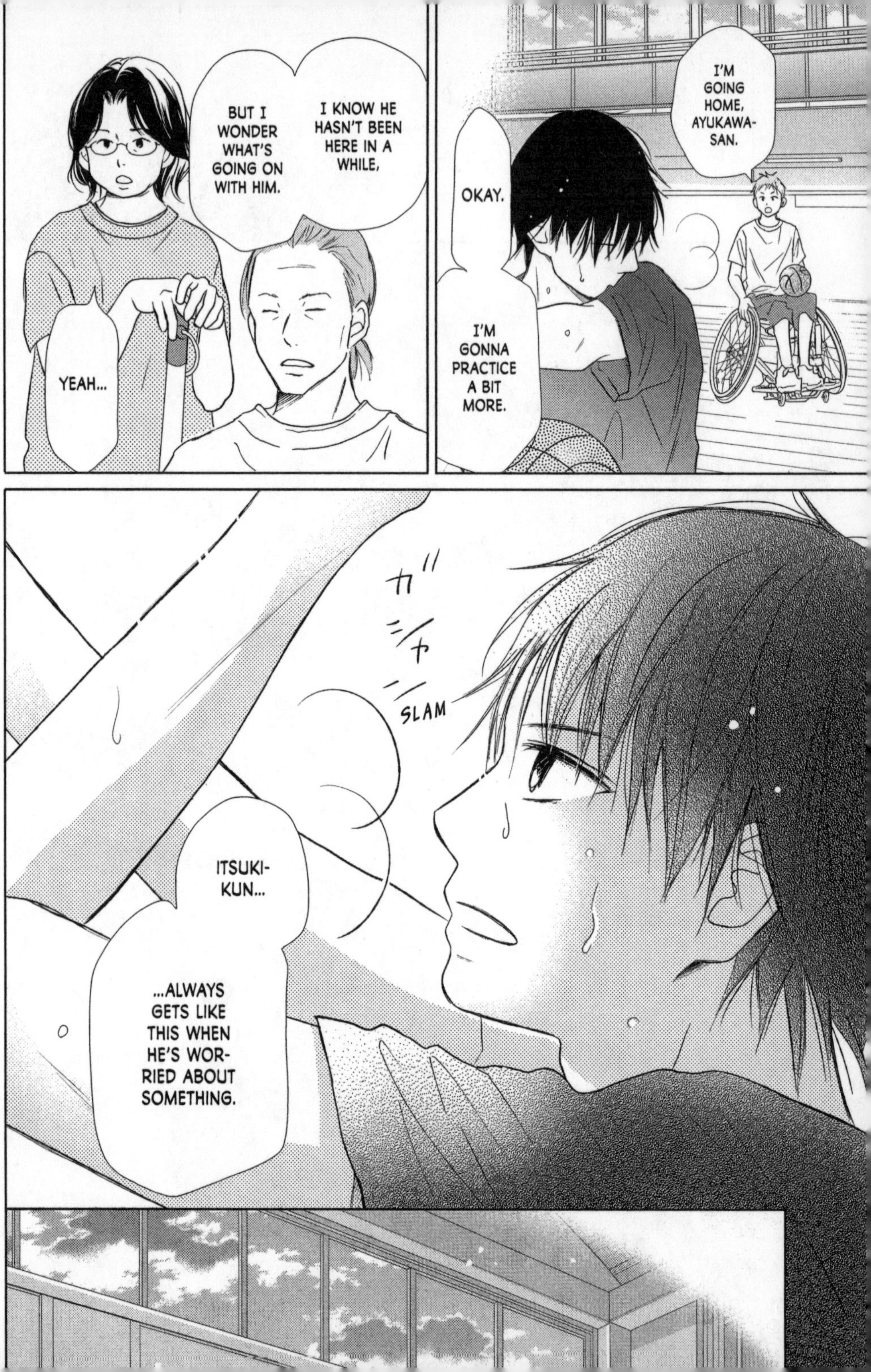
I'M GOING HOME, AYUKAWA-SAN.
OKAY.
I'M GONNA PRACTICE A BIT MORE.
I KNOW HE HASN'T BEEN HERE IN A WHILE,
BUT I WONDER WHAT'S GOING ON WITH HIM.
YEAH...
ガシャ
SLAM
ITSUKI-KUN...
...ALWAYS GETS LIKE THIS WHEN HE'S WOR-RIED ABOUT SOMETHING.

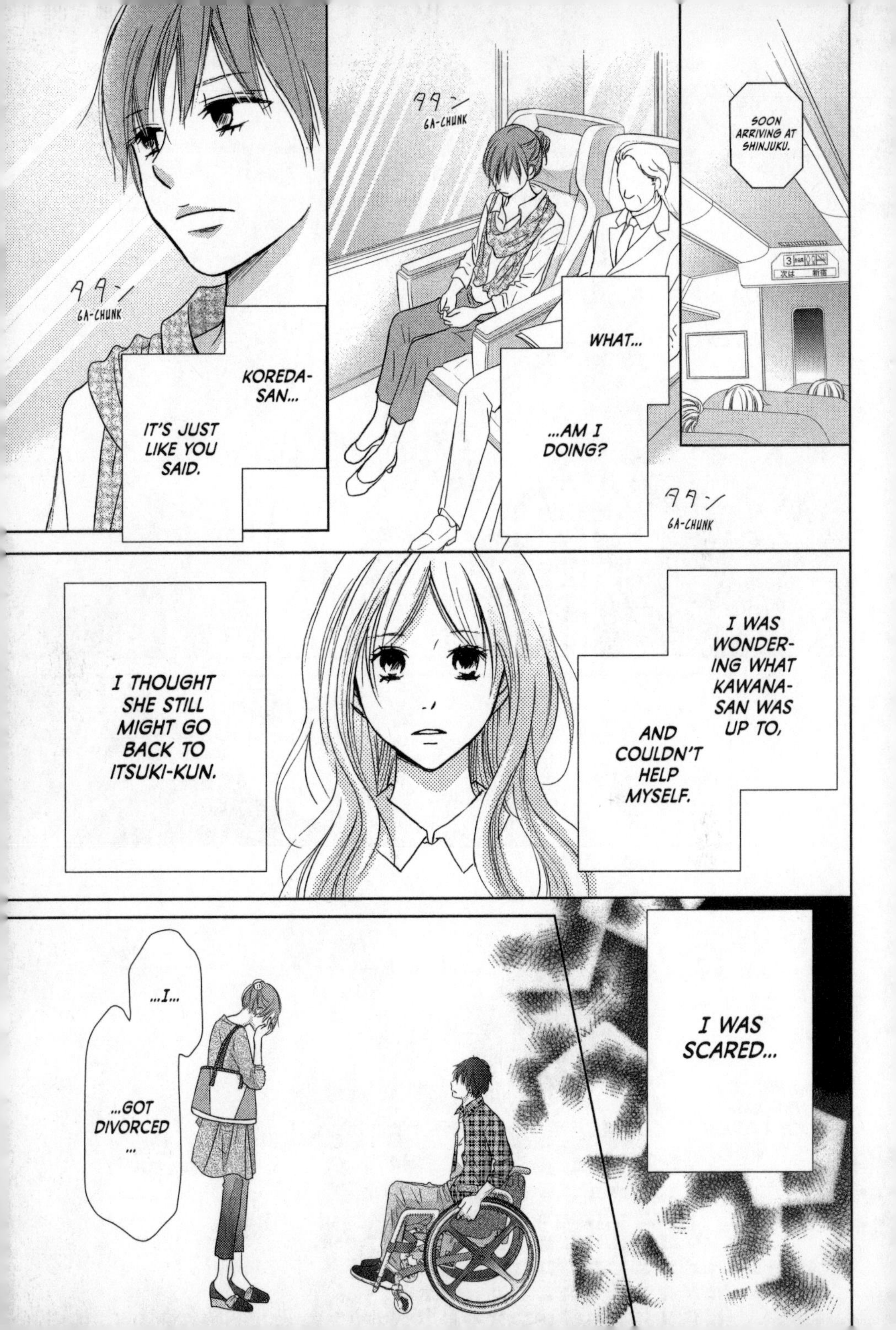
SOON ARRIVING AT SHINJUKU.
タタン
GA-CHUNK
WHAT...
...AM I DOING?
タタン
GA-CHUNK
タタン
GA-CHUNK
KOREDA-SAN...
IT'S JUST LIKE YOU SAID.
I WAS WONDERING WHAT KAWANA-SAN WAS UP TO,
AND COULDN'T HELP MYSELF.
I THOUGHT SHE STILL MIGHT GO BACK TO ITSUKI-KUN.
I WAS SCARED...
...I...
...GOT DIVORCED...

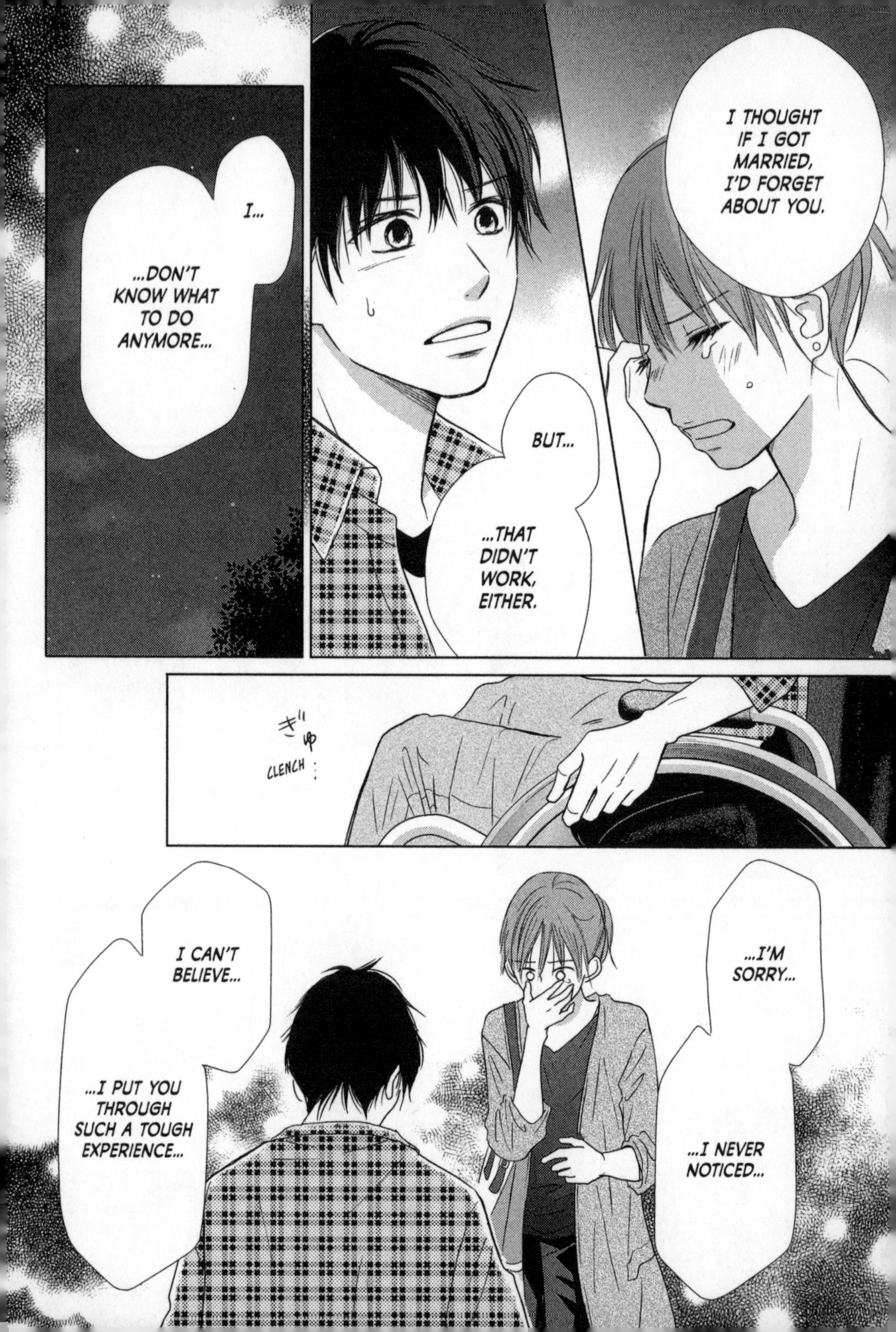
I THOUGHT IF I GOT MARRIED, I'D FORGET ABOUT YOU.
BUT...
...THAT DIDN'T WORK, EITHER.
I...
...DON'T KNOW WHAT TO DO ANYMORE...
ぎゅ
CLENCH
...I'M SORRY...
...I NEVER NOTICED...
I CAN'T BELIEVE...
...I PUT YOU THROUGH SUCH A TOUGH EXPERIENCE...

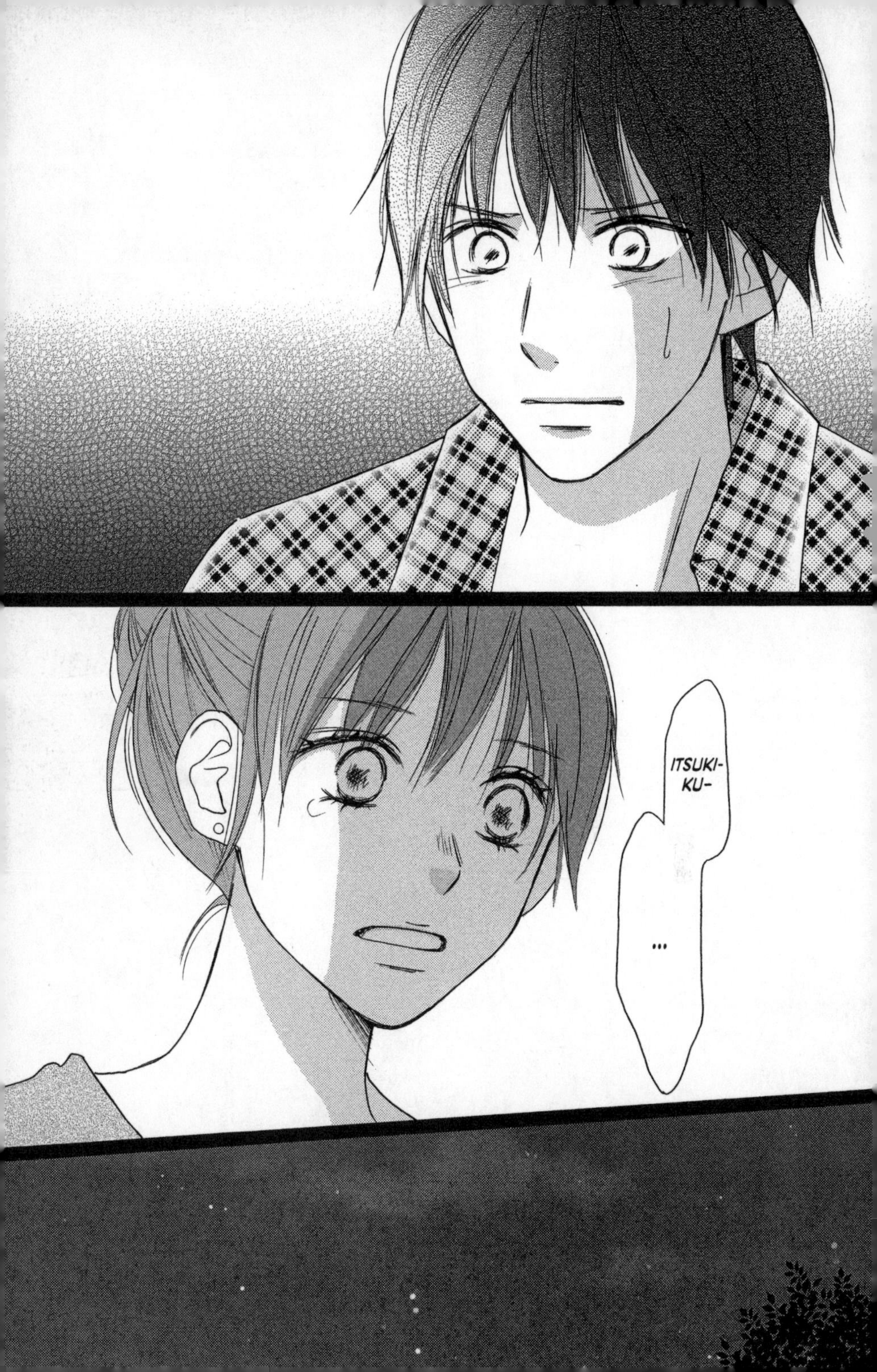
ITSUKI-KU-
...

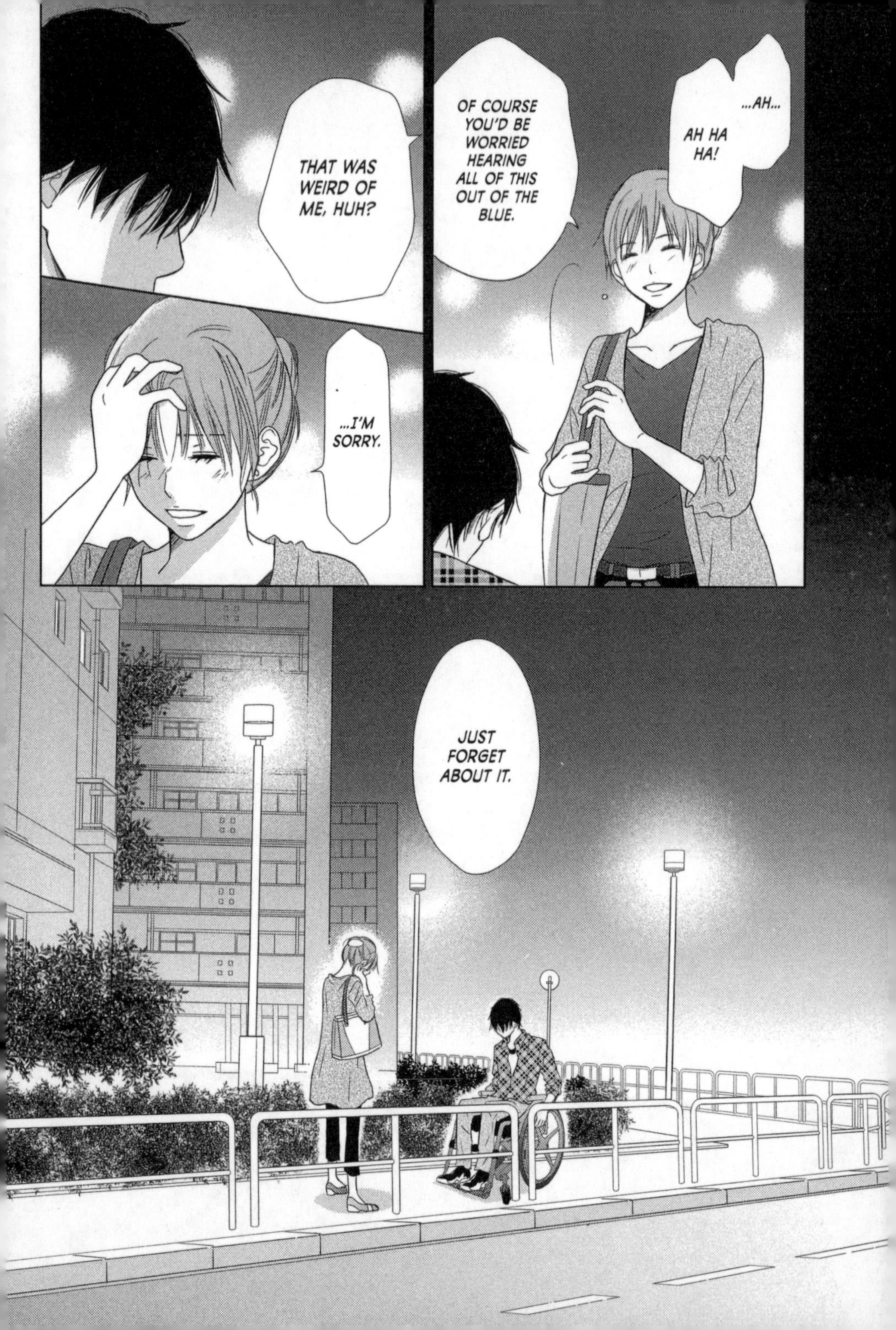
...AH...
AH HA HA!
OF COURSE YOU'D BE WORRIED HEARING ALL OF THIS OUT OF THE BLUE.
THAT WAS WEIRD OF ME, HUH?
...I'M SORRY.
JUST FORGET ABOUT IT.

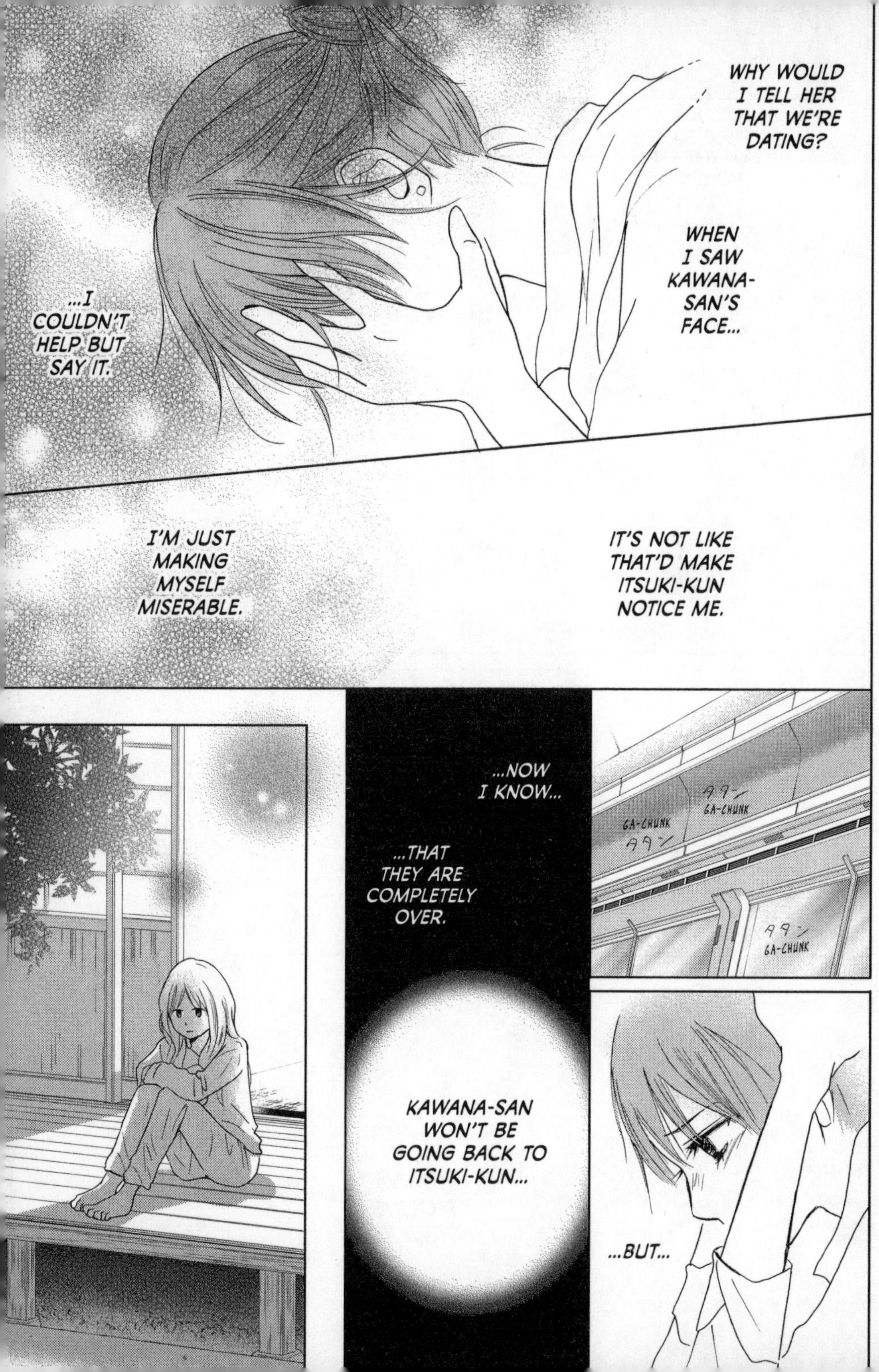
WHY WOULD I TELL HER THAT WE'RE DATING?
WHEN I SAW KAWANA-SAN'S FACE...
...I COULDN'T HELP BUT SAY IT.
IT'S NOT LIKE THAT'D MAKE ITSUKI-KUN NOTICE ME.
I'M JUST MAKING MYSELF MISERABLE.
タタン
GA-CHUNK
GA-CHUNK
タタン
タタン
GA-CHUNK
...BUT...
...NOW I KNOW...
...THAT THEY ARE COMPLETELY OVER.
KAWANA-SAN WON'T BE GOING BACK TO ITSUKI-KUN...

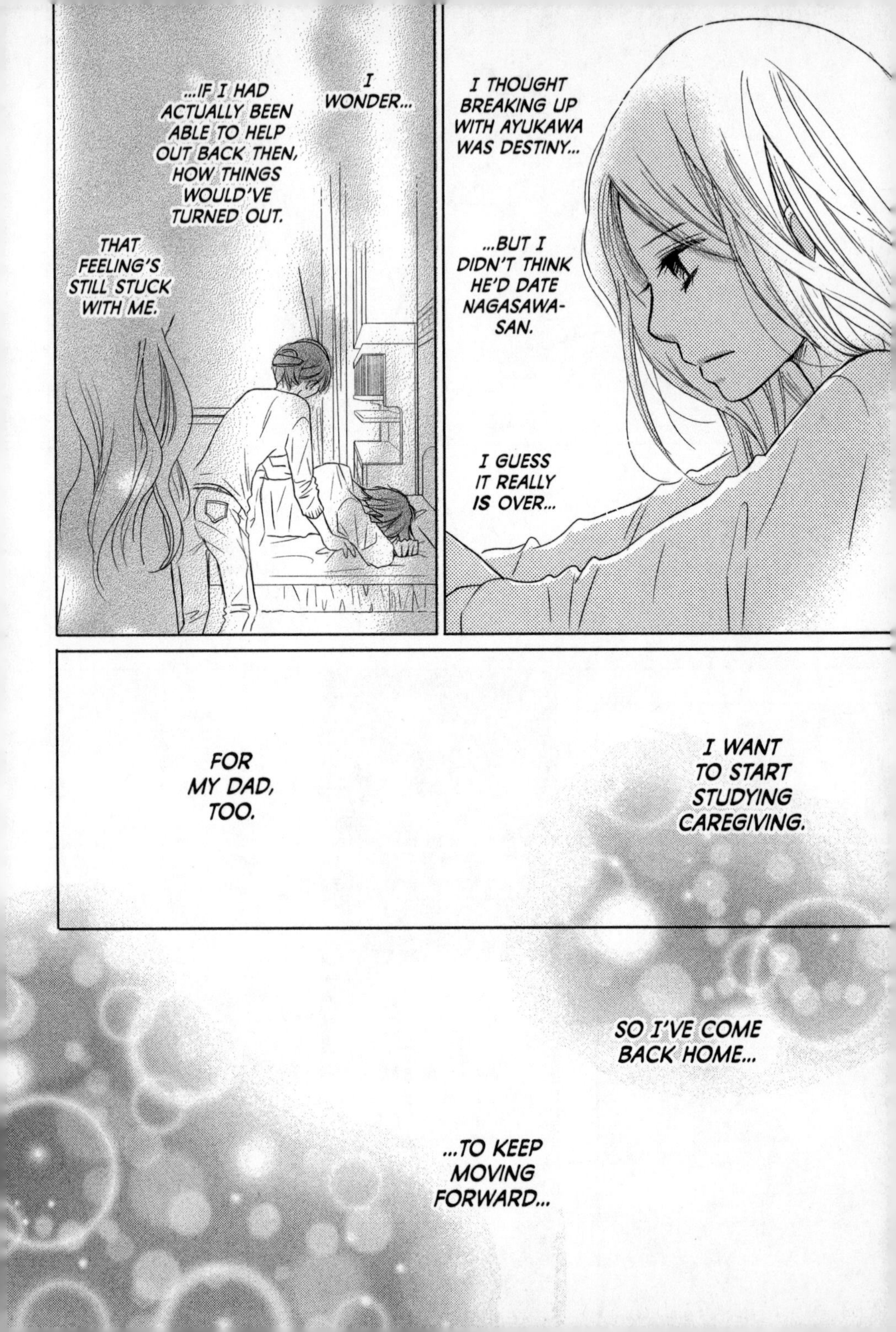
I THOUGHT BREAKING UP WITH AYUKAWA WAS DESTINY...
...BUT I DIDN'T THINK HE'D DATE NAGASAWA-SAN.
I GUESS IT REALLY IS OVER...
I WONDER...
...IF I HAD ACTUALLY BEEN ABLE TO HELP OUT BACK THEN, HOW THINGS WOULD'VE TURNED OUT.
THAT FEELING'S STILL STUCK WITH ME.
I WANT TO START STUDYING CAREGIVING.
FOR MY DAD, TOO.
SO I'VE COME BACK HOME...
...TO KEEP MOVING FORWARD...

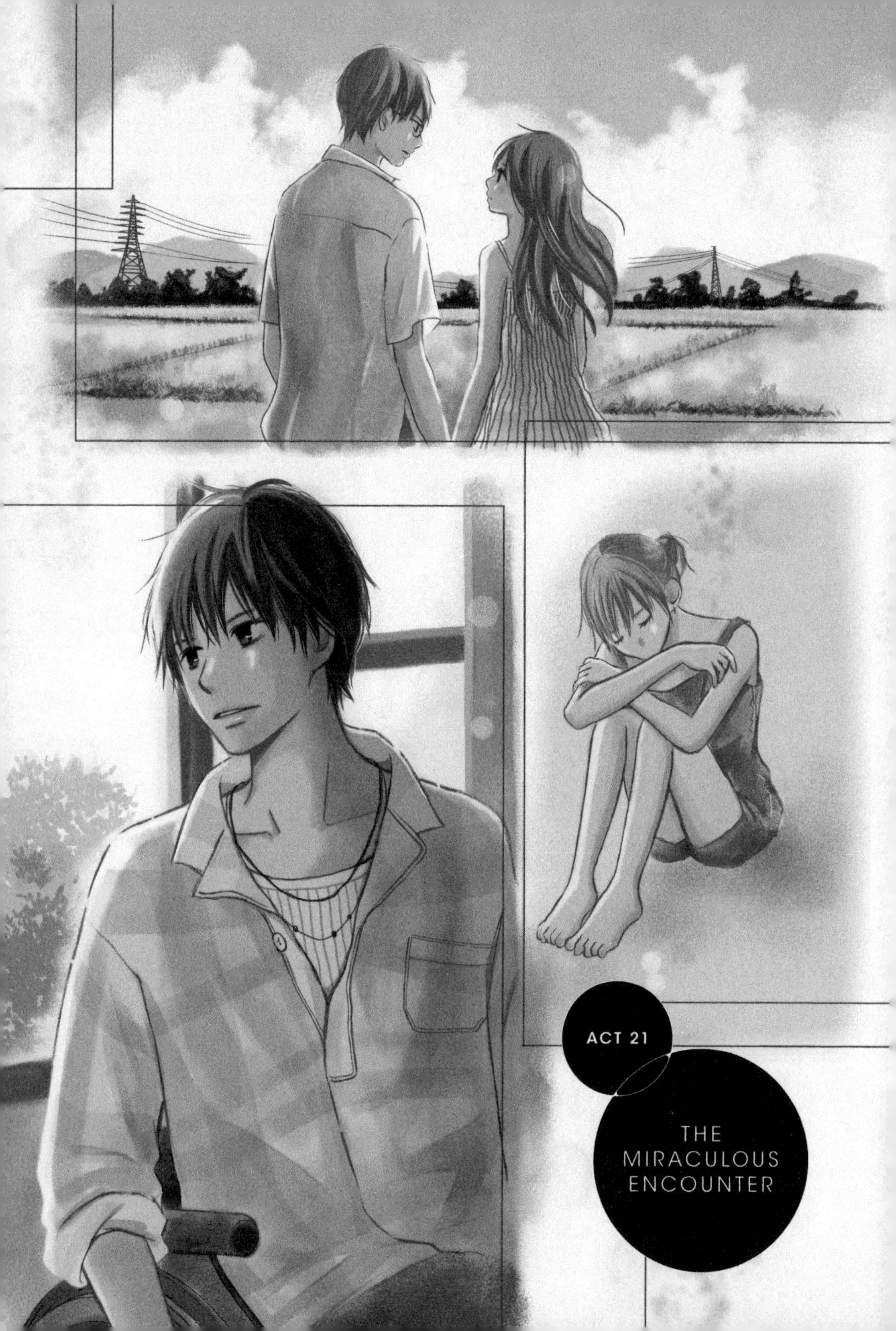
ACT 21
THE MIRACULOUS ENCOUNTER

PERFECT WORLD

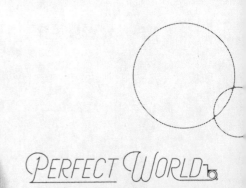

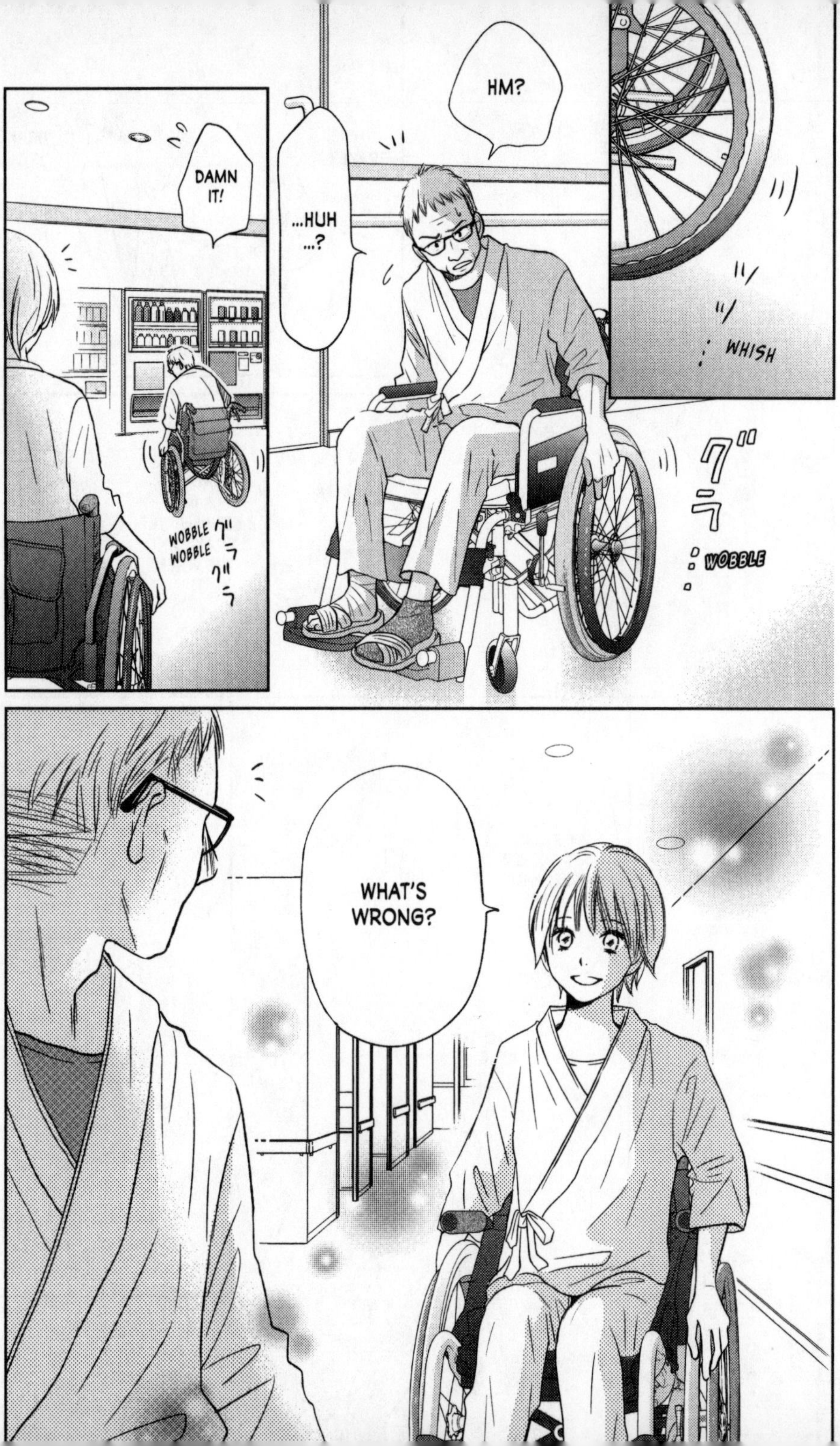
WHISH
HM?
...HUH ...?
グラ
WOBBLE
DAMN IT!
WOBBLE WOBBLE
グラグラ
WHAT'S WRONG?

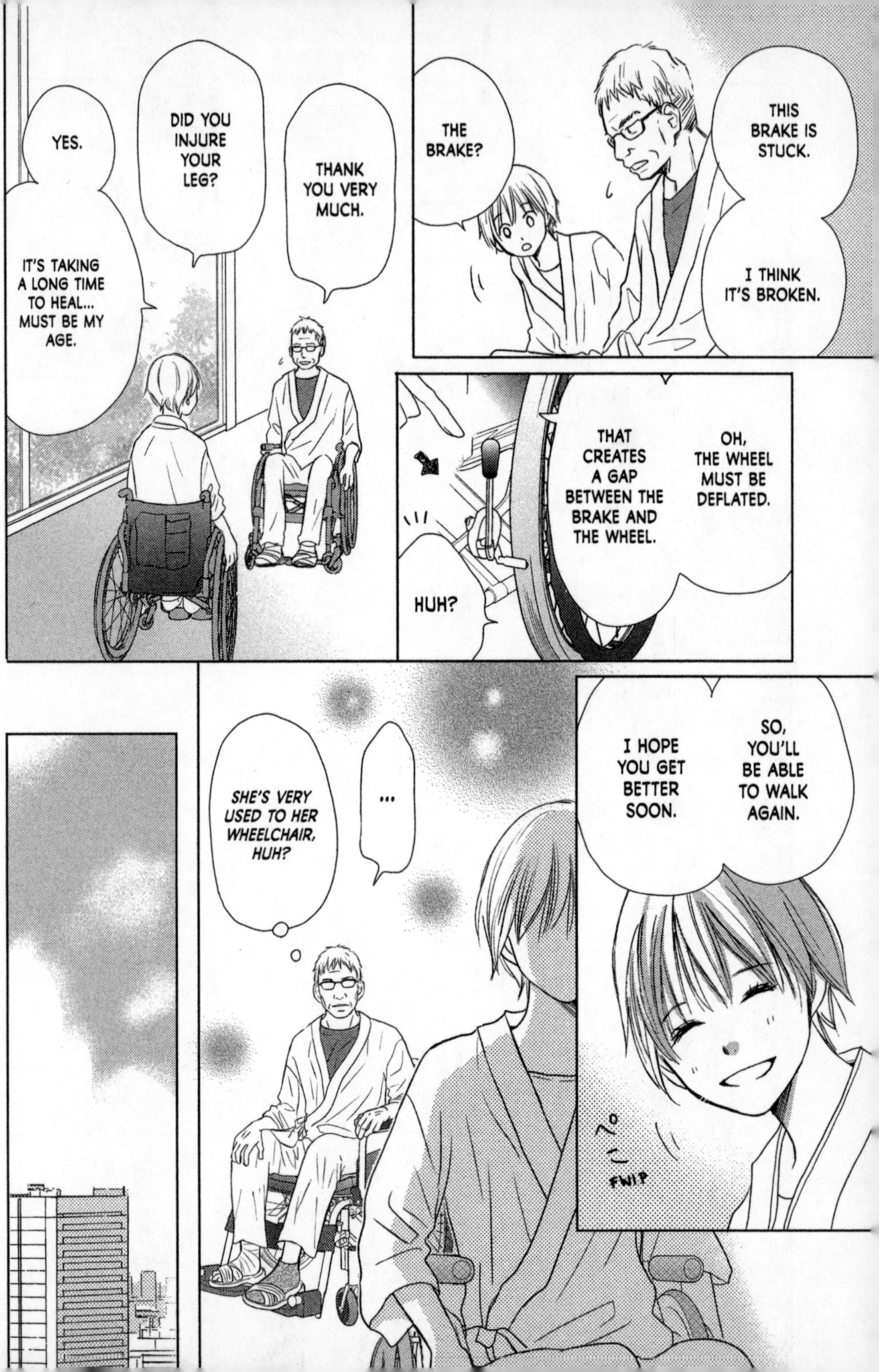
THIS BRAKE IS STUCK.
I THINK IT'S BROKEN.
THE BRAKE?
OH, THE WHEEL MUST BE DEFLATED.
THAT CREATES A GAP BETWEEN THE BRAKE AND THE WHEEL.
HUH?
THANK YOU VERY MUCH.
DID YOU INJURE YOUR LEG?
YES.
IT'S TAKING A LONG TIME TO HEAL... MUST BE MY AGE.
SO, YOU'LL BE ABLE TO WALK AGAIN.
I HOPE YOU GET BETTER SOON.
FWIP
...
SHE'S VERY USED TO HER WHEELCHAIR, HUH?

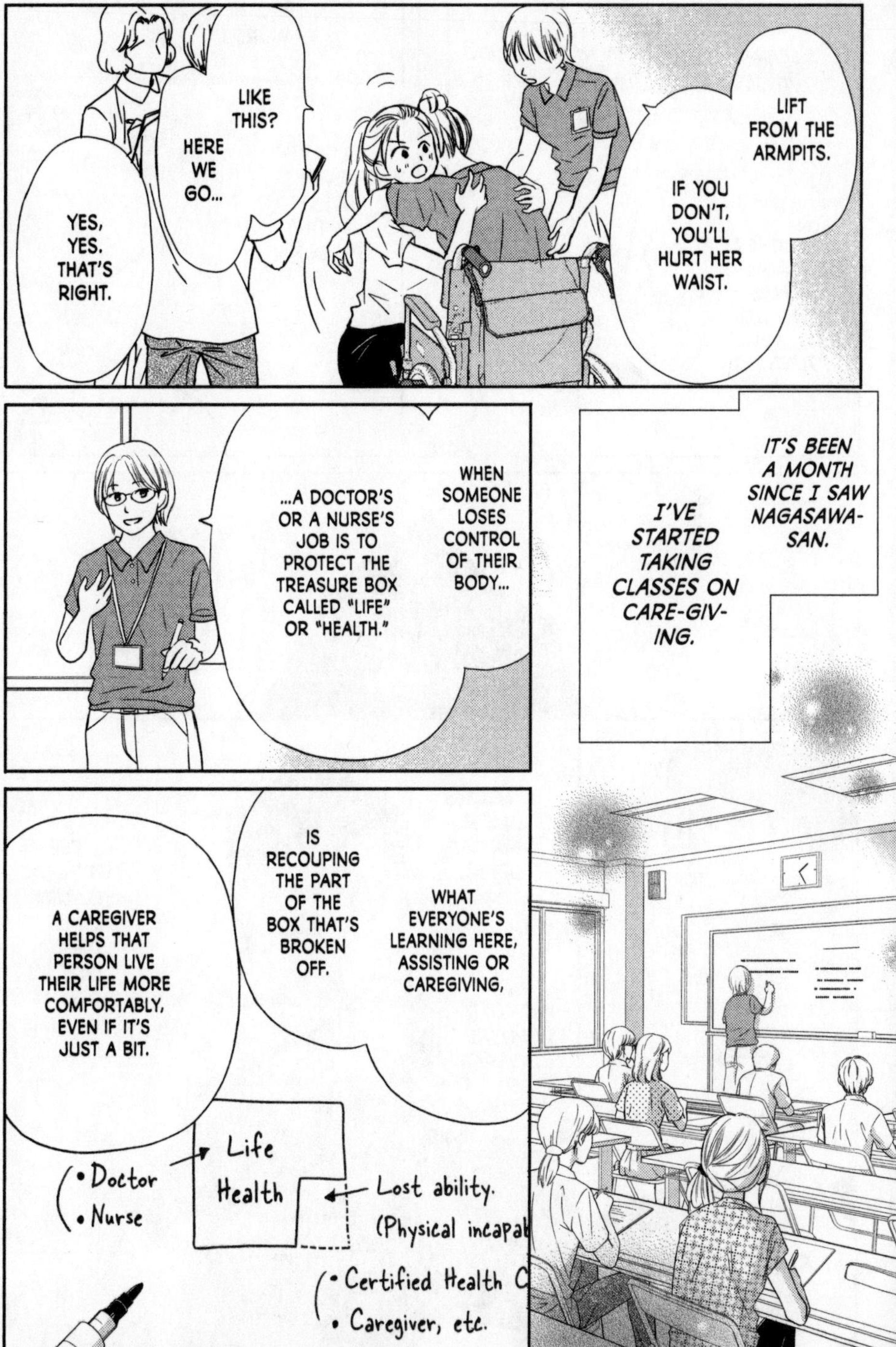
LIFT FROM THE ARMPITS.
IF YOU DON'T, YOU'LL HURT HER WAIST.
LIKE THIS?
HERE WE GO...
YES, YES. THAT'S RIGHT.
IT'S BEEN A MONTH SINCE I SAW NAGASAWA-SAN.
I'VE STARTED TAKING CLASSES ON CARE-GIVING.
WHEN SOMEONE LOSES CONTROL OF THEIR BODY...
...A DOCTOR'S OR A NURSE'S JOB IS TO PROTECT THE TREASURE BOX CALLED "LIFE" OR "HEALTH."
WHAT EVERYONE'S LEARNING HERE, ASSISTING OR CAREGIVING,
IS RECOUPING THE PART OF THE BOX THAT'S BROKEN OFF.
A CAREGIVER HELPS THAT PERSON LIVE THEIR LIFE MORE COMFORTABLY, EVEN IF IT'S JUST A BIT.
Life
Health
• Doctor
• Nurse
Lost ability.
(Physical incapab
• Certified Health C
• Caregiver, etc.

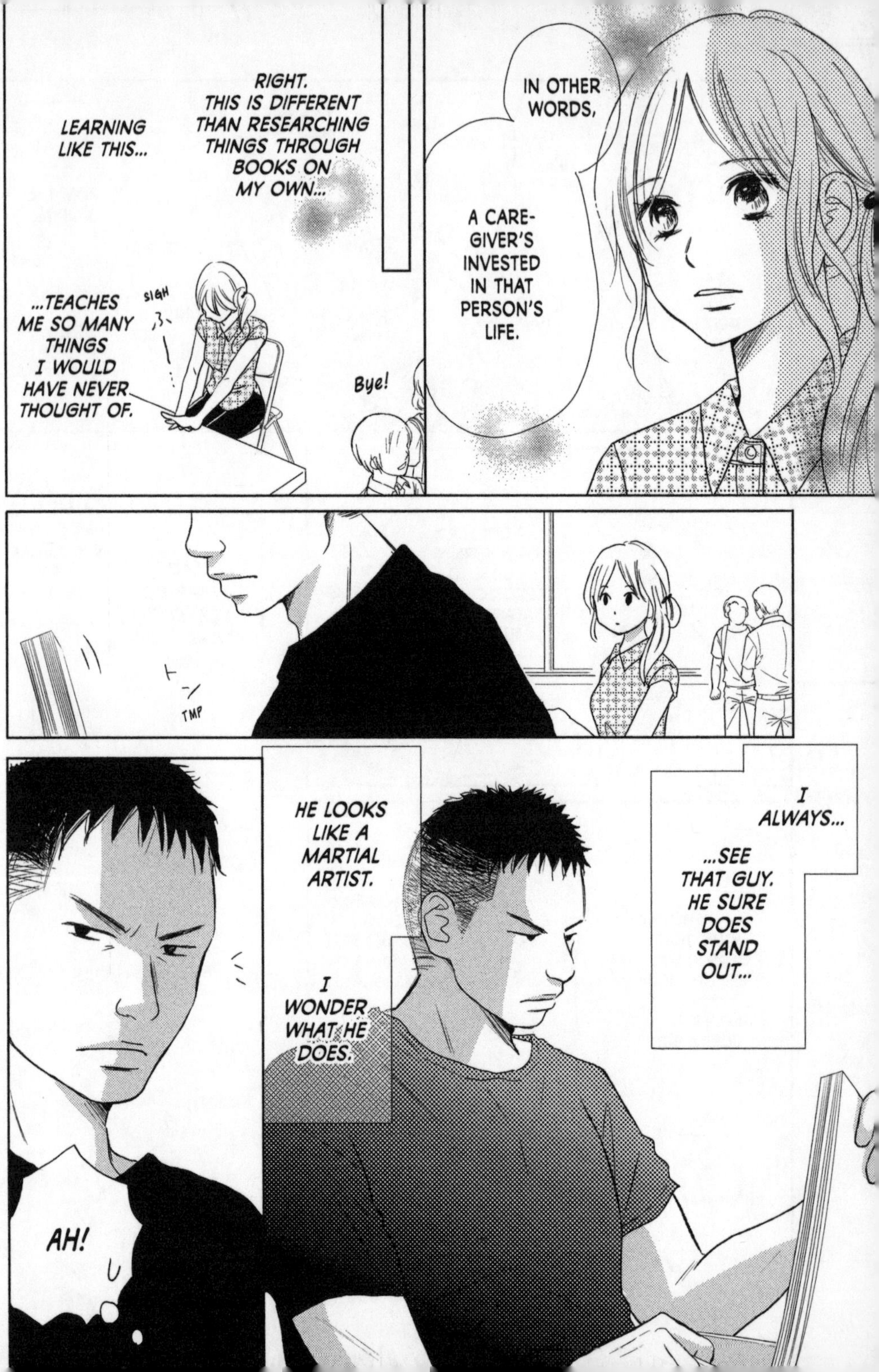
IN OTHER WORDS,
A CARE-GIVER'S INVESTED IN THAT PERSON'S LIFE.
RIGHT. THIS IS DIFFERENT THAN RESEARCHING THINGS THROUGH BOOKS ON MY OWN...
LEARNING LIKE THIS...
...TEACHES ME SO MANY THINGS I WOULD HAVE NEVER THOUGHT OF.
SIGH
Bye!
TMP
I ALWAYS...
...SEE THAT GUY. HE SURE DOES STAND OUT...
HE LOOKS LIKE A MARTIAL ARTIST.
I WONDER WHAT HE DOES.
AH!

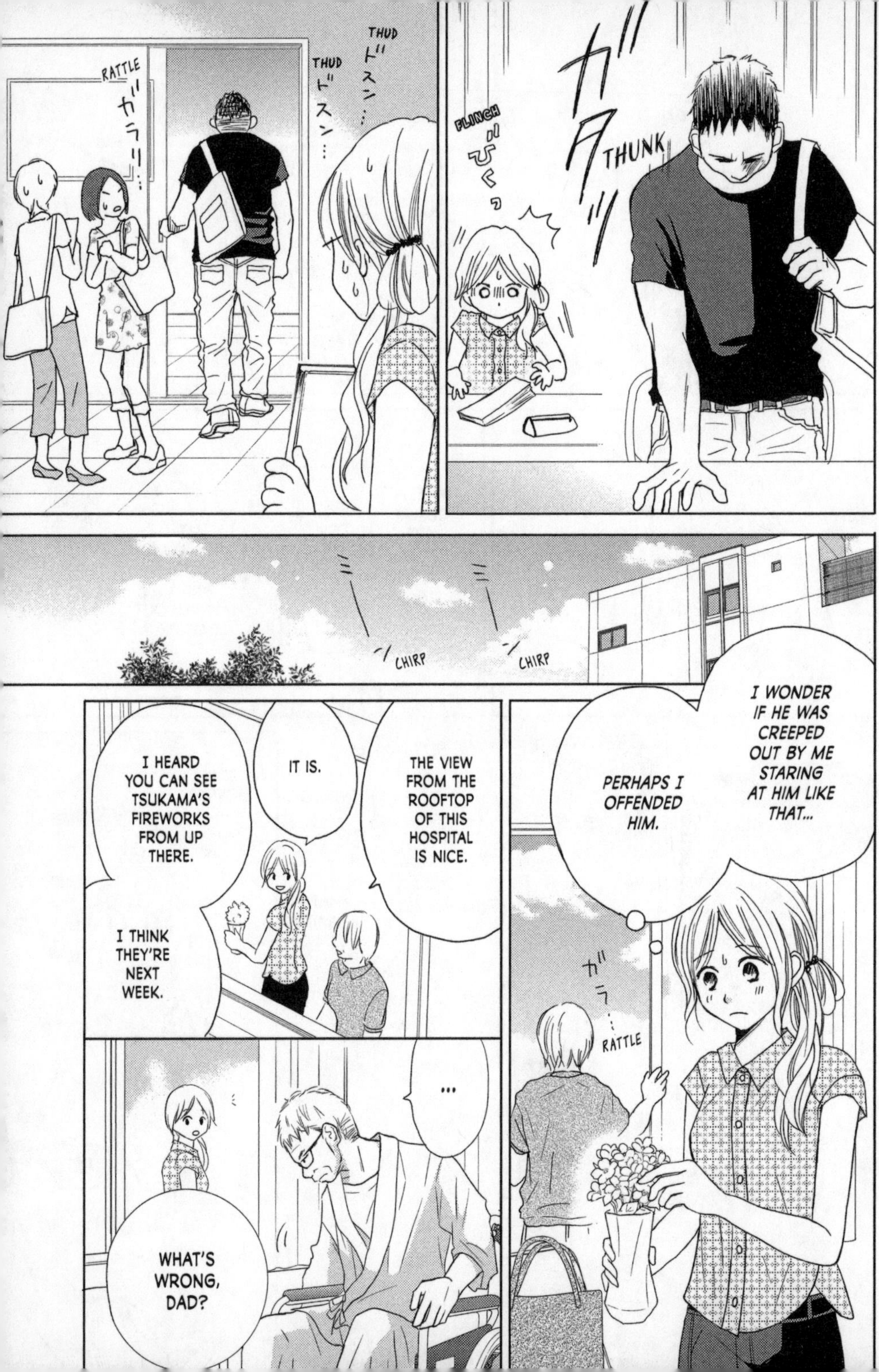
ガタッ
THUNK
FLINCH
びくっ
RATTLE
ガラリ…
THUD
ドスン…
THUD
ドスン…
CHIRP
CHIRP
I WONDER IF HE WAS CREEPED OUT BY ME STARING AT HIM LIKE THAT...
PERHAPS I OFFENDED HIM.
ガラ…
RATTLE
THE VIEW FROM THE ROOFTOP OF THIS HOSPITAL IS NICE.
IT IS.
I HEARD YOU CAN SEE TSUKAMA'S FIREWORKS FROM UP THERE.
I THINK THEY'RE NEXT WEEK.
...
WHAT'S WRONG, DAD?

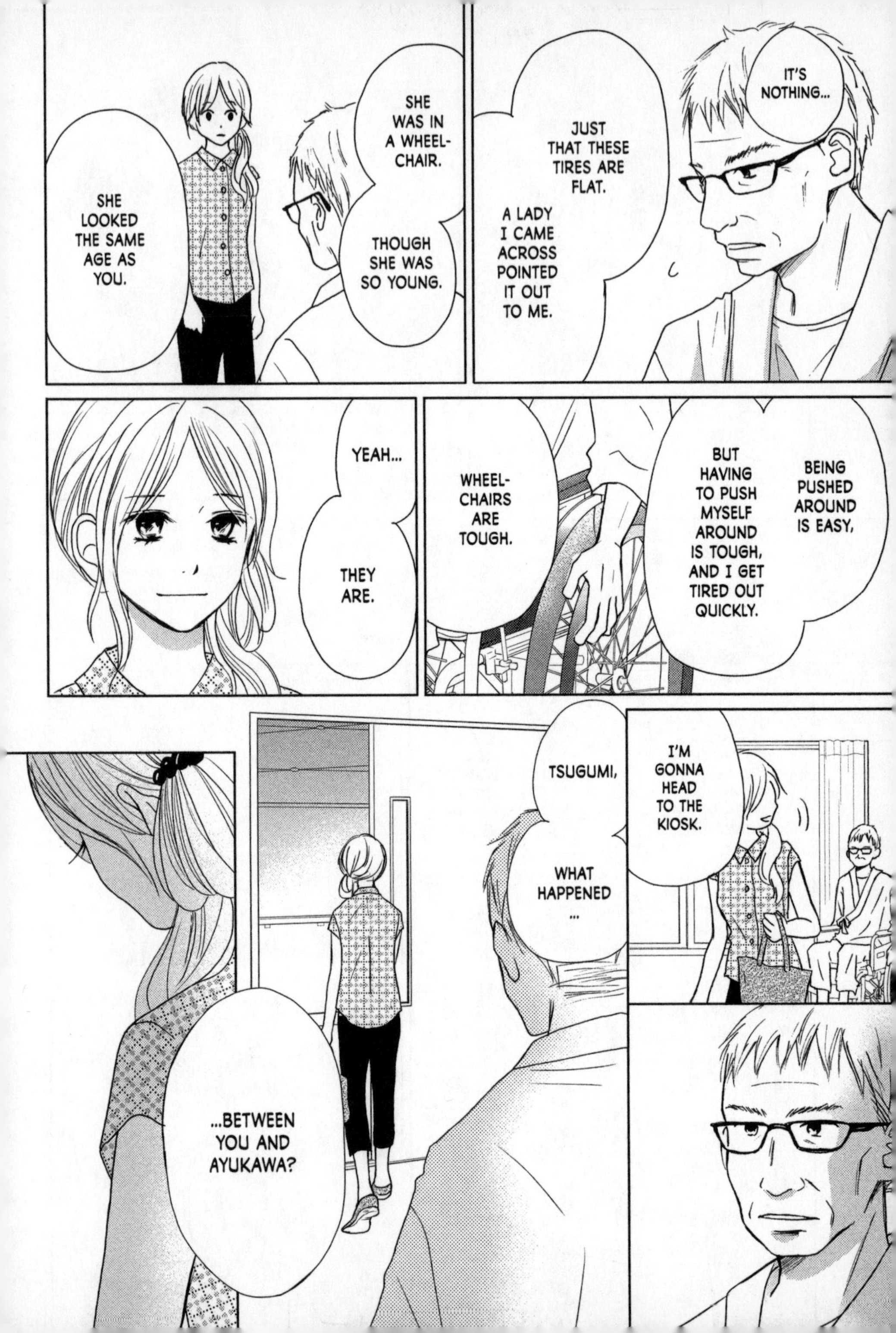
IT'S NOTHING...
JUST THAT THESE TIRES ARE FLAT.
A LADY I CAME ACROSS POINTED IT OUT TO ME.
SHE WAS IN A WHEEL-CHAIR.
THOUGH SHE WAS SO YOUNG.
SHE LOOKED THE SAME AGE AS YOU.
BEING PUSHED AROUND IS EASY,
BUT HAVING TO PUSH MYSELF AROUND IS TOUGH, AND I GET TIRED OUT QUICKLY.
WHEEL-CHAIRS ARE TOUGH.
YEAH...
THEY ARE.
I'M GONNA HEAD TO THE KIOSK.
TSUGUMI,
WHAT HAPPENED ...
...BETWEEN YOU AND AYUKAWA?

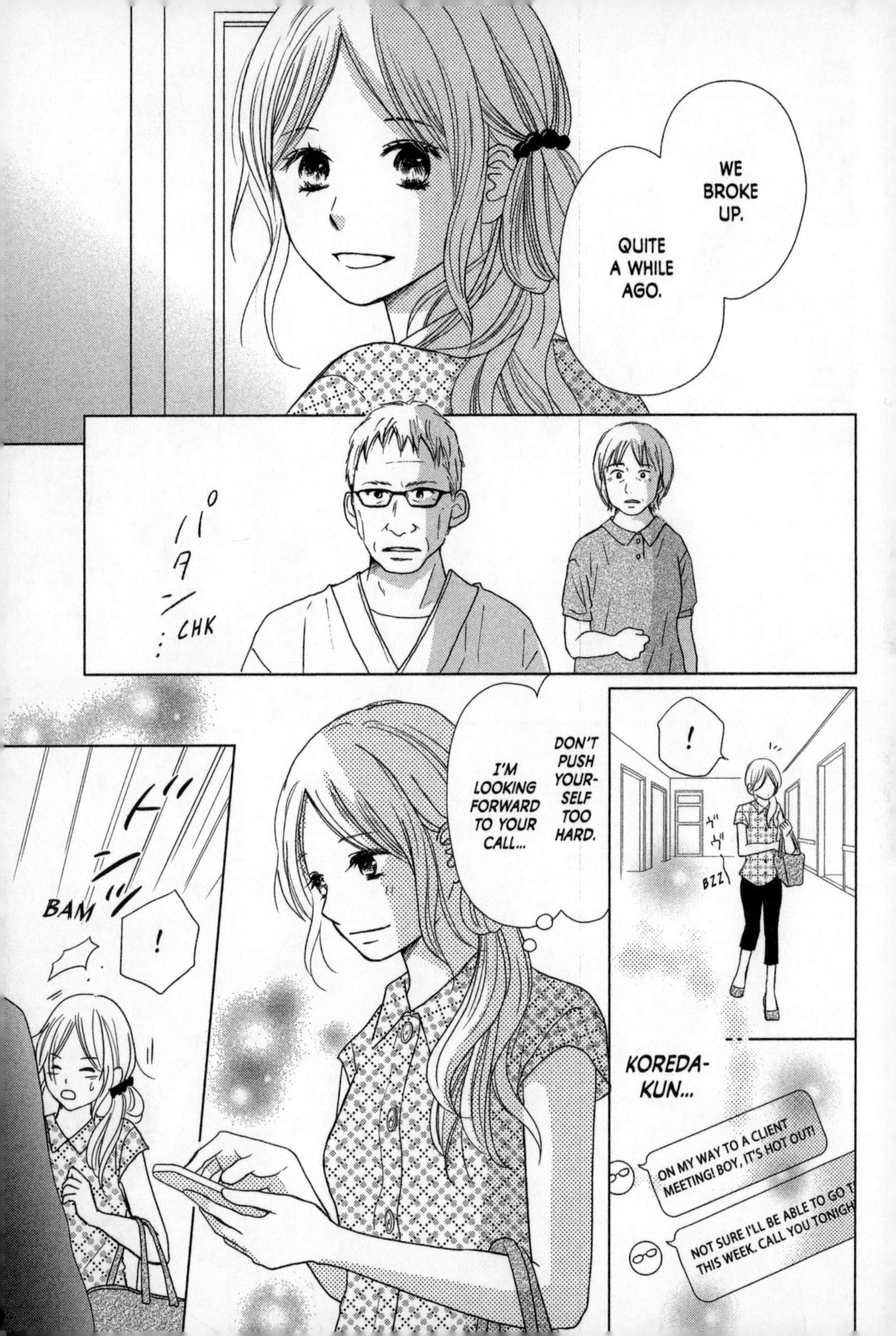

WE BROKE UP.
QUITE A WHILE AGO.
パタン
CHK
!
ヴヴ
BZZ
DON'T PUSH YOURSELF TOO HARD.
I'M LOOKING FORWARD TO YOUR CALL...
KOREDA-KUN...
ON MY WAY TO A CLIENT MEETING! BOY, IT'S HOT OUT!
NOT SURE I'LL BE ABLE TO GO T
THIS WEEK. CALL YOU TONIGH
BAM
!

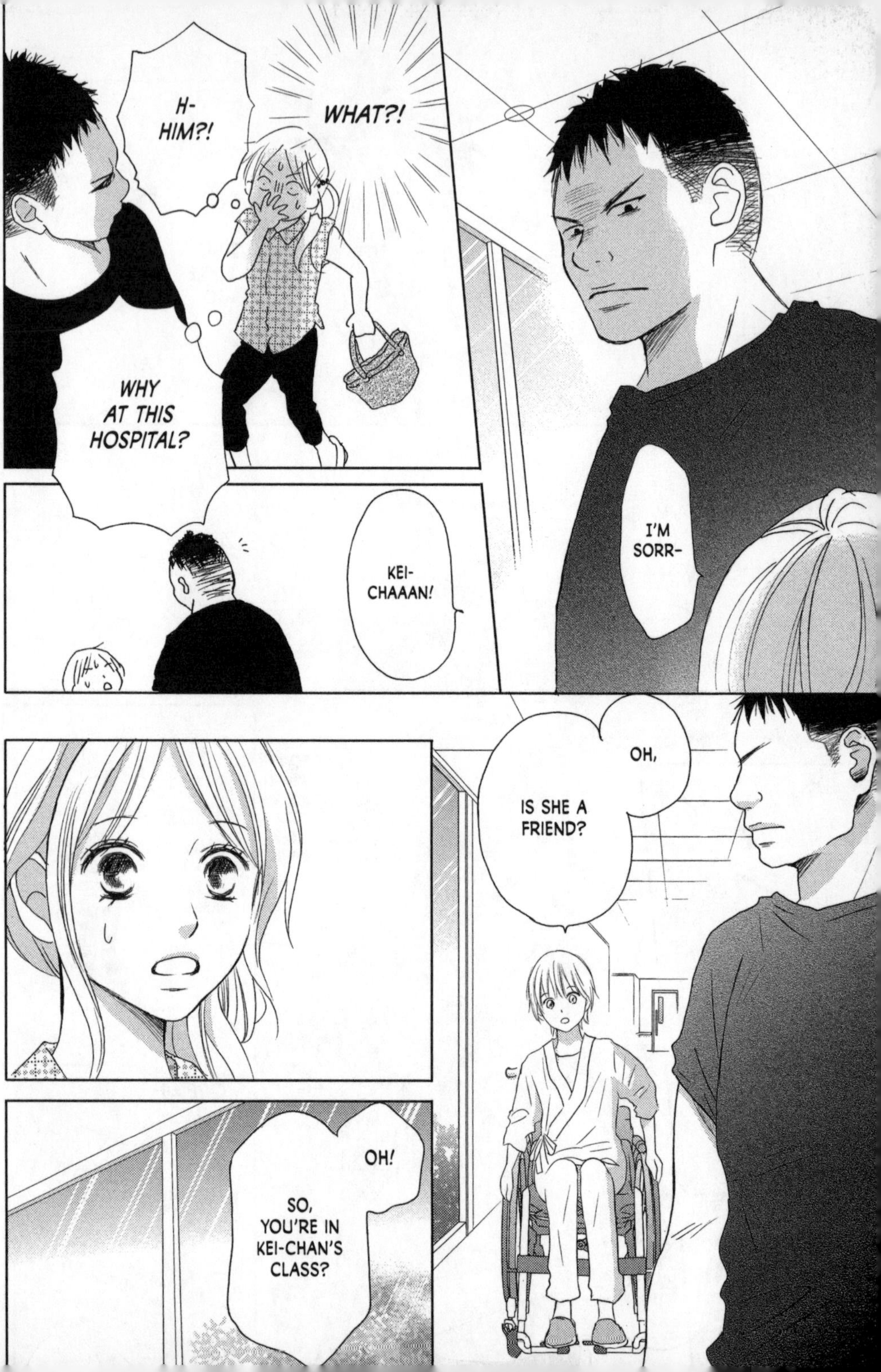
I'M SORR-
WHAT?!
H-HIM?!
WHY AT THIS HOSPITAL?
KEI-CHAAAN!
OH, IS SHE A FRIEND?
OH! SO, YOU'RE IN KEI-CHAN'S CLASS?

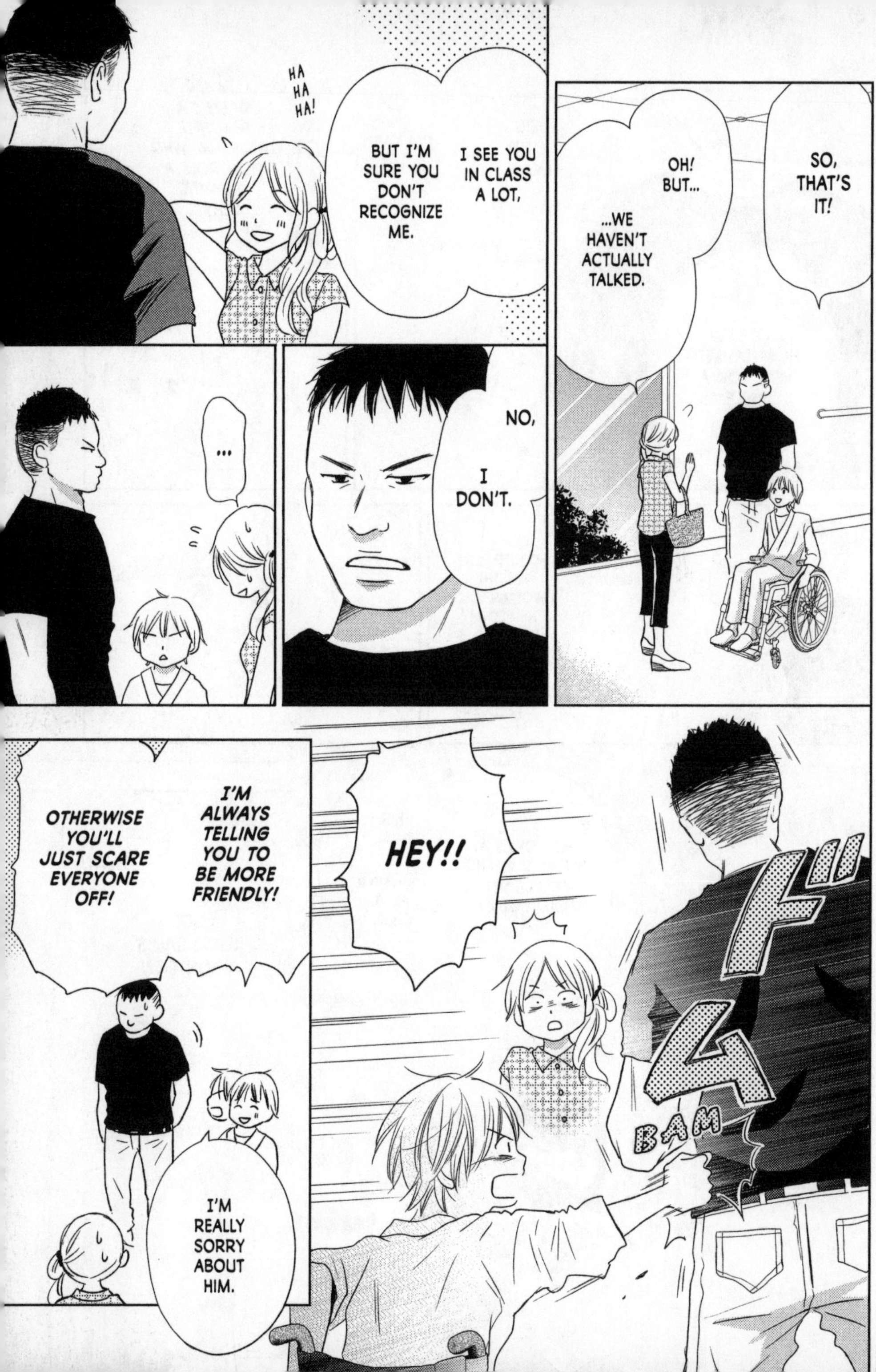
SO, THAT'S IT!
OH! BUT...
...WE HAVEN'T ACTUALLY TALKED.
I SEE YOU IN CLASS A LOT,
BUT I'M SURE YOU DON'T RECOGNIZE ME.
HA HA HA!
NO,
I DON'T.
...
HEY!!
ドム
BAM
I'M ALWAYS TELLING YOU TO BE MORE FRIENDLY!
OTHERWISE YOU'LL JUST SCARE EVERYONE OFF!
I'M REALLY SORRY ABOUT HIM.

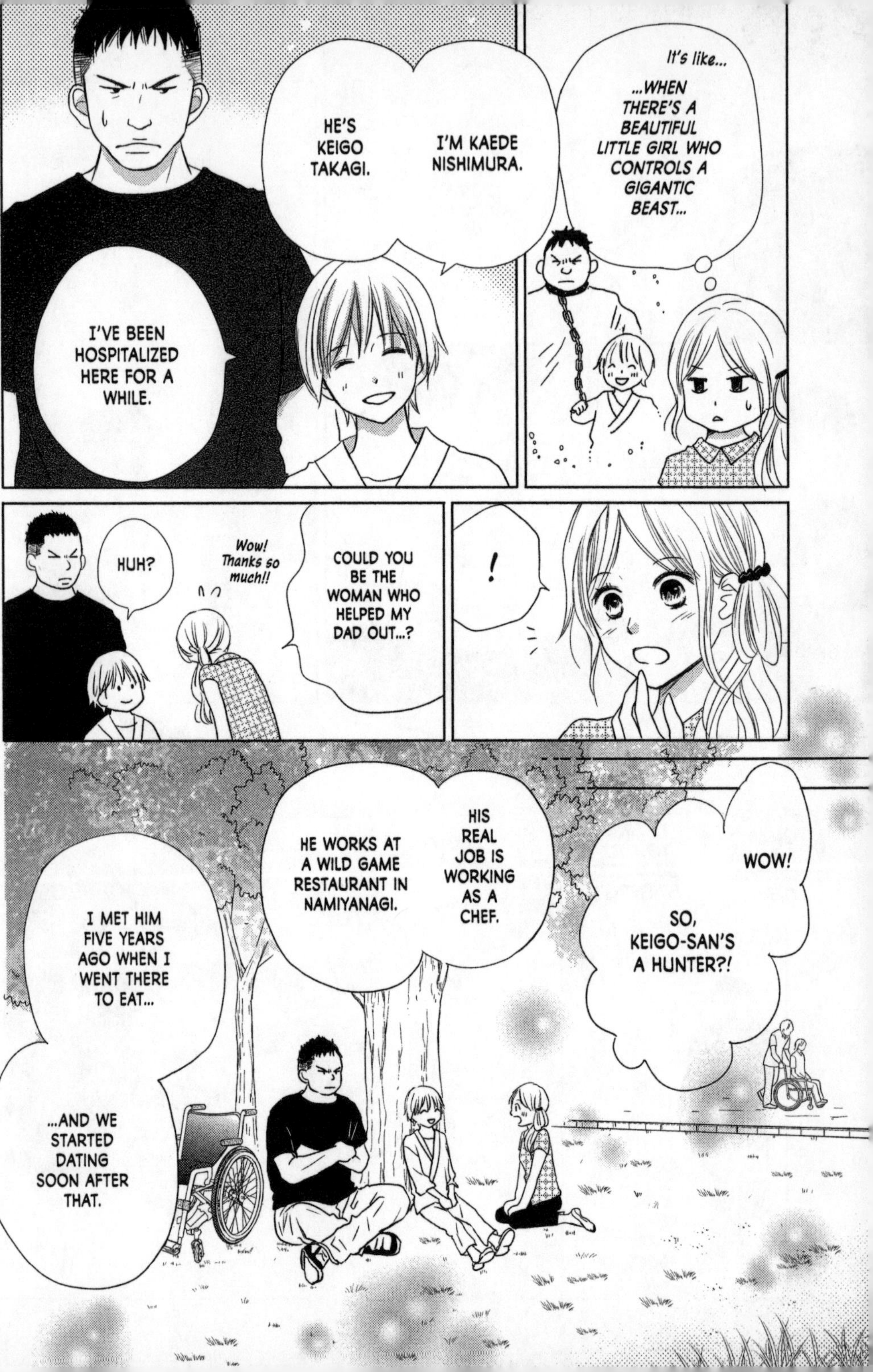
It's like...
...WHEN THERE'S A BEAUTIFUL LITTLE GIRL WHO CONTROLS A GIGANTIC BEAST...
I'M KAEDE NISHIMURA.
HE'S KEIGO TAKAGI.
I'VE BEEN HOSPITALIZED HERE FOR A WHILE.
!
COULD YOU BE THE WOMAN WHO HELPED MY DAD OUT...?
Wow! Thanks so much!!
HUH?
WOW!
SO, KEIGO-SAN'S A HUNTER?!
HIS REAL JOB IS WORKING AS A CHEF.
HE WORKS AT A WILD GAME RESTAURANT IN NAMIYANAGI.
I MET HIM FIVE YEARS AGO WHEN I WENT THERE TO EAT...
...AND WE STARTED DATING SOON AFTER THAT.

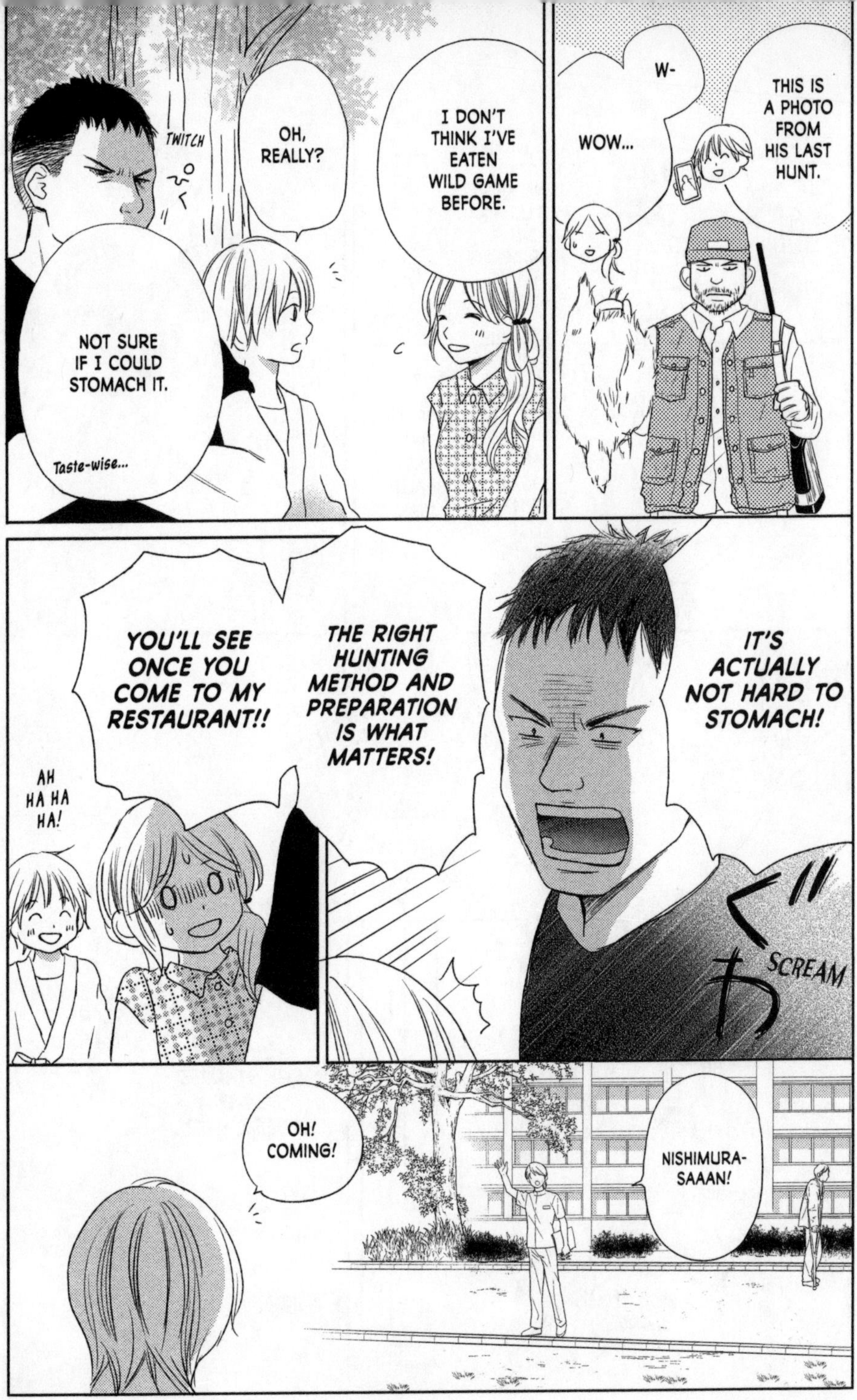

THIS IS A PHOTO FROM HIS LAST HUNT.
W-
WOW...
I DON'T THINK I'VE EATEN WILD GAME BEFORE.
OH, REALLY?
TWITCH
Taste-wise...
NOT SURE IF I COULD STOMACH IT.
IT'S ACTUALLY NOT HARD TO STOMACH!
SCREAM
THE RIGHT HUNTING METHOD AND PREPARATION IS WHAT MATTERS!
YOU'LL SEE ONCE YOU COME TO MY RESTAURANT!!
AH HA HA HA!
NISHIMURA-SAAAN!
OH! COMING!

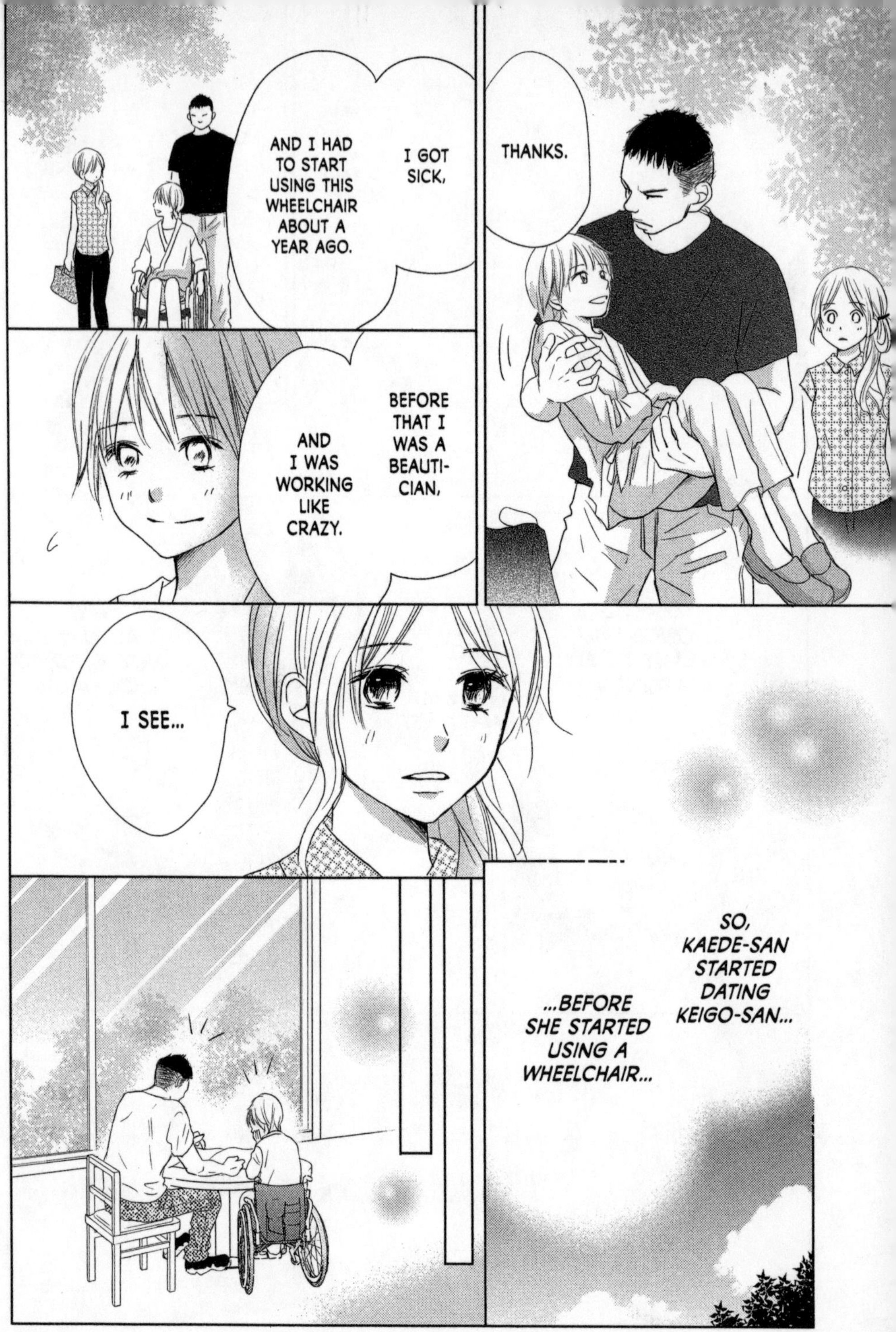
THANKS.
I GOT SICK,
AND I HAD TO START USING THIS WHEELCHAIR ABOUT A YEAR AGO.
BEFORE THAT I WAS A BEAUTI-CIAN,
AND I WAS WORKING LIKE CRAZY.
I SEE...
SO, KAEDE-SAN STARTED DATING KEIGO-SAN...
...BEFORE SHE STARTED USING A WHEELCHAIR...

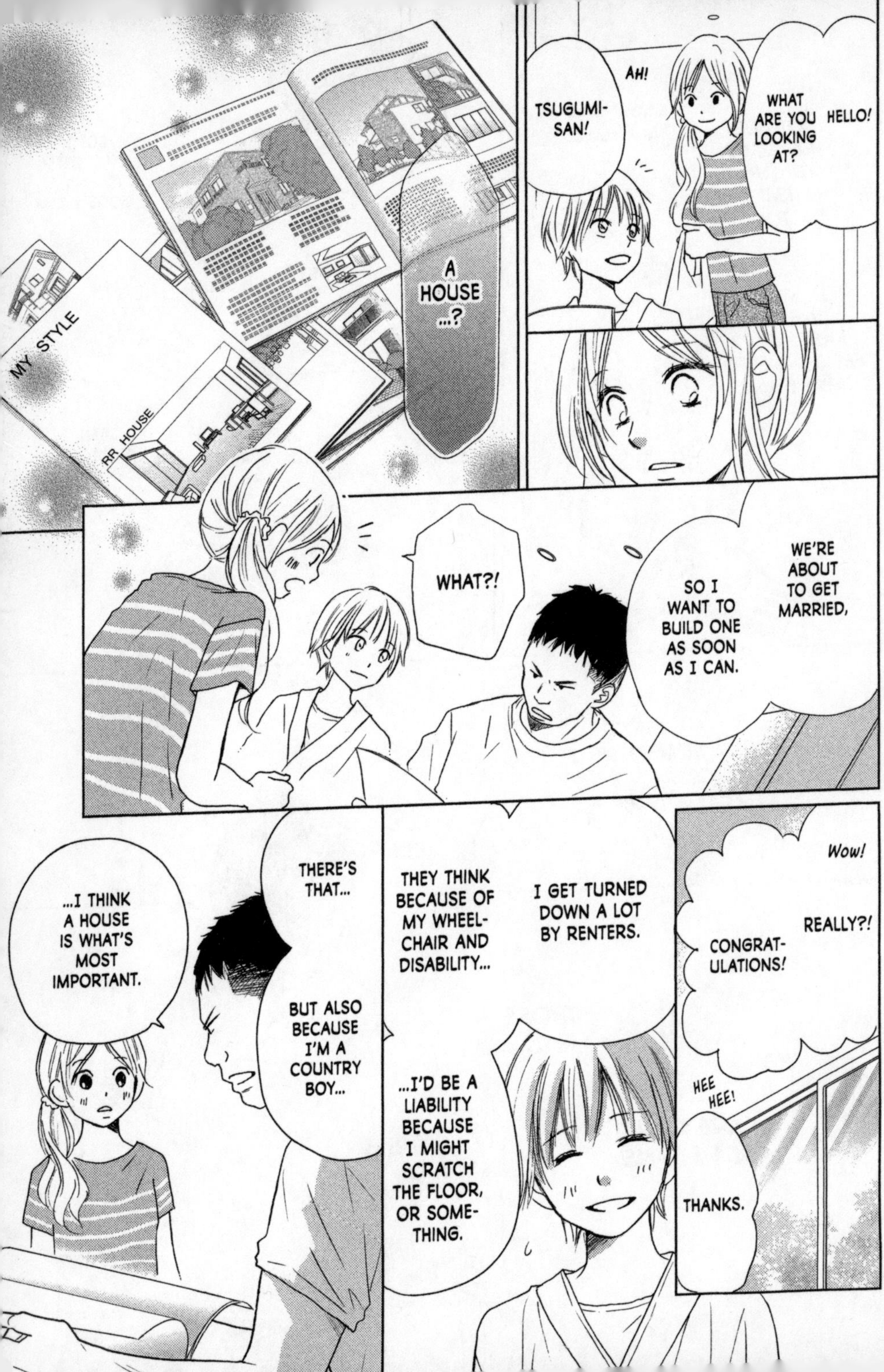
HELLO!
WHAT ARE YOU LOOKING AT?
AH!
TSUGUMI-SAN!
A HOUSE ...?
MY STYLE
RR HOUSE
WE'RE ABOUT TO GET MARRIED,
SO I WANT TO BUILD ONE AS SOON AS I CAN.
WHAT?!
Wow!
REALLY?!
CONGRAT-ULATIONS!
HEE HEE!
THANKS.
I GET TURNED DOWN A LOT BY RENTERS.
THEY THINK BECAUSE OF MY WHEEL-CHAIR AND DISABILITY...
...I'D BE A LIABILITY BECAUSE I MIGHT SCRATCH THE FLOOR, OR SOME-THING.
THERE'S THAT...
BUT ALSO BECAUSE I'M A COUNTRY BOY...
...I THINK A HOUSE IS WHAT'S MOST IMPORTANT.

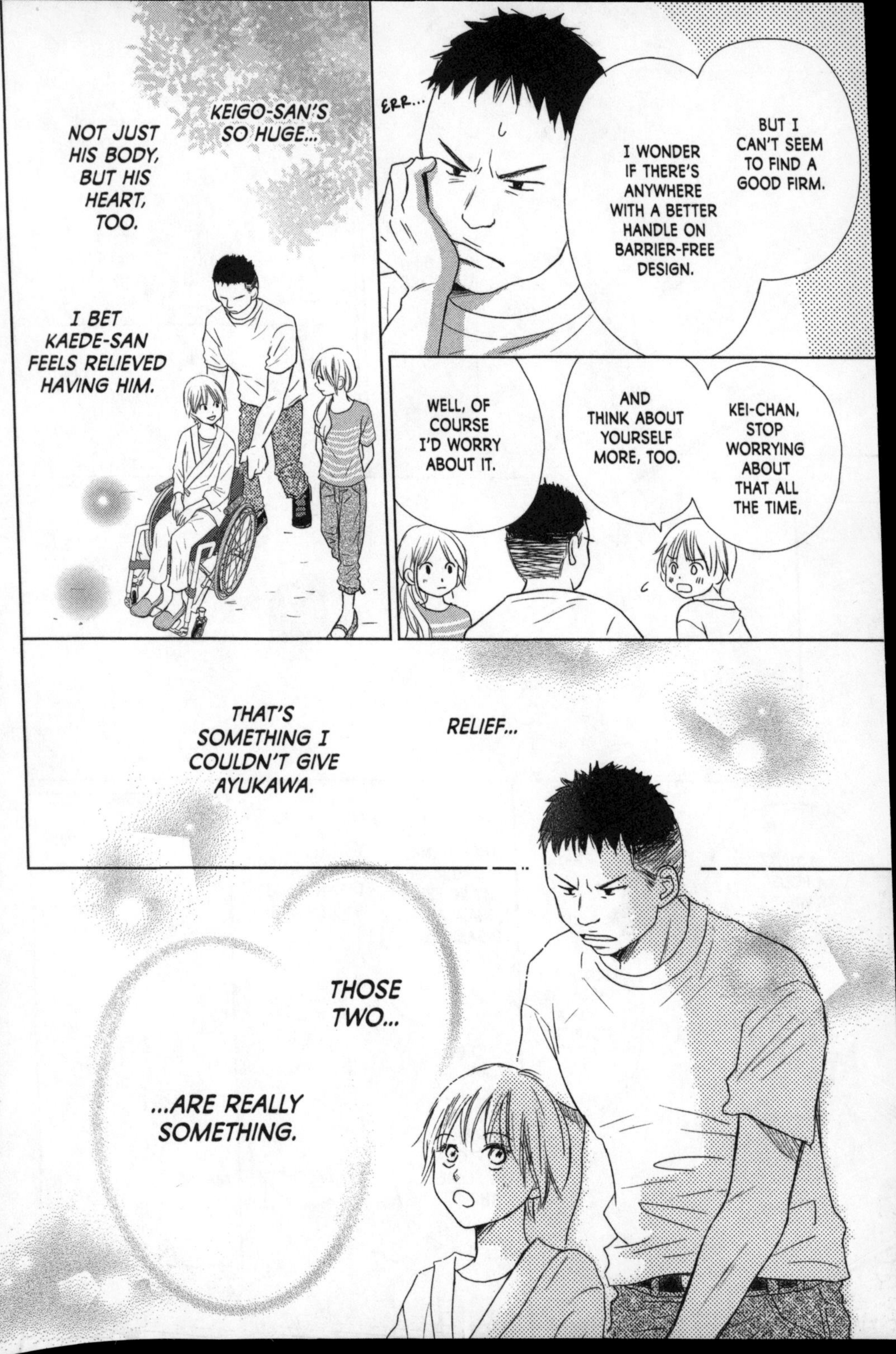
BUT I CAN'T SEEM TO FIND A GOOD FIRM.
I WONDER IF THERE'S ANYWHERE WITH A BETTER HANDLE ON BARRIER-FREE DESIGN.
ERR...
KEI-CHAN, STOP WORRYING ABOUT THAT ALL THE TIME,
AND THINK ABOUT YOURSELF MORE, TOO.
WELL, OF COURSE I'D WORRY ABOUT IT.
KEIGO-SAN'S SO HUGE...
NOT JUST HIS BODY, BUT HIS HEART, TOO.
I BET KAEDE-SAN FEELS RELIEVED HAVING HIM.
RELIEF...
THAT'S SOMETHING I COULDN'T GIVE AYUKAWA.
THOSE TWO...
...ARE REALLY SOMETHING.

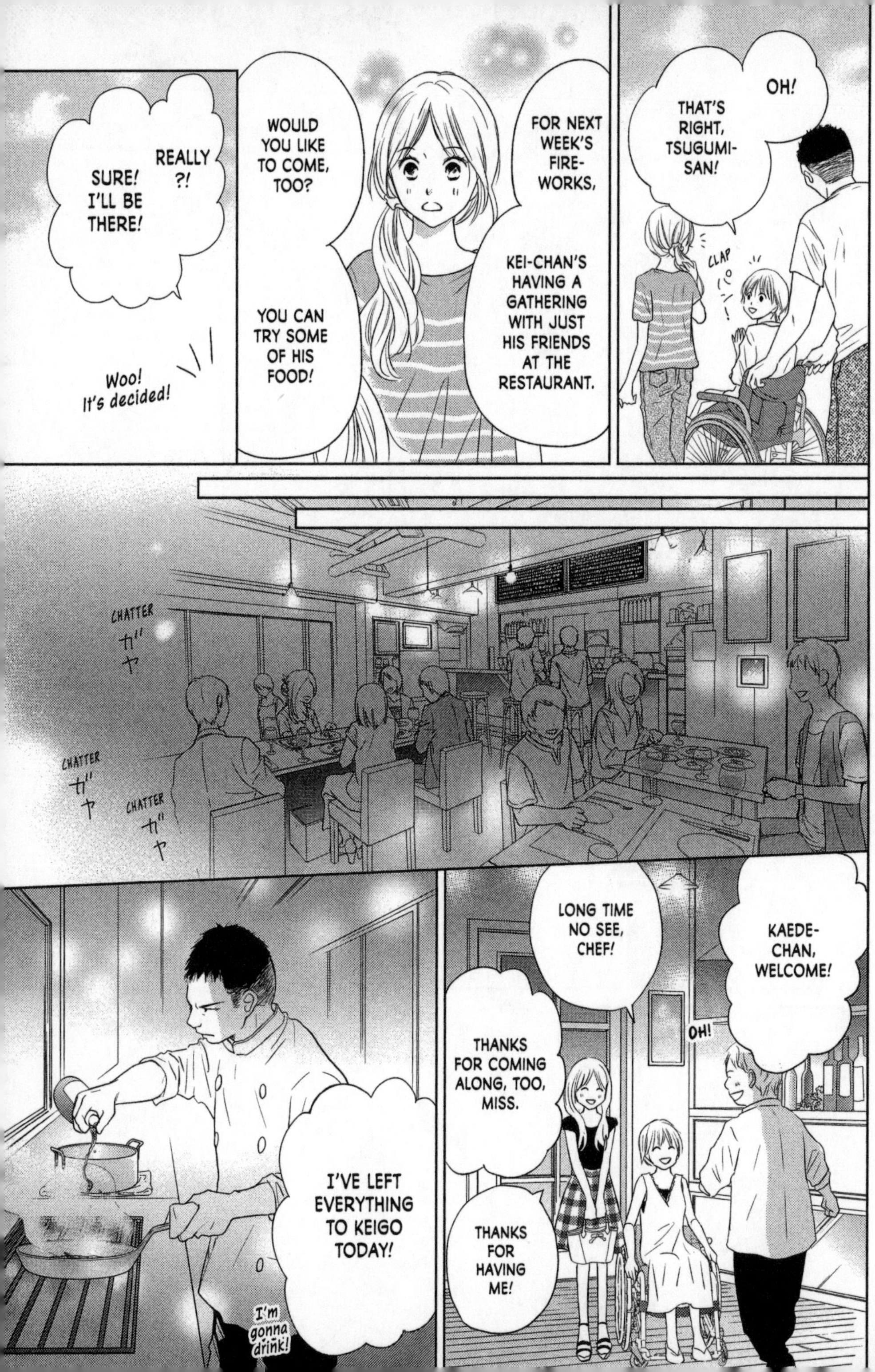
OH!
THAT'S RIGHT, TSUGUMI-SAN!
CLAP
FOR NEXT WEEK'S FIRE-WORKS,
KEI-CHAN'S HAVING A GATHERING WITH JUST HIS FRIENDS AT THE RESTAURANT.
WOULD YOU LIKE TO COME, TOO?
YOU CAN TRY SOME OF HIS FOOD!
REALLY ?!
SURE! I'LL BE THERE!
Woo! It's decided!
CHATTER
CHATTER
CHATTER
KAEDE-CHAN, WELCOME!
OH!
LONG TIME NO SEE, CHEF!
THANKS FOR COMING ALONG, TOO, MISS.
THANKS FOR HAVING ME!
I'VE LEFT EVERYTHING TO KEIGO TODAY!
I'm gonna drink!

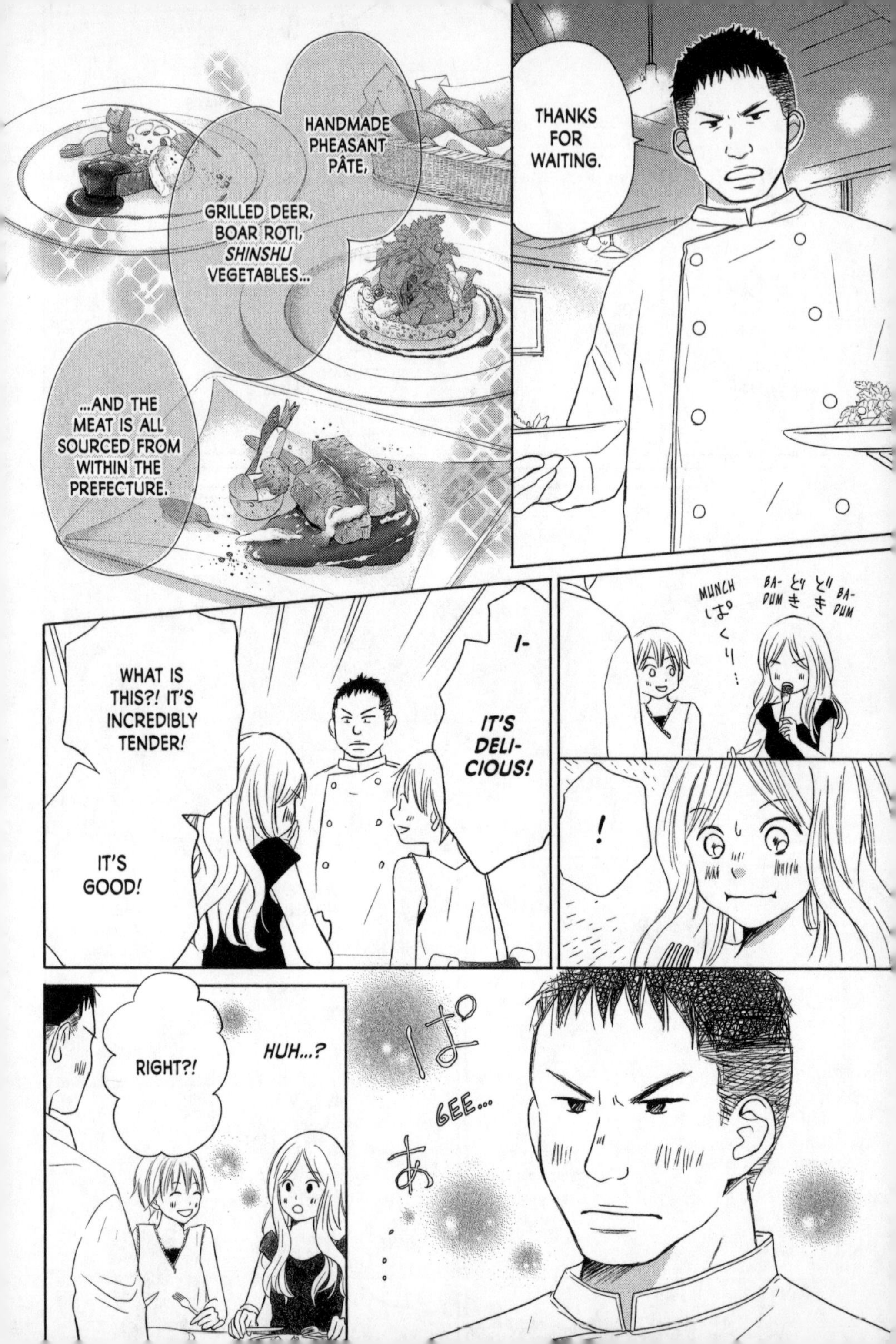
THANKS FOR WAITING.
HANDMADE PHEASANT PÂTE,
GRILLED DEER, BOAR ROTI, *SHINSHU* VEGETABLES...
...AND THE MEAT IS ALL SOURCED FROM WITHIN THE PREFECTURE.
BA-DUM BA-DUM
どきどき
MUNCH
ぱくり…
!
I-
IT'S DELICIOUS!
WHAT IS THIS?! IT'S INCREDIBLY TENDER!
IT'S GOOD!
GEE....
はあ…
HUH...?
RIGHT?!

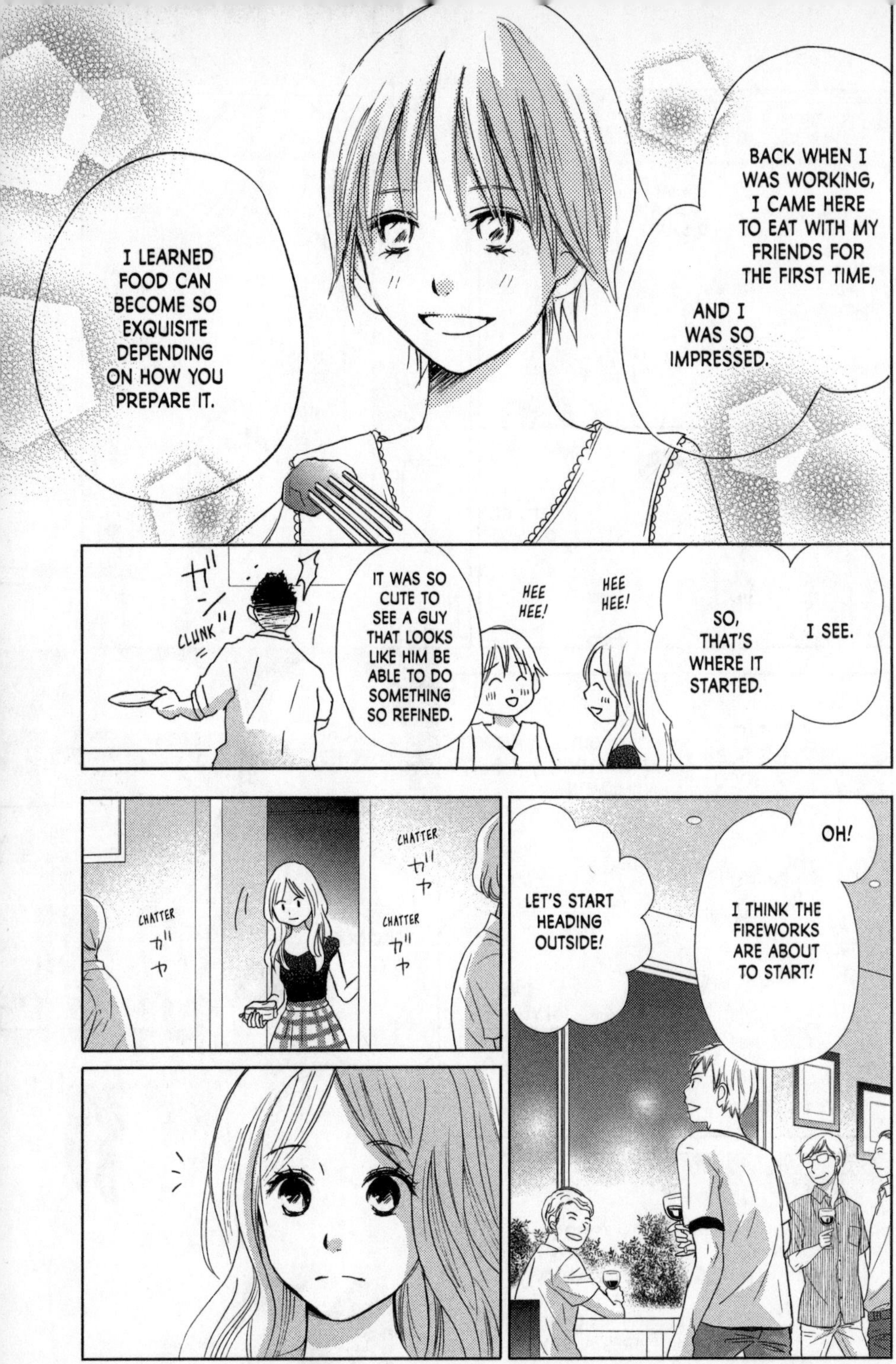
BACK WHEN I WAS WORKING, I CAME HERE TO EAT WITH MY FRIENDS FOR THE FIRST TIME,
AND I WAS SO IMPRESSED.
I LEARNED FOOD CAN BECOME SO EXQUISITE DEPENDING ON HOW YOU PREPARE IT.
I SEE.
SO, THAT'S WHERE IT STARTED.
HEE HEE!
HEE HEE!
IT WAS SO CUTE TO SEE A GUY THAT LOOKS LIKE HIM BE ABLE TO DO SOMETHING SO REFINED.
ガ
CLUNK
OH!
I THINK THE FIREWORKS ARE ABOUT TO START!
LET'S START HEADING OUTSIDE!
CHATTER
ガヤ
CHATTER
ガヤ
CHATTER
ガヤ

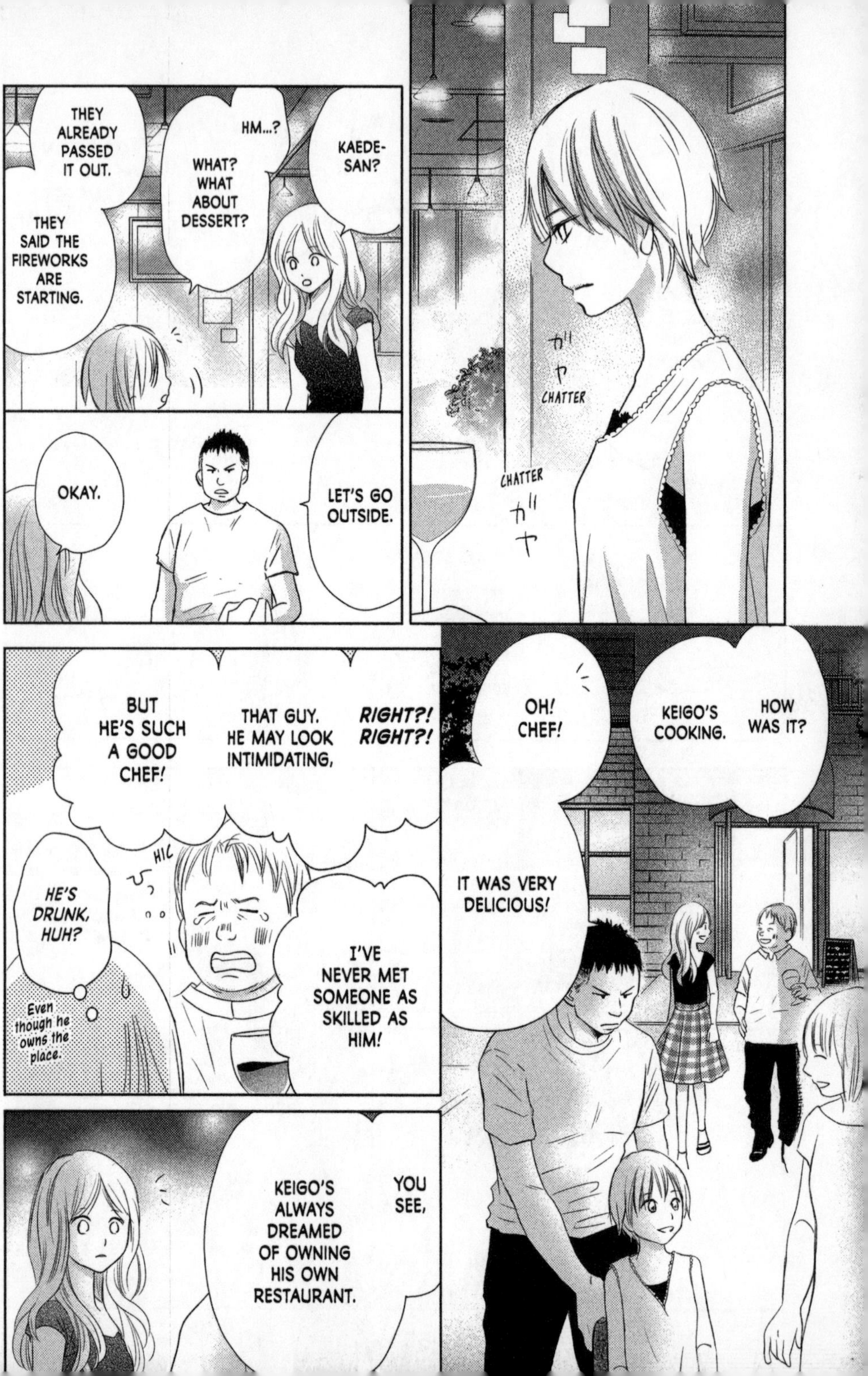
ガヤ
CHATTER
CHATTER
ガヤ
KAEDE-SAN?
HM...?
WHAT? WHAT ABOUT DESSERT?
THEY ALREADY PASSED IT OUT.
THEY SAID THE FIREWORKS ARE STARTING.
LET'S GO OUTSIDE.
OKAY.
HOW WAS IT?
KEIGO'S COOKING.
OH! CHEF!
IT WAS VERY DELICIOUS!
RIGHT?! RIGHT?!
THAT GUY. HE MAY LOOK INTIMIDATING,
BUT HE'S SUCH A GOOD CHEF!
HIC
I'VE NEVER MET SOMEONE AS SKILLED AS HIM!
HE'S DRUNK, HUH?
Even though he owns the place.
YOU SEE,
KEIGO'S ALWAYS DREAMED OF OWNING HIS OWN RESTAURANT.

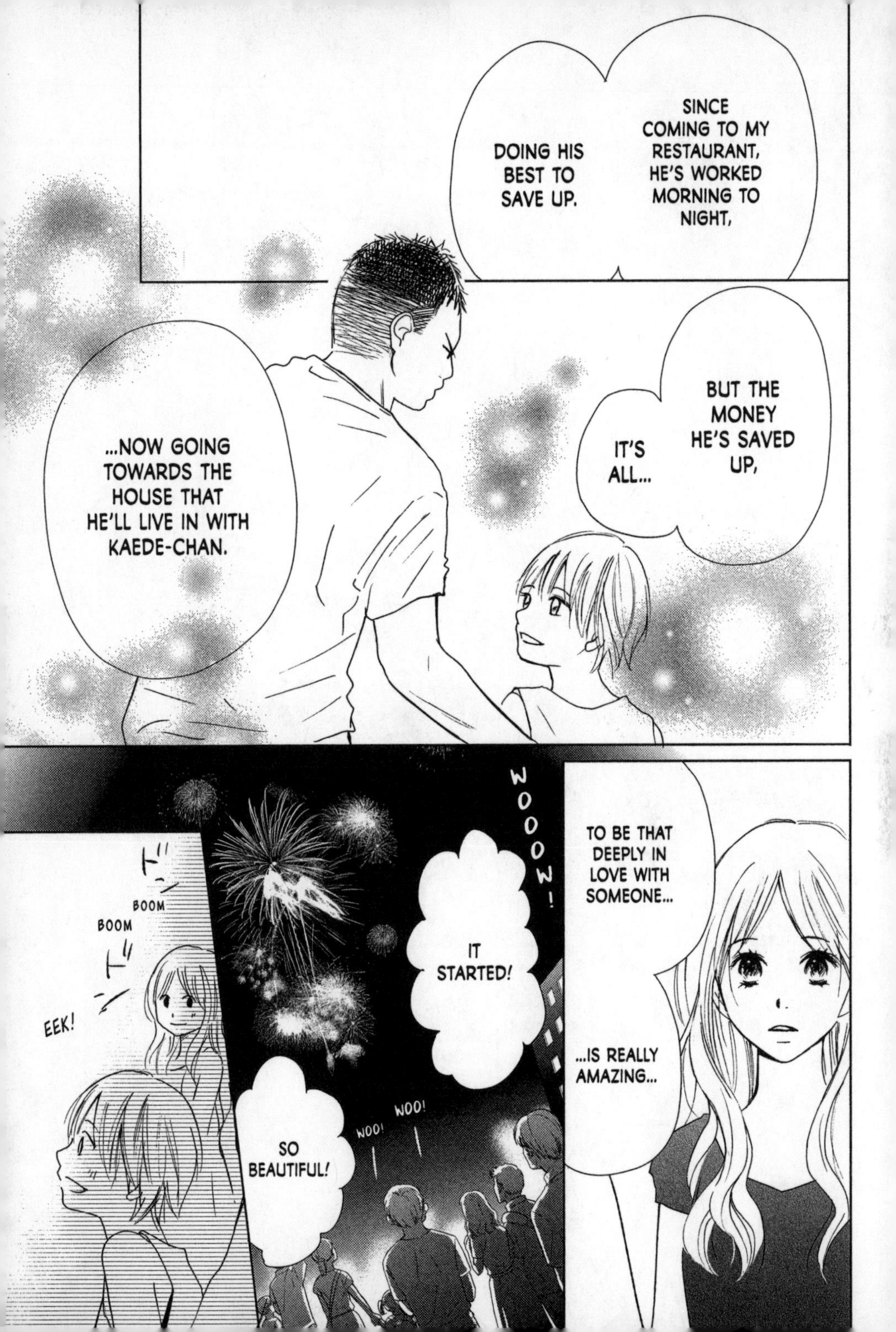
SINCE COMING TO MY RESTAURANT, HE'S WORKED MORNING TO NIGHT,
DOING HIS BEST TO SAVE UP.
BUT THE MONEY HE'S SAVED UP,
IT'S ALL...
...NOW GOING TOWARDS THE HOUSE THAT HE'LL LIVE IN WITH KAEDE-CHAN.
TO BE THAT DEEPLY IN LOVE WITH SOMEONE...
...IS REALLY AMAZING...
WOOOOW!
IT STARTED!
WOO!
WOO!
SO BEAUTIFUL!
BOOM
BOOM
EEK!

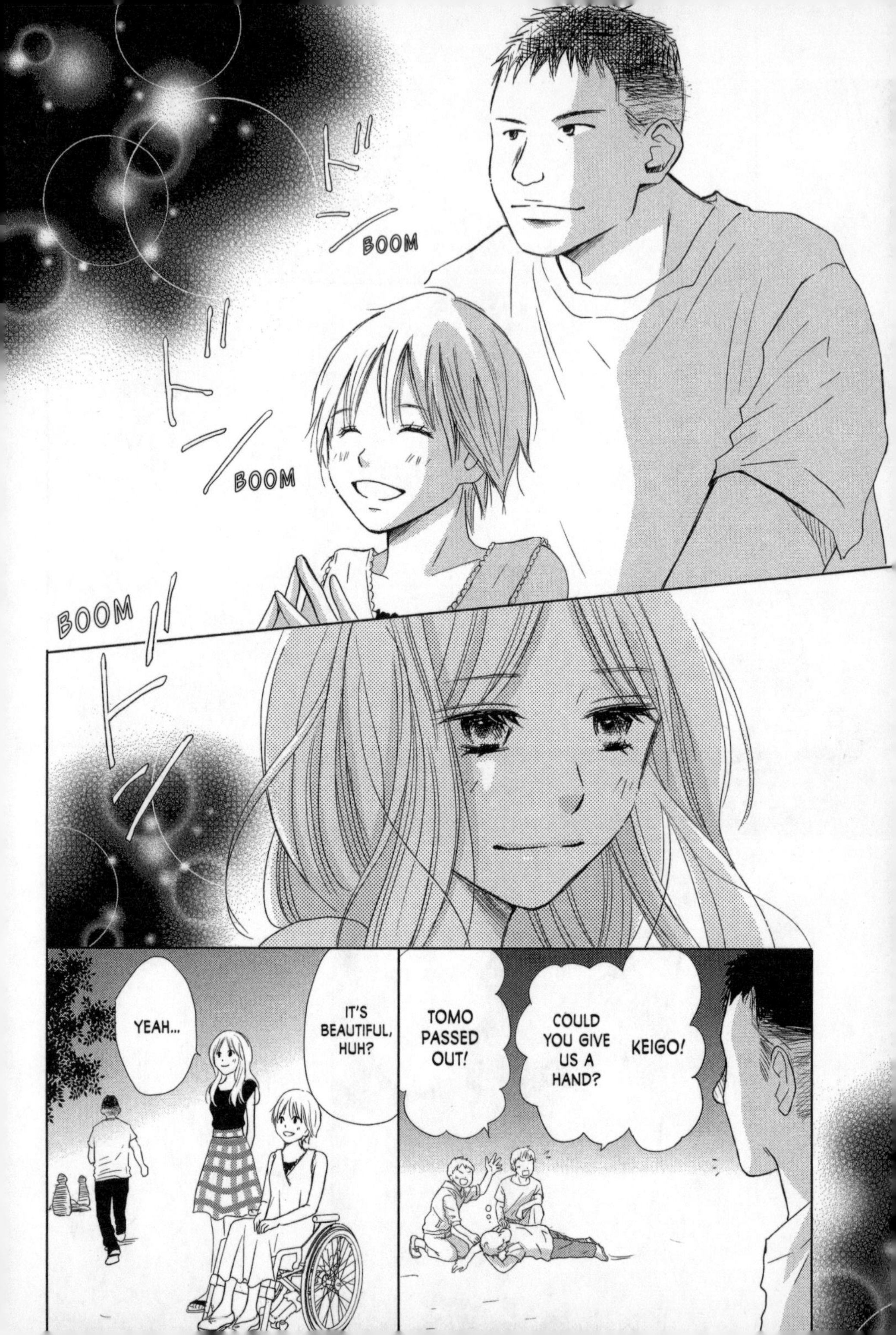
ドーン
BOOM
ドーン
BOOM
ドーン
BOOM
KEIGO!
COULD YOU GIVE US A HAND?
TOMO PASSED OUT!
IT'S BEAUTIFUL, HUH?
YEAH...

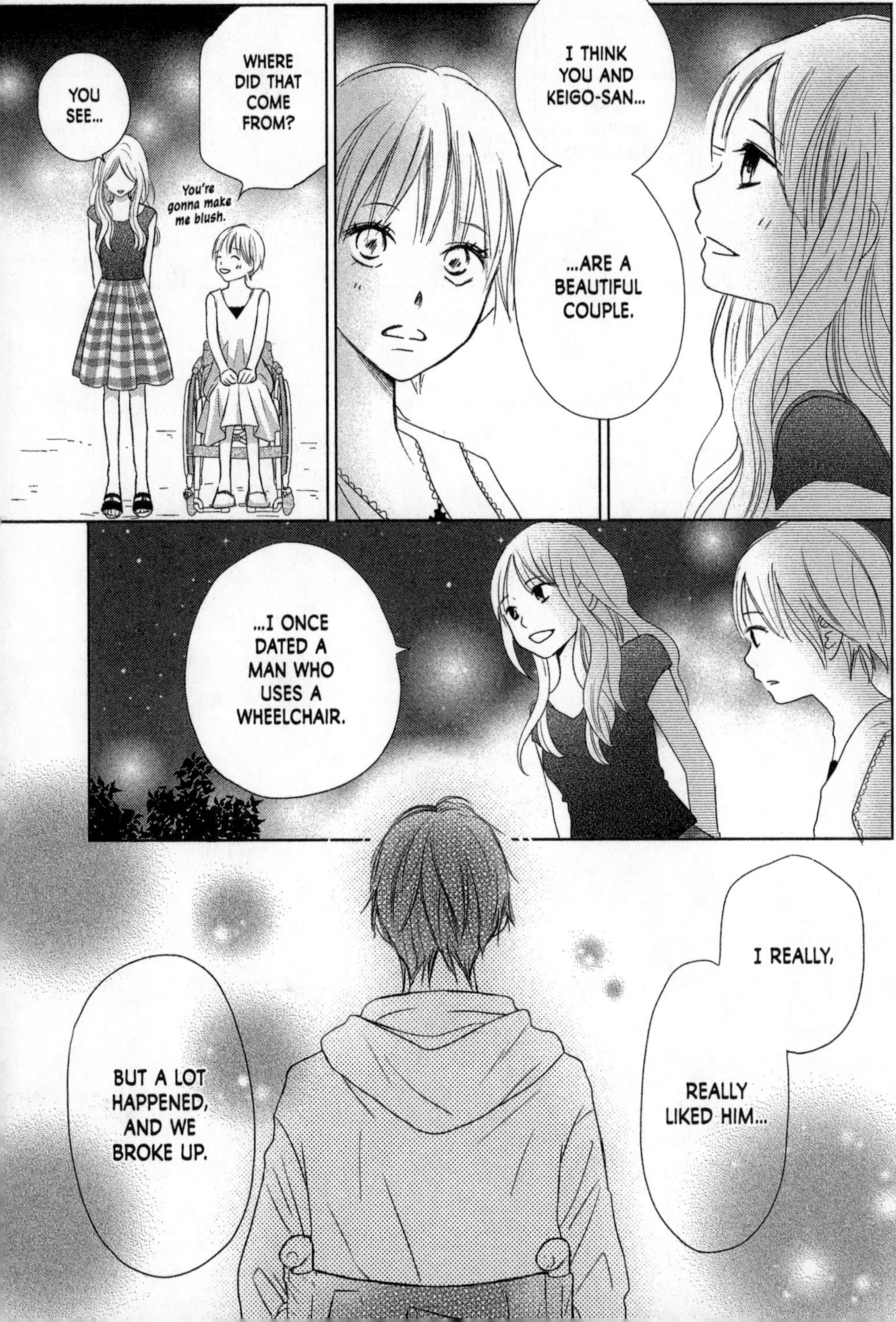
I THINK YOU AND KEIGO-SAN...
...ARE A BEAUTIFUL COUPLE.
WHERE DID THAT COME FROM?
You're gonna make me blush.
YOU SEE...
...I ONCE DATED A MAN WHO USES A WHEELCHAIR.
I REALLY,
REALLY LIKED HIM...
BUT A LOT HAPPENED, AND WE BROKE UP.

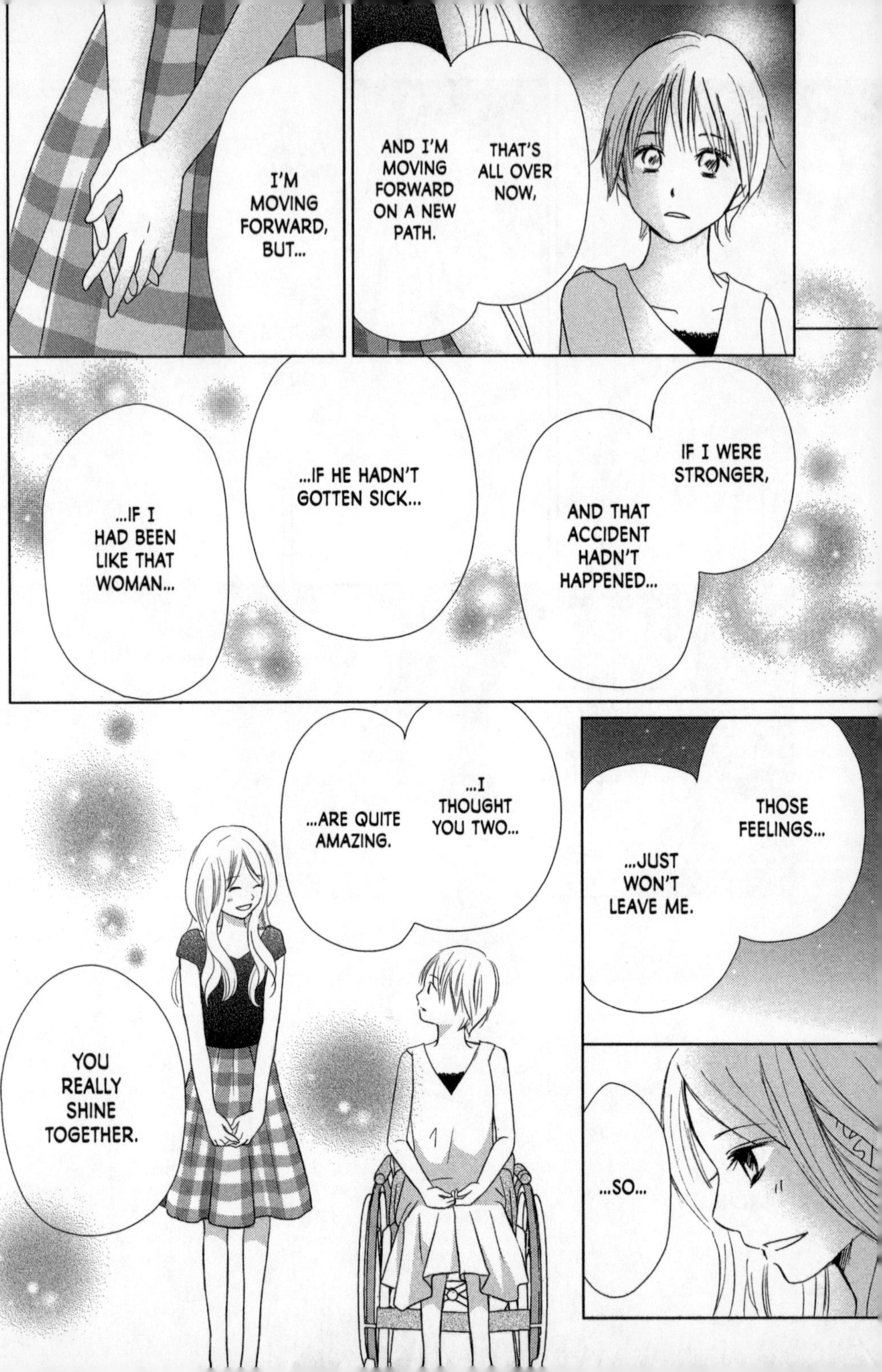
THAT'S ALL OVER NOW,
AND I'M MOVING FORWARD ON A NEW PATH.
I'M MOVING FORWARD, BUT...
IF I WERE STRONGER,
AND THAT ACCIDENT HADN'T HAPPENED...
...IF HE HADN'T GOTTEN SICK...
...IF I HAD BEEN LIKE THAT WOMAN...
THOSE FEELINGS...
...JUST WON'T LEAVE ME.
...SO...
...I THOUGHT YOU TWO...
...ARE QUITE AMAZING.
YOU REALLY SHINE TOGETHER.

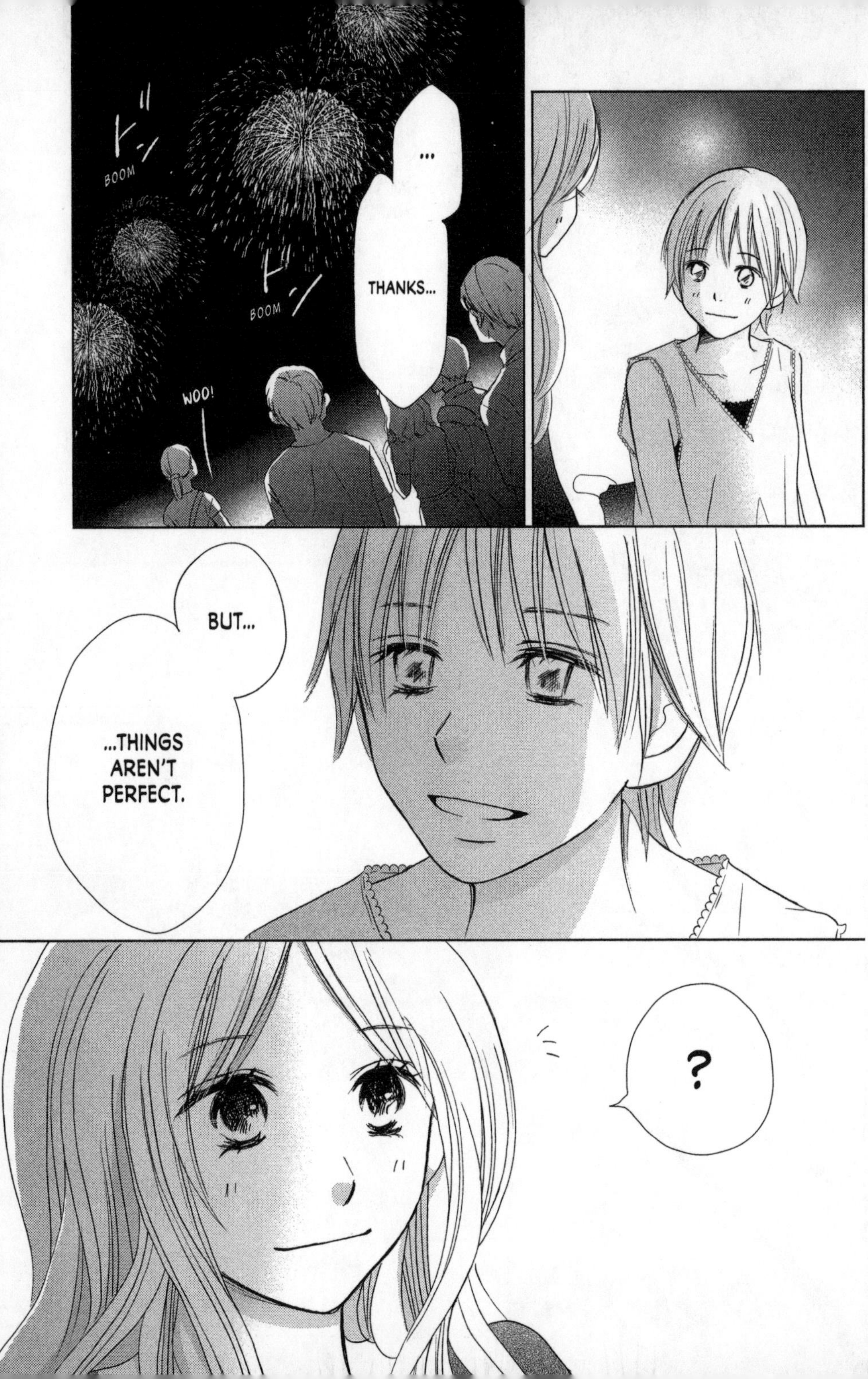
...
THANKS...
ドン
BOOM
ドン
BOOM
WOO!
BUT...
...THINGS AREN'T PERFECT.
?

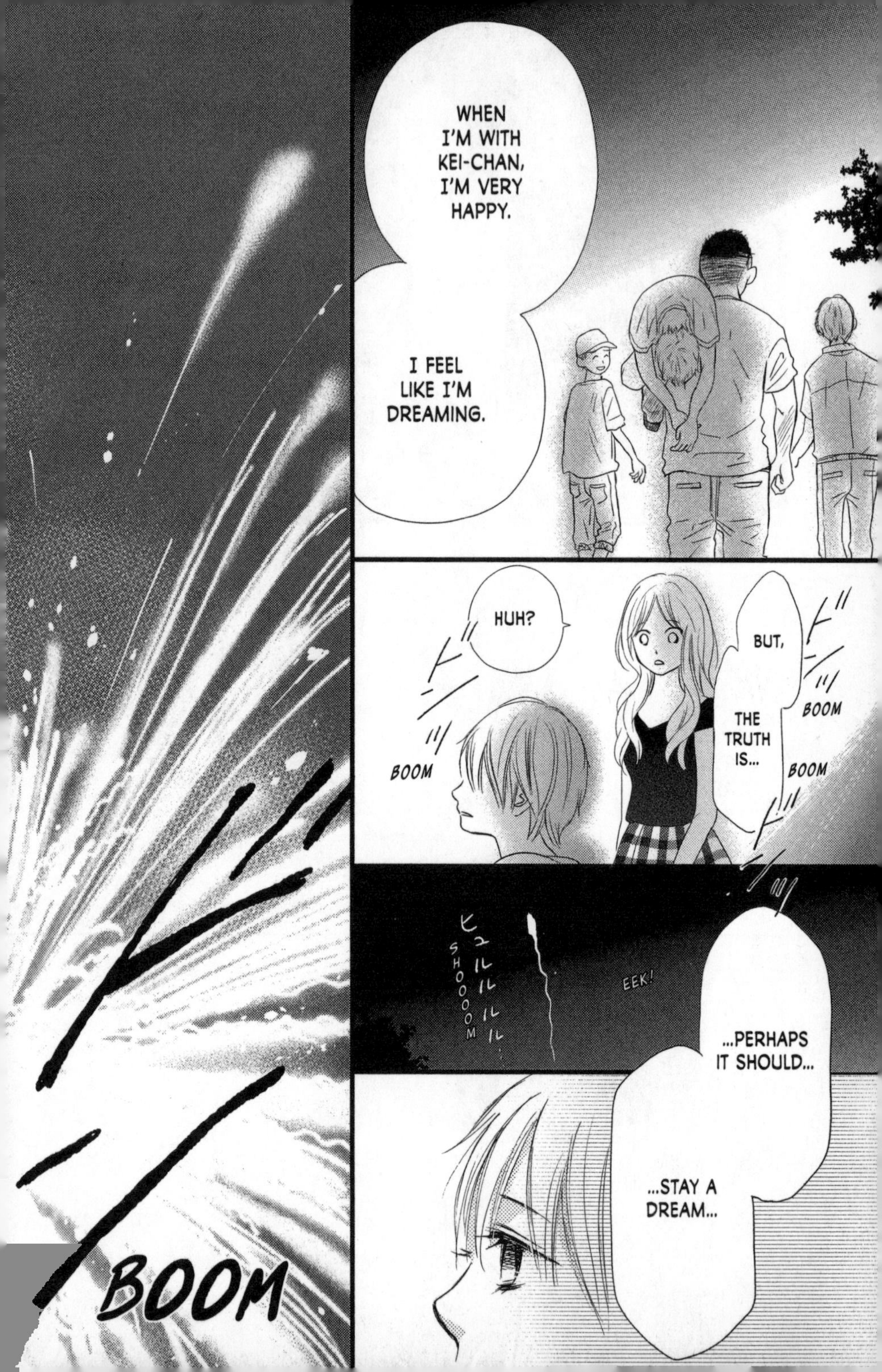

WHEN I'M WITH KEI-CHAN, I'M VERY HAPPY.
I FEEL LIKE I'M DREAMING.
HUH?
BUT,
THE TRUTH IS...
BOOM
BOOM
BOOM
SHOOOOM
EEK!
...PERHAPS IT SHOULD...
...STAY A DREAM...
BOOM

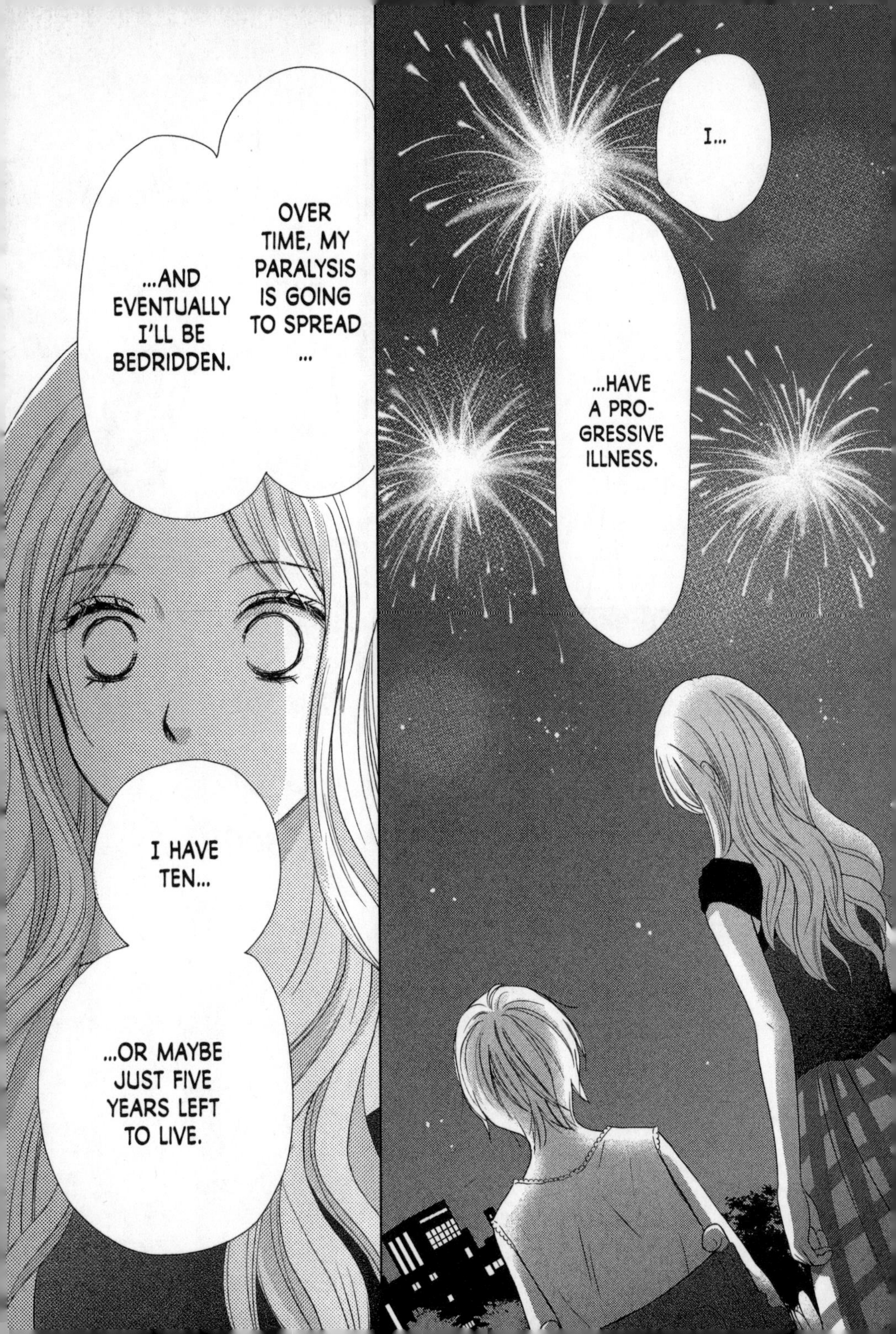
I...
...HAVE A PRO-GRESSIVE ILLNESS.
OVER TIME, MY PARALYSIS IS GOING TO SPREAD ...
...AND EVENTUALLY I'LL BE BEDRIDDEN.
I HAVE TEN...
...OR MAYBE JUST FIVE YEARS LEFT TO LIVE.

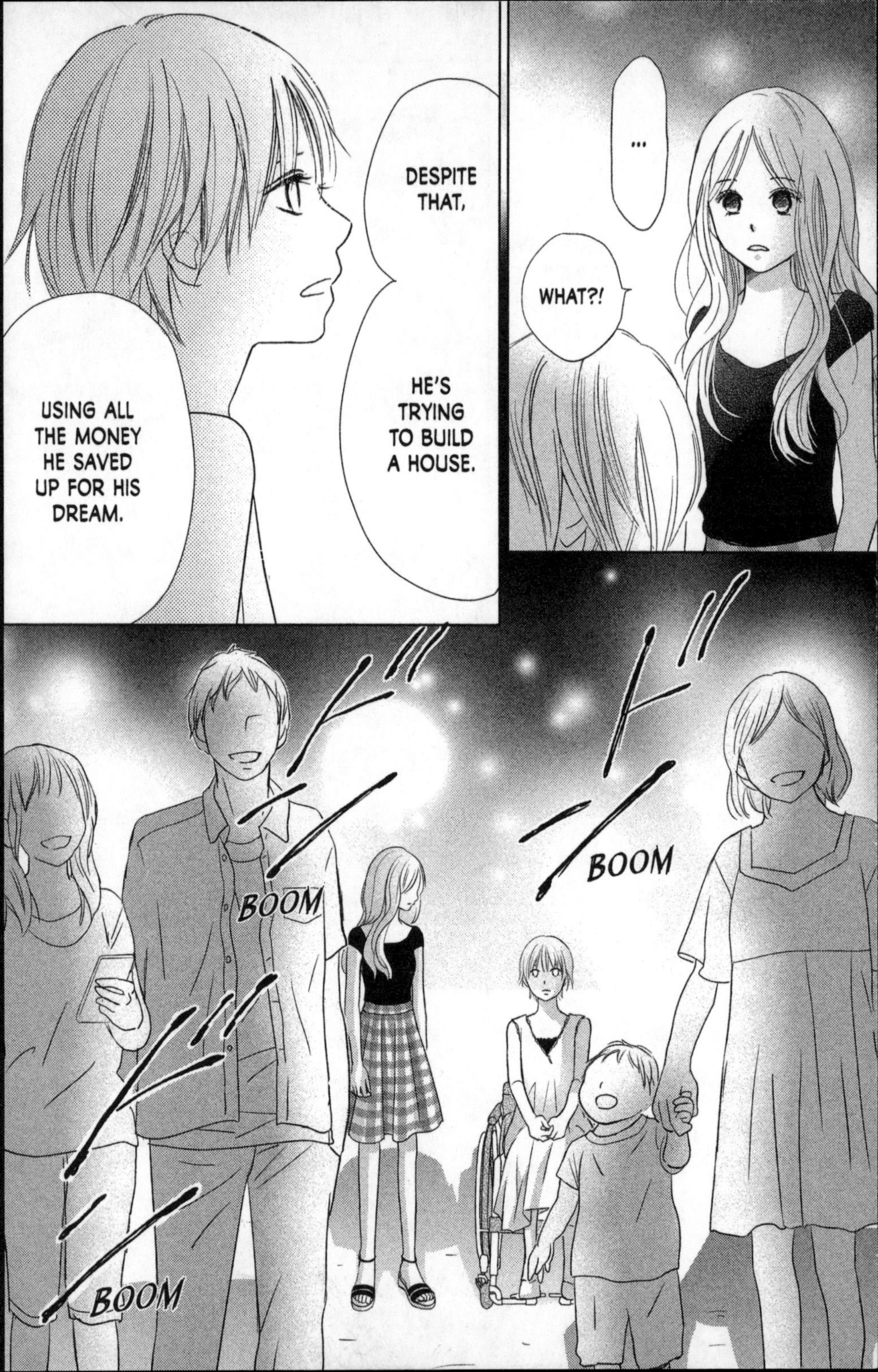
...
WHAT?!
DESPITE THAT,
HE'S TRYING TO BUILD A HOUSE.
USING ALL THE MONEY HE SAVED UP FOR HIS DREAM.
BOOM
BOOM
BOOM

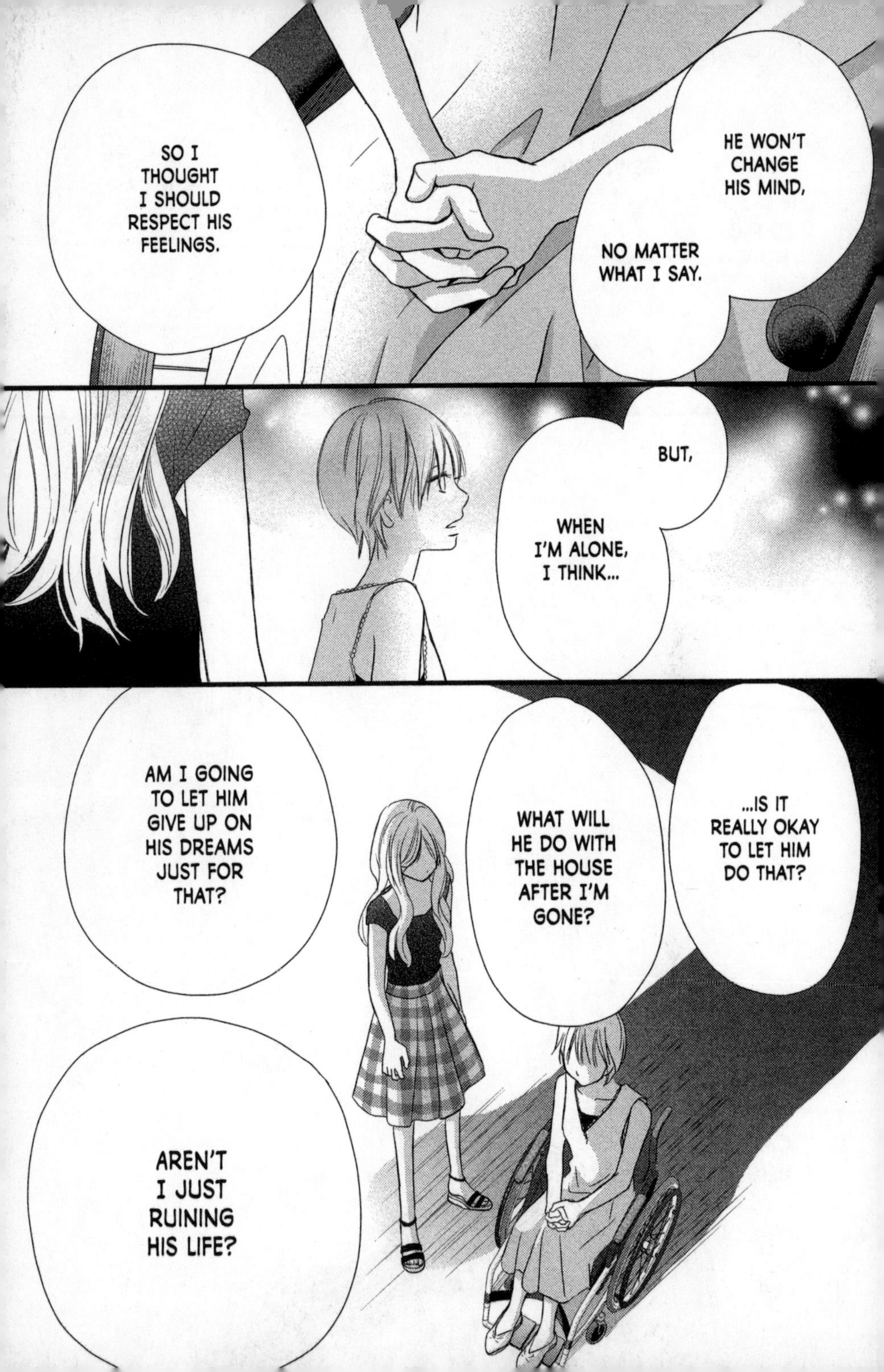
HE WON'T CHANGE HIS MIND,
NO MATTER WHAT I SAY.
SO I THOUGHT I SHOULD RESPECT HIS FEELINGS.
BUT,
WHEN I'M ALONE, I THINK...
...IS IT REALLY OKAY TO LET HIM DO THAT?
WHAT WILL HE DO WITH THE HOUSE AFTER I'M GONE?
AM I GOING TO LET HIM GIVE UP ON HIS DREAMS JUST FOR THAT?
AREN'T I JUST RUINING HIS LIFE?

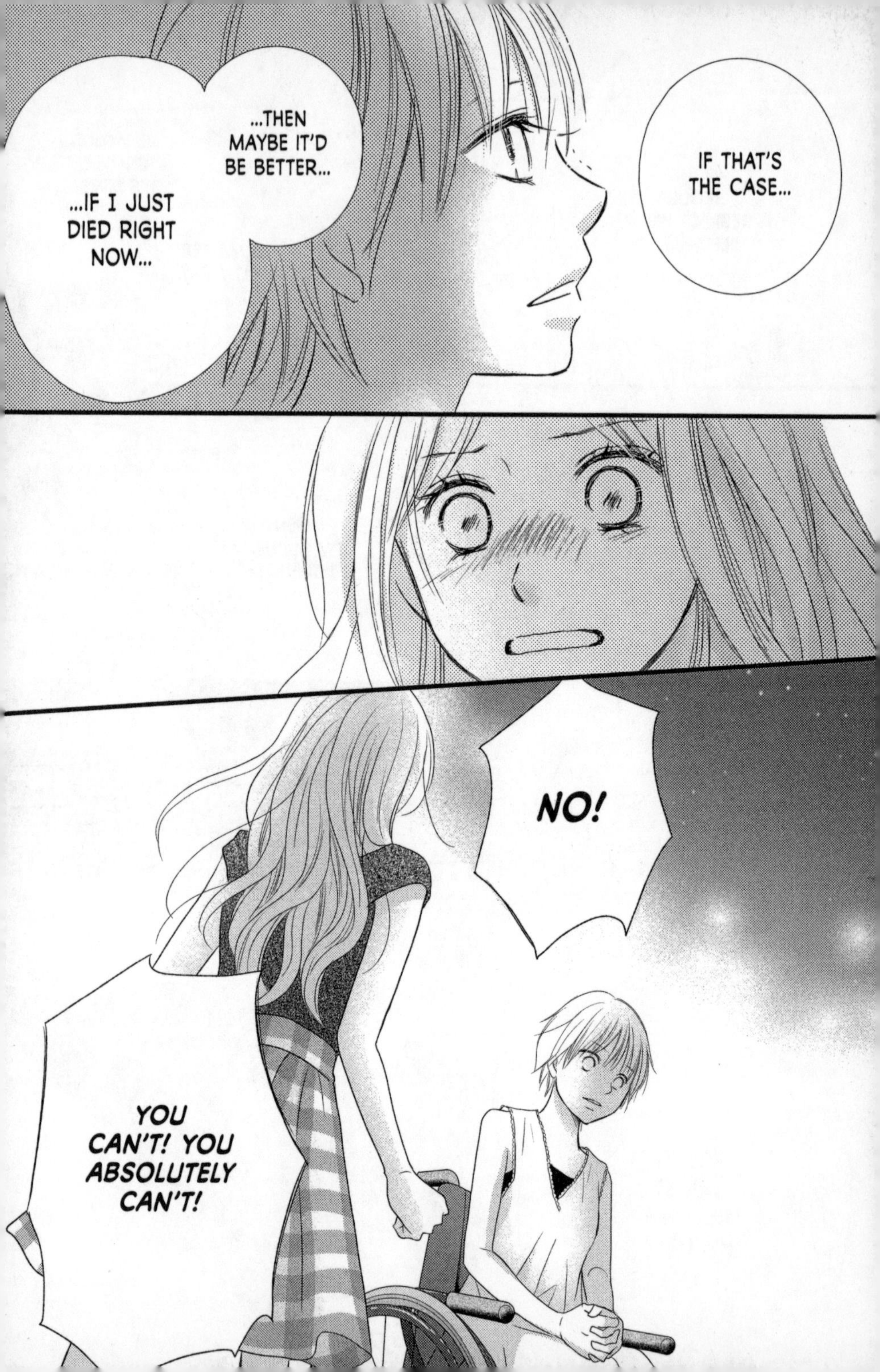
IF THAT'S THE CASE...
...THEN MAYBE IT'D BE BETTER...
...IF I JUST DIED RIGHT NOW...
NO!
YOU CAN'T! YOU ABSOLUTELY CAN'T!

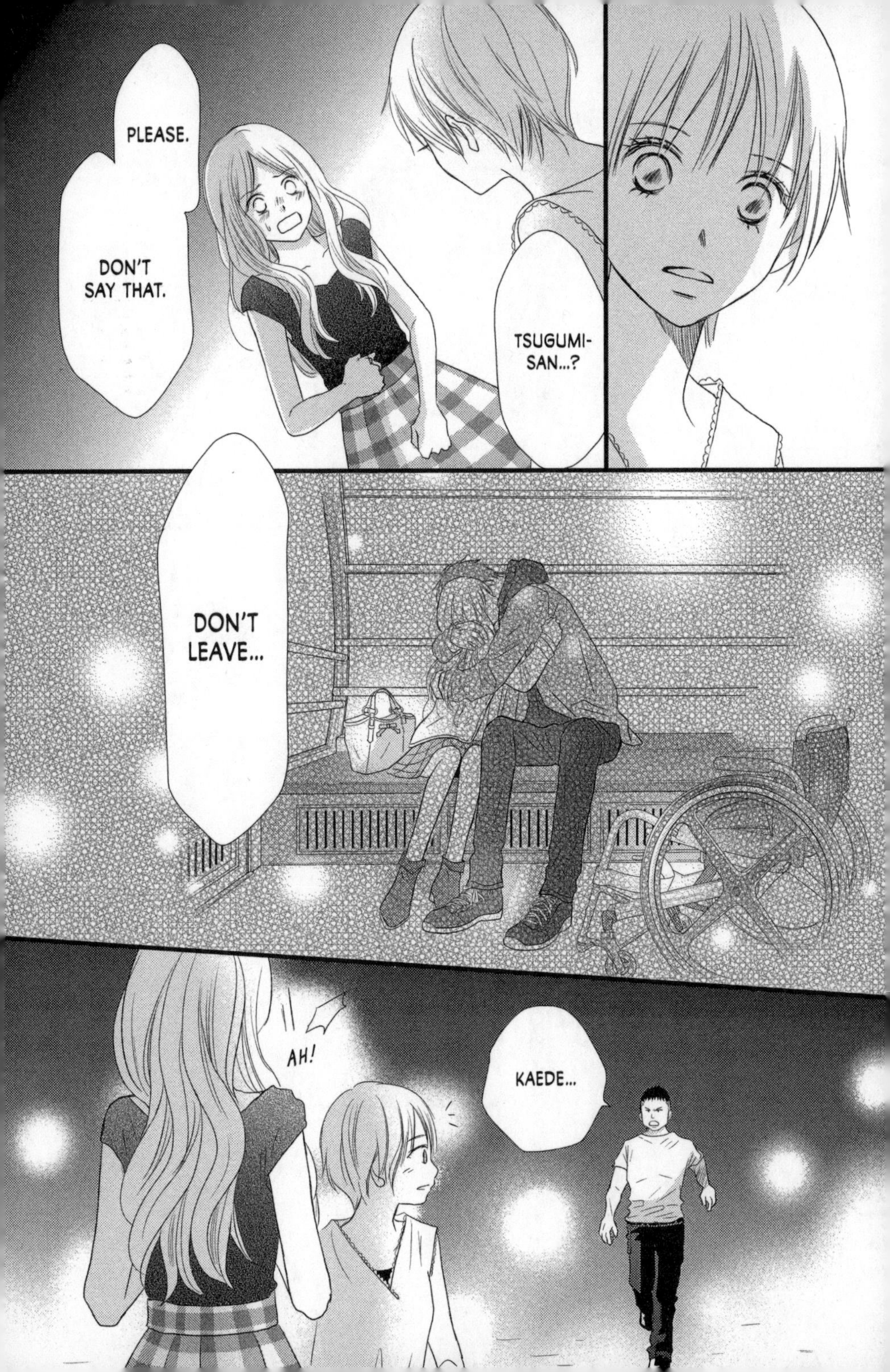
TSUGUMI-SAN...?
PLEASE.
DON'T SAY THAT.
DON'T LEAVE...
KAEDE...
AH!

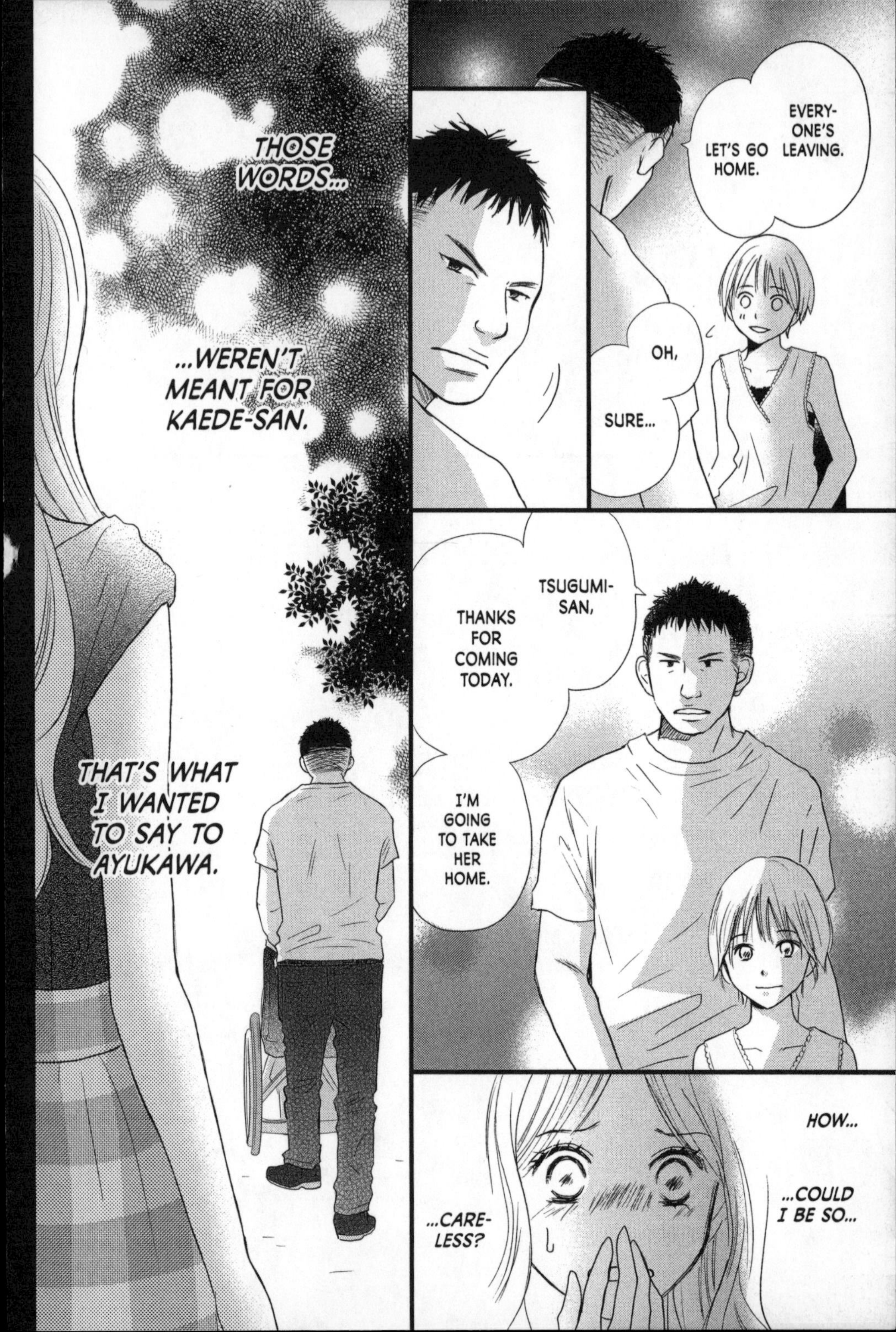
EVERYONE'S LEAVING.
LET'S GO HOME.
OH,
SURE...
TSUGUMI-SAN,
THANKS FOR COMING TODAY.
I'M GOING TO TAKE HER HOME.
HOW...
...COULD I BE SO...
...CARELESS?
THOSE WORDS...
...WEREN'T MEANT FOR KAEDE-SAN.
THAT'S WHAT I WANTED TO SAY TO AYUKAWA.

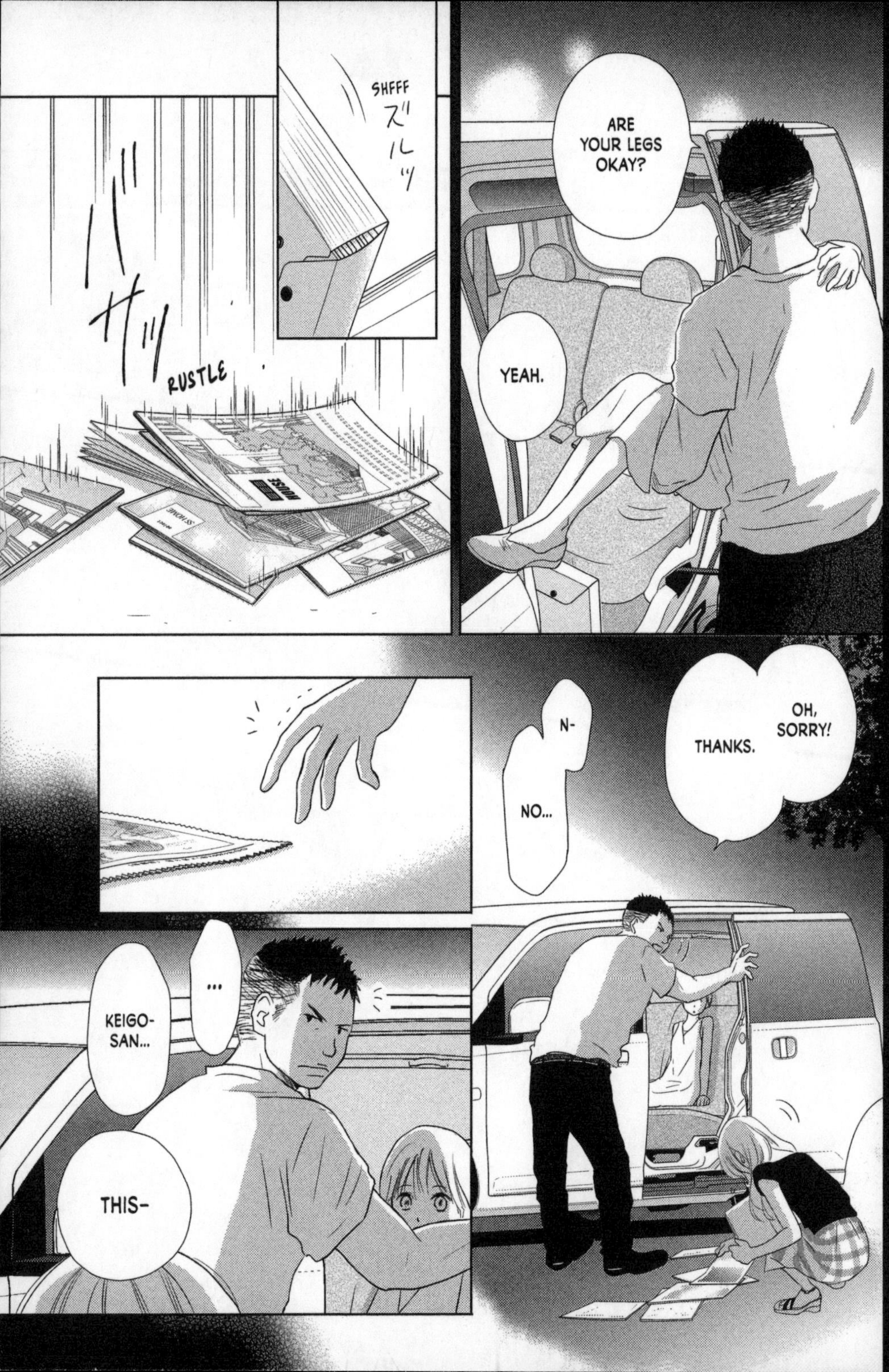
ARE YOUR LEGS OKAY?
YEAH.
SHFFF
ズルッ
ザッ
RUSTLE
OH, SORRY!
THANKS.
N-
NO...
...
KEIGO-SAN...
THIS-

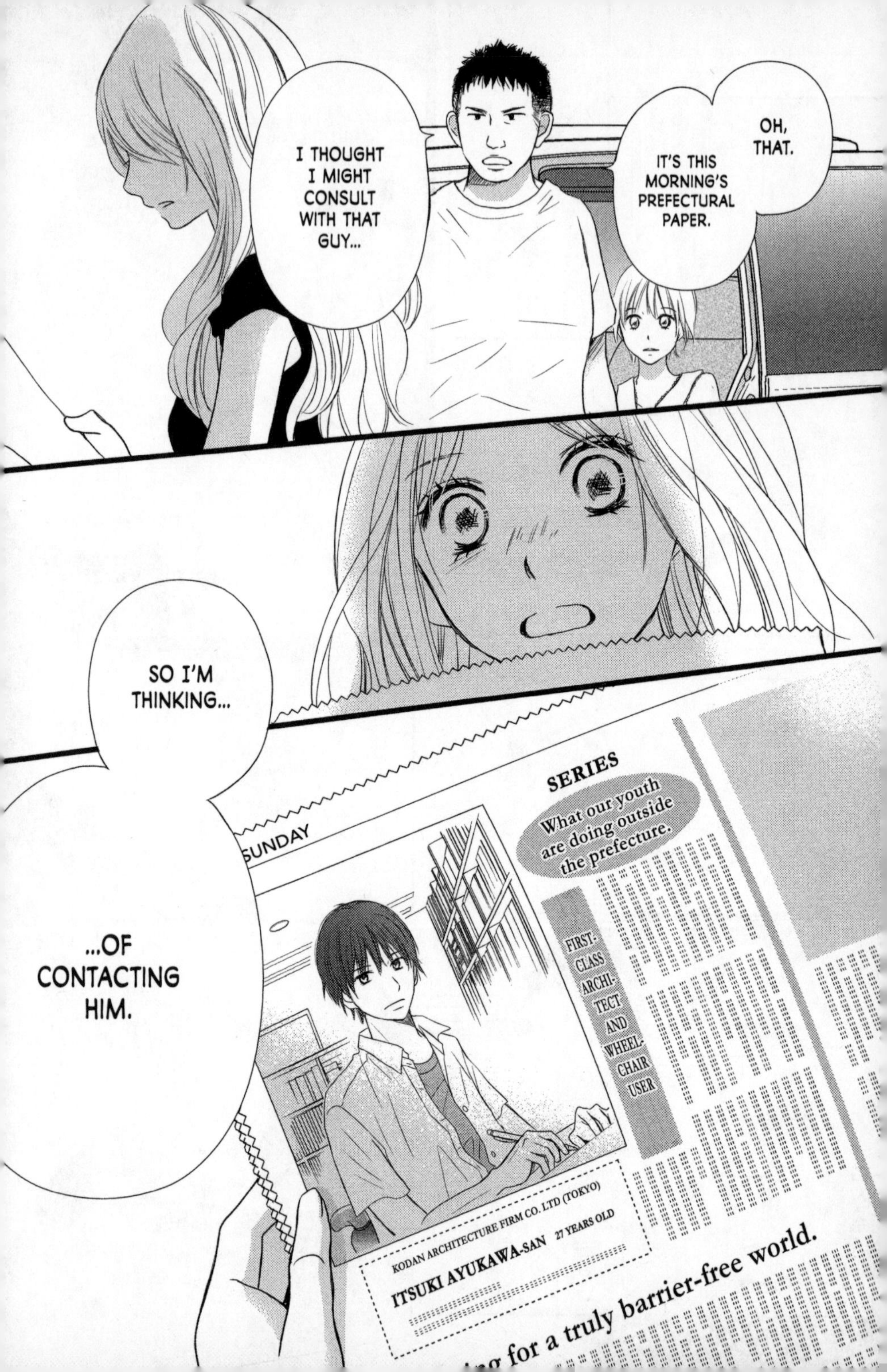
OH, THAT.
IT'S THIS MORNING'S PREFECTURAL PAPER.
I THOUGHT I MIGHT CONSULT WITH THAT GUY...
SO I'M THINKING...
...OF CONTACTING HIM.
SERIES
What our youth are doing outside the prefecture.
SUNDAY
FIRST-CLASS ARCHITECT AND WHEELCHAIR USER
KODAN ARCHITECTURE FIRM CO. LTD (TOKYO)
ITSUKI AYUKAWA-SAN 27 YEARS OLD
for a truly barrier-free world.

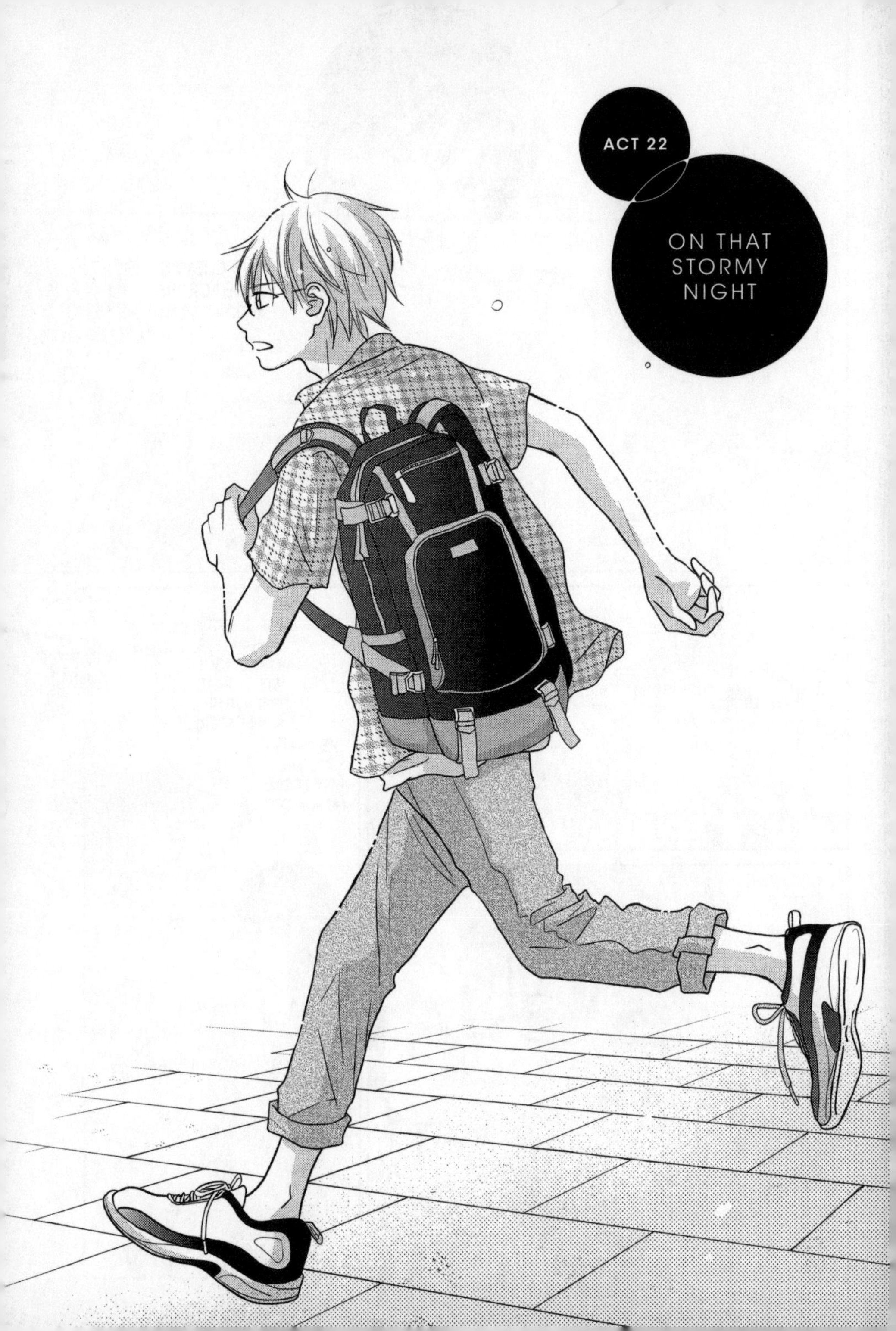
ACT 22
ON THAT STORMY NIGHT

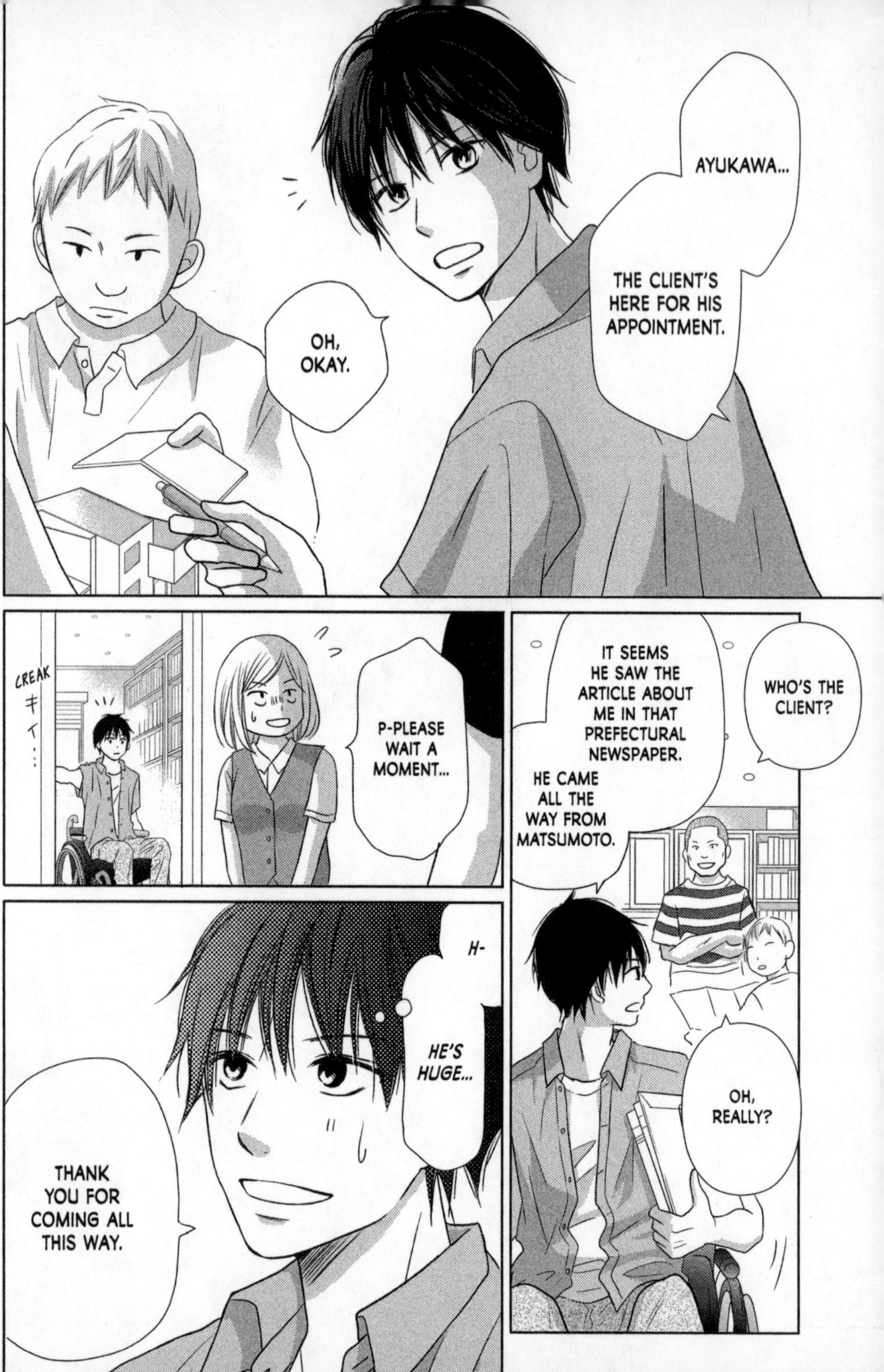
AYUKAWA...
THE CLIENT'S HERE FOR HIS APPOINTMENT.
OH, OKAY.
WHO'S THE CLIENT?
IT SEEMS HE SAW THE ARTICLE ABOUT ME IN THAT PREFECTURAL NEWSPAPER.
HE CAME ALL THE WAY FROM MATSUMOTO.
OH, REALLY?
P-PLEASE WAIT A MOMENT...
CREAK
キイ…
H-
HE'S HUGE...
THANK YOU FOR COMING ALL THIS WAY.

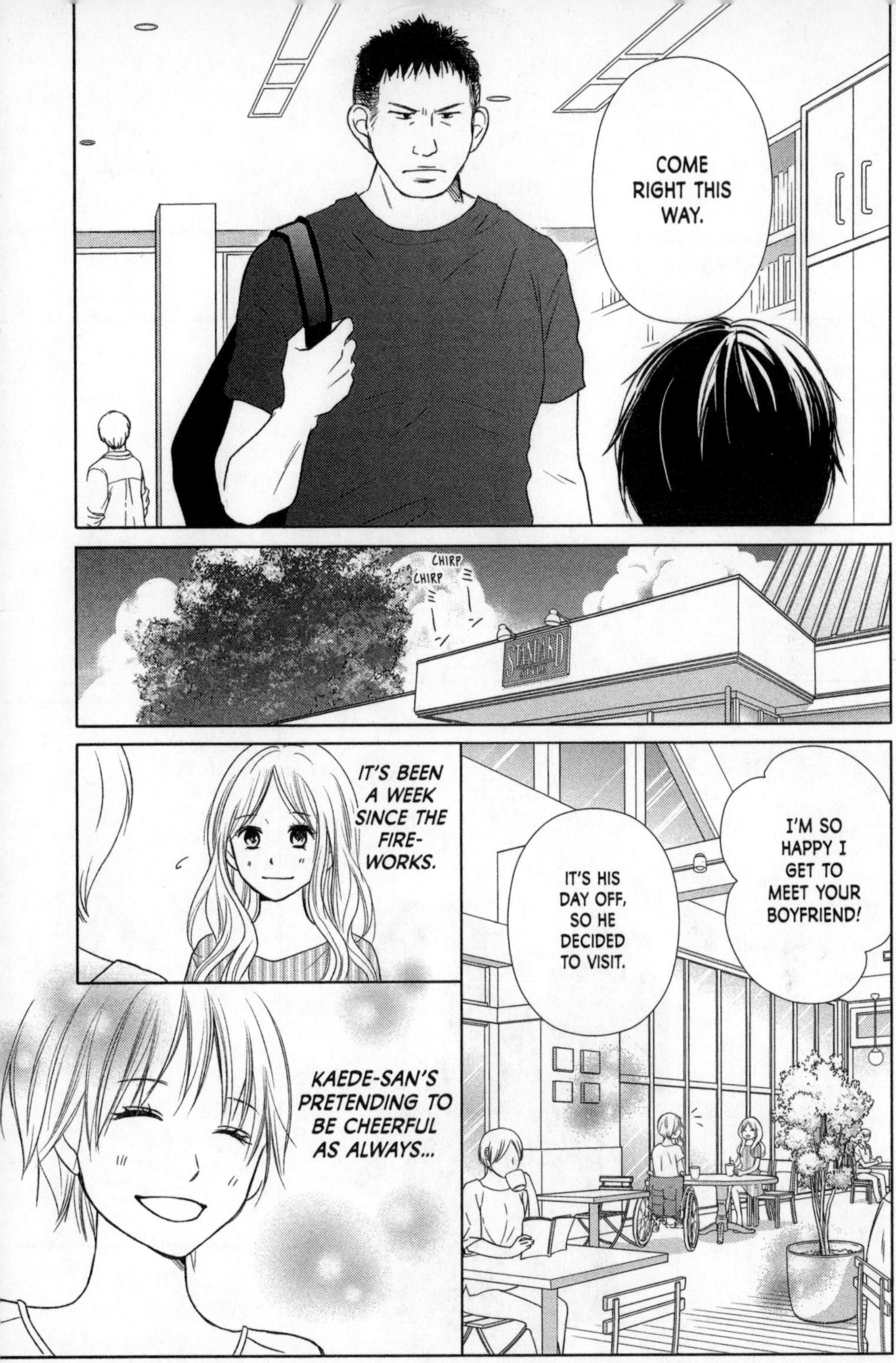
COME RIGHT THIS WAY.
CHIRP
CHIRP
I'M SO HAPPY I GET TO MEET YOUR BOYFRIEND!
IT'S HIS DAY OFF, SO HE DECIDED TO VISIT.
IT'S BEEN A WEEK SINCE THE FIRE-WORKS.
KAEDE-SAN'S PRETENDING TO BE CHEERFUL AS ALWAYS...

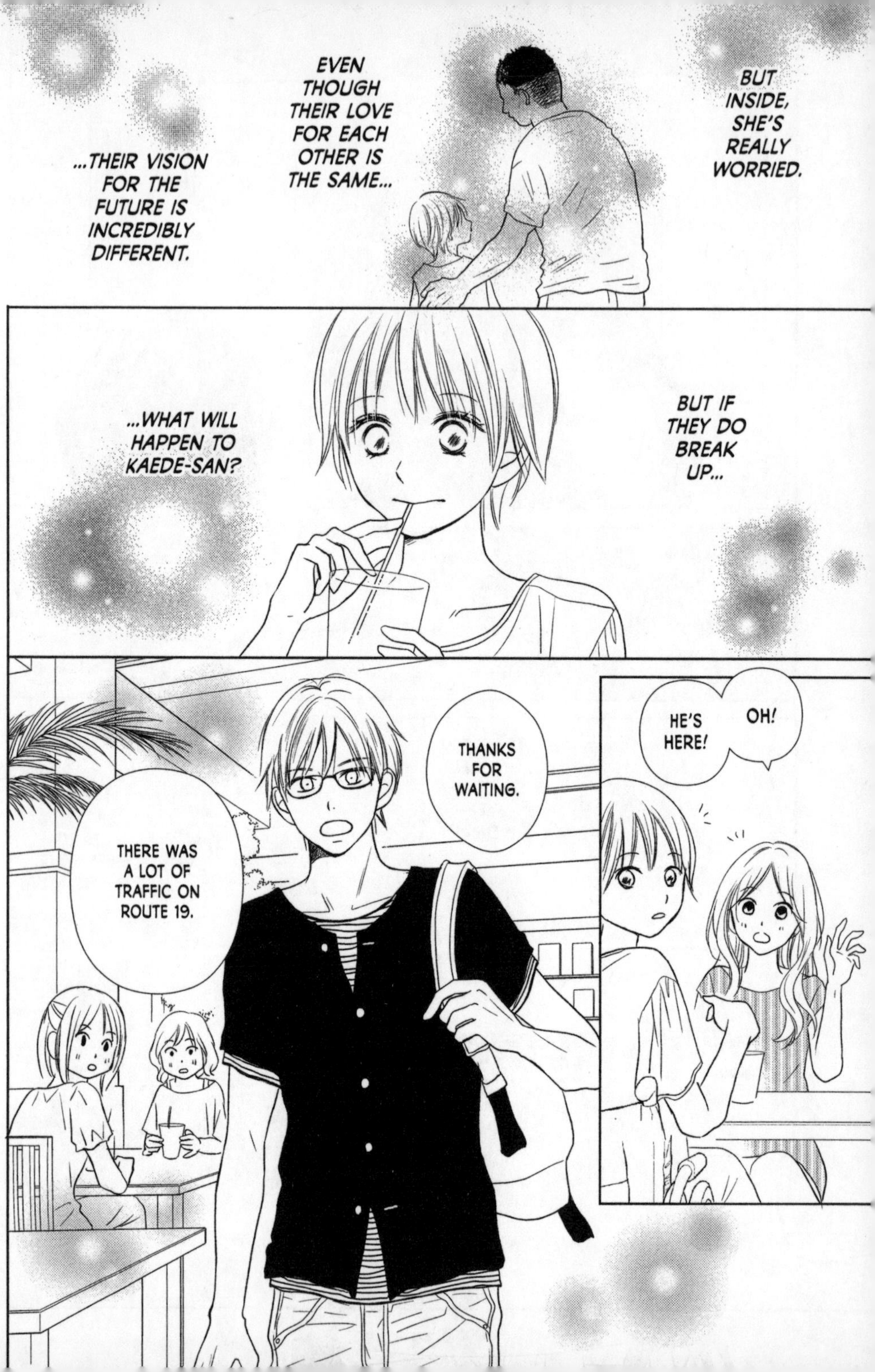
BUT INSIDE, SHE'S REALLY WORRIED.
EVEN THOUGH THEIR LOVE FOR EACH OTHER IS THE SAME...
...THEIR VISION FOR THE FUTURE IS INCREDIBLY DIFFERENT.
BUT IF THEY DO BREAK UP...
...WHAT WILL HAPPEN TO KAEDE-SAN?
OH!
HE'S HERE!
THANKS FOR WAITING.
THERE WAS A LOT OF TRAFFIC ON ROUTE 19.

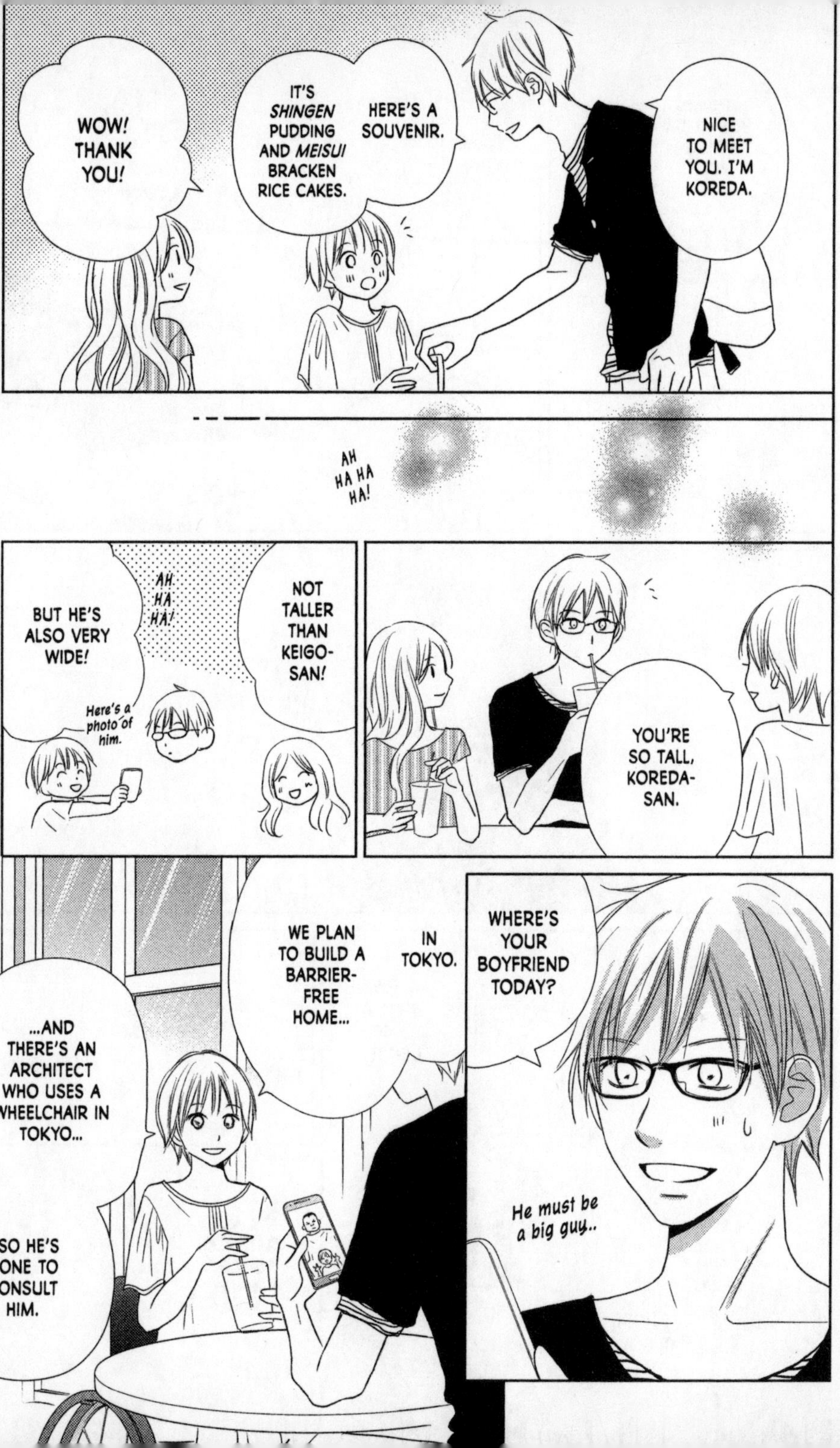
NICE TO MEET YOU. I'M KOREDA.
HERE'S A SOUVENIR.
IT'S *SHINGEN* PUDDING AND *MEISUI* BRACKEN RICE CAKES.
WOW! THANK YOU!
AH HA HA HA!
YOU'RE SO TALL, KOREDA-SAN.
NOT TALLER THAN KEIGO-SAN!
AH HA HA!
BUT HE'S ALSO VERY WIDE!
Here's a photo of him.
WHERE'S YOUR BOYFRIEND TODAY?
He must be a big guy..
IN TOKYO.
WE PLAN TO BUILD A BARRIER-FREE HOME...
...AND THERE'S AN ARCHITECT WHO USES A WHEELCHAIR IN TOKYO...
...SO HE'S GONE TO CONSULT HIM.

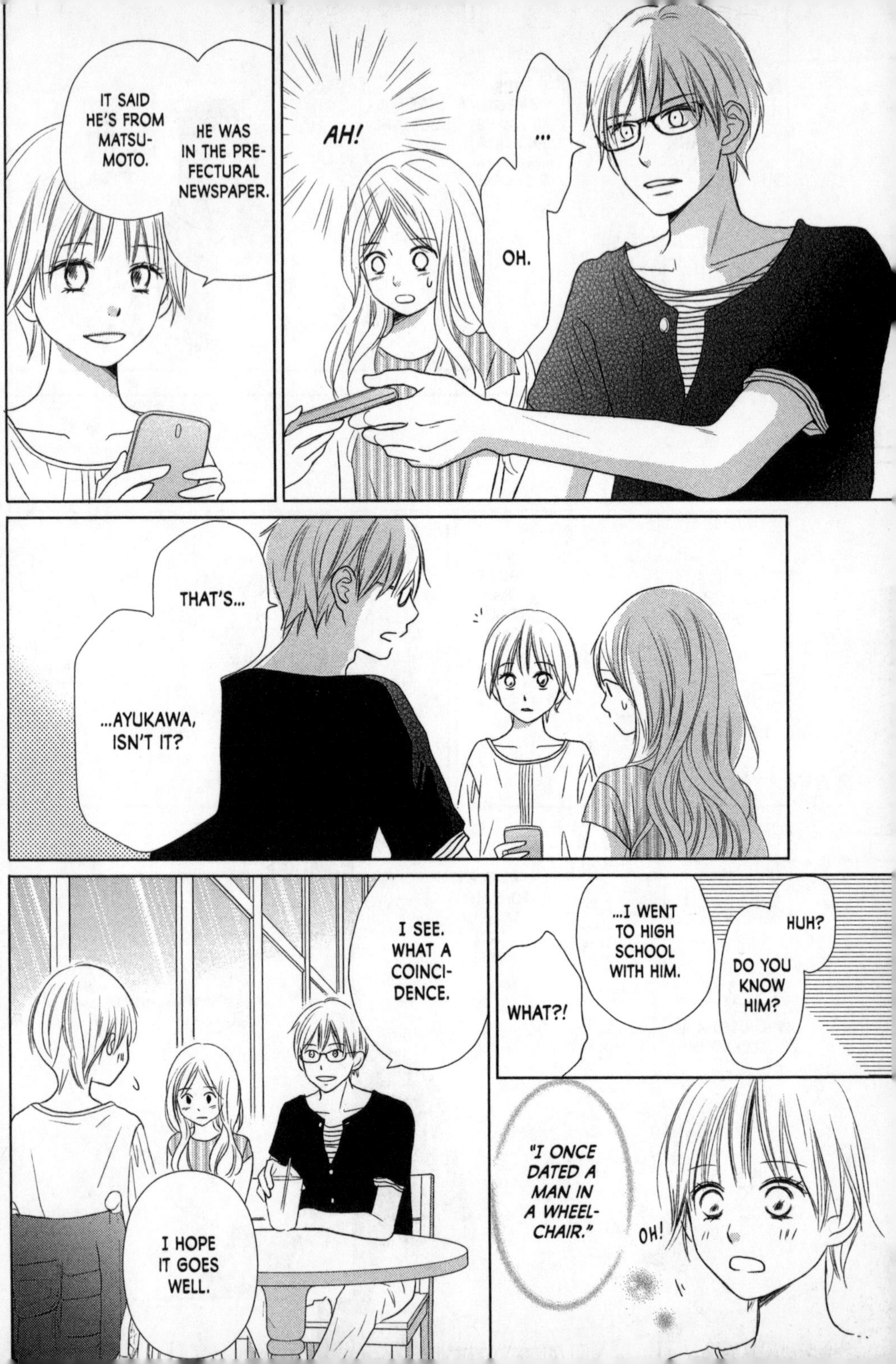
...
OH.
AH!
HE WAS IN THE PRE-FECTURAL NEWSPAPER.
IT SAID HE'S FROM MATSU-MOTO.
THAT'S...
...AYUKAWA, ISN'T IT?
HUH?
DO YOU KNOW HIM?
...I WENT TO HIGH SCHOOL WITH HIM.
WHAT?!
"I ONCE DATED A MAN IN A WHEEL-CHAIR."
OH!
I SEE. WHAT A COINCI-DENCE.
I HOPE IT GOES WELL.

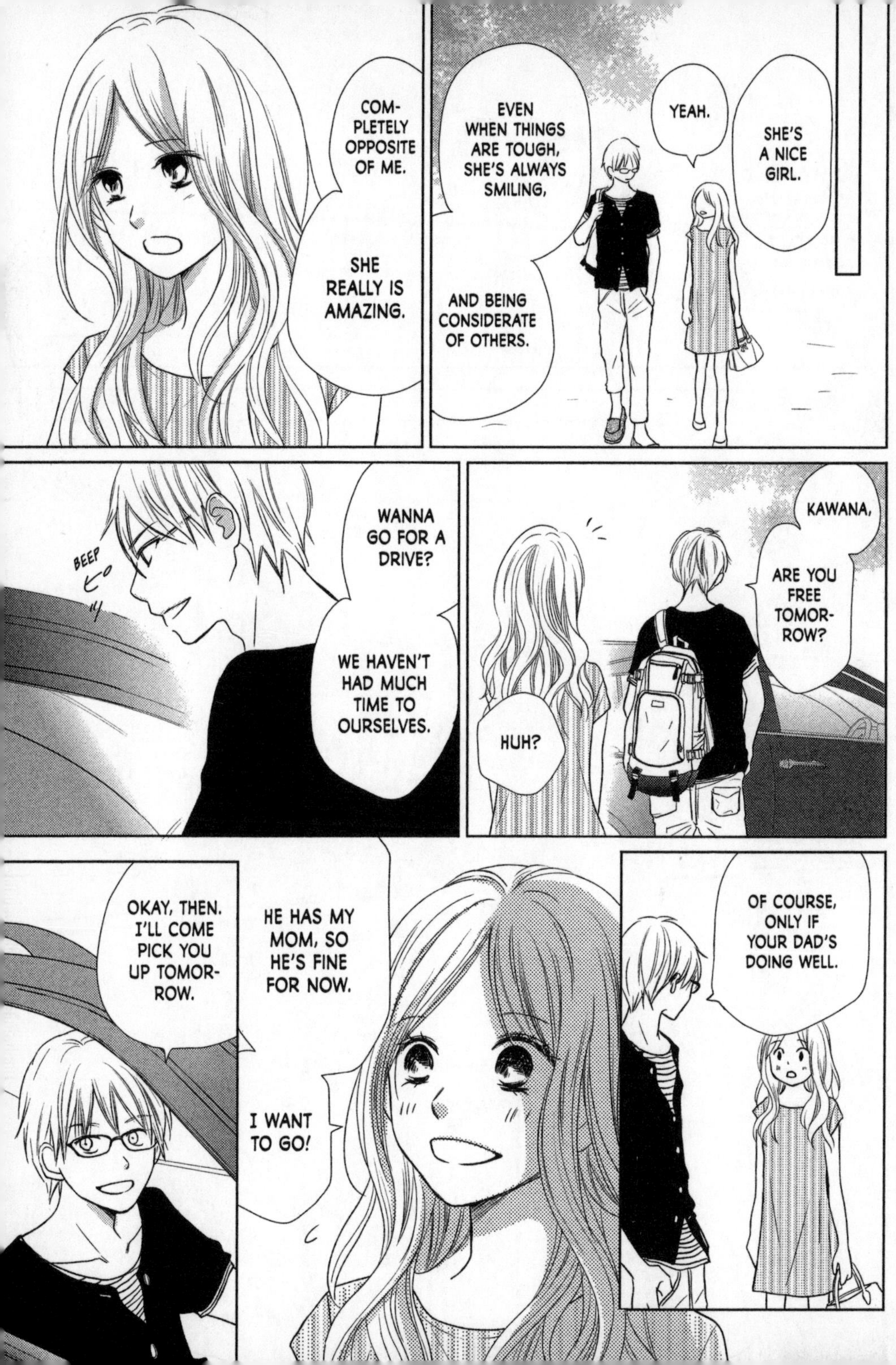
SHE'S A NICE GIRL.
YEAH.
EVEN WHEN THINGS ARE TOUGH, SHE'S ALWAYS SMILING,
AND BEING CONSIDERATE OF OTHERS.
COM-PLETELY OPPOSITE OF ME.
SHE REALLY IS AMAZING.
KAWANA,
ARE YOU FREE TOMOR-ROW?
HUH?
BEEP
WANNA GO FOR A DRIVE?
WE HAVEN'T HAD MUCH TIME TO OURSELVES.
OF COURSE, ONLY IF YOUR DAD'S DOING WELL.
HE HAS MY MOM, SO HE'S FINE FOR NOW.
I WANT TO GO!
OKAY, THEN. I'LL COME PICK YOU UP TOMOR-ROW.

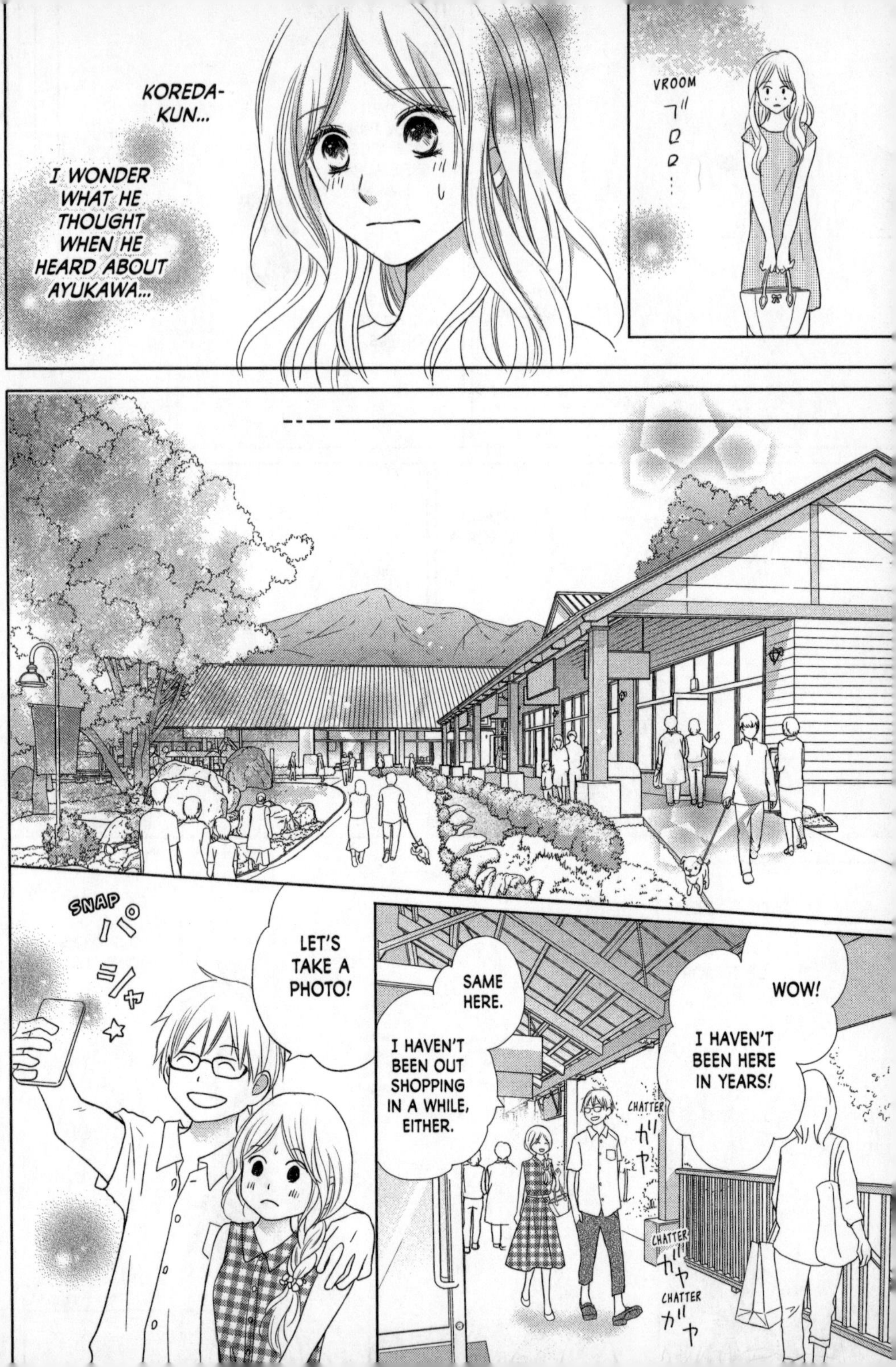
VROOM
ブロロ…
KOREDA-KUN...
I WONDER WHAT HE THOUGHT WHEN HE HEARD ABOUT AYUKAWA...
WOW!
I HAVEN'T BEEN HERE IN YEARS!
SAME HERE.
I HAVEN'T BEEN OUT SHOPPING IN A WHILE, EITHER.
CHATTER
ガヤ
CHATTER
ガヤ
CHATTER
ガヤ
LET'S TAKE A PHOTO!
SNAP
パシャ

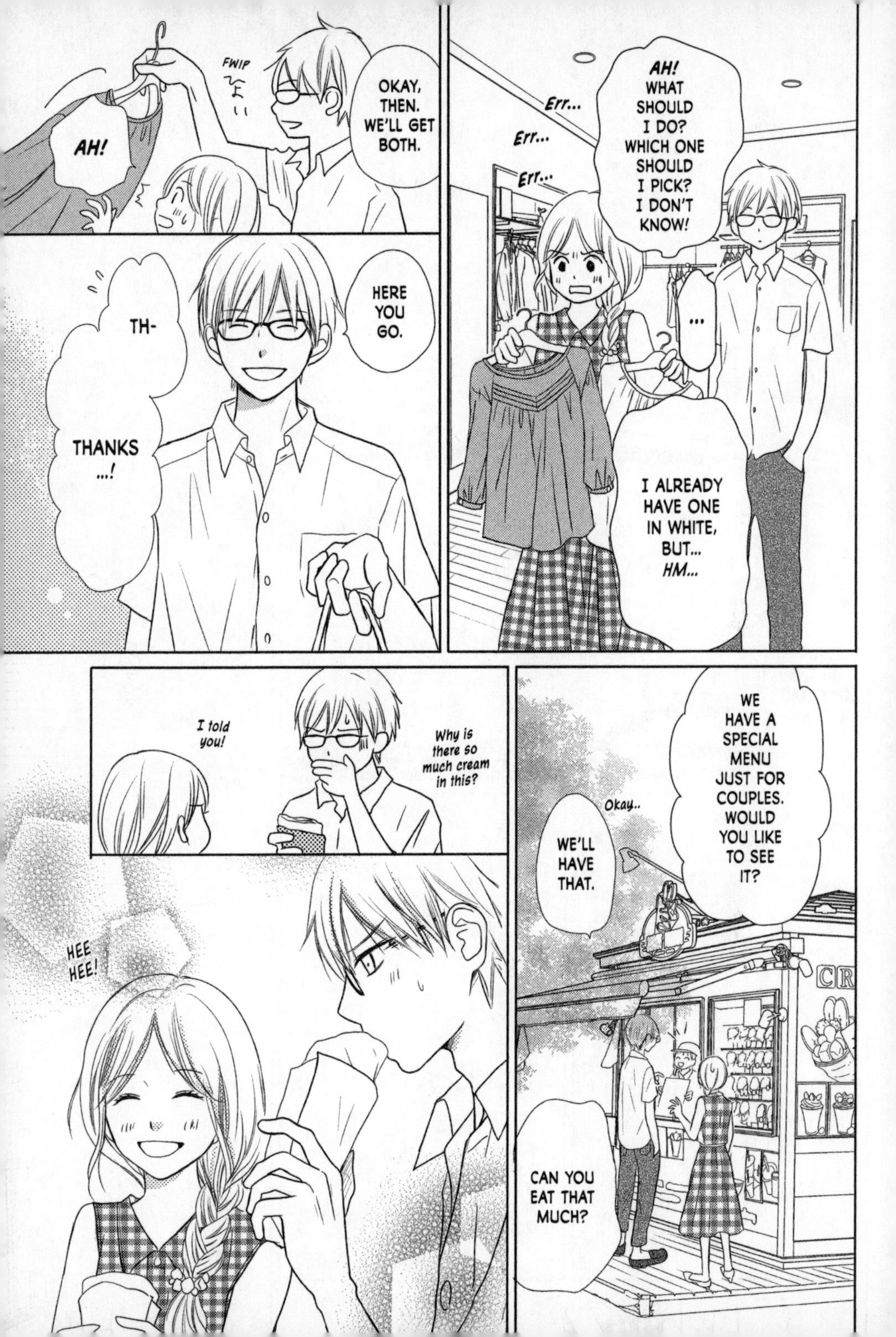
Err...
Err...
Err...
AH! WHAT SHOULD I DO? WHICH ONE SHOULD I PICK? I DON'T KNOW!
...
I ALREADY HAVE ONE IN WHITE, BUT... HM...
OKAY, THEN. WE'LL GET BOTH.
FWIP
AH!
HERE YOU GO.
TH-
THANKS ...!
WE HAVE A SPECIAL MENU JUST FOR COUPLES. WOULD YOU LIKE TO SEE IT?
Okay..
WE'LL HAVE THAT.
CAN YOU EAT THAT MUCH?
Why is there so much cream in this?
I told you!
HEE HEE!

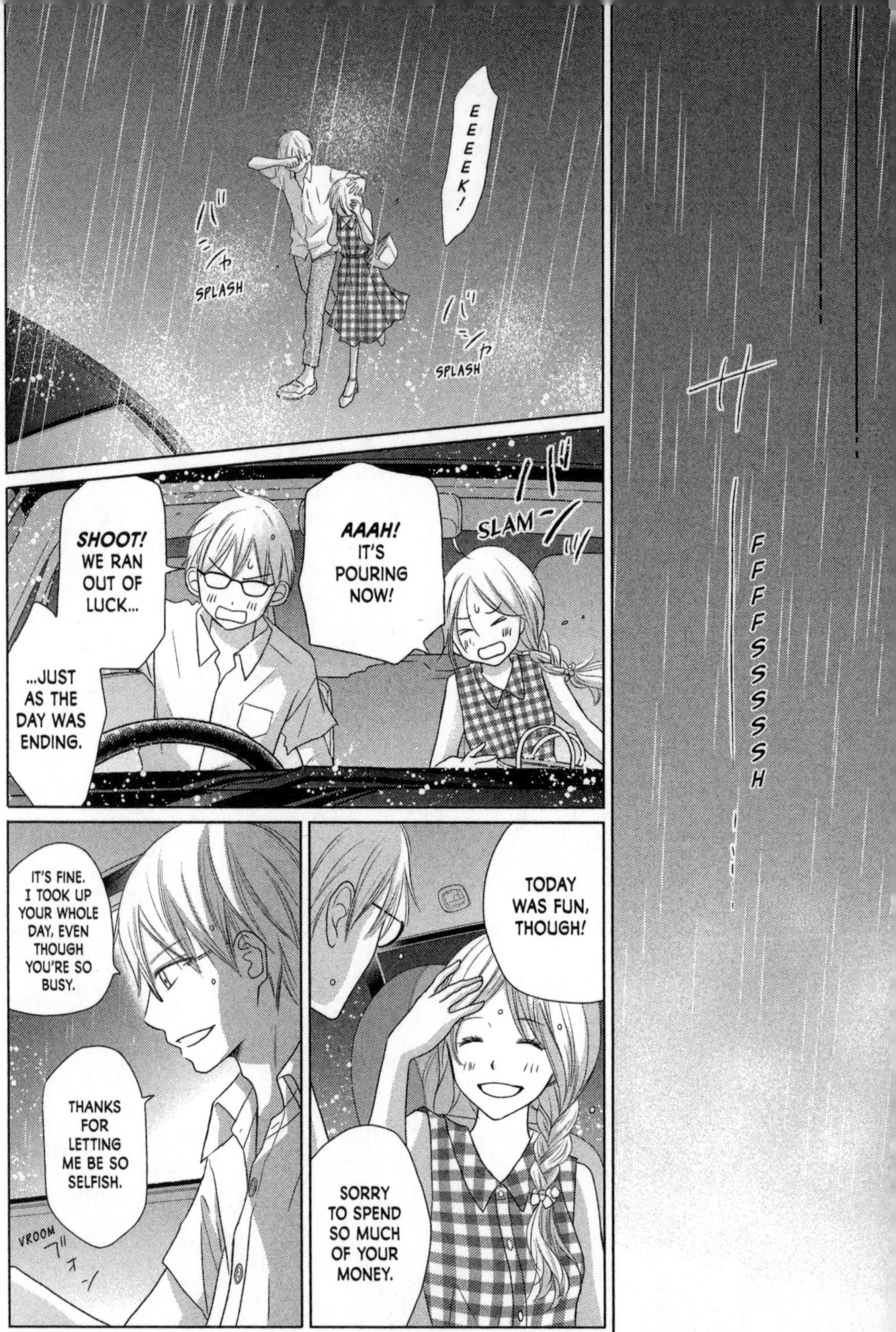
FFFFSSSSSH
EEEEEK!
SPLASH
SPLASH
SLAM
AAAH! IT'S POURING NOW!
SHOOT! WE RAN OUT OF LUCK...
...JUST AS THE DAY WAS ENDING.
TODAY WAS FUN, THOUGH!
SORRY TO SPEND SO MUCH OF YOUR MONEY.
IT'S FINE. I TOOK UP YOUR WHOLE DAY, EVEN THOUGH YOU'RE SO BUSY.
THANKS FOR LETTING ME BE SO SELFISH.
VROOM

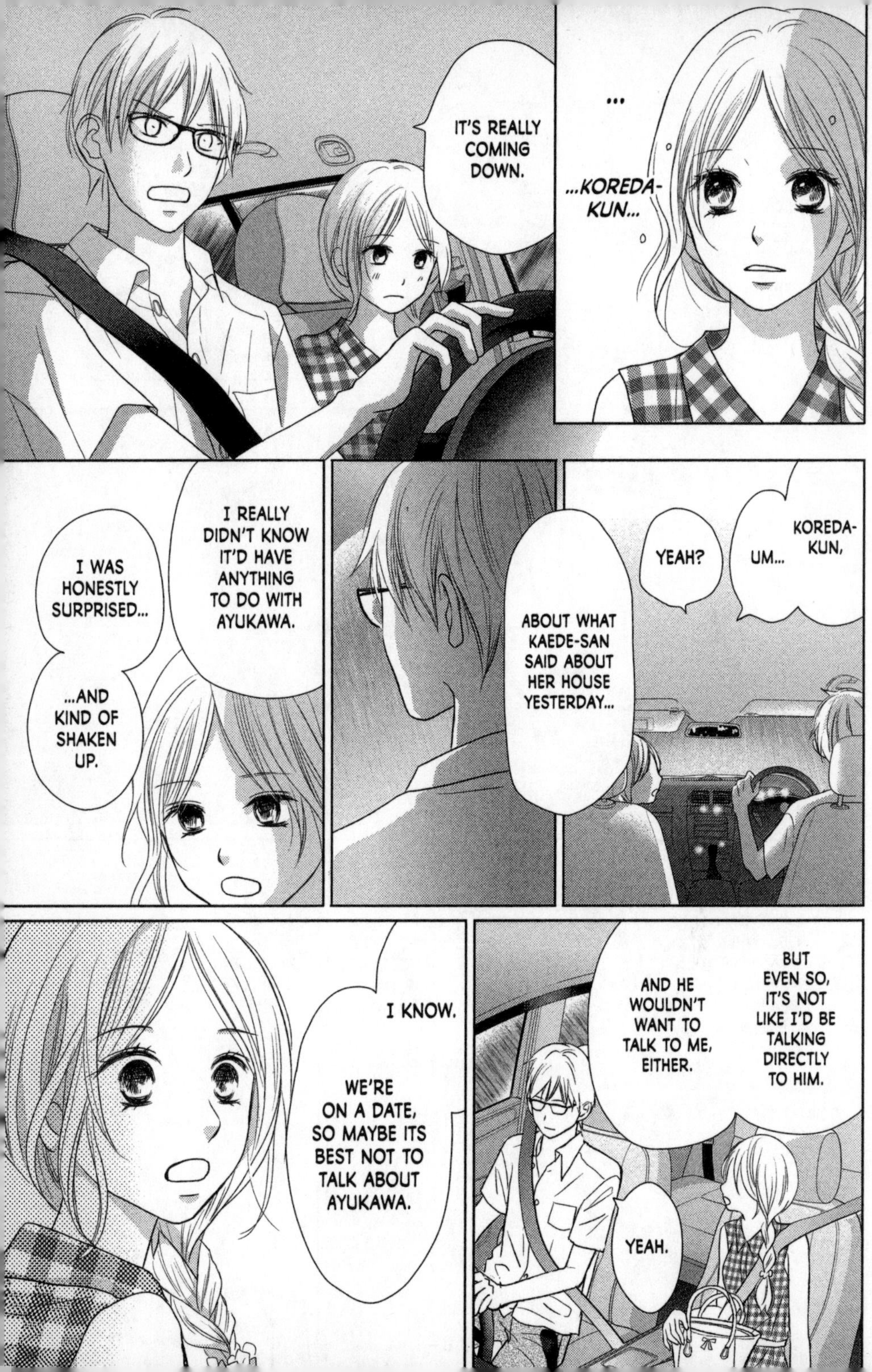
...
...KOREDA-KUN...
IT'S REALLY COMING DOWN.
KOREDA-KUN,
UM...
YEAH?
ABOUT WHAT KAEDE-SAN SAID ABOUT HER HOUSE YESTERDAY...
I REALLY DIDN'T KNOW IT'D HAVE ANYTHING TO DO WITH AYUKAWA.
I WAS HONESTLY SURPRISED...
...AND KIND OF SHAKEN UP.
BUT EVEN SO, IT'S NOT LIKE I'D BE TALKING DIRECTLY TO HIM.
AND HE WOULDN'T WANT TO TALK TO ME, EITHER.
YEAH.
I KNOW.
WE'RE ON A DATE, SO MAYBE ITS BEST NOT TO TALK ABOUT AYUKAWA.

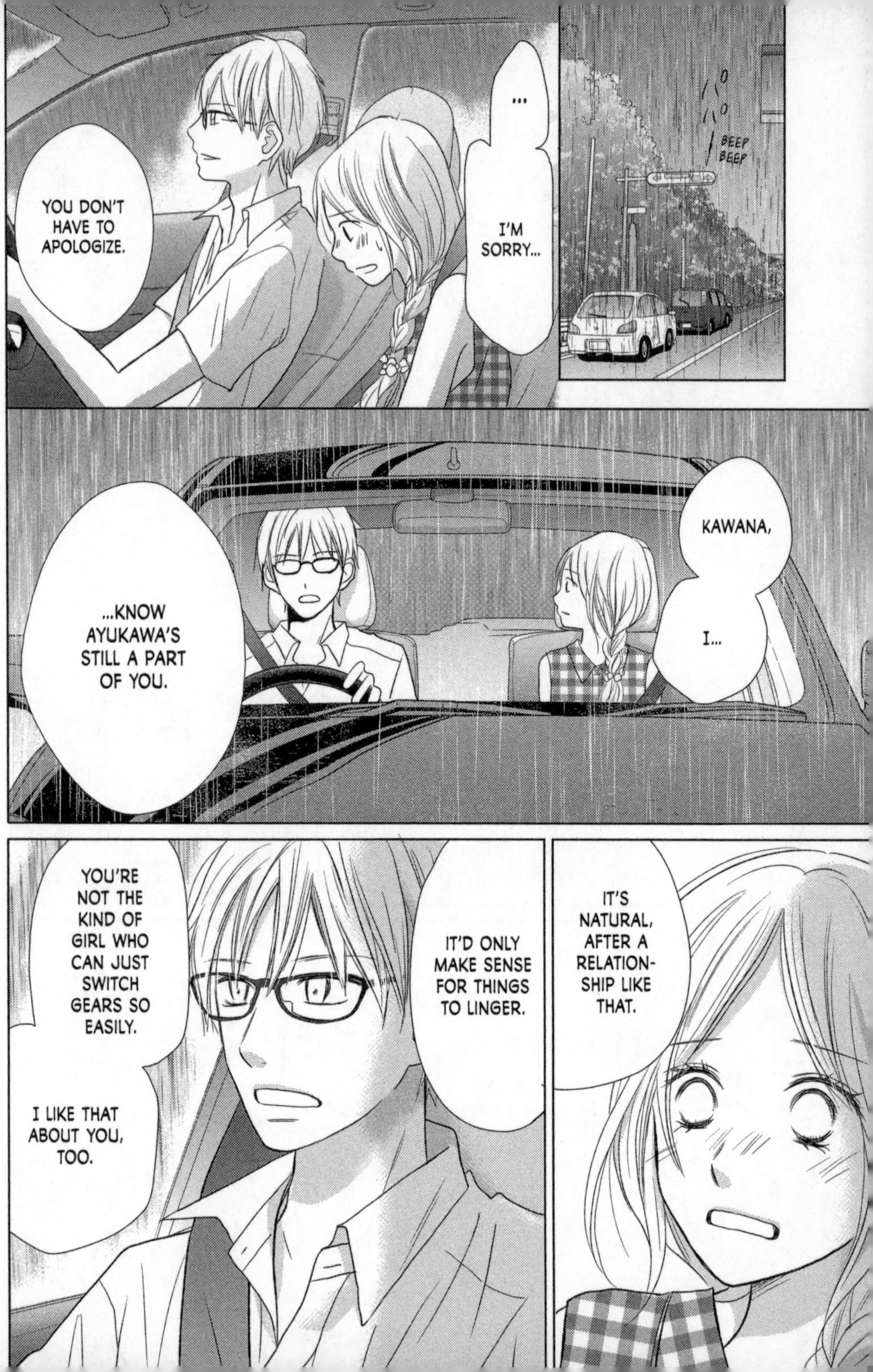

BEEP BEEP
...
I'M SORRY...
YOU DON'T HAVE TO APOLOGIZE.
KAWANA,
I...
...KNOW AYUKAWA'S STILL A PART OF YOU.
IT'S NATURAL, AFTER A RELATION-SHIP LIKE THAT.
IT'D ONLY MAKE SENSE FOR THINGS TO LINGER.
YOU'RE NOT THE KIND OF GIRL WHO CAN JUST SWITCH GEARS SO EASILY.
I LIKE THAT ABOUT YOU, TOO.

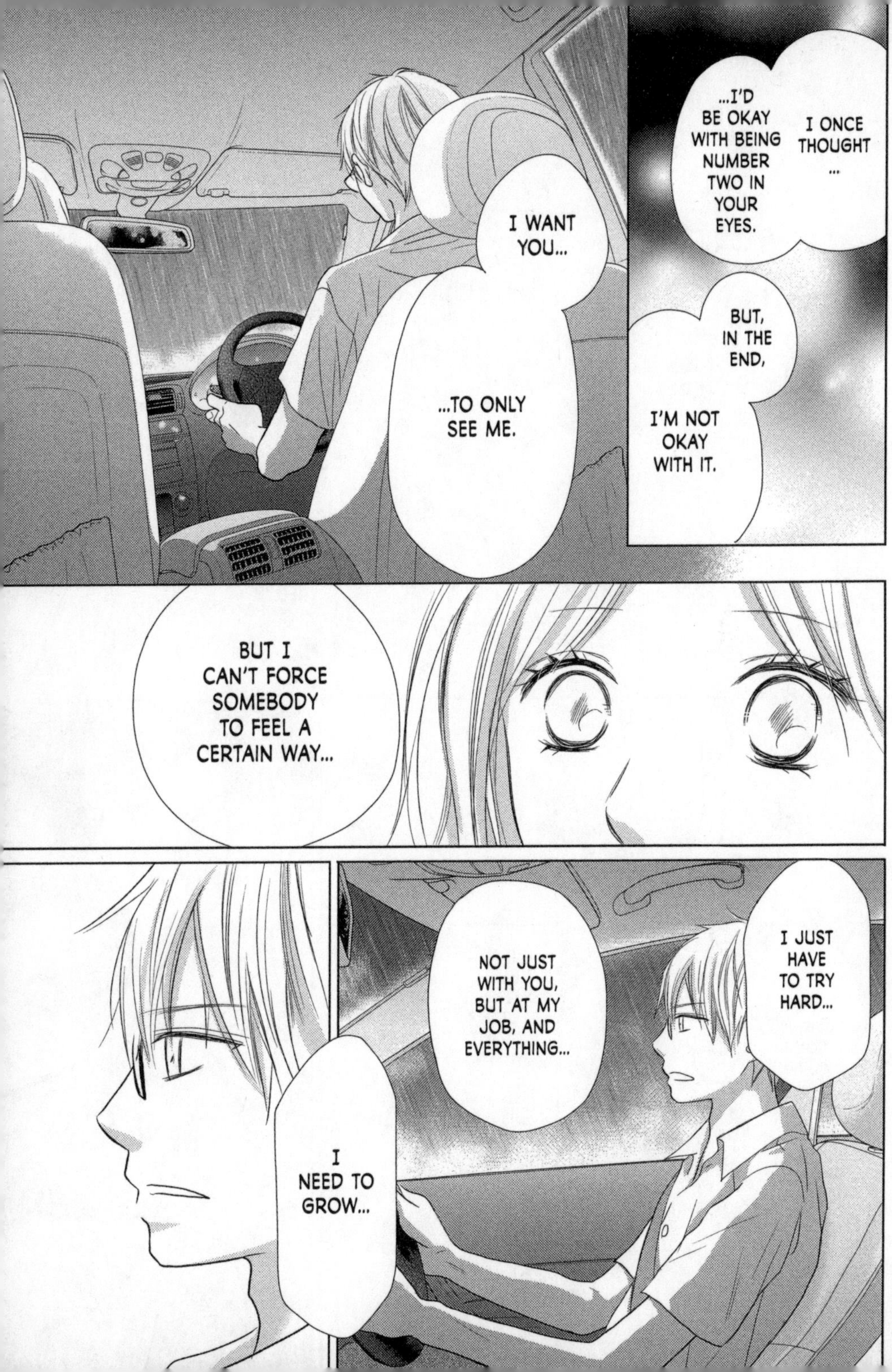
I ONCE THOUGHT...
...I'D BE OKAY WITH BEING NUMBER TWO IN YOUR EYES.
BUT, IN THE END,
I'M NOT OKAY WITH IT.
I WANT YOU...
...TO ONLY SEE ME.
BUT I CAN'T FORCE SOMEBODY TO FEEL A CERTAIN WAY...
I JUST HAVE TO TRY HARD...
NOT JUST WITH YOU, BUT AT MY JOB, AND EVERYTHING...
I NEED TO GROW...

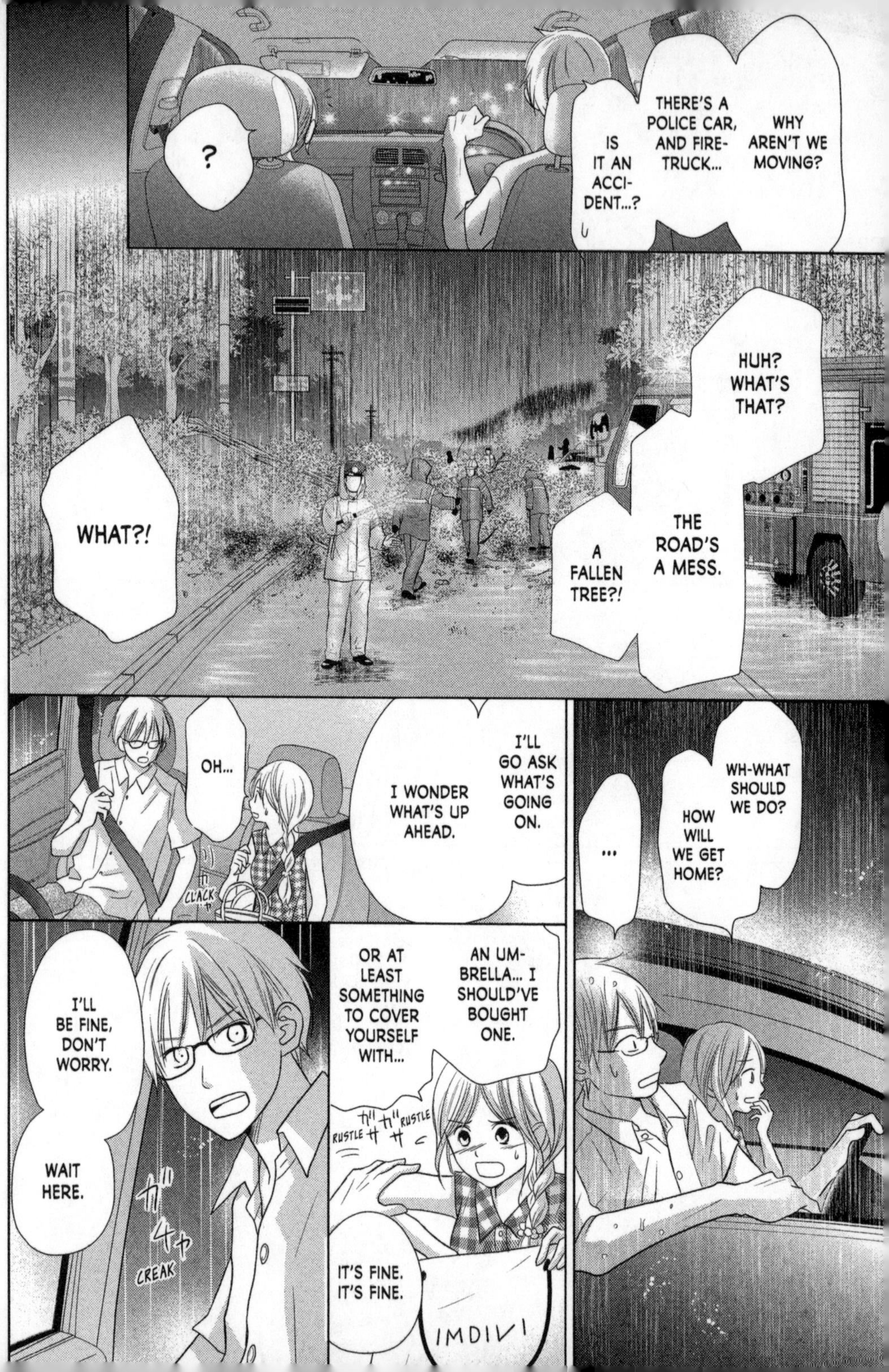
WHY AREN'T WE MOVING?
THERE'S A POLICE CAR, AND FIRE-TRUCK...
IS IT AN ACCI-DENT...?
?
HUH? WHAT'S THAT?
THE ROAD'S A MESS.
A FALLEN TREE?!
WHAT?!
WH-WHAT SHOULD WE DO?
HOW WILL WE GET HOME?
...
I'LL GO ASK WHAT'S GOING ON.
I WONDER WHAT'S UP AHEAD.
OH...
CLACK
AN UM-BRELLA... I SHOULD'VE BOUGHT ONE.
OR AT LEAST SOMETHING TO COVER YOURSELF WITH...
RUSTLE
RUSTLE
IT'S FINE. IT'S FINE.
IMDIVI
I'LL BE FINE, DON'T WORRY.
WAIT HERE.
CREAK

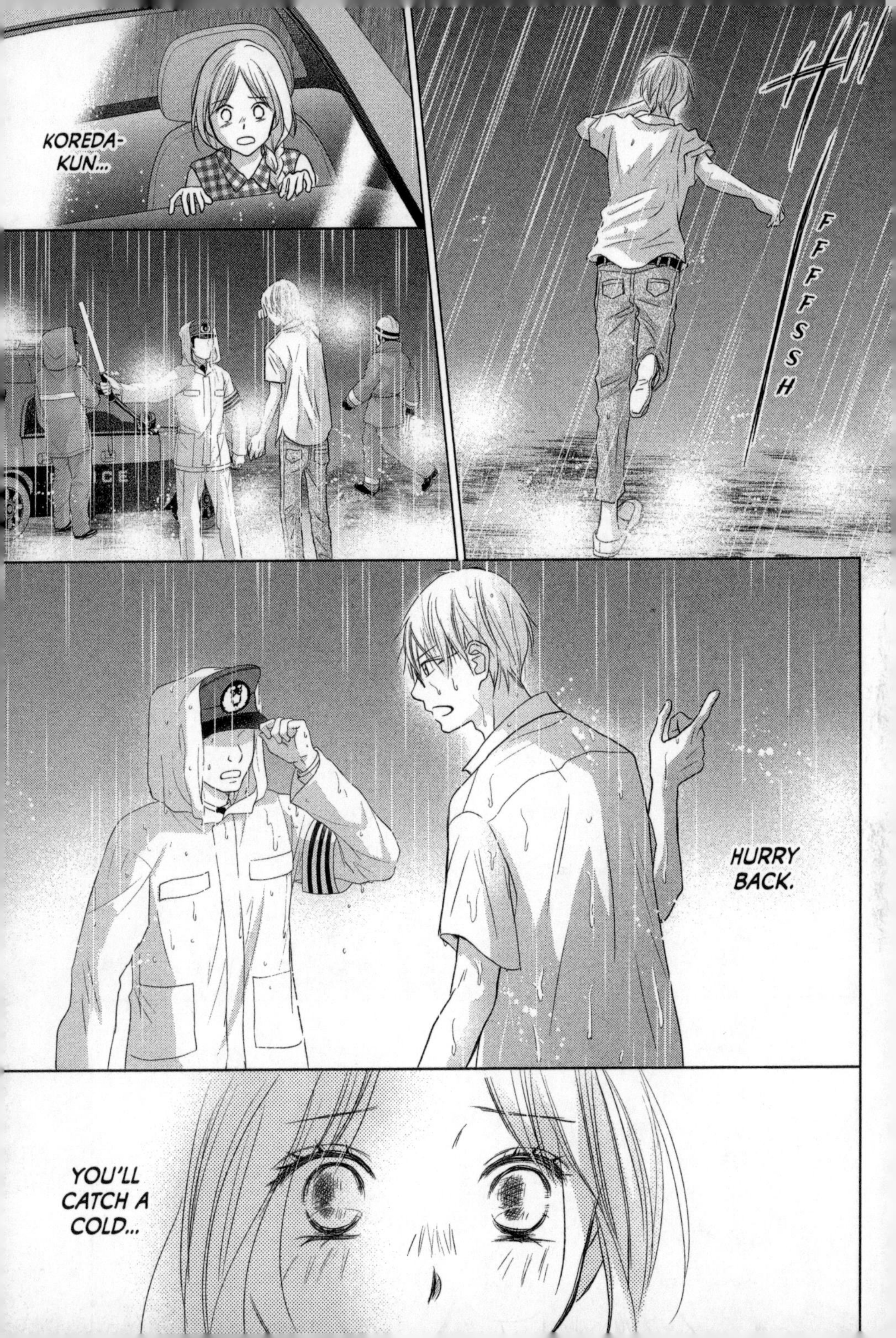
FFFFSSH
KOREDA-KUN...
HURRY BACK.
YOU'LL CATCH A COLD...

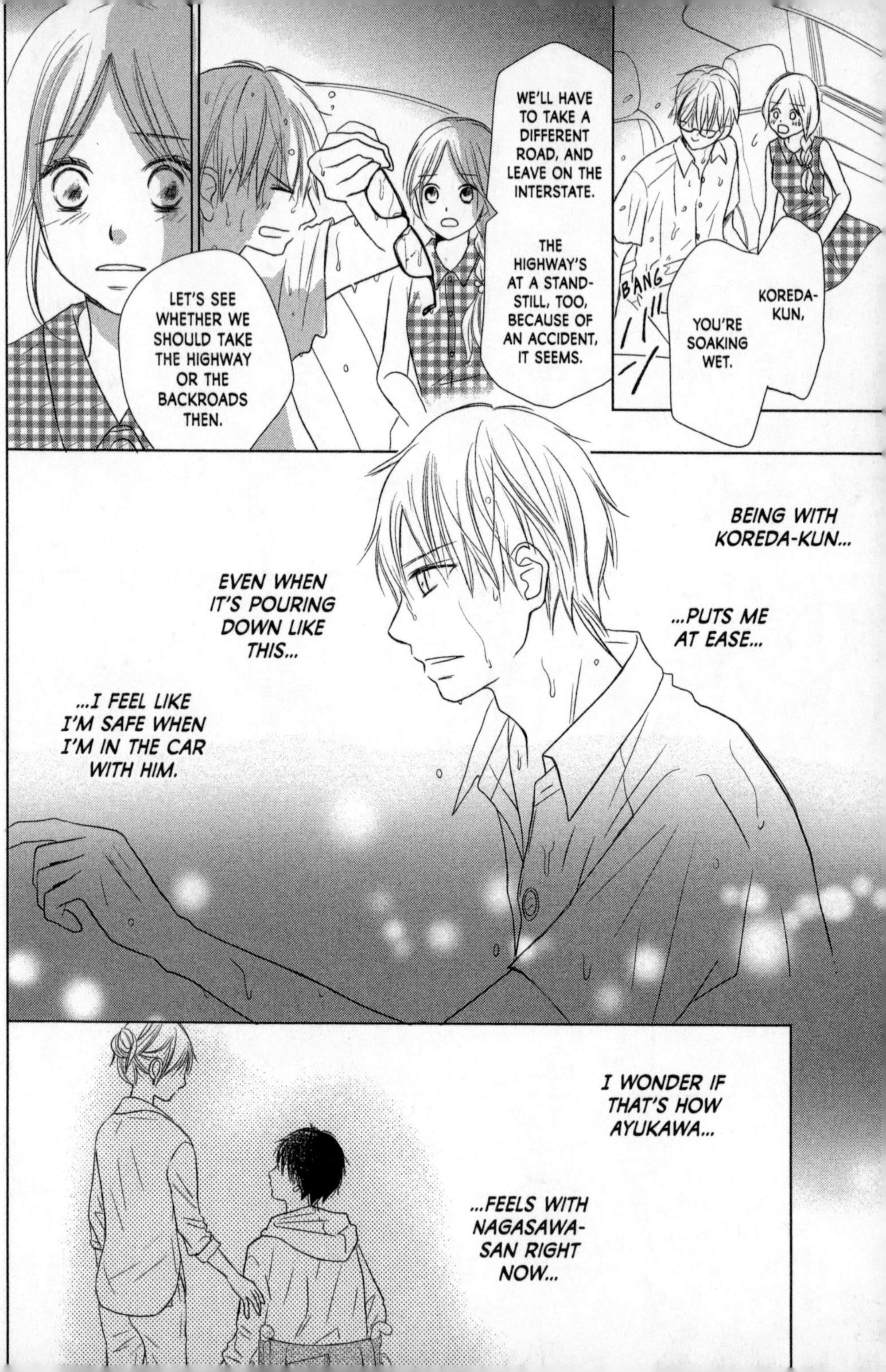

KOREDA-KUN,
YOU'RE SOAKING WET.
BANG
WE'LL HAVE TO TAKE A DIFFERENT ROAD, AND LEAVE ON THE INTERSTATE.
THE HIGHWAY'S AT A STAND-STILL, TOO, BECAUSE OF AN ACCIDENT, IT SEEMS.
LET'S SEE WHETHER WE SHOULD TAKE THE HIGHWAY OR THE BACKROADS THEN.
BEING WITH KOREDA-KUN...
...PUTS ME AT EASE...
EVEN WHEN IT'S POURING DOWN LIKE THIS...
...I FEEL LIKE I'M SAFE WHEN I'M IN THE CAR WITH HIM.
I WONDER IF THAT'S HOW AYUKAWA...
...FEELS WITH NAGASAWA-SAN RIGHT NOW...

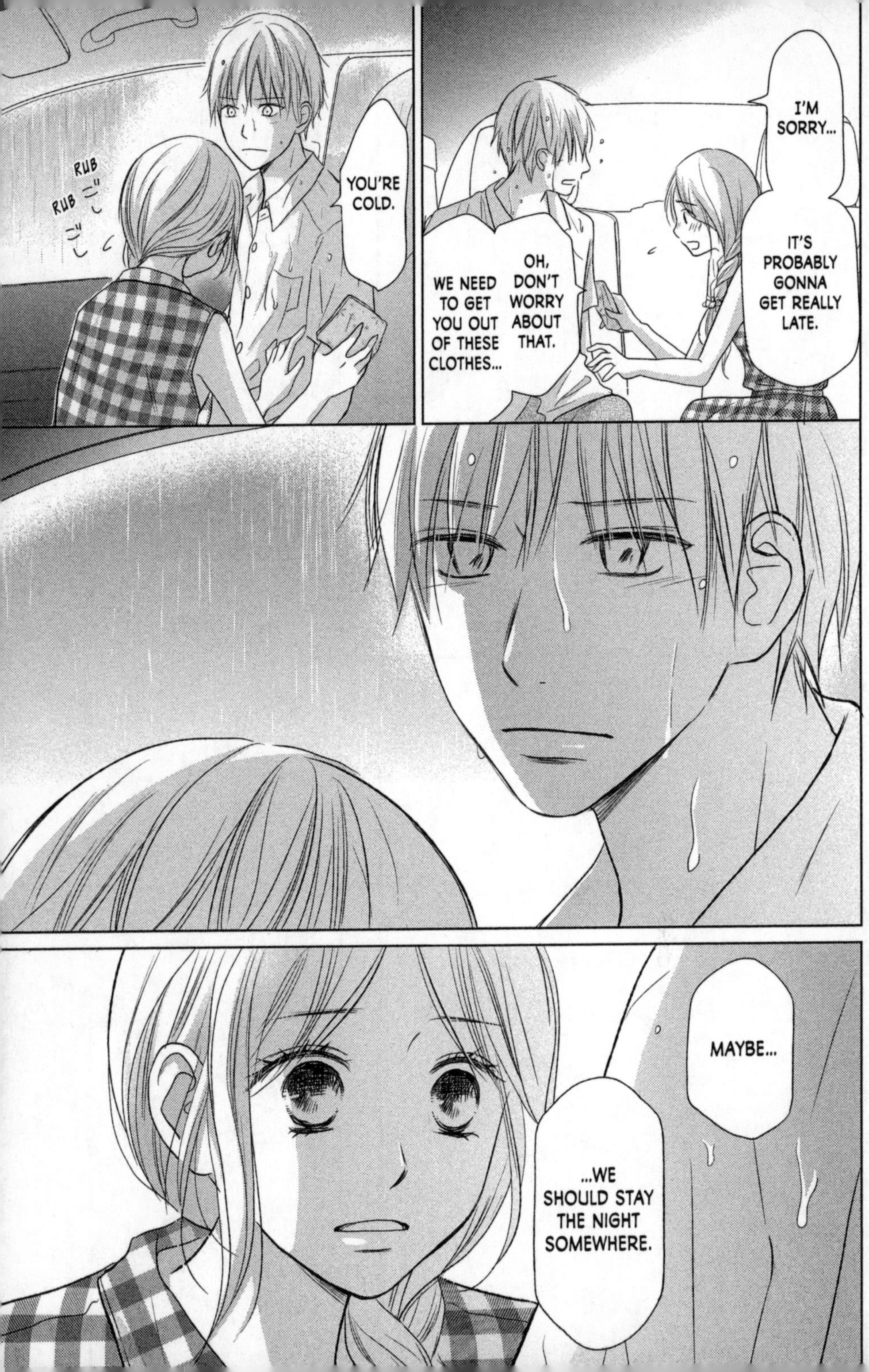
I'M SORRY...
IT'S PROBABLY GONNA GET REALLY LATE.
OH, DON'T WORRY ABOUT THAT.
WE NEED TO GET YOU OUT OF THESE CLOTHES...
RUB RUB
ごし ごし
YOU'RE COLD.
MAYBE...
...WE SHOULD STAY THE NIGHT SOMEWHERE.

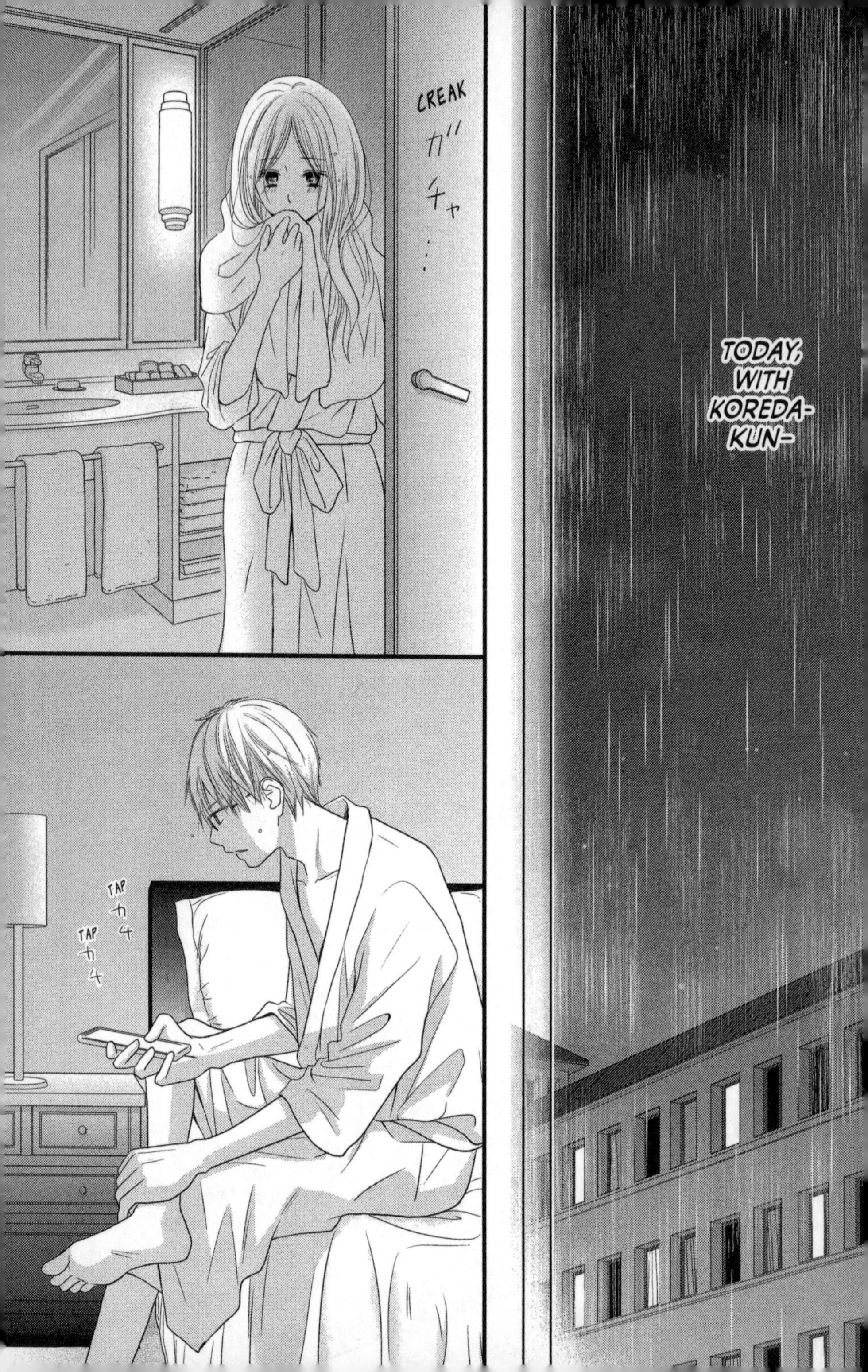
TODAY, WITH KOREDA-KUN-
CREAK
ガチャ…
TAP
TAP

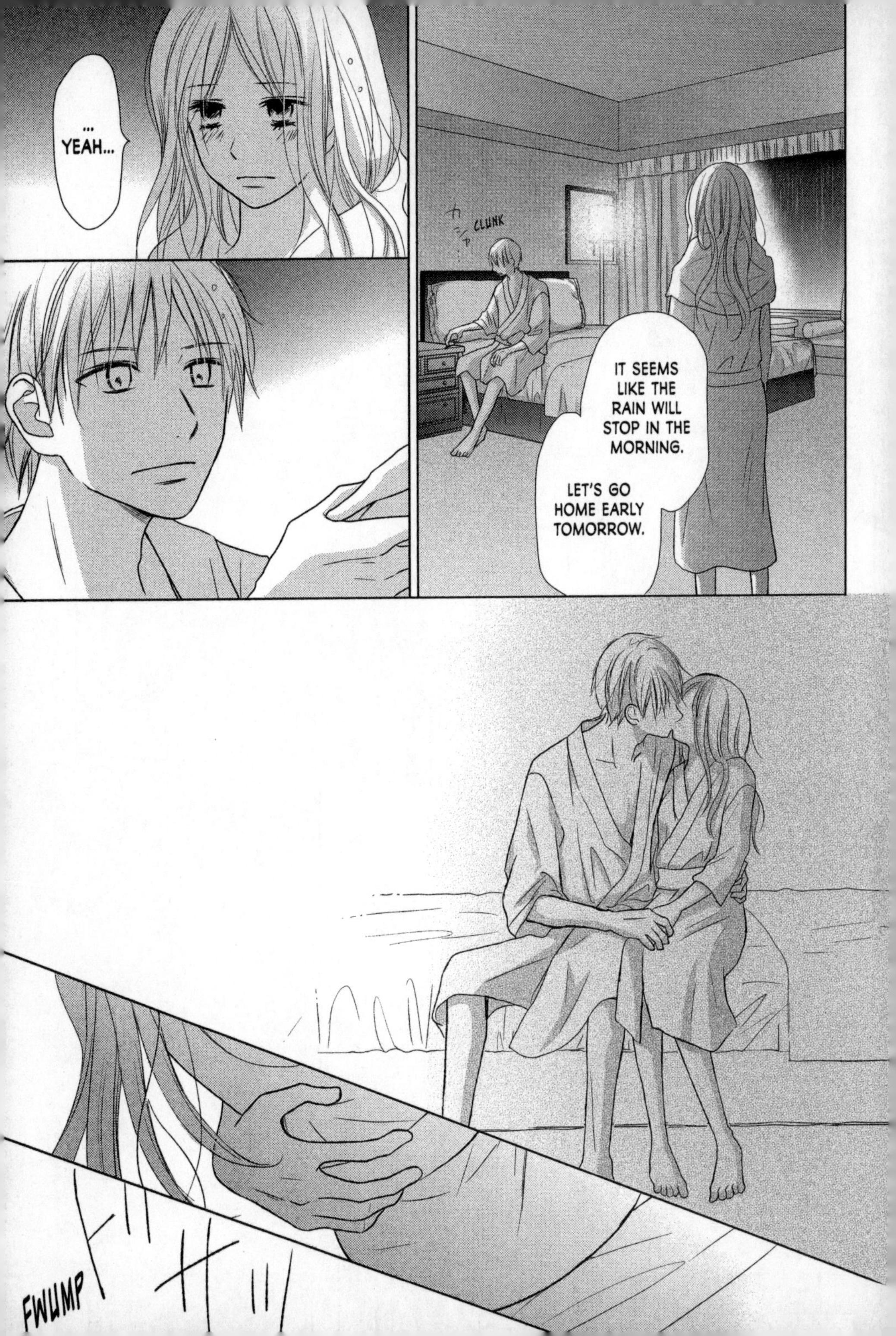
カシャ
CLUNK
IT SEEMS LIKE THE RAIN WILL STOP IN THE MORNING.
LET'S GO HOME EARLY TOMORROW.
... YEAH...
FWUMP

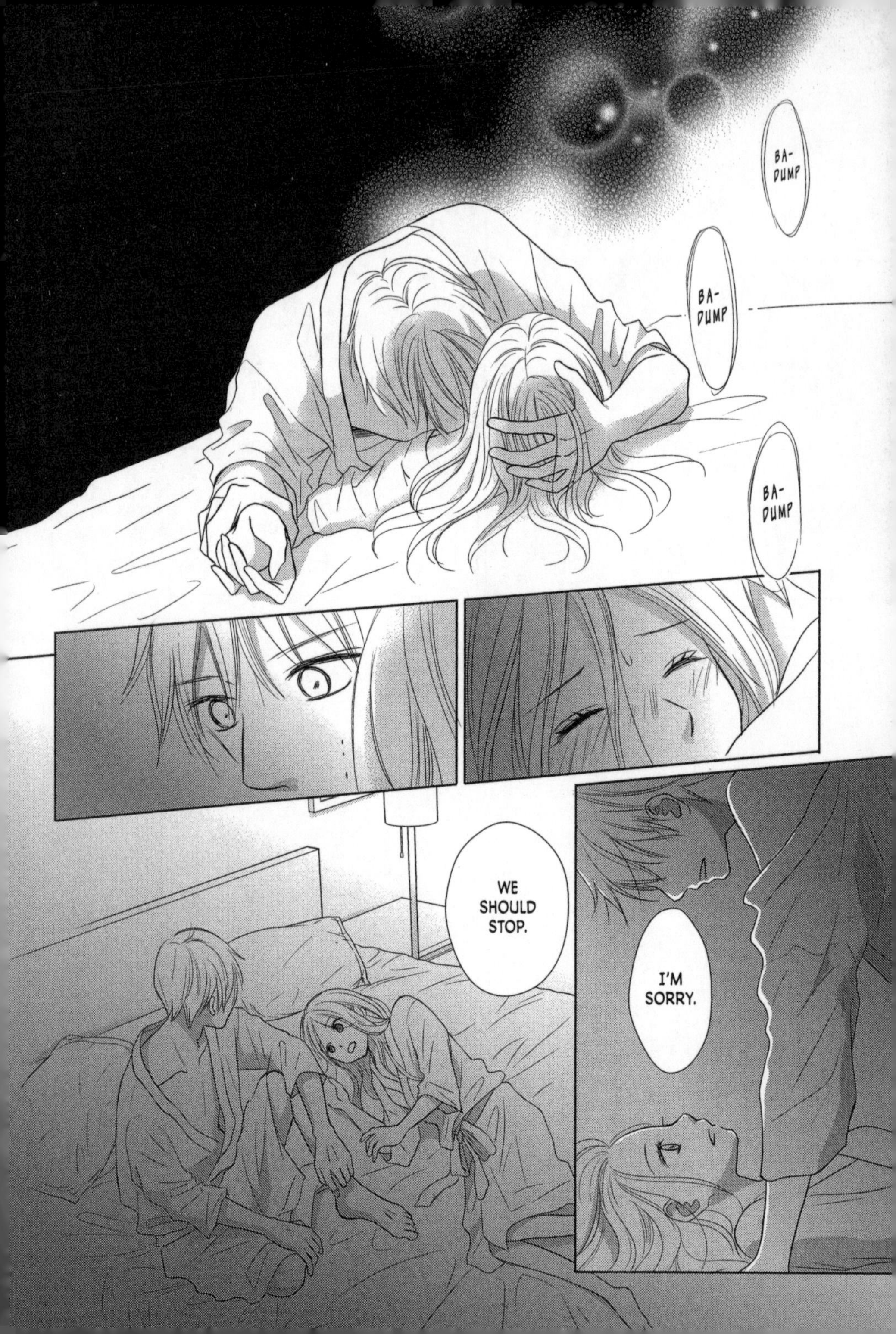
BA-DUMP
BA-DUMP
BA-DUMP
I'M SORRY.
WE SHOULD STOP.

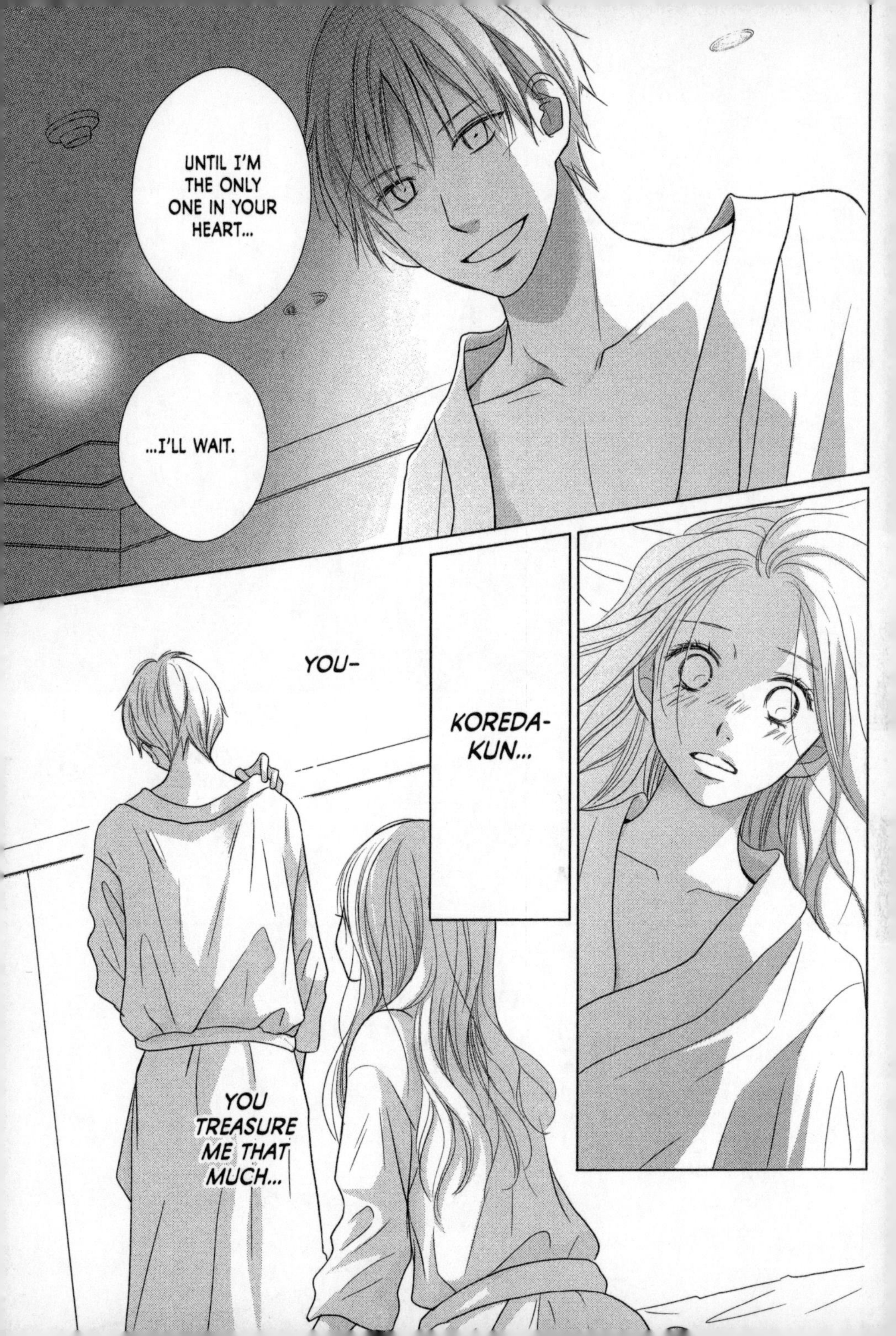
UNTIL I'M THE ONLY ONE IN YOUR HEART...
...I'LL WAIT.
KOREDA-KUN...
YOU-
YOU TREASURE ME THAT MUCH...

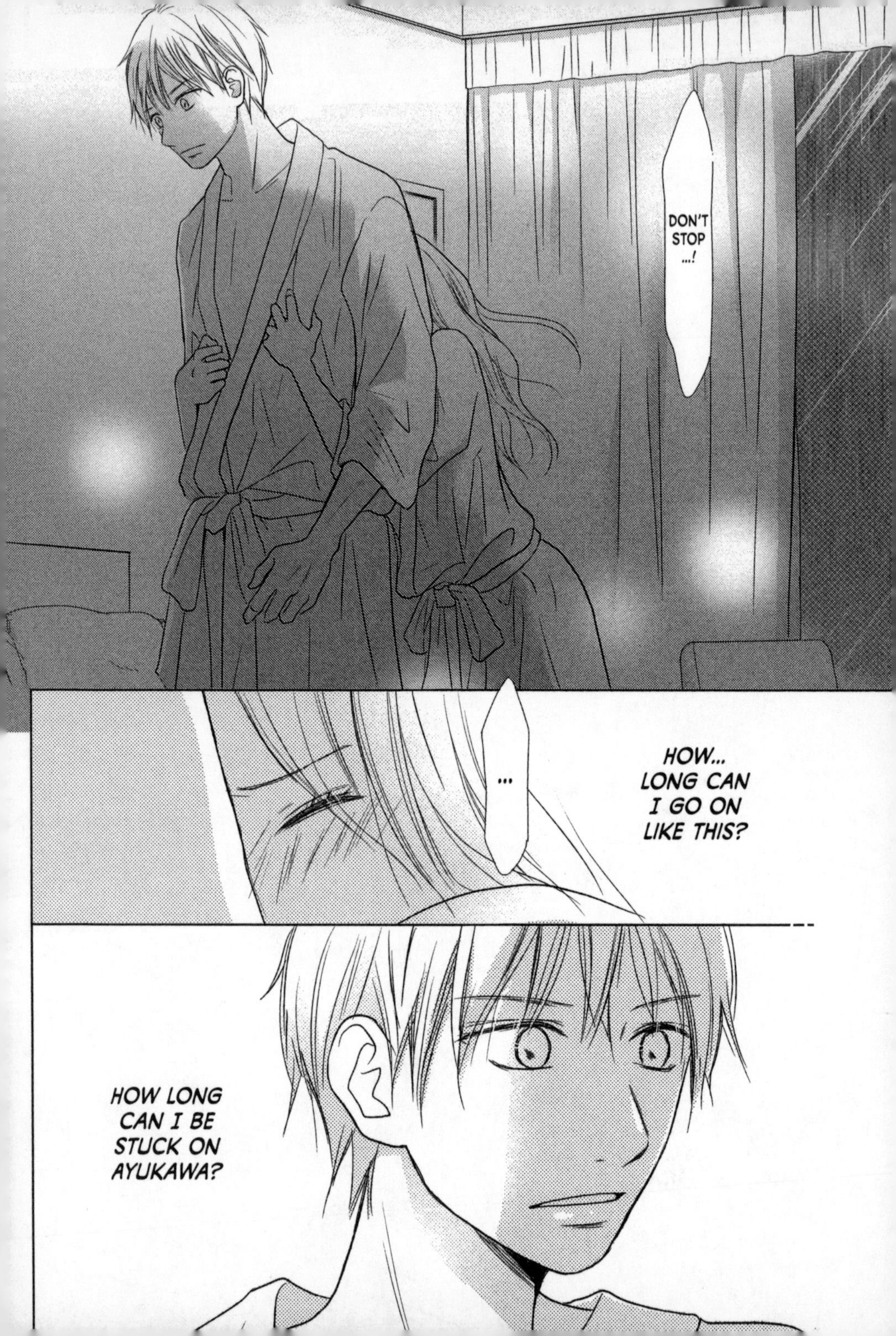

DON'T STOP ...!
...
HOW... LONG CAN I GO ON LIKE THIS?
HOW LONG CAN I BE STUCK ON AYUKAWA?

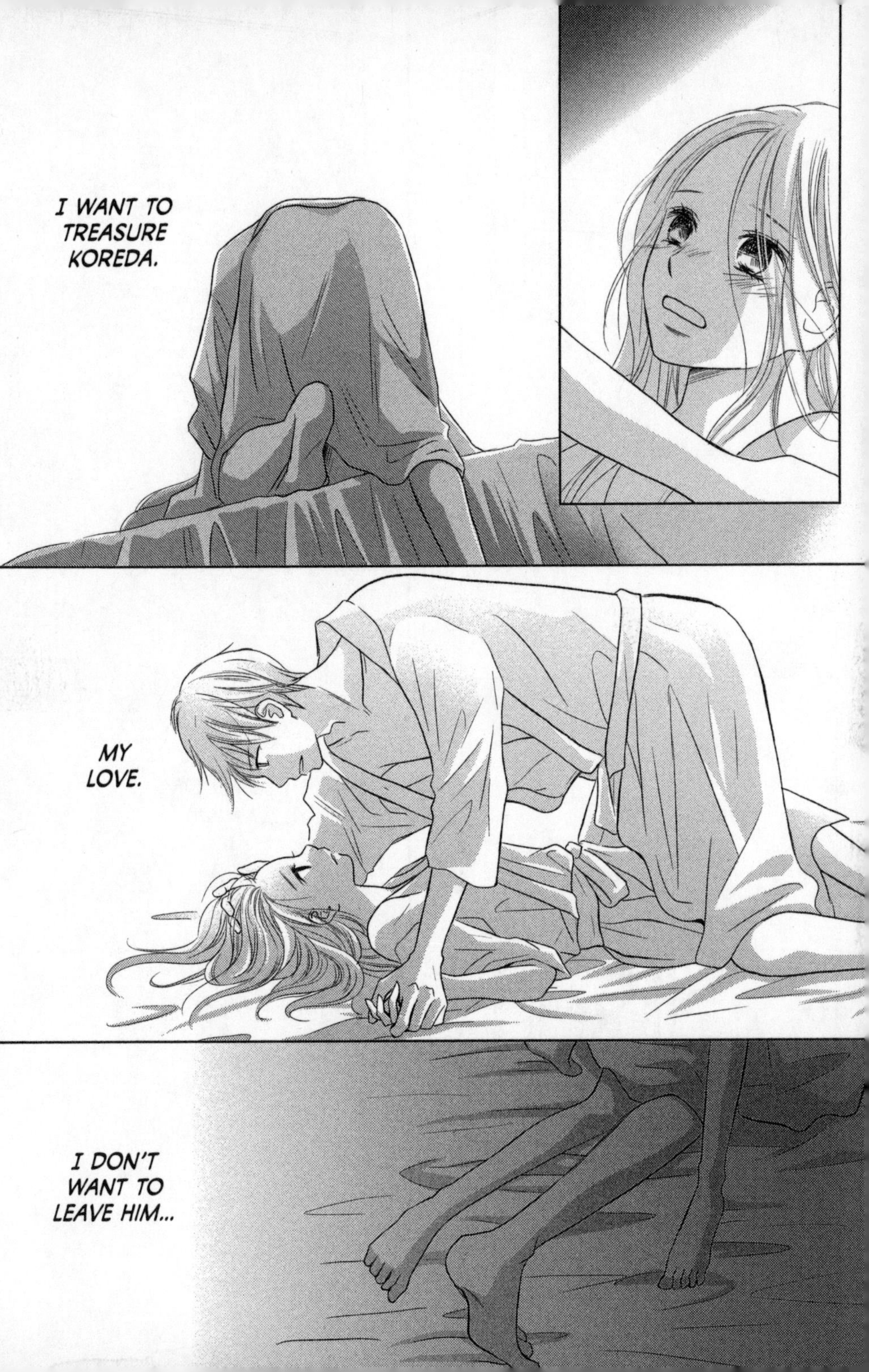
I WANT TO TREASURE KOREDA.
MY LOVE.
I DON'T WANT TO LEAVE HIM...

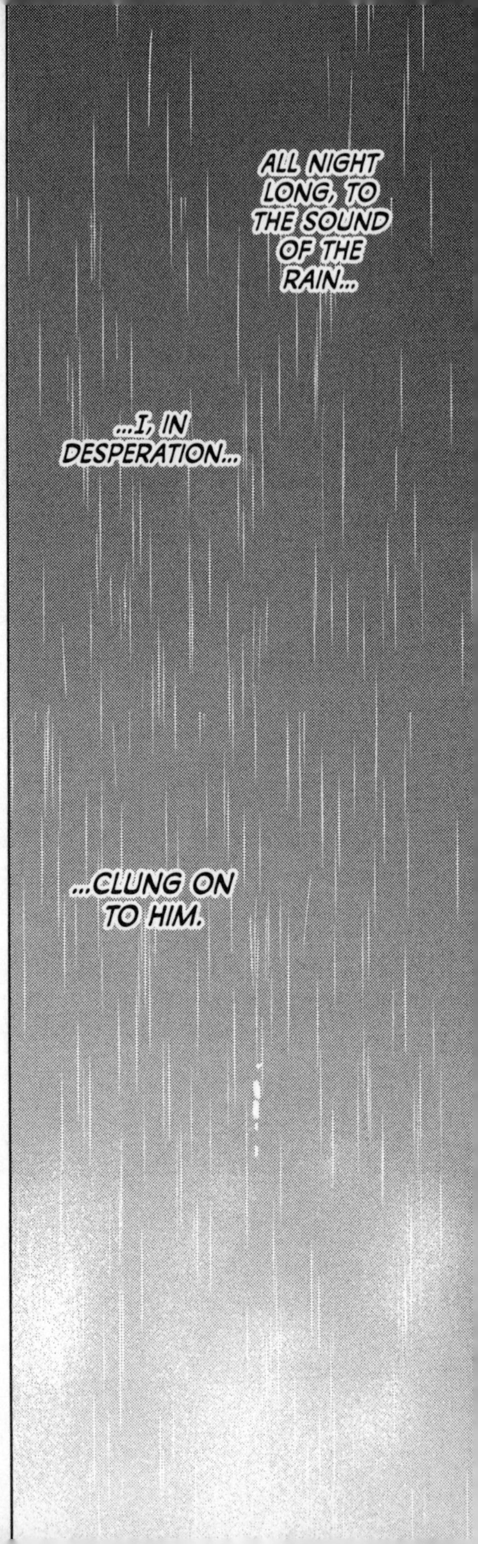
ALL NIGHT LONG, TO THE SOUND OF THE RAIN...
...I, IN DESPERATION...
...CLUNG ON TO HIM.

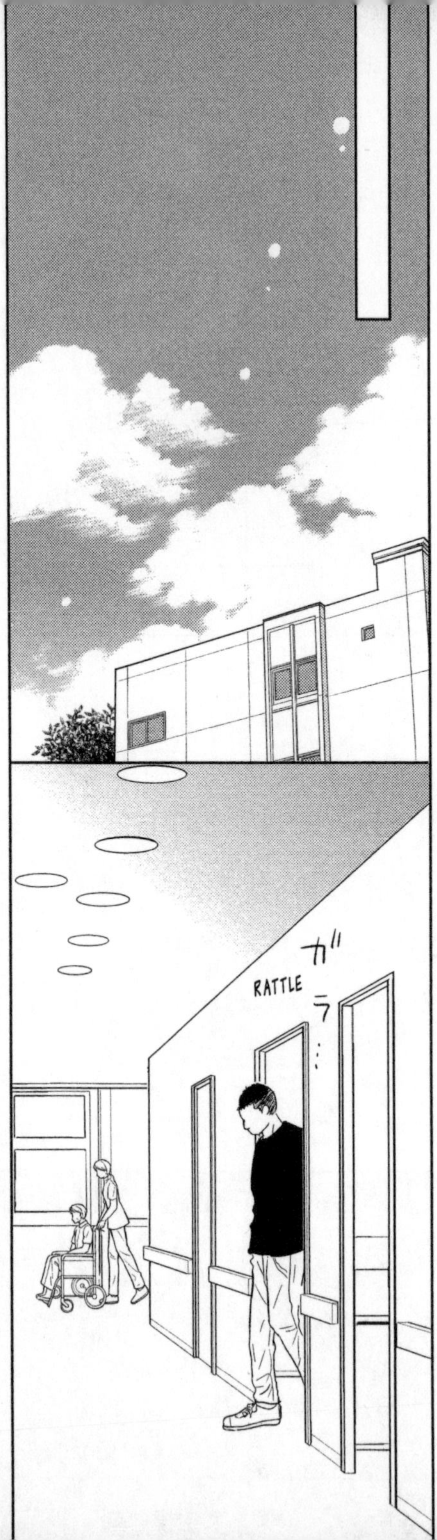
ガラ…
RATTLE

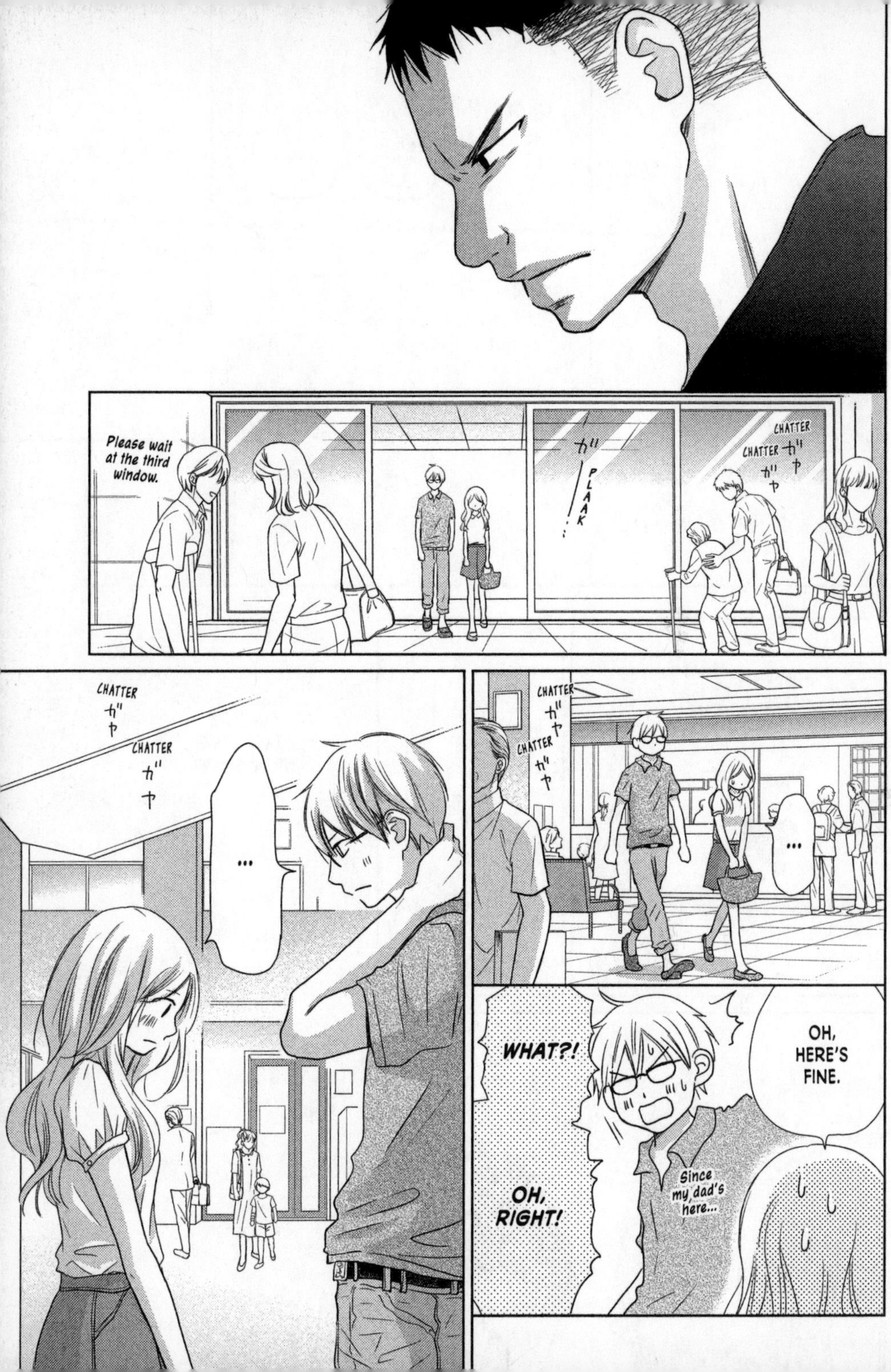
CHATTER
ガヤ
CHATTER
ガヤ
ガ
PLAAK
Please wait at the third window.
CHATTER
ガヤ
CHATTER
ガヤ
...
OH, HERE'S FINE.
Since my dad's here...
WHAT?!
OH, RIGHT!
CHATTER
ガヤ
CHATTER
ガヤ
...

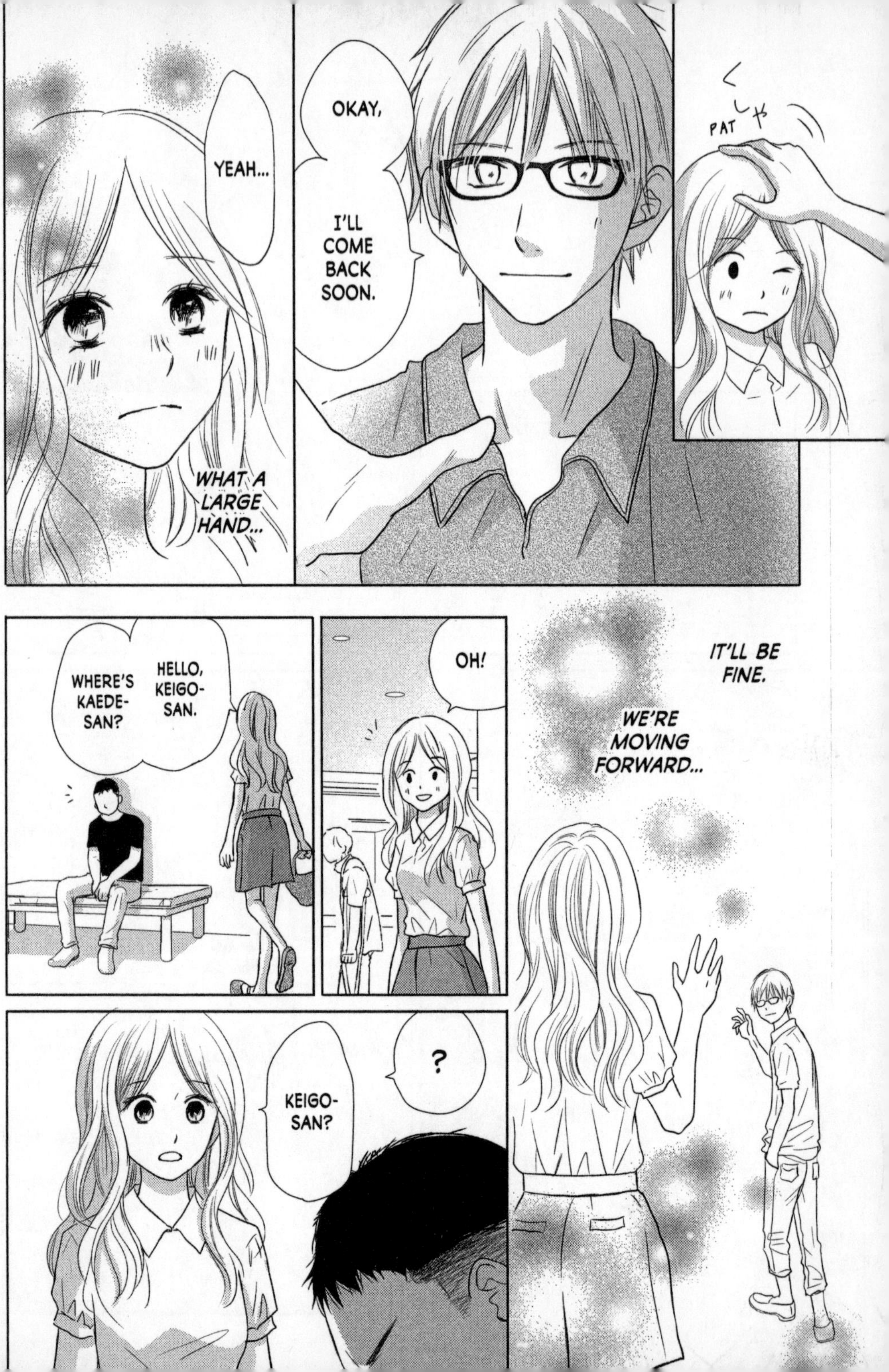
くしゃ
PAT
OKAY,
I'LL COME BACK SOON.
YEAH...
WHAT A LARGE HAND...
IT'LL BE FINE.
WE'RE MOVING FORWARD...
OH!
HELLO, KEIGO-SAN.
WHERE'S KAEDE-SAN?
?
KEIGO-SAN?

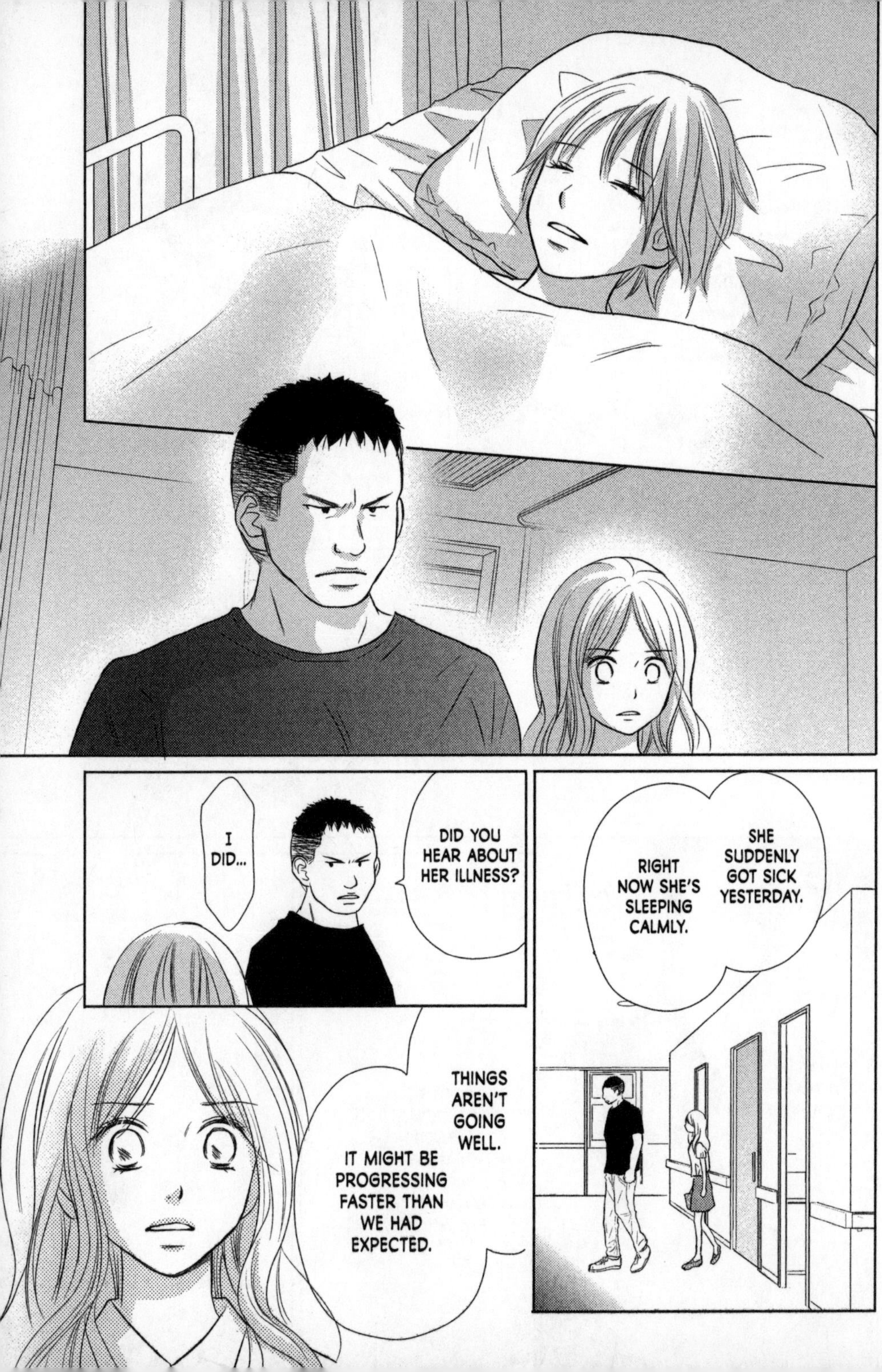
SHE SUDDENLY GOT SICK YESTERDAY.
RIGHT NOW SHE'S SLEEPING CALMLY.
DID YOU HEAR ABOUT HER ILLNESS?
I DID...
THINGS AREN'T GOING WELL.
IT MIGHT BE PROGRESSING FASTER THAN WE HAD EXPECTED.

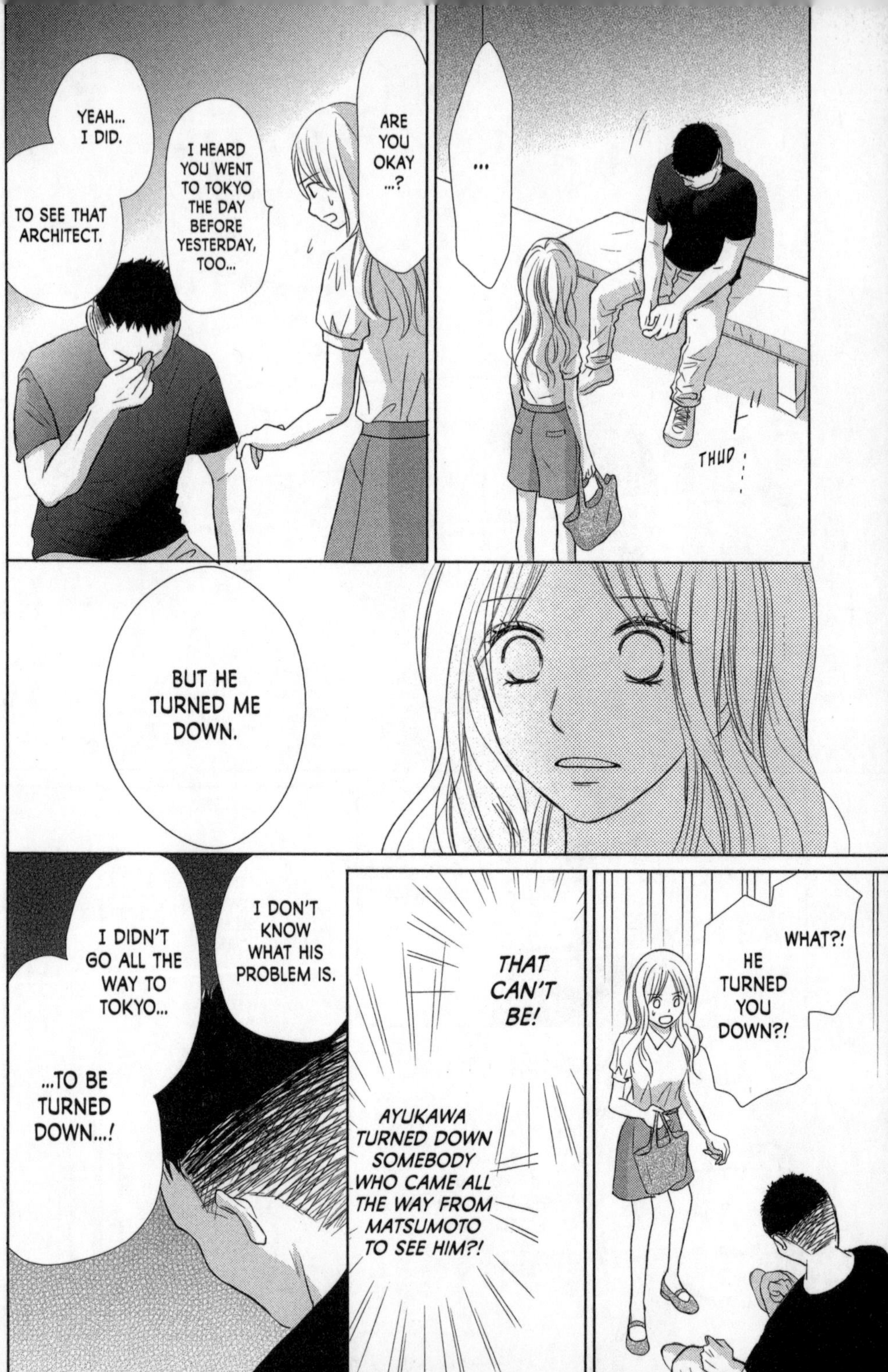
...
THUD
ARE YOU OKAY ...?
I HEARD YOU WENT TO TOKYO THE DAY BEFORE YESTERDAY, TOO...
YEAH... I DID.
TO SEE THAT ARCHITECT.
BUT HE TURNED ME DOWN.
WHAT?! HE TURNED YOU DOWN?!
THAT CAN'T BE!
AYUKAWA TURNED DOWN SOMEBODY WHO CAME ALL THE WAY FROM MATSUMOTO TO SEE HIM?!
I DON'T KNOW WHAT HIS PROBLEM IS.
I DIDN'T GO ALL THE WAY TO TOKYO...
...TO BE TURNED DOWN...!

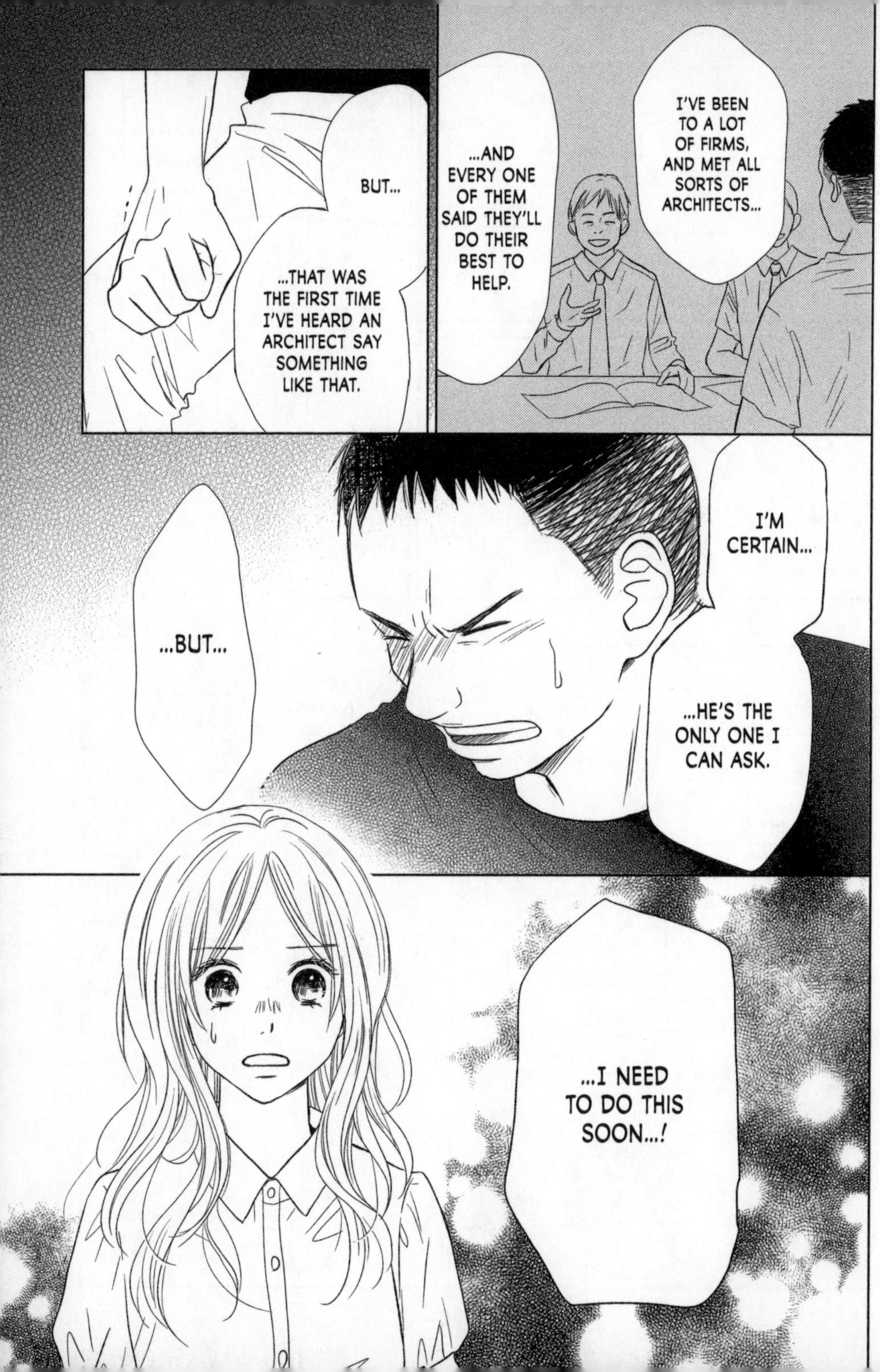
I'VE BEEN TO A LOT OF FIRMS, AND MET ALL SORTS OF ARCHITECTS...
...AND EVERY ONE OF THEM SAID THEY'LL DO THEIR BEST TO HELP.
BUT...
...THAT WAS THE FIRST TIME I'VE HEARD AN ARCHITECT SAY SOMETHING LIKE THAT.
I'M CERTAIN...
...HE'S THE ONLY ONE I CAN ASK.
...BUT...
...I NEED TO DO THIS SOON...!

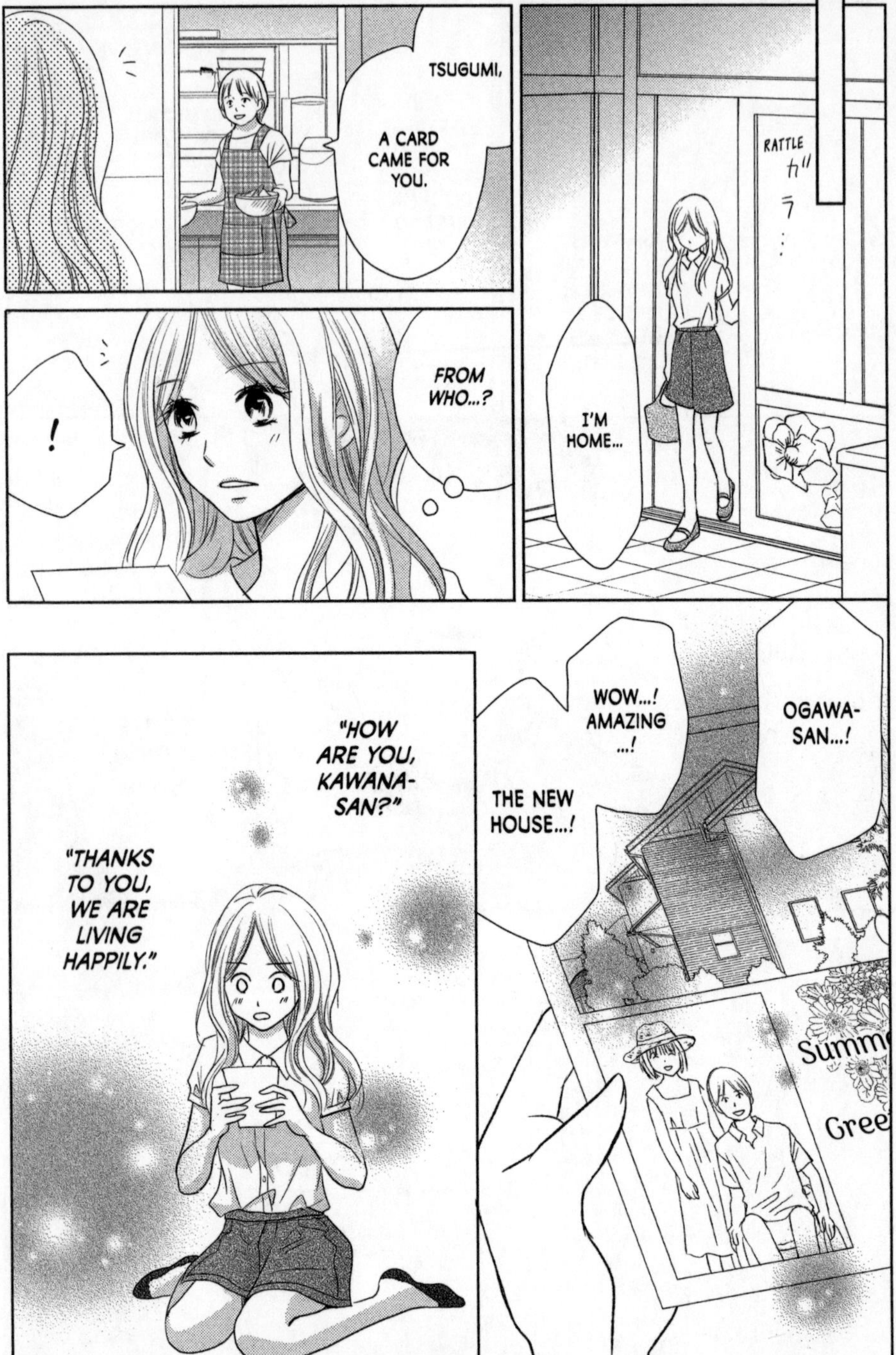
RATTLE
ガラ…
I'M HOME...
TSUGUMI,
A CARD CAME FOR YOU.
FROM WHO...?
!
OGAWA-SAN...!
WOW...! AMAZING ...!
THE NEW HOUSE...!
"HOW ARE YOU, KAWANA-SAN?"
"THANKS TO YOU, WE ARE LIVING HAPPILY."

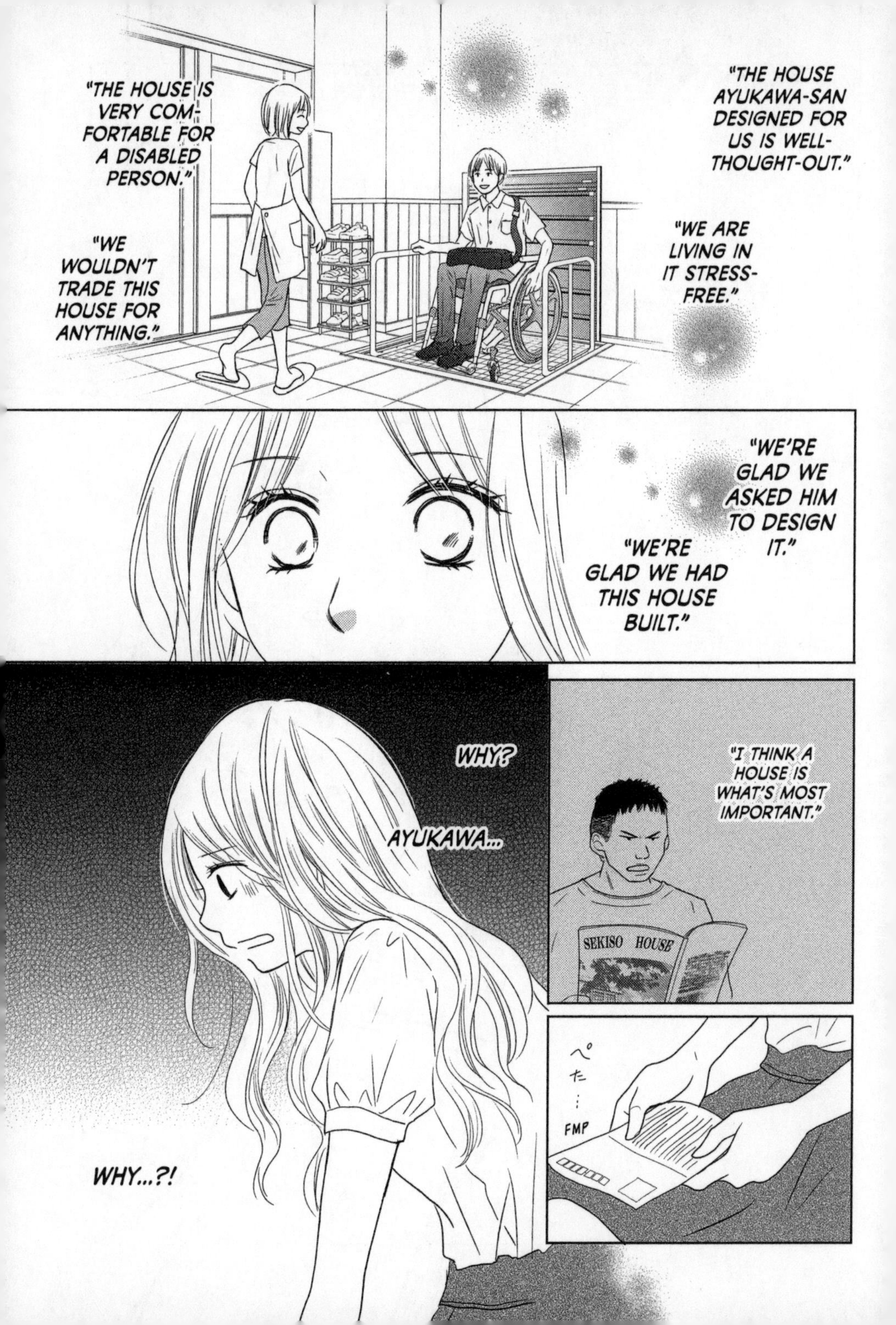
"THE HOUSE AYUKAWA-SAN DESIGNED FOR US IS WELL-THOUGHT-OUT."
"WE ARE LIVING IN IT STRESS-FREE."
"THE HOUSE IS VERY COM-FORTABLE FOR A DISABLED PERSON."
"WE WOULDN'T TRADE THIS HOUSE FOR ANYTHING."
"WE'RE GLAD WE ASKED HIM TO DESIGN IT."
"WE'RE GLAD WE HAD THIS HOUSE BUILT."
"I THINK A HOUSE IS WHAT'S MOST IMPORTANT."
SEKISO HOUSE
ぺた…
FMP
WHY?
AYUKAWA...
WHY...?!

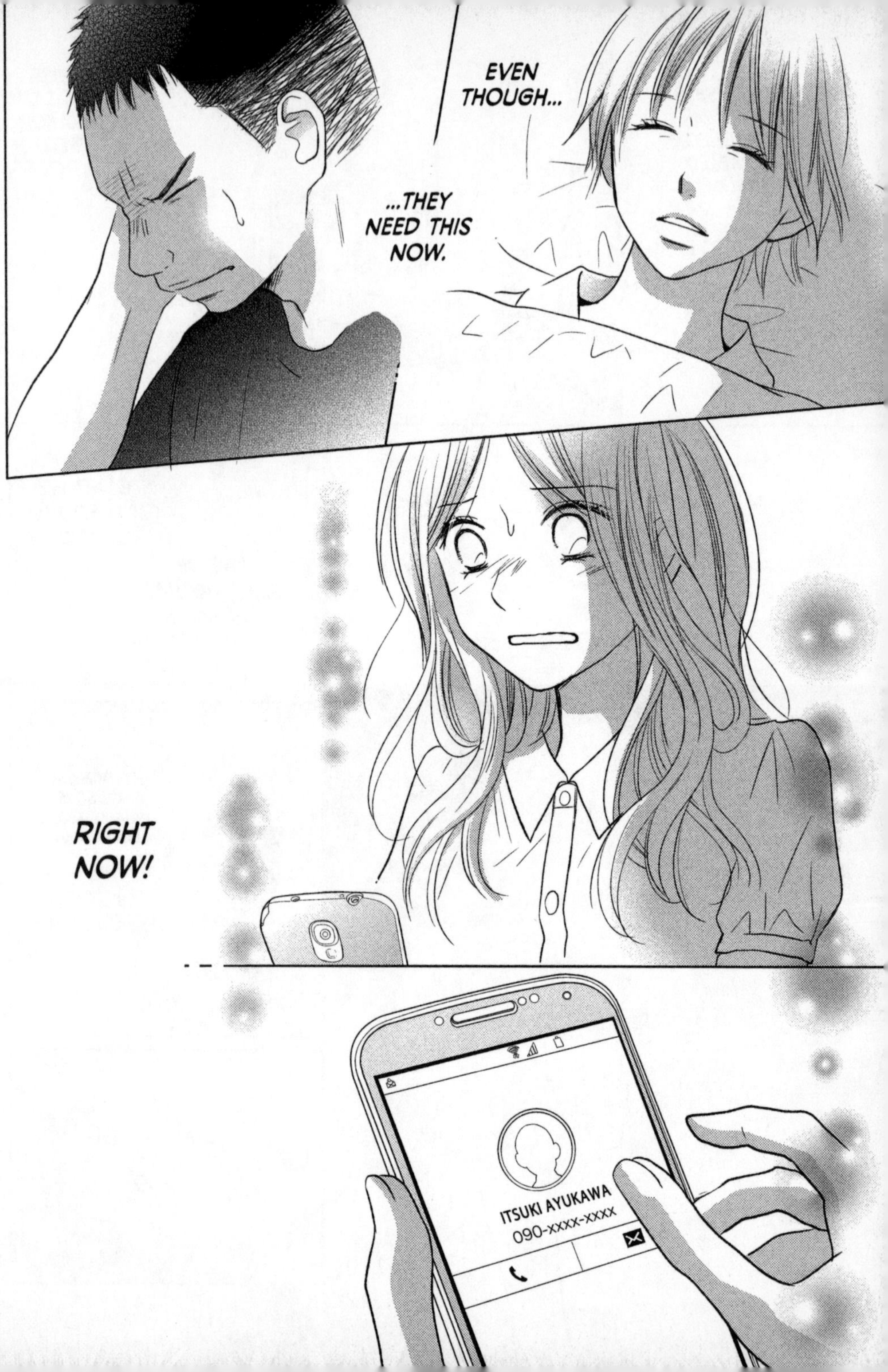
EVEN THOUGH...
...THEY NEED THIS NOW.
RIGHT NOW!
ITSUKI AYUKAWA
090-xxxx-xxxx

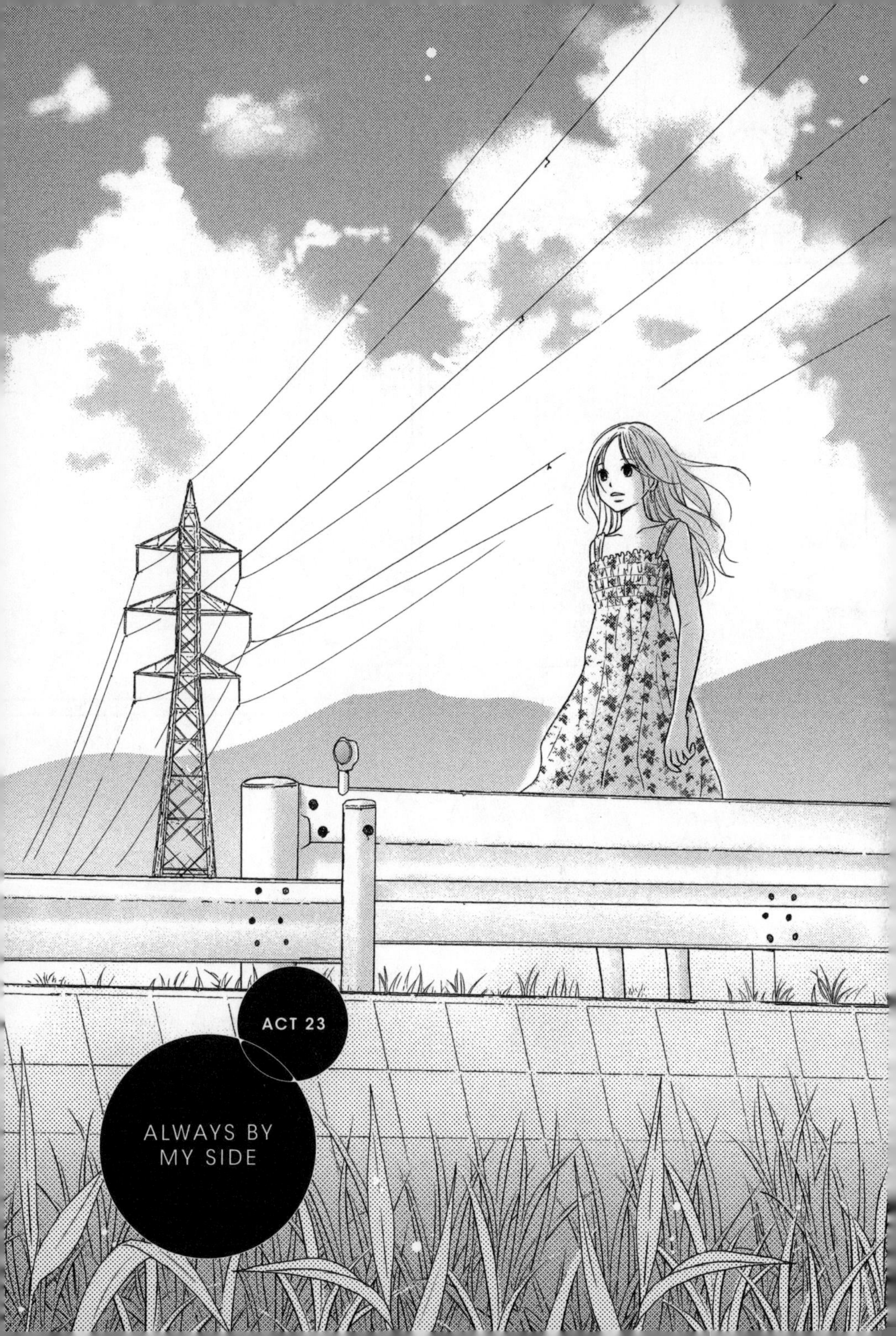
ACT 23
ALWAYS BY MY SIDE

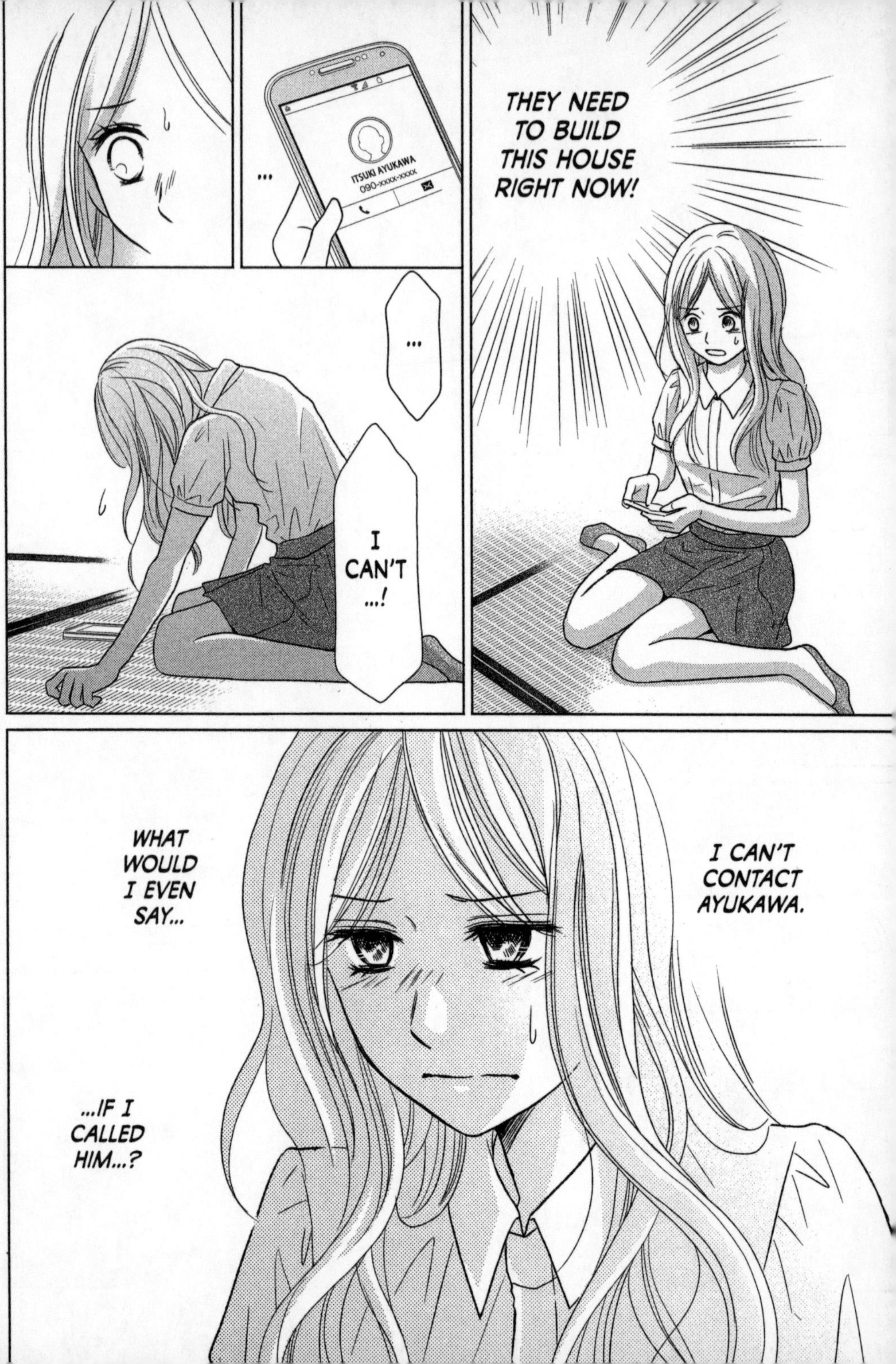
THEY NEED TO BUILD THIS HOUSE RIGHT NOW!
ITSUKI AYUKAWA
090-xxxx-xxxx
...
...
I CAN'T ...!
I CAN'T CONTACT AYUKAWA.
WHAT WOULD I EVEN SAY...
...IF I CALLED HIM...?

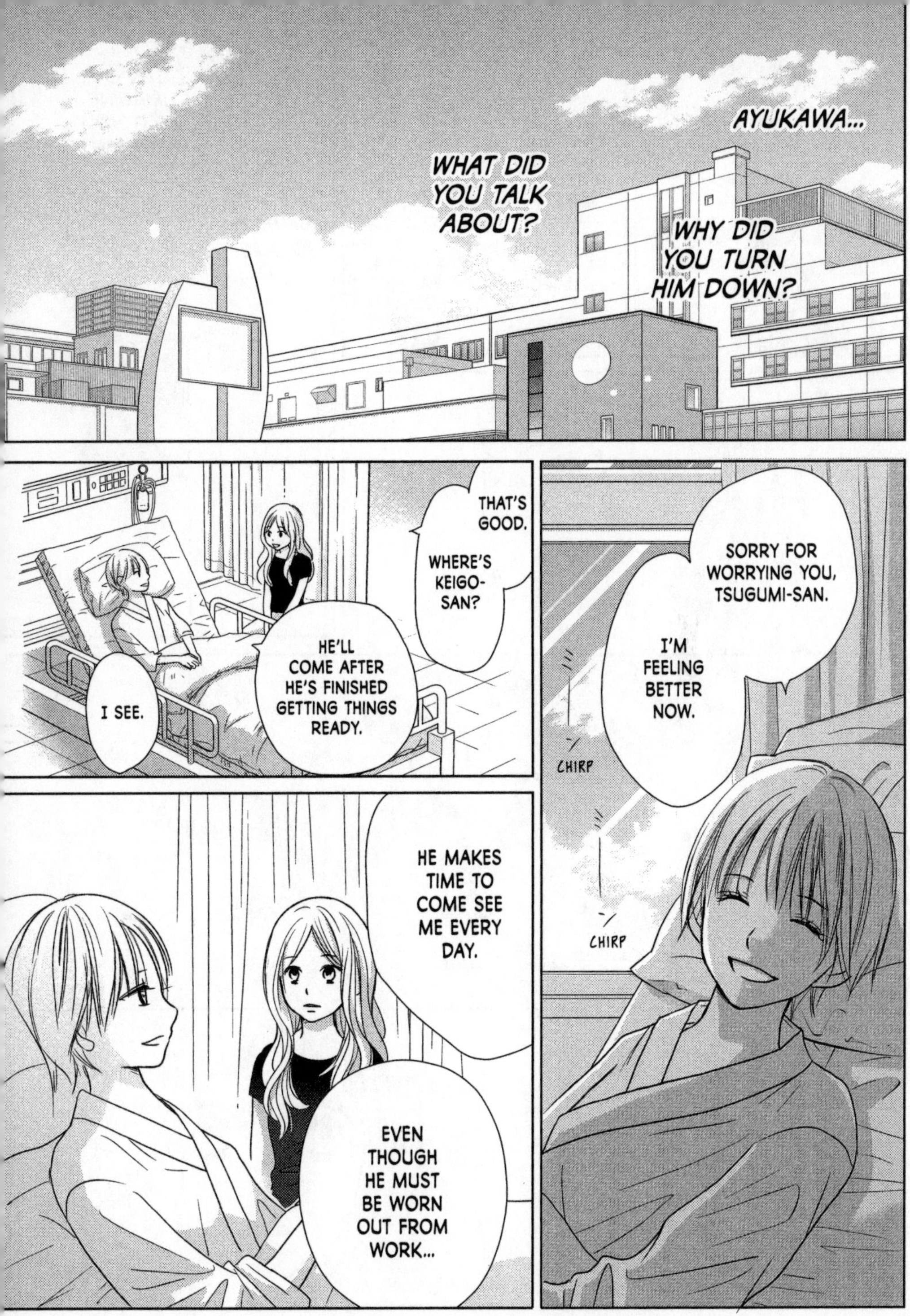
AYUKAWA...
WHAT DID YOU TALK ABOUT?
WHY DID YOU TURN HIM DOWN?
SORRY FOR WORRYING YOU, TSUGUMI-SAN.
I'M FEELING BETTER NOW.
CHIRP
CHIRP
THAT'S GOOD.
WHERE'S KEIGO-SAN?
HE'LL COME AFTER HE'S FINISHED GETTING THINGS READY.
I SEE.
HE MAKES TIME TO COME SEE ME EVERY DAY.
EVEN THOUGH HE MUST BE WORN OUT FROM WORK...

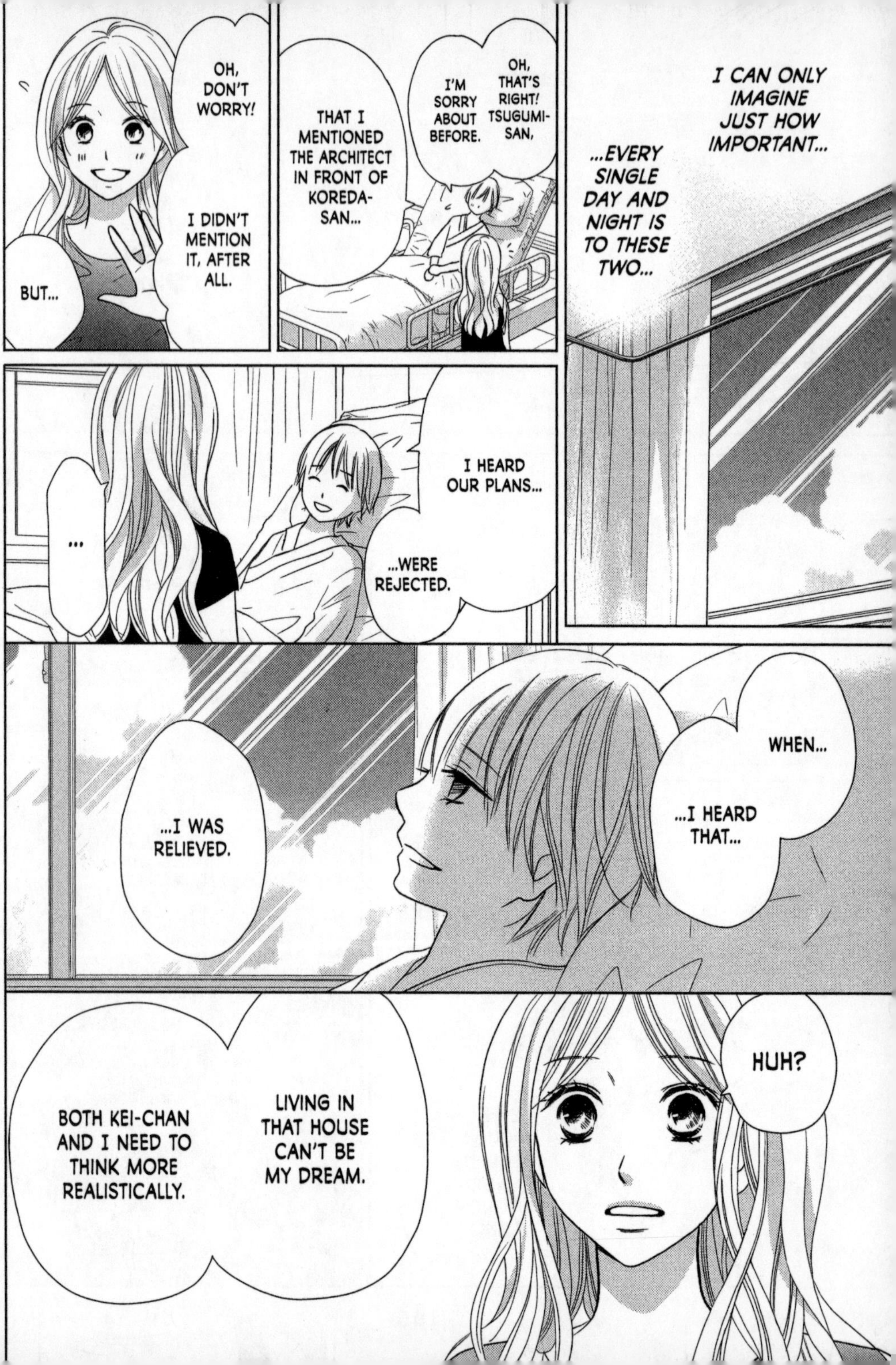
I CAN ONLY IMAGINE JUST HOW IMPORTANT...
...EVERY SINGLE DAY AND NIGHT IS TO THESE TWO...
OH, THAT'S RIGHT! TSUGUMI-SAN,
I'M SORRY ABOUT BEFORE.
THAT I MENTIONED THE ARCHITECT IN FRONT OF KOREDA-SAN...
OH, DON'T WORRY!
I DIDN'T MENTION IT, AFTER ALL.
BUT...
I HEARD OUR PLANS...
...WERE REJECTED.
...
WHEN...
...I HEARD THAT...
...I WAS RELIEVED.
HUH?
LIVING IN THAT HOUSE CAN'T BE MY DREAM.
BOTH KEI-CHAN AND I NEED TO THINK MORE REALISTICALLY.

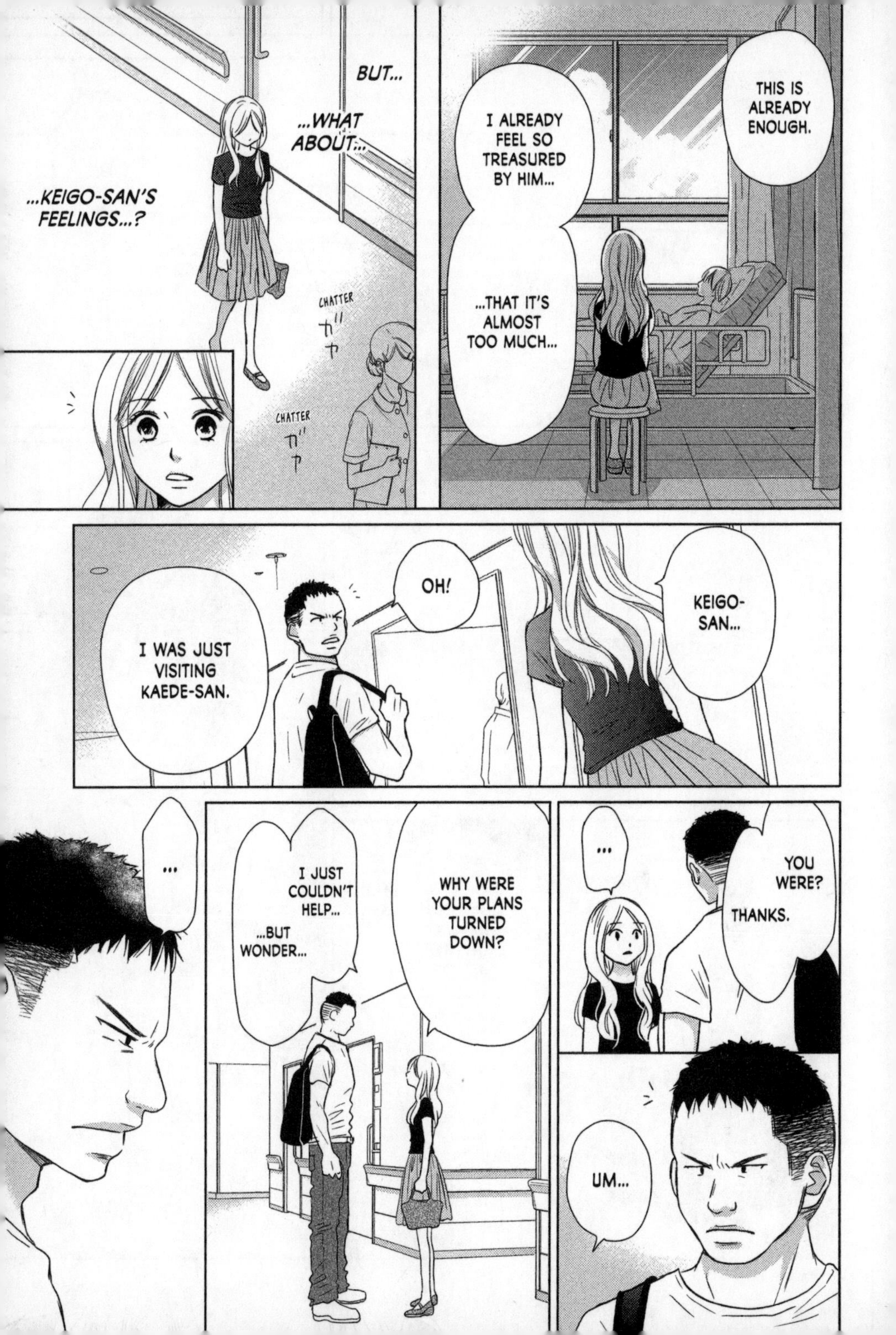
THIS IS ALREADY ENOUGH.
I ALREADY FEEL SO TREASURED BY HIM...
...THAT IT'S ALMOST TOO MUCH...
BUT...
...WHAT ABOUT...
...KEIGO-SAN'S FEELINGS...?
CHATTER ガヤ
CHATTER ガヤ
KEIGO-SAN...
OH!
I WAS JUST VISITING KAEDE-SAN.
YOU WERE? THANKS.
...
UM...
WHY WERE YOUR PLANS TURNED DOWN?
I JUST COULDN'T HELP... ...BUT WONDER...
...

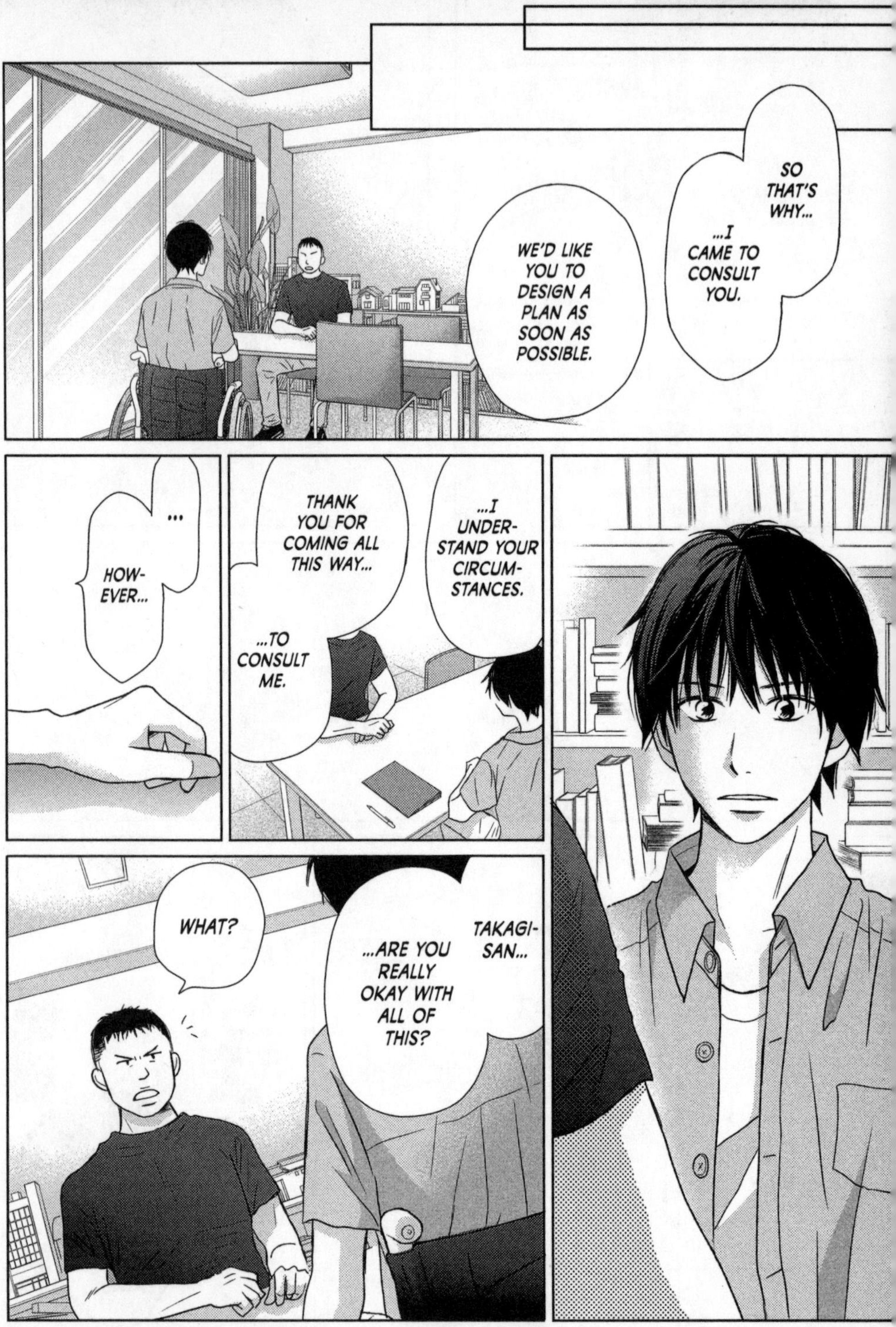
SO THAT'S WHY...
...I CAME TO CONSULT YOU.
WE'D LIKE YOU TO DESIGN A PLAN AS SOON AS POSSIBLE.
...I UNDER-STAND YOUR CIRCUM-STANCES.
THANK YOU FOR COMING ALL THIS WAY...
...TO CONSULT ME.
...
HOW-EVER...
TAKAGI-SAN...
...ARE YOU REALLY OKAY WITH ALL OF THIS?
WHAT?

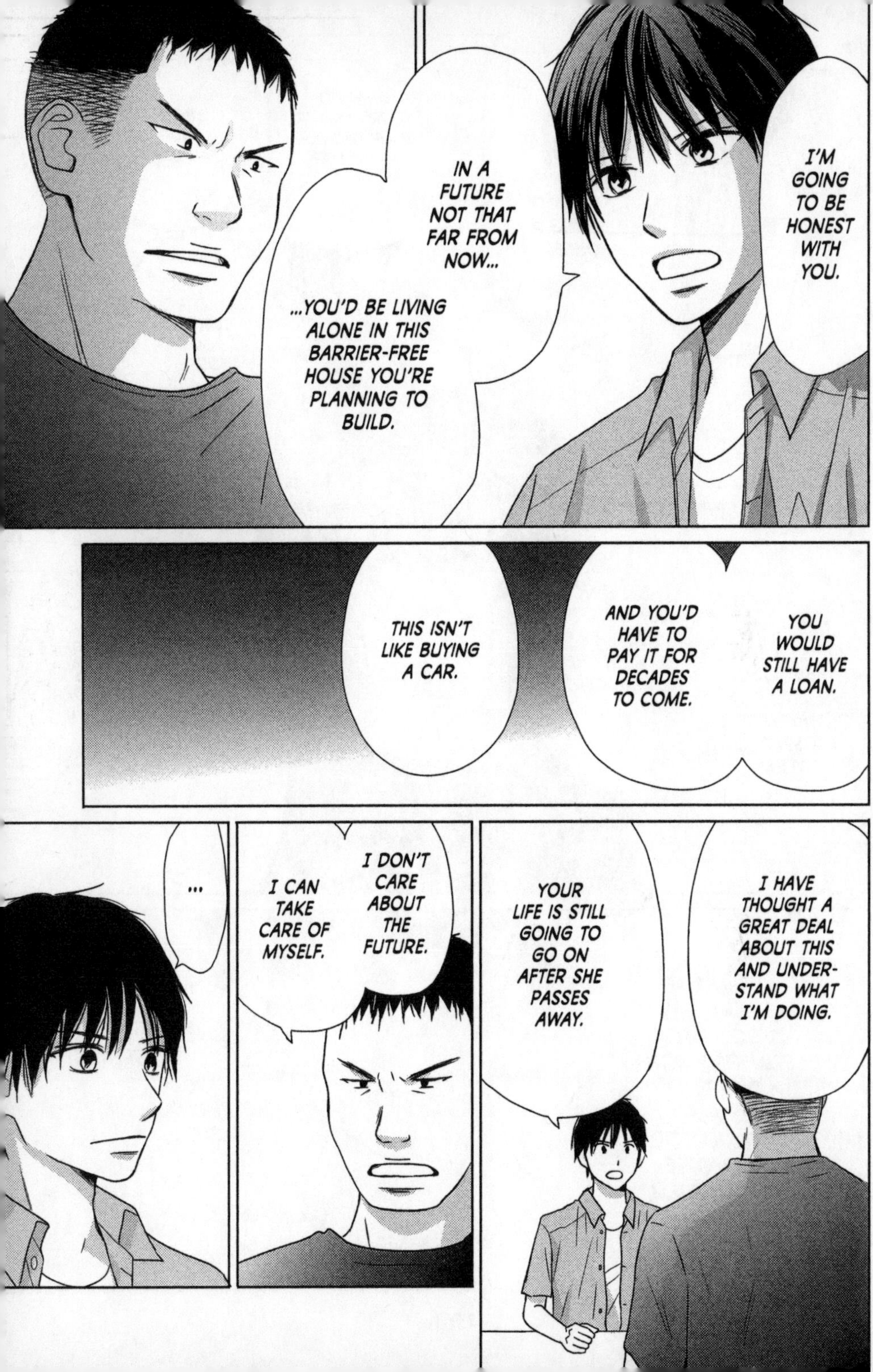
I'M GOING TO BE HONEST WITH YOU.
IN A FUTURE NOT THAT FAR FROM NOW...
...YOU'D BE LIVING ALONE IN THIS BARRIER-FREE HOUSE YOU'RE PLANNING TO BUILD.
YOU WOULD STILL HAVE A LOAN.
AND YOU'D HAVE TO PAY IT FOR DECADES TO COME.
THIS ISN'T LIKE BUYING A CAR.
I HAVE THOUGHT A GREAT DEAL ABOUT THIS AND UNDER-STAND WHAT I'M DOING.
YOUR LIFE IS STILL GOING TO GO ON AFTER SHE PASSES AWAY.
I DON'T CARE ABOUT THE FUTURE.
I CAN TAKE CARE OF MYSELF.
...

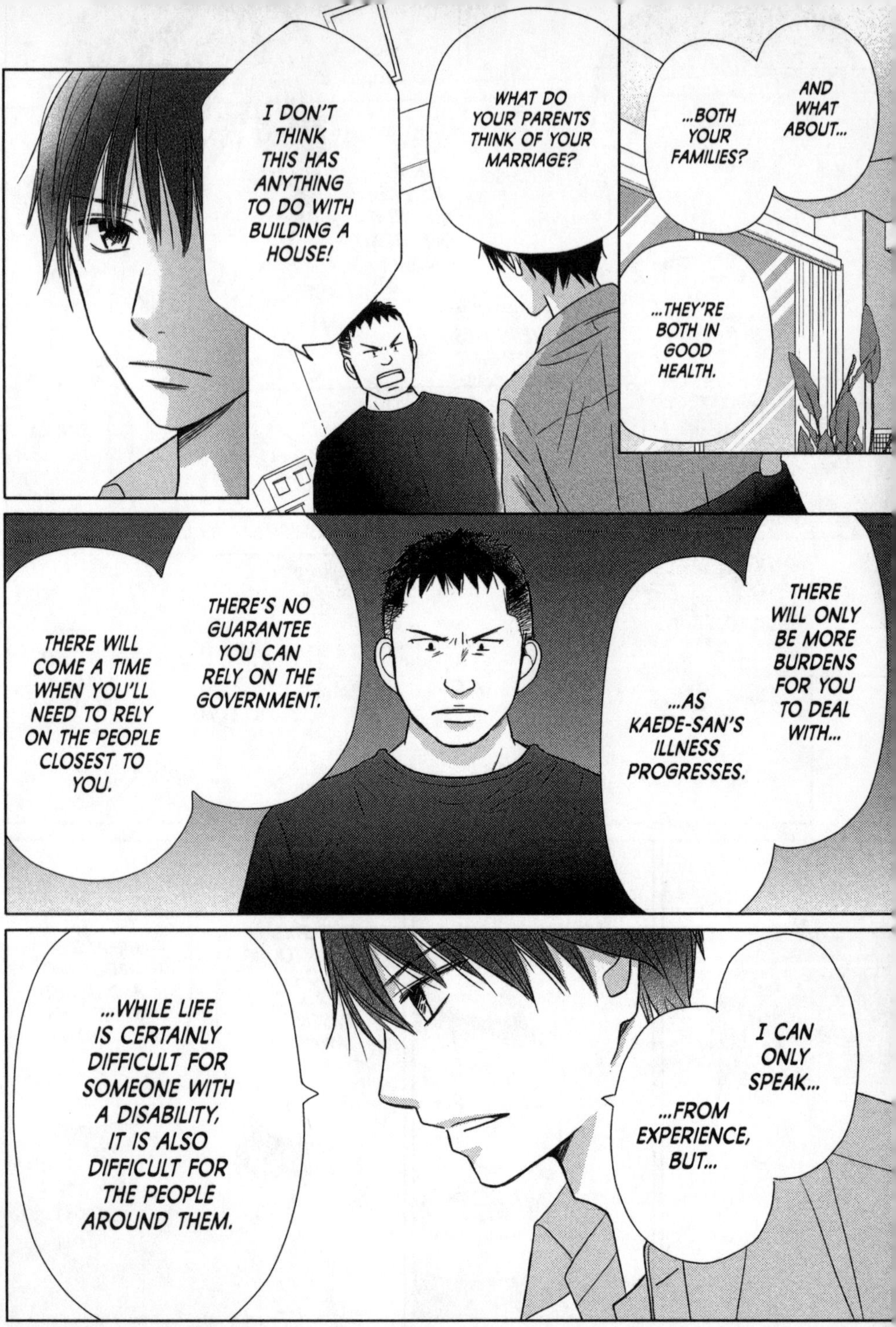

AND WHAT ABOUT...
...BOTH YOUR FAMILIES?
...THEY'RE BOTH IN GOOD HEALTH.
WHAT DO YOUR PARENTS THINK OF YOUR MARRIAGE?
I DON'T THINK THIS HAS ANYTHING TO DO WITH BUILDING A HOUSE!
THERE WILL ONLY BE MORE BURDENS FOR YOU TO DEAL WITH...
...AS KAEDE-SAN'S ILLNESS PROGRESSES.
THERE'S NO GUARANTEE YOU CAN RELY ON THE GOVERNMENT.
THERE WILL COME A TIME WHEN YOU'LL NEED TO RELY ON THE PEOPLE CLOSEST TO YOU.
I CAN ONLY SPEAK...
...FROM EXPERIENCE, BUT...
...WHILE LIFE IS CERTAINLY DIFFICULT FOR SOMEONE WITH A DISABILITY, IT IS ALSO DIFFICULT FOR THE PEOPLE AROUND THEM.

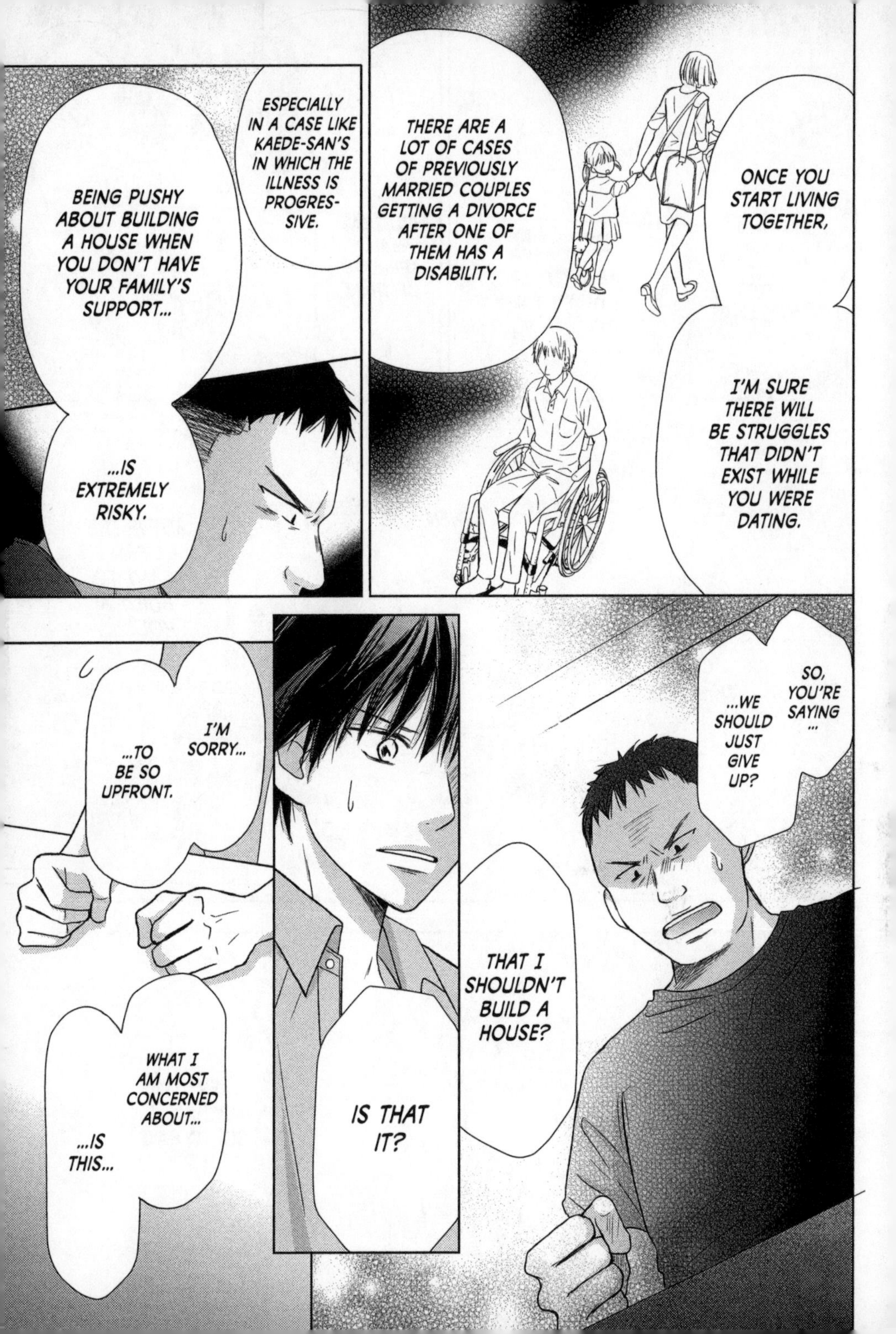

ONCE YOU START LIVING TOGETHER,
I'M SURE THERE WILL BE STRUGGLES THAT DIDN'T EXIST WHILE YOU WERE DATING.
THERE ARE A LOT OF CASES OF PREVIOUSLY MARRIED COUPLES GETTING A DIVORCE AFTER ONE OF THEM HAS A DISABILITY.
ESPECIALLY IN A CASE LIKE KAEDE-SAN'S IN WHICH THE ILLNESS IS PROGRESSIVE.
BEING PUSHY ABOUT BUILDING A HOUSE WHEN YOU DON'T HAVE YOUR FAMILY'S SUPPORT...
...IS EXTREMELY RISKY.
SO, YOU'RE SAYING...
...WE SHOULD JUST GIVE UP?
THAT I SHOULDN'T BUILD A HOUSE?
IS THAT IT?
I'M SORRY...
...TO BE SO UPFRONT.
WHAT I AM MOST CONCERNED ABOUT...
...IS THIS...

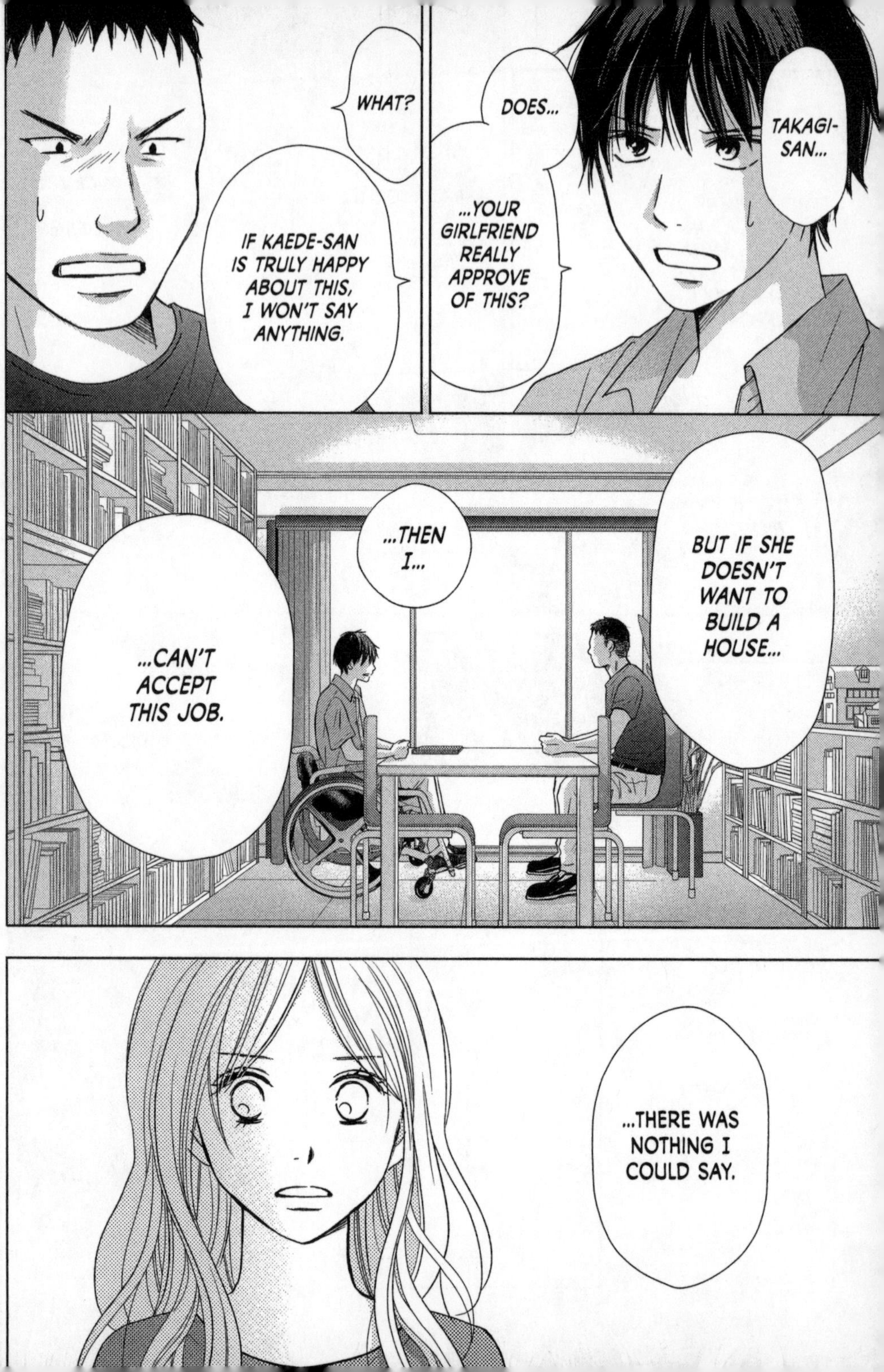
TAKAGI-SAN...
DOES...
...YOUR GIRLFRIEND REALLY APPROVE OF THIS?
WHAT?
IF KAEDE-SAN IS TRULY HAPPY ABOUT THIS, I WON'T SAY ANYTHING.
BUT IF SHE DOESN'T WANT TO BUILD A HOUSE...
...THEN I...
...CAN'T ACCEPT THIS JOB.
...THERE WAS NOTHING I COULD SAY.

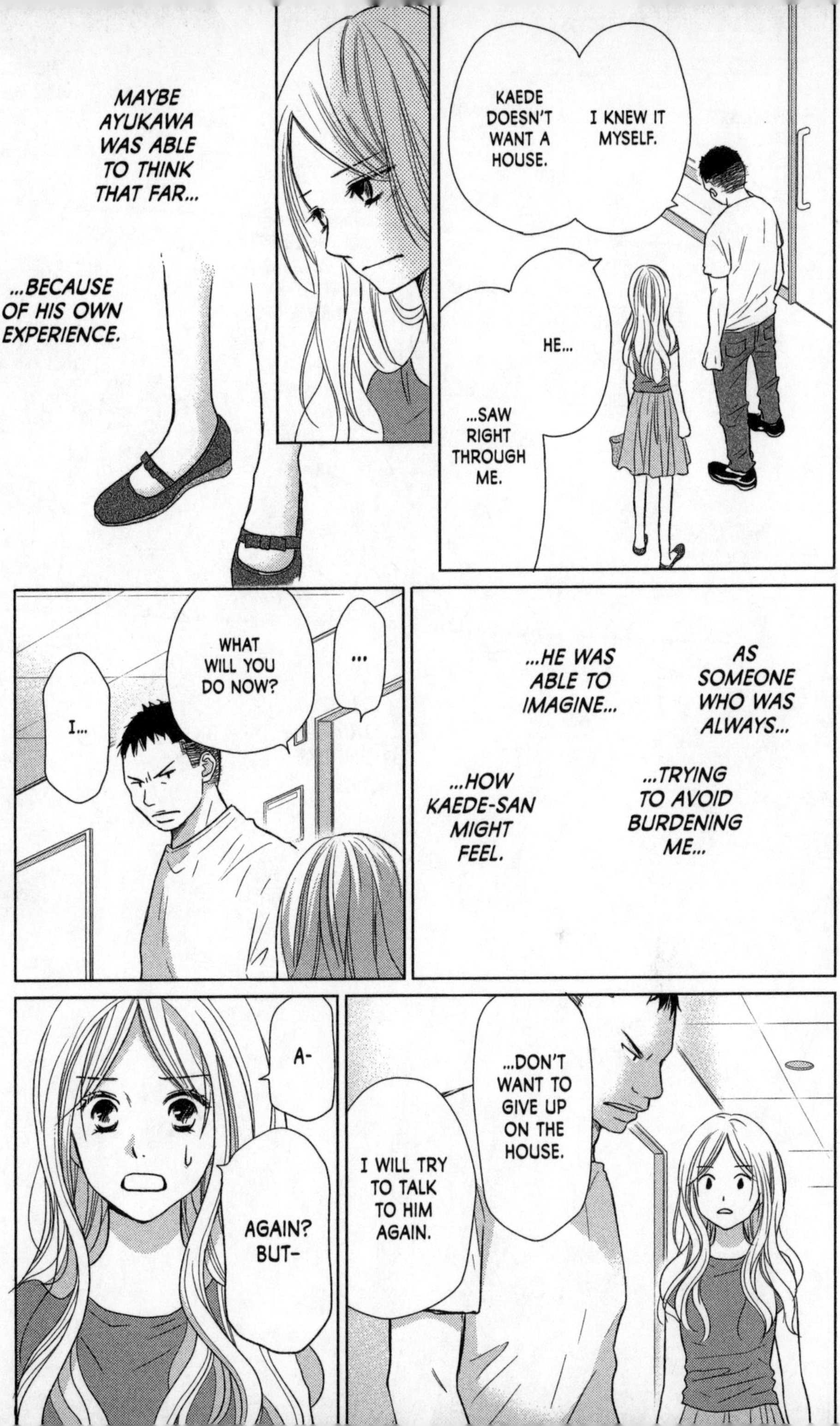
KAEDE DOESN'T WANT A HOUSE. I KNEW IT MYSELF.
HE...
...SAW RIGHT THROUGH ME.
MAYBE AYUKAWA WAS ABLE TO THINK THAT FAR...
...BECAUSE OF HIS OWN EXPERIENCE.
AS SOMEONE WHO WAS ALWAYS...
...TRYING TO AVOID BURDENING ME...
...HE WAS ABLE TO IMAGINE...
...HOW KAEDE-SAN MIGHT FEEL.
...
WHAT WILL YOU DO NOW?
I...
...DON'T WANT TO GIVE UP ON THE HOUSE.
I WILL TRY TO TALK TO HIM AGAIN.
A-
AGAIN? BUT-

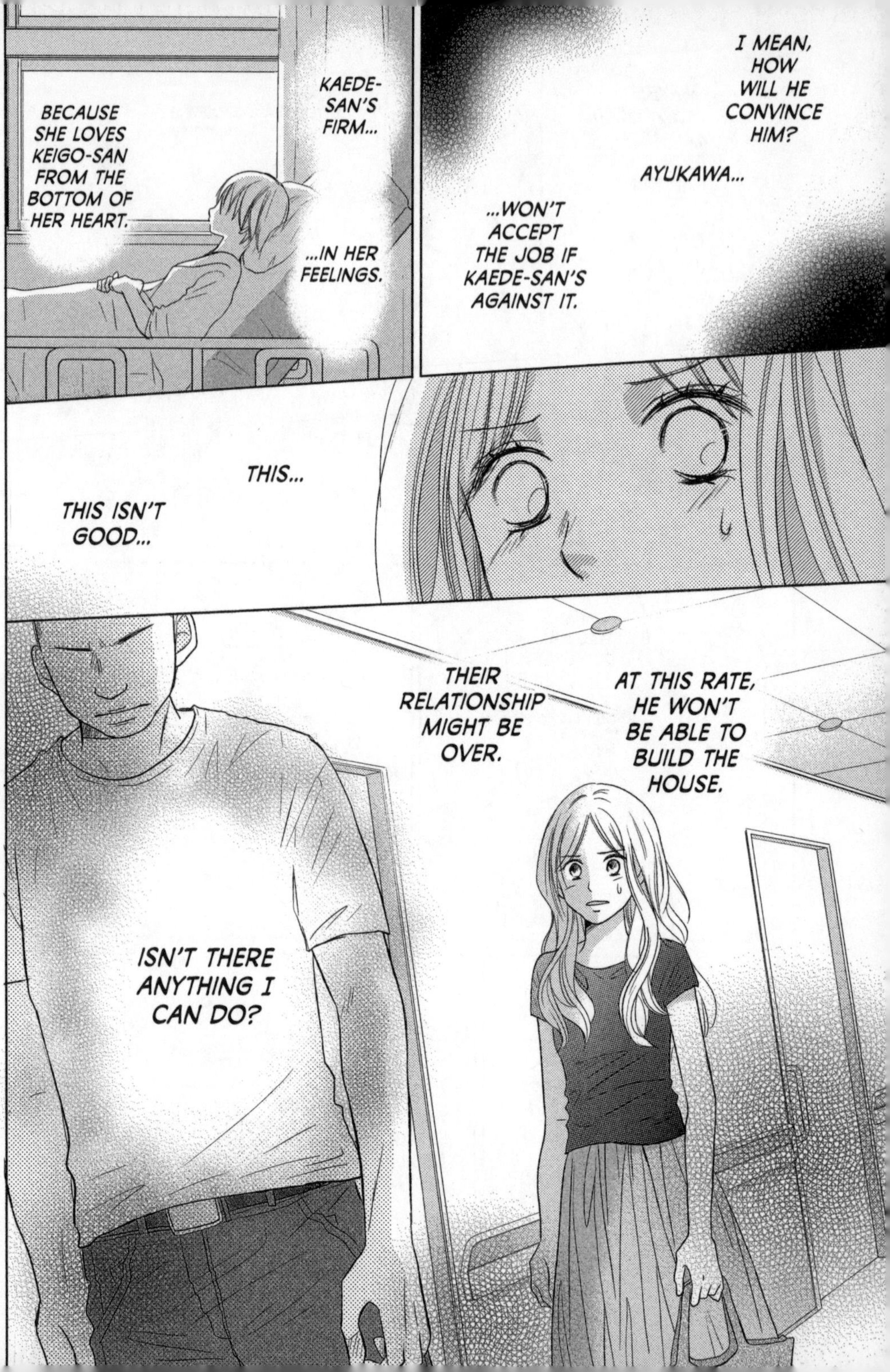
I MEAN, HOW WILL HE CONVINCE HIM?
AYUKAWA...
...WON'T ACCEPT THE JOB IF KAEDE-SAN'S AGAINST IT.
KAEDE-SAN'S FIRM...
...IN HER FEELINGS.
BECAUSE SHE LOVES KEIGO-SAN FROM THE BOTTOM OF HER HEART.
THIS...
THIS ISN'T GOOD...
AT THIS RATE, HE WON'T BE ABLE TO BUILD THE HOUSE.
THEIR RELATIONSHIP MIGHT BE OVER.
ISN'T THERE ANYTHING I CAN DO?

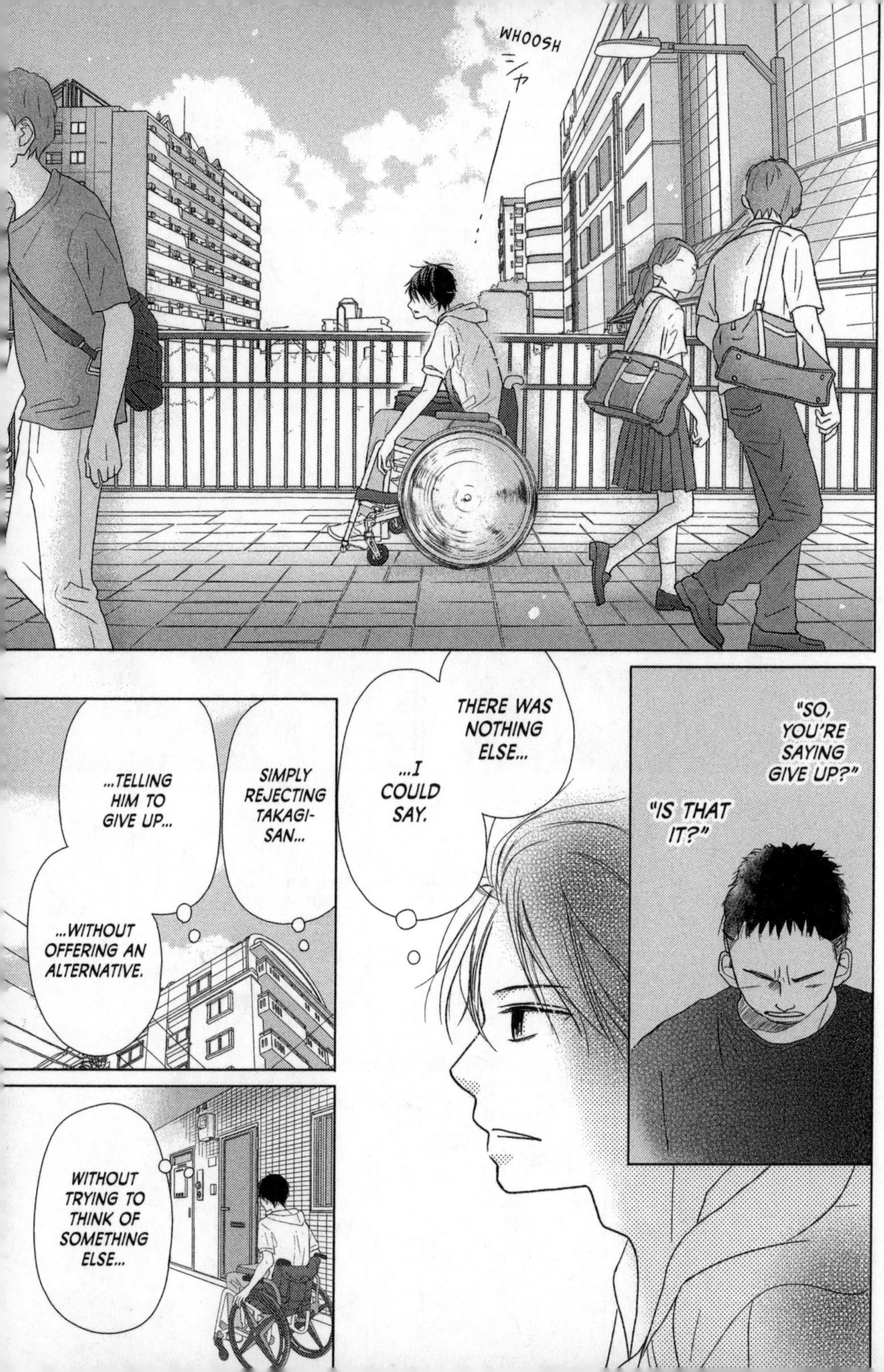
WHOOSH
シャ
"SO, YOU'RE SAYING GIVE UP?"
"IS THAT IT?"
THERE WAS NOTHING ELSE...
...I COULD SAY.
SIMPLY REJECTING TAKAGI-SAN...
...TELLING HIM TO GIVE UP...
...WITHOUT OFFERING AN ALTERNATIVE.
WITHOUT TRYING TO THINK OF SOMETHING ELSE...

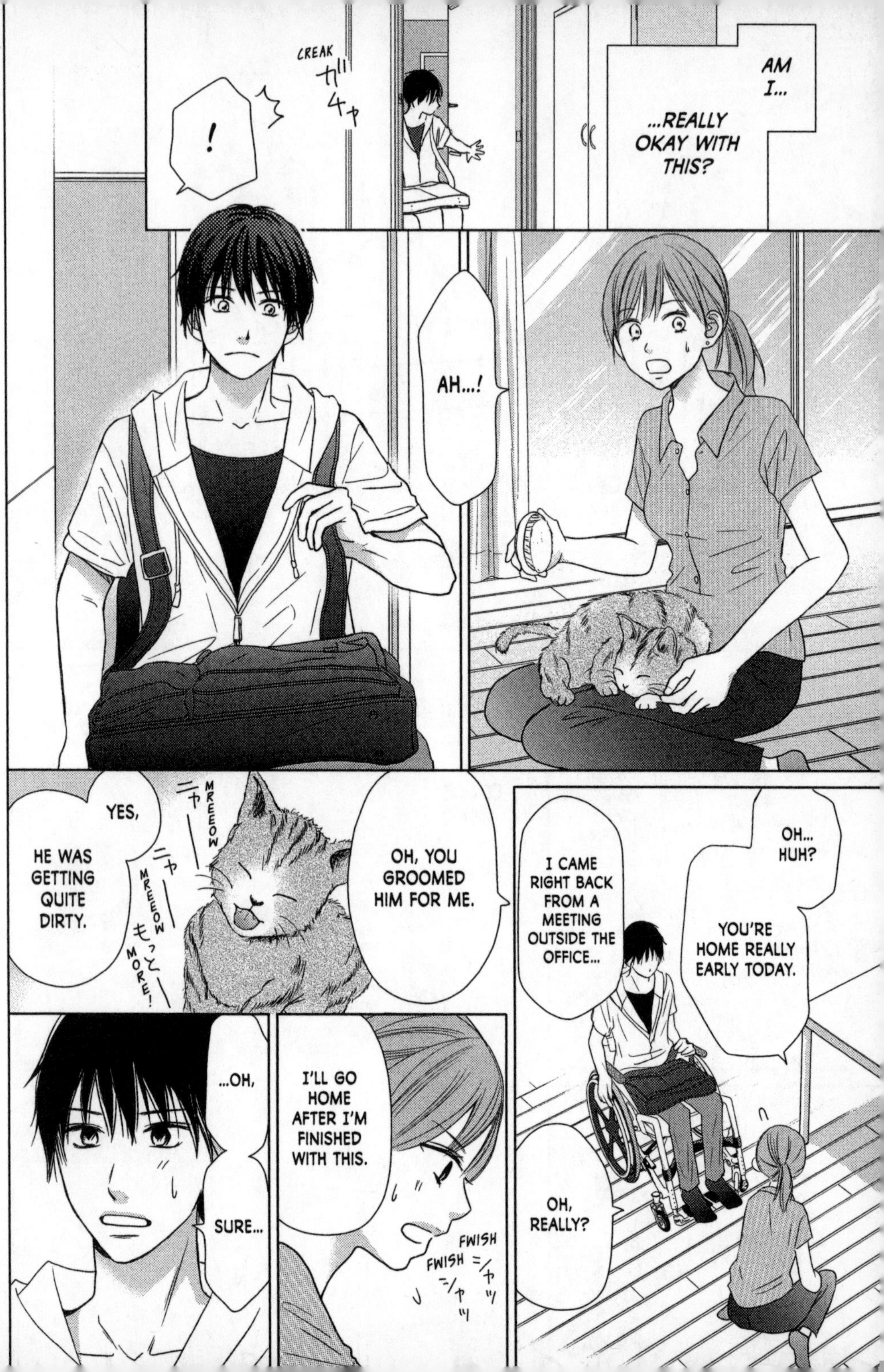
AM I...
...REALLY OKAY WITH THIS?
CREAK
ガルチャ
!
AH...!
OH... HUH?
YOU'RE HOME REALLY EARLY TODAY.
I CAME RIGHT BACK FROM A MEETING OUTSIDE THE OFFICE...
OH, REALLY?
OH, YOU GROOMED HIM FOR ME.
ニャー MREEOW
ニャー MREEOW
もっと MORE!
YES, HE WAS GETTING QUITE DIRTY.
I'LL GO HOME AFTER I'M FINISHED WITH THIS.
FWISH シャッ
FWISH シャッ
...OH,
SURE...

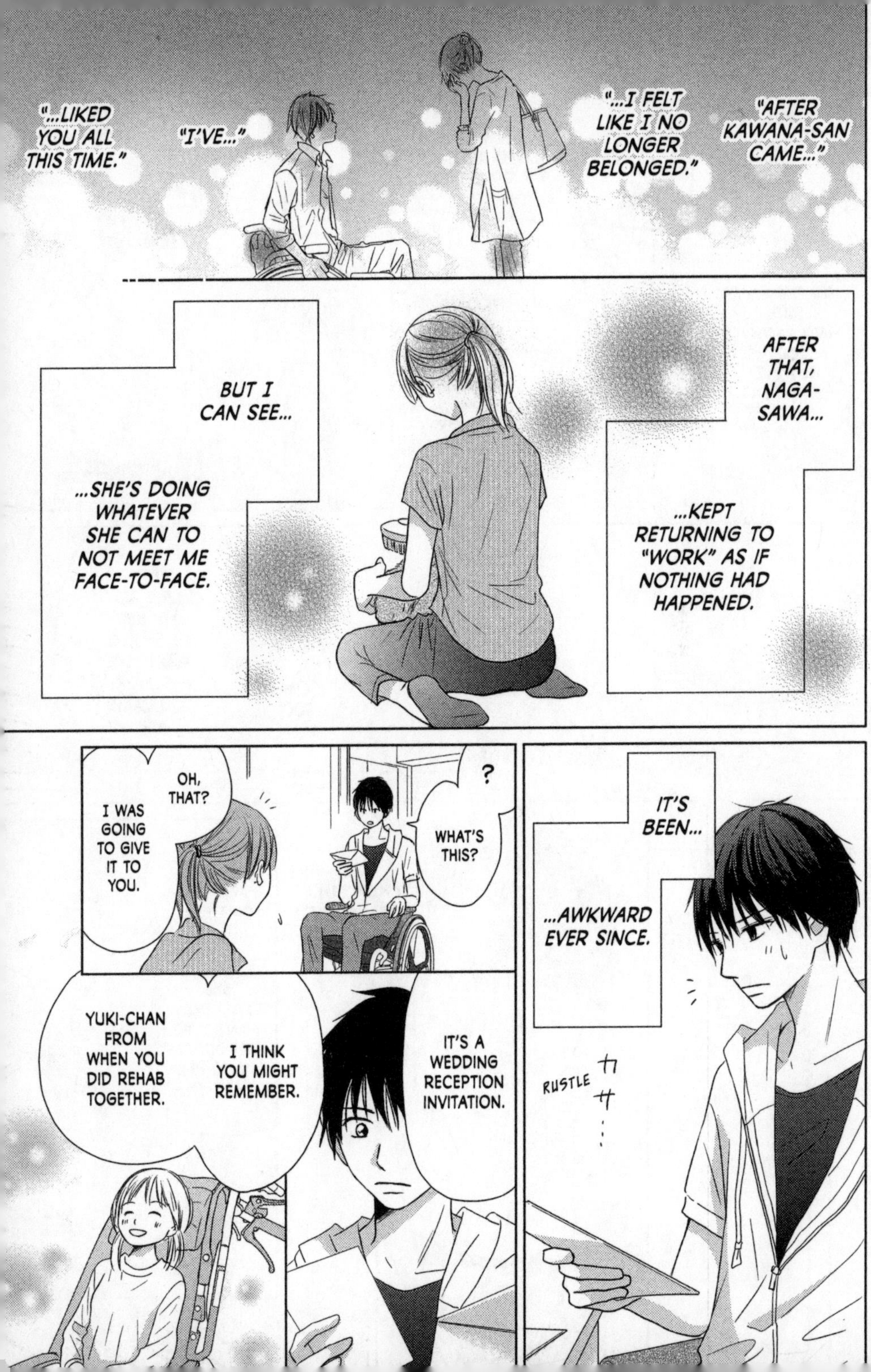
"AFTER KAWANA-SAN CAME..."
"...I FELT LIKE I NO LONGER BELONGED."
"I'VE..."
"...LIKED YOU ALL THIS TIME."
AFTER THAT, NAGA-SAWA...
...KEPT RETURNING TO "WORK" AS IF NOTHING HAD HAPPENED.
BUT I CAN SEE...
...SHE'S DOING WHATEVER SHE CAN TO NOT MEET ME FACE-TO-FACE.
IT'S BEEN...
...AWKWARD EVER SINCE.
RUSTLE
?
WHAT'S THIS?
OH, THAT?
I WAS GOING TO GIVE IT TO YOU.
IT'S A WEDDING RECEPTION INVITATION.
I THINK YOU MIGHT REMEMBER.
YUKI-CHAN FROM WHEN YOU DID REHAB TOGETHER.

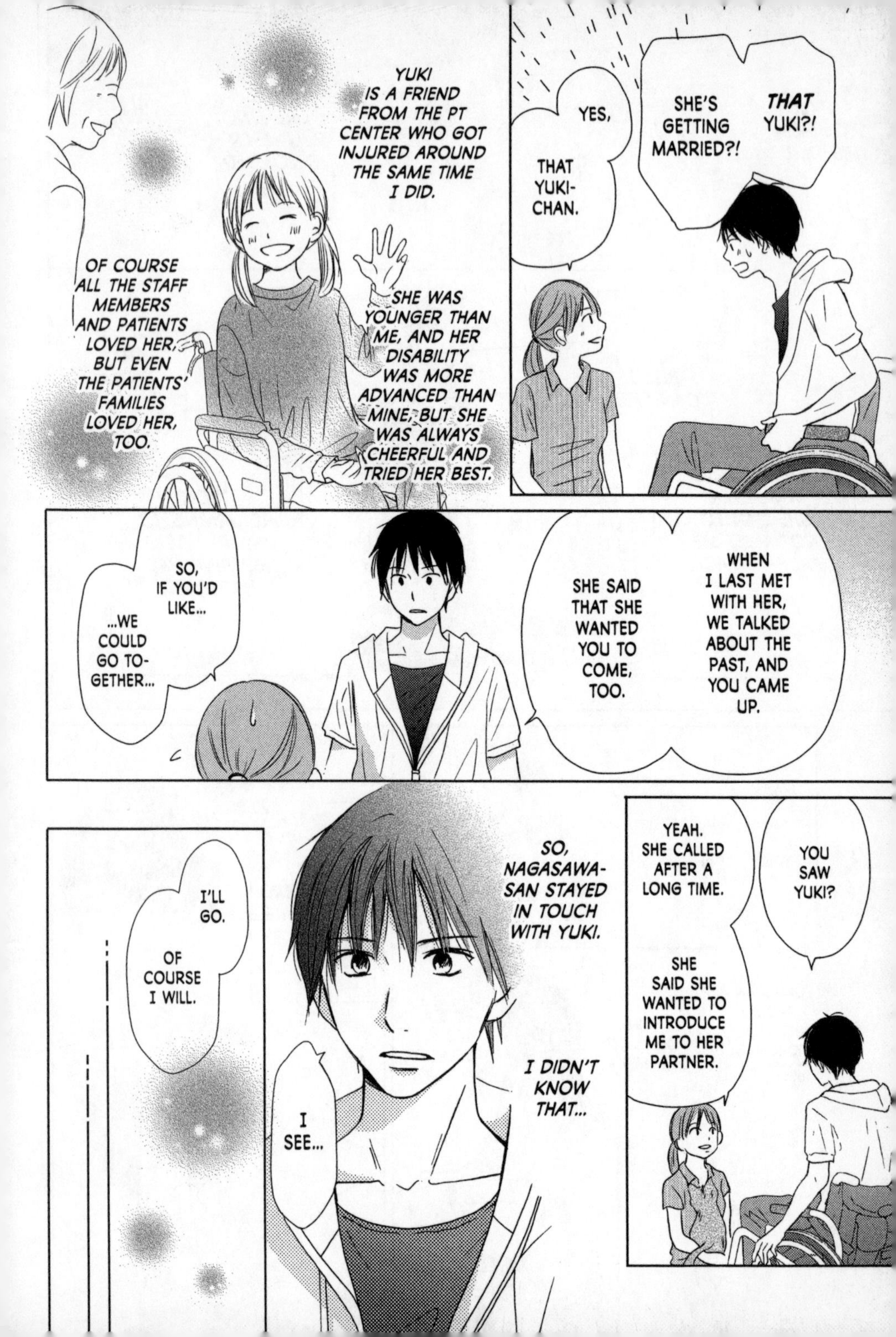
THAT YUKI?!
SHE'S GETTING MARRIED?!
YES,
THAT YUKI-CHAN.
YUKI IS A FRIEND FROM THE PT CENTER WHO GOT INJURED AROUND THE SAME TIME I DID.
SHE WAS YOUNGER THAN ME, AND HER DISABILITY WAS MORE ADVANCED THAN MINE, BUT SHE WAS ALWAYS CHEERFUL AND TRIED HER BEST.
OF COURSE ALL THE STAFF MEMBERS AND PATIENTS LOVED HER, BUT EVEN THE PATIENTS' FAMILIES LOVED HER, TOO.
WHEN I LAST MET WITH HER, WE TALKED ABOUT THE PAST, AND YOU CAME UP.
SHE SAID THAT SHE WANTED YOU TO COME, TOO.
SO, IF YOU'D LIKE...
...WE COULD GO TO-GETHER...
YOU SAW YUKI?
YEAH. SHE CALLED AFTER A LONG TIME.
SHE SAID SHE WANTED TO INTRODUCE ME TO HER PARTNER.
SO, NAGASAWA-SAN STAYED IN TOUCH WITH YUKI.
I DIDN'T KNOW THAT...
I SEE...
I'LL GO.
OF COURSE I WILL.

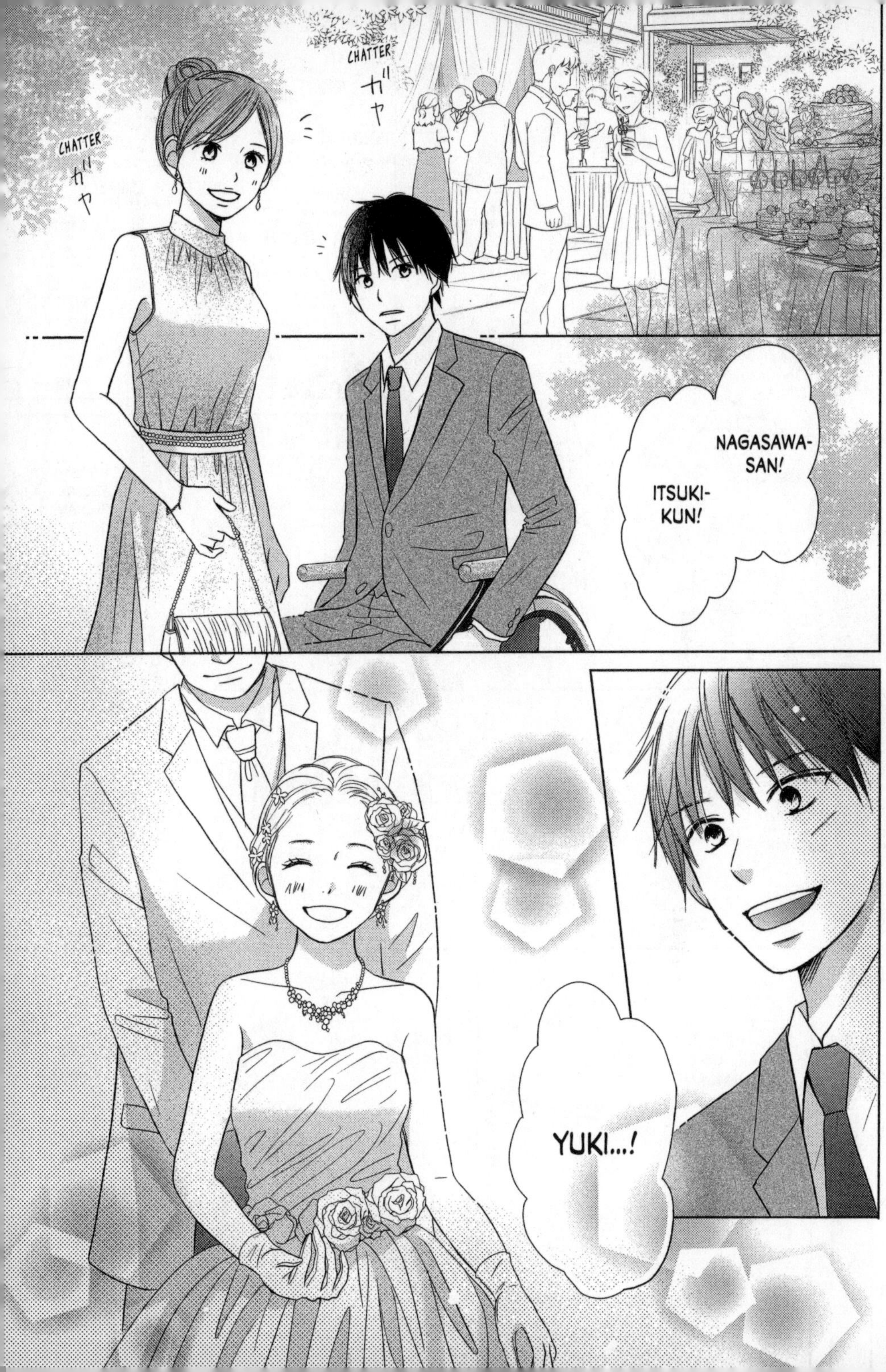
CHATTER
ガヤ
CHATTER
ガヤ
NAGASAWA-SAN!
ITSUKI-KUN!
YUKI...!

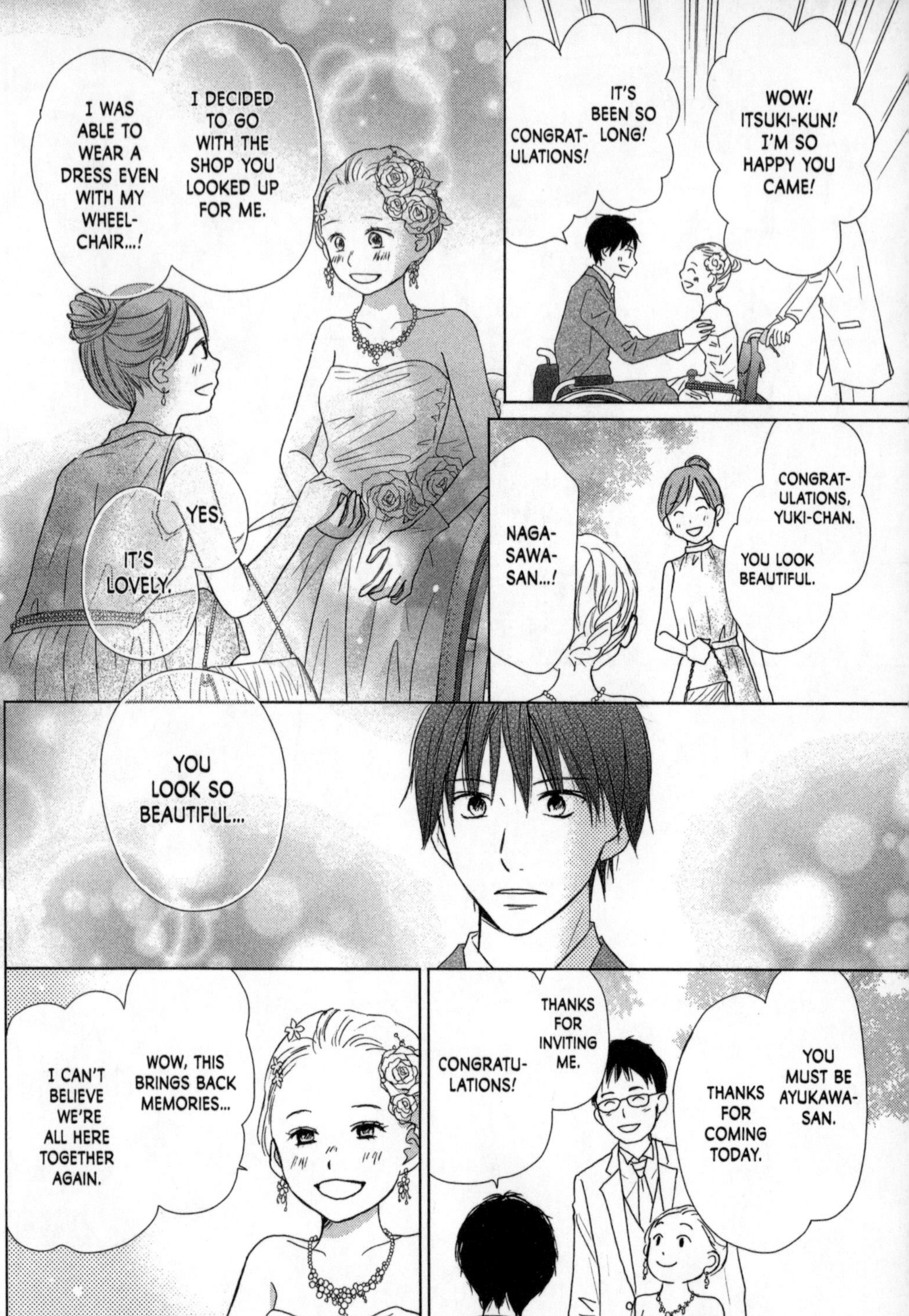
WOW! ITSUKI-KUN! I'M SO HAPPY YOU CAME!
IT'S BEEN SO LONG!
CONGRATULATIONS!
CONGRATULATIONS, YUKI-CHAN.
YOU LOOK BEAUTIFUL.
NAGASAWA-SAN...!
I DECIDED TO GO WITH THE SHOP YOU LOOKED UP FOR ME.
I WAS ABLE TO WEAR A DRESS EVEN WITH MY WHEELCHAIR...!
YES, IT'S LOVELY.
YOU LOOK SO BEAUTIFUL...
YOU MUST BE AYUKAWA-SAN.
THANKS FOR COMING TODAY.
THANKS FOR INVITING ME.
CONGRATULATIONS!
WOW, THIS BRINGS BACK MEMORIES...
I CAN'T BELIEVE WE'RE ALL HERE TOGETHER AGAIN.

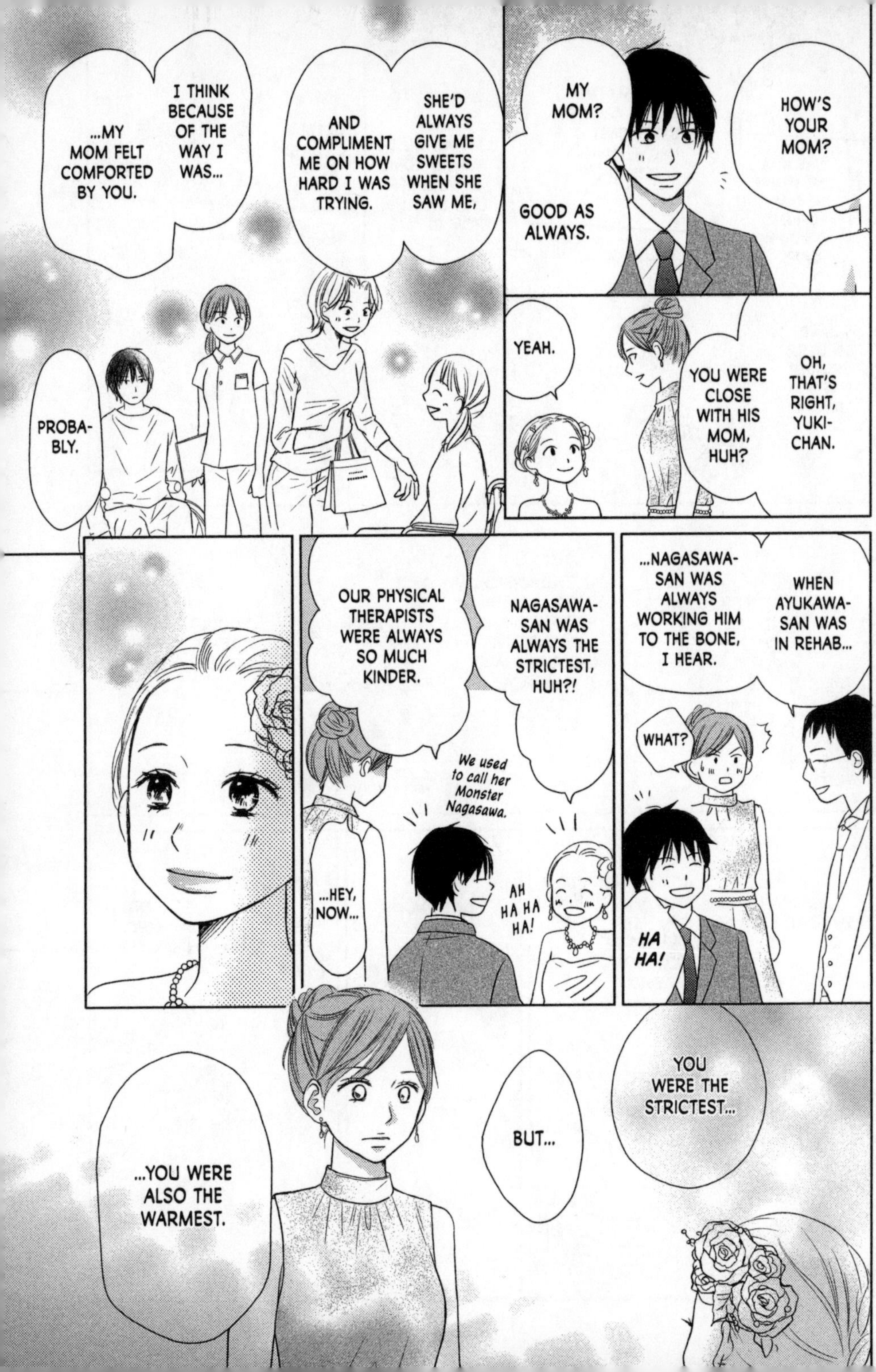
HOW'S YOUR MOM?
MY MOM?
GOOD AS ALWAYS.
OH, THAT'S RIGHT, YUKI-CHAN.
YOU WERE CLOSE WITH HIS MOM, HUH?
YEAH.
SHE'D ALWAYS GIVE ME SWEETS WHEN SHE SAW ME,
AND COMPLIMENT ME ON HOW HARD I WAS TRYING.
I THINK BECAUSE OF THE WAY I WAS...
...MY MOM FELT COMFORTED BY YOU.
PROBA-BLY.
WHEN AYUKAWA-SAN WAS IN REHAB...
...NAGASAWA-SAN WAS ALWAYS WORKING HIM TO THE BONE, I HEAR.
WHAT?
HA HA!
NAGASAWA-SAN WAS ALWAYS THE STRICTEST, HUH?!
We used to call her Monster Nagasawa.
OUR PHYSICAL THERAPISTS WERE ALWAYS SO MUCH KINDER.
AH HA HA HA!
...HEY, NOW...
YOU WERE THE STRICTEST...
BUT...
...YOU WERE ALSO THE WARMEST.

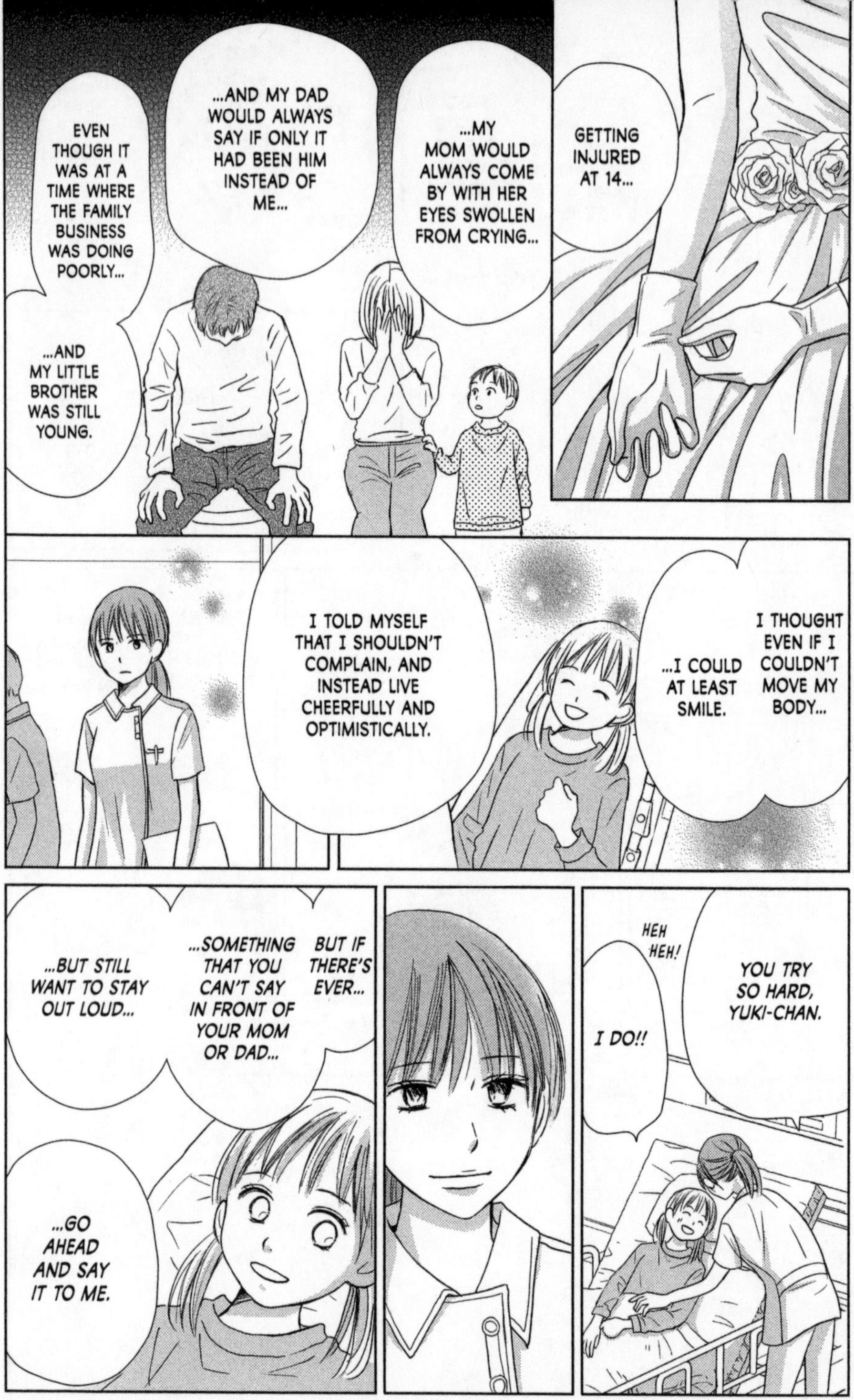
GETTING INJURED AT 14...
...MY MOM WOULD ALWAYS COME BY WITH HER EYES SWOLLEN FROM CRYING...
...AND MY DAD WOULD ALWAYS SAY IF ONLY IT HAD BEEN HIM INSTEAD OF ME...
EVEN THOUGH IT WAS AT A TIME WHERE THE FAMILY BUSINESS WAS DOING POORLY...
...AND MY LITTLE BROTHER WAS STILL YOUNG.
I THOUGHT EVEN IF I COULDN'T MOVE MY BODY...
...I COULD AT LEAST SMILE.
I TOLD MYSELF THAT I SHOULDN'T COMPLAIN, AND INSTEAD LIVE CHEERFULLY AND OPTIMISTICALLY.
YOU TRY SO HARD, YUKI-CHAN.
HEH HEH!
I DO!!
BUT IF THERE'S EVER...
...SOMETHING THAT YOU CAN'T SAY IN FRONT OF YOUR MOM OR DAD...
...BUT STILL WANT TO STAY OUT LOUD...
...GO AHEAD AND SAY IT TO ME.

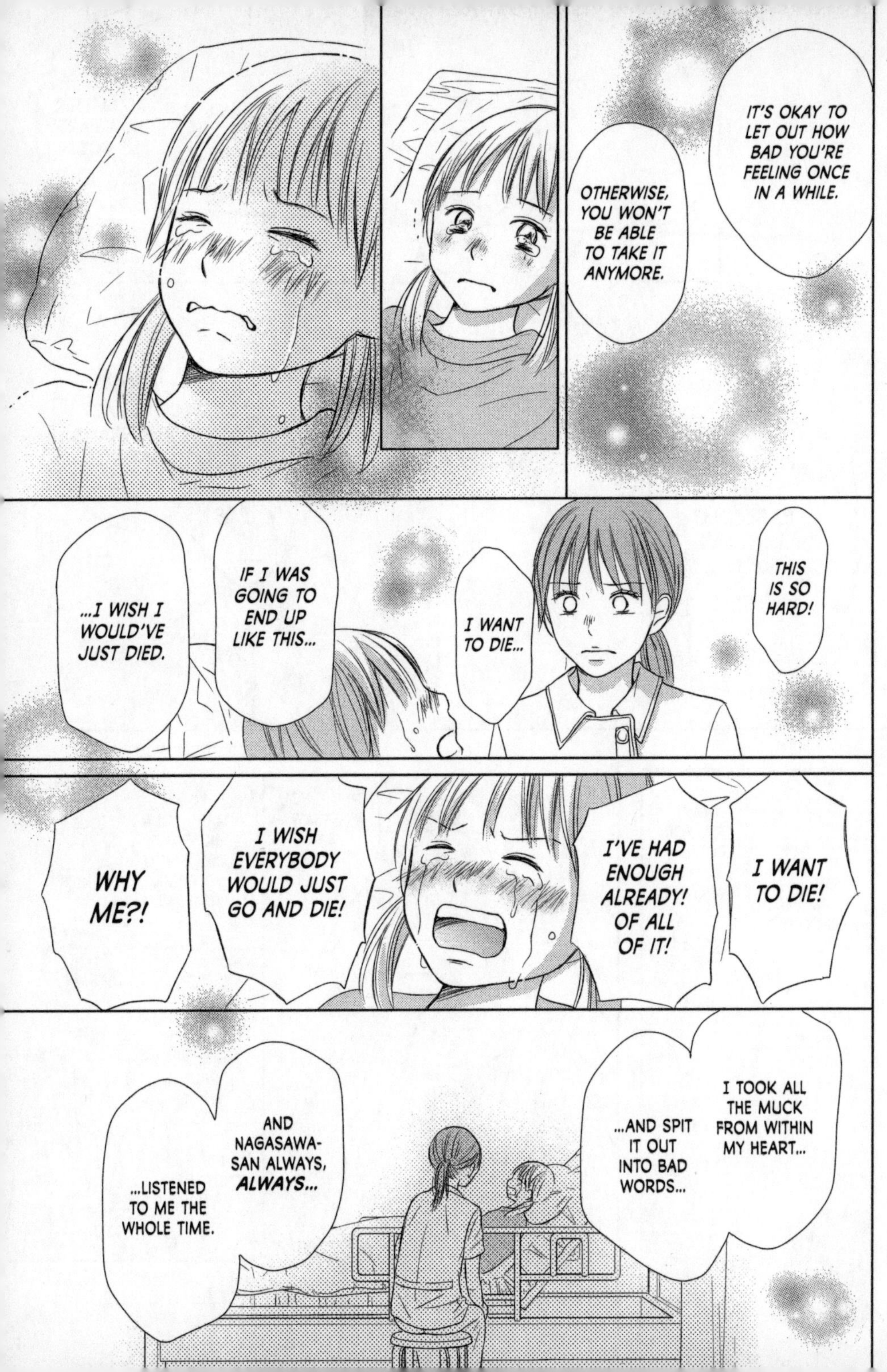
IT'S OKAY TO LET OUT HOW BAD YOU'RE FEELING ONCE IN A WHILE.
OTHERWISE, YOU WON'T BE ABLE TO TAKE IT ANYMORE.
THIS IS SO HARD!
I WANT TO DIE...
IF I WAS GOING TO END UP LIKE THIS...
...I WISH I WOULD'VE JUST DIED.
I WANT TO DIE!
I'VE HAD ENOUGH ALREADY! OF ALL OF IT!
I WISH EVERYBODY WOULD JUST GO AND DIE!
WHY ME?!
I TOOK ALL THE MUCK FROM WITHIN MY HEART...
...AND SPIT IT OUT INTO BAD WORDS...
AND NAGASAWA-SAN ALWAYS, **ALWAYS...**
...LISTENED TO ME THE WHOLE TIME.

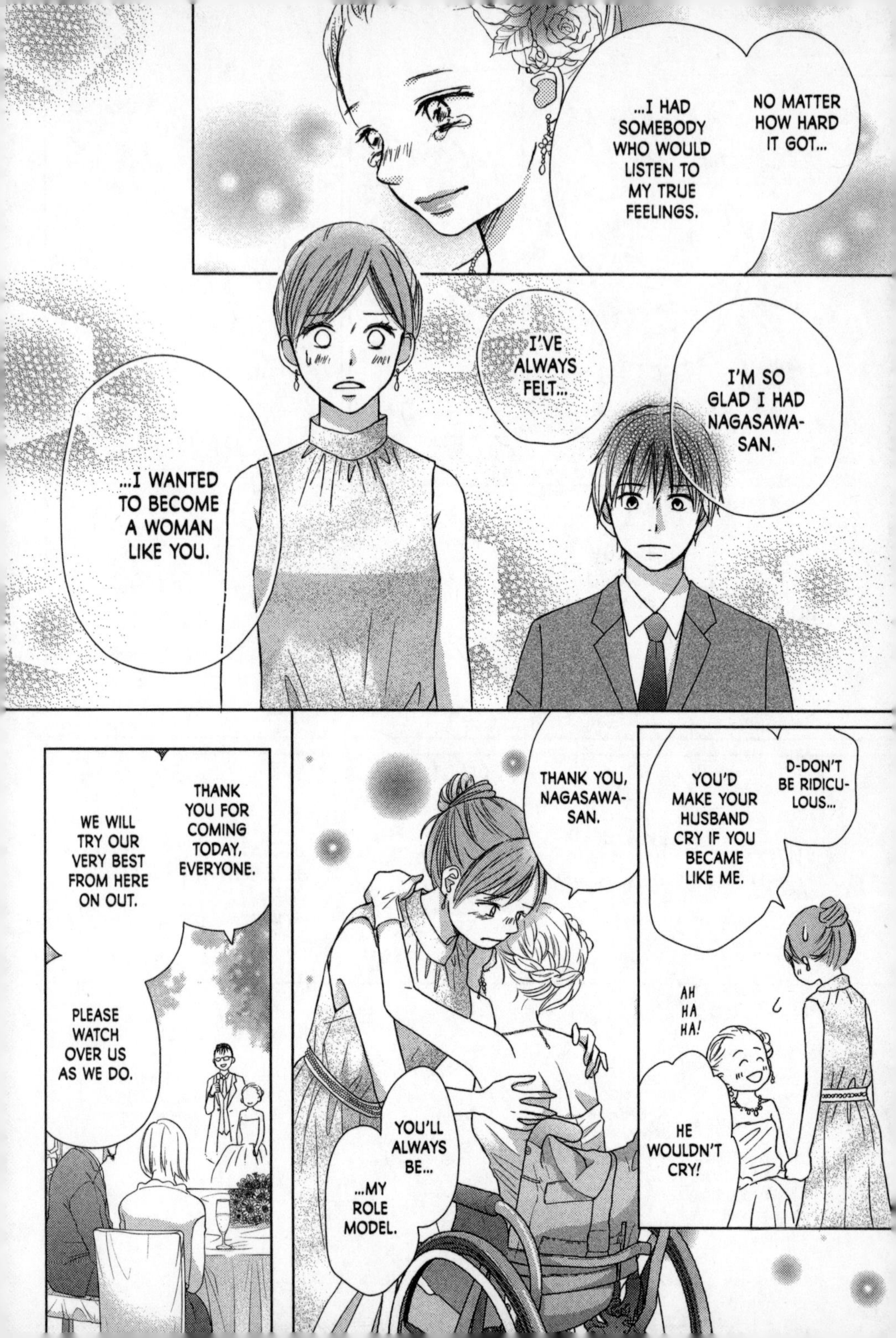
NO MATTER HOW HARD IT GOT...
...I HAD SOMEBODY WHO WOULD LISTEN TO MY TRUE FEELINGS.
I'M SO GLAD I HAD NAGASAWA-SAN.
I'VE ALWAYS FELT...
...I WANTED TO BECOME A WOMAN LIKE YOU.
D-DON'T BE RIDICU-LOUS...
YOU'D MAKE YOUR HUSBAND CRY IF YOU BECAME LIKE ME.
AH HA HA!
HE WOULDN'T CRY!
THANK YOU, NAGASAWA-SAN.
YOU'LL ALWAYS BE...
...MY ROLE MODEL.
THANK YOU FOR COMING TODAY, EVERYONE.
WE WILL TRY OUR VERY BEST FROM HERE ON OUT.
PLEASE WATCH OVER US AS WE DO.

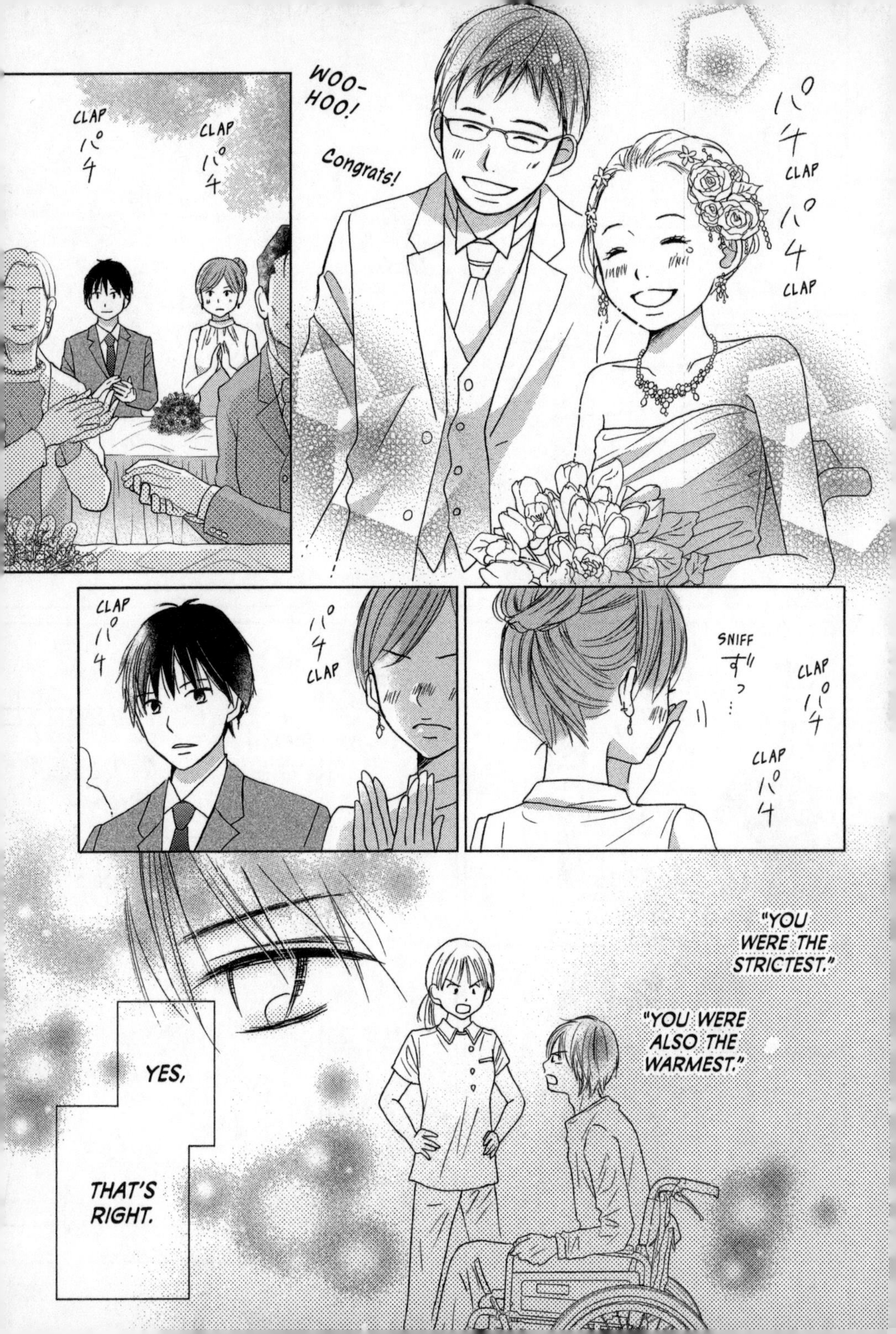
パチ
CLAP
パチ
CLAP
WOO-HOO!
Congrats!
CLAP
パチ
CLAP
パチ
CLAP
パチ
CLAP
パチ
SNIFF
ずっ…
パチ
CLAP
CLAP
パチ
"YOU WERE THE STRICTEST."
"YOU WERE ALSO THE WARMEST."
YES,
THAT'S RIGHT.

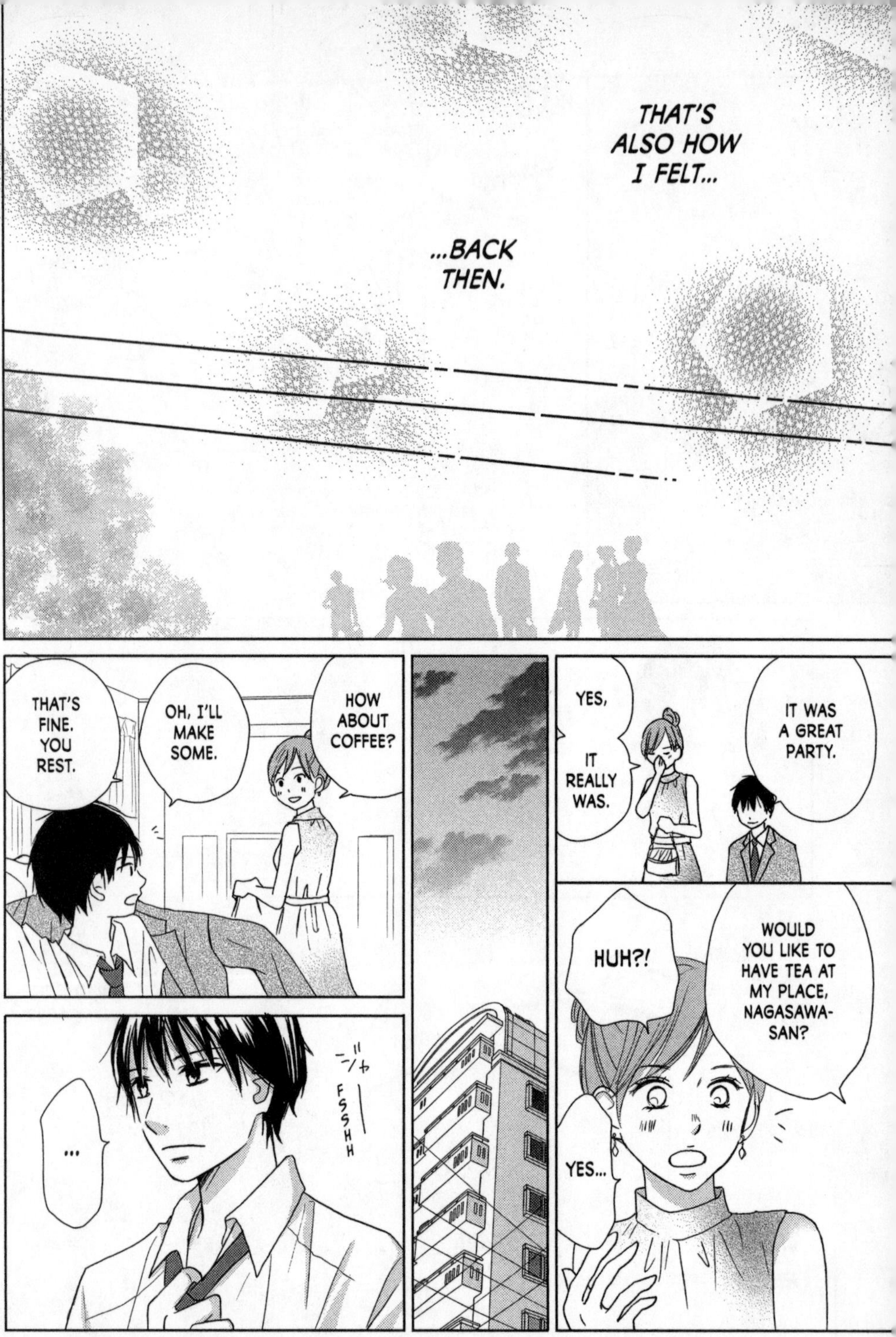
THAT'S ALSO HOW I FELT...
...BACK THEN.
IT WAS A GREAT PARTY.
YES,
IT REALLY WAS.
WOULD YOU LIKE TO HAVE TEA AT MY PLACE, NAGASAWA-SAN?
HUH?!
YES...
HOW ABOUT COFFEE?
OH, I'LL MAKE SOME.
THAT'S FINE. YOU REST.
FSSHH
...

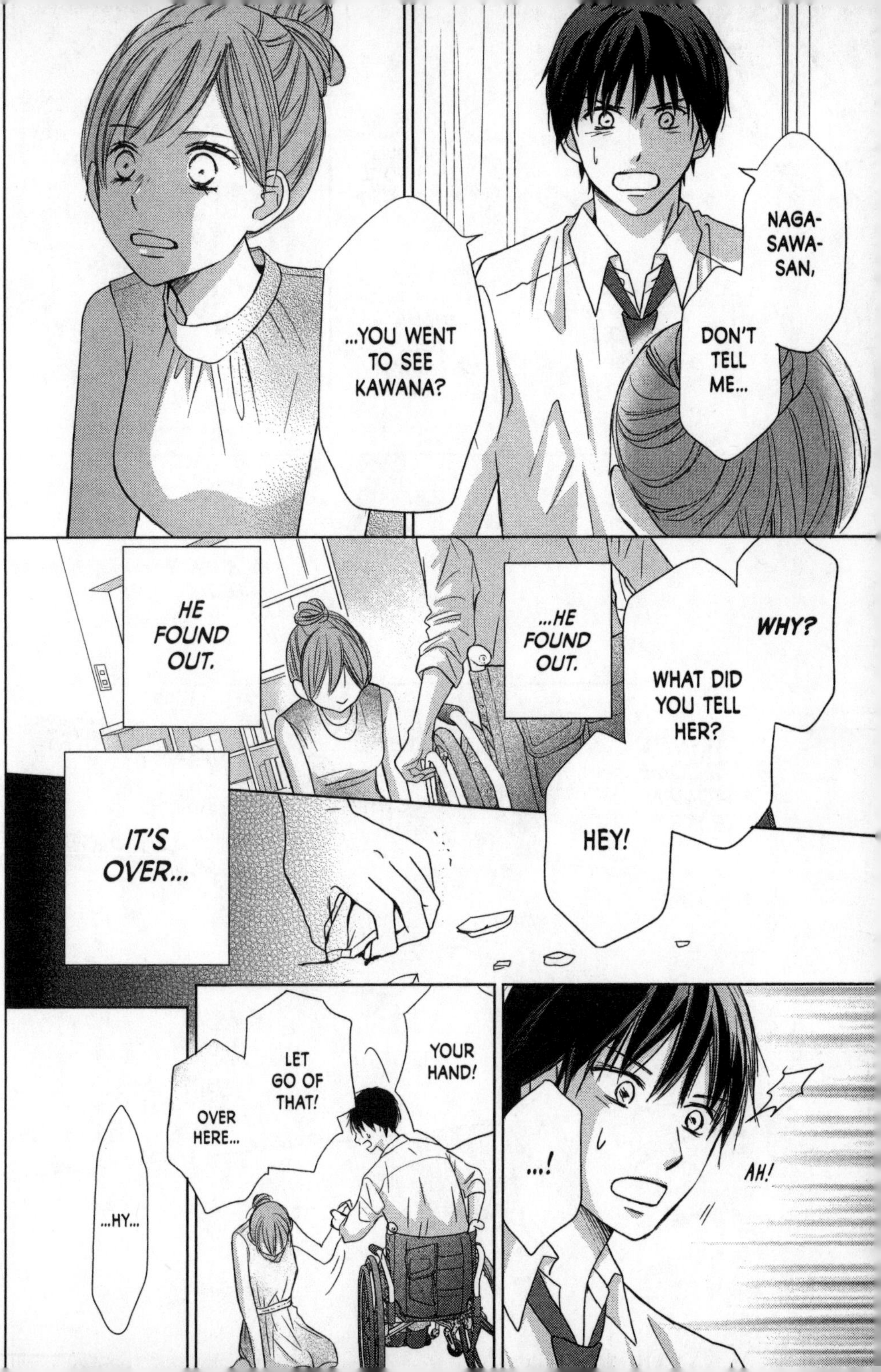
NAGA-SAWA-SAN,
DON'T TELL ME...
...YOU WENT TO SEE KAWANA?
WHY?
WHAT DID YOU TELL HER?
HEY!
...HE FOUND OUT.
HE FOUND OUT.
IT'S OVER...
AH!
...!
YOUR HAND!
LET GO OF THAT!
OVER HERE...
...HY...

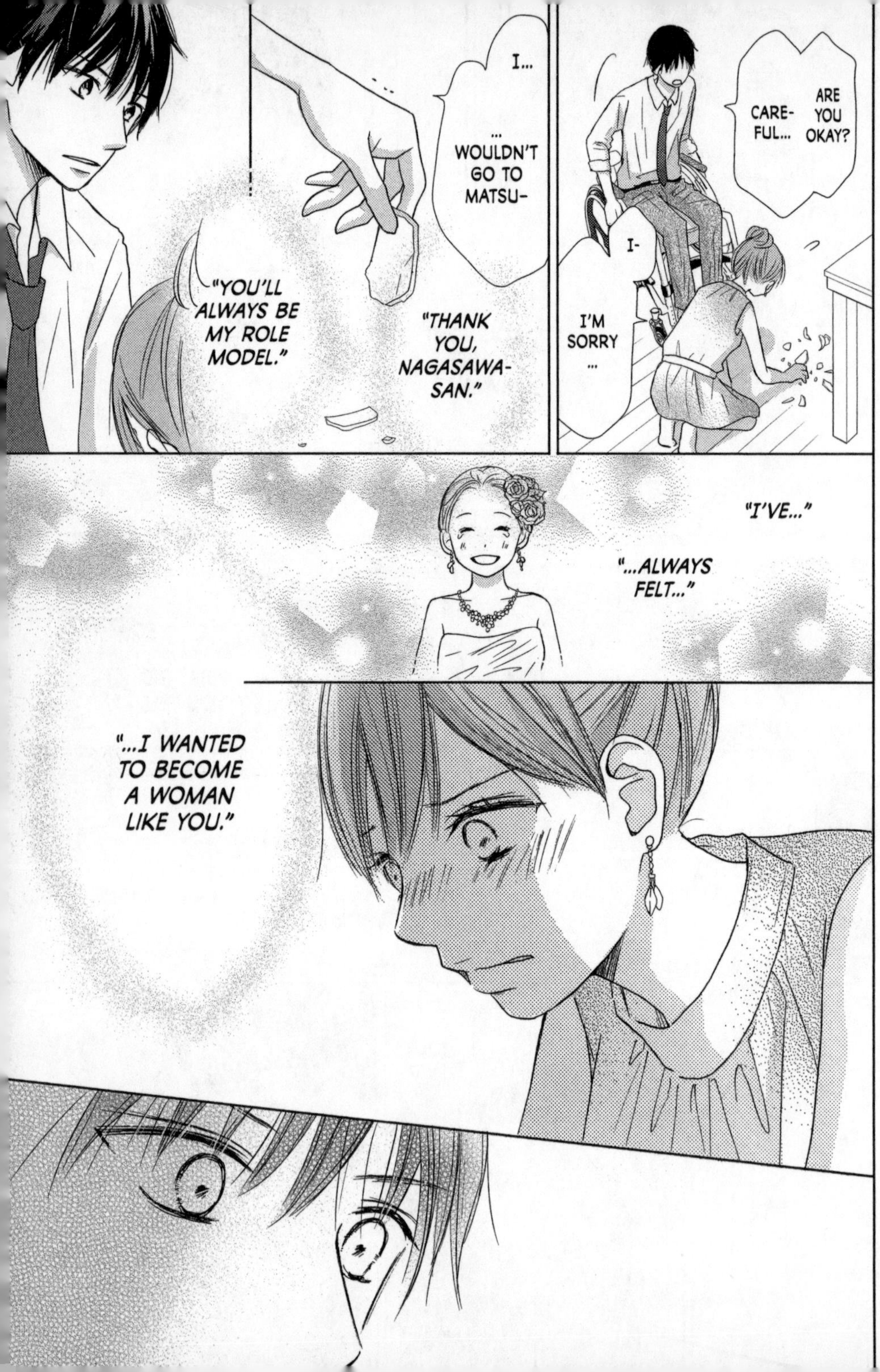
ARE YOU OKAY?
CARE-FUL...
I-
I'M SORRY ...
I...
... WOULDN'T GO TO MATSU-
"THANK YOU, NAGASAWA-SAN."
"YOU'LL ALWAYS BE MY ROLE MODEL."
"I'VE..."
"...ALWAYS FELT..."
"...I WANTED TO BECOME A WOMAN LIKE YOU."

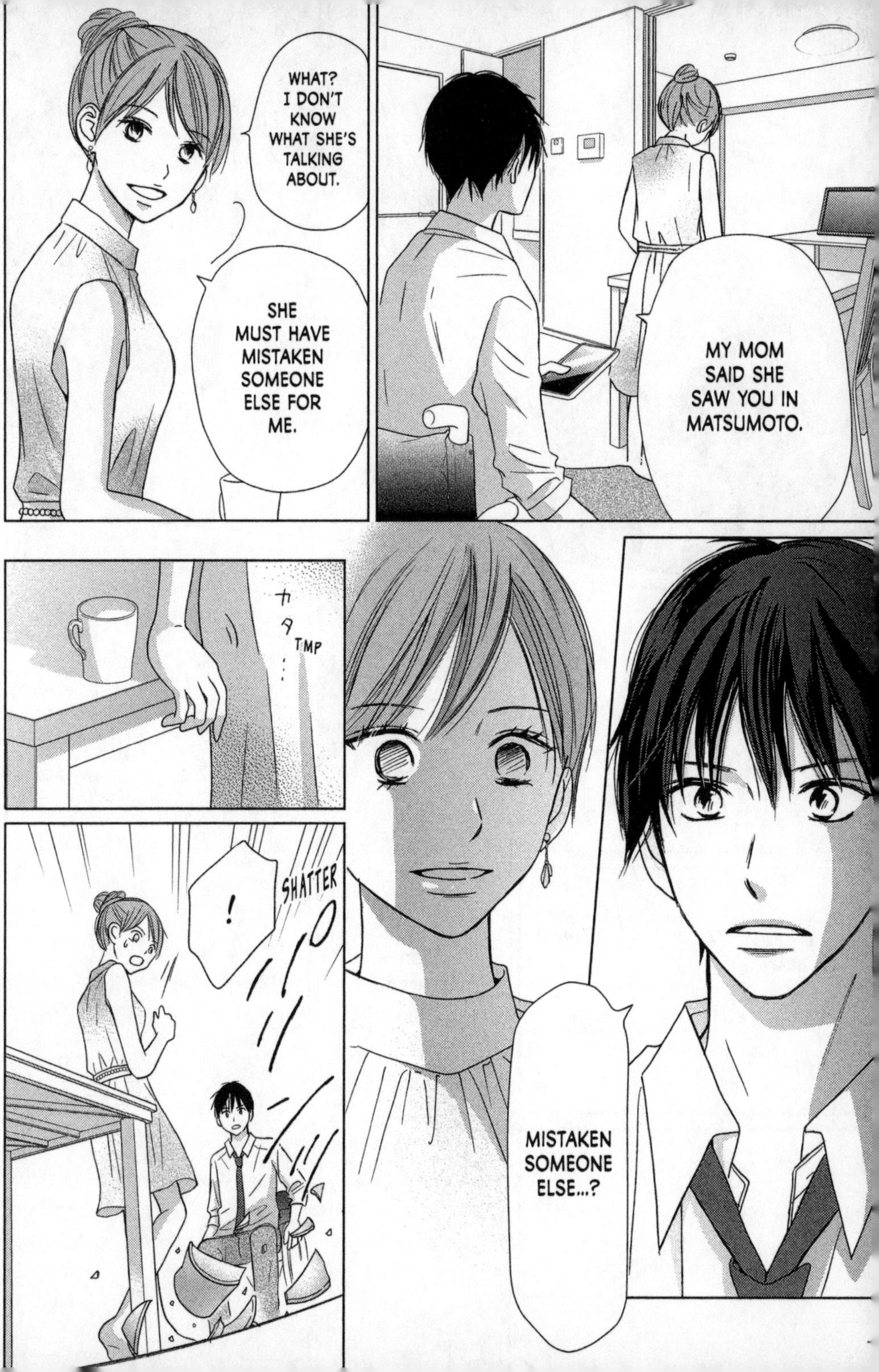
MY MOM SAID SHE SAW YOU IN MATSUMOTO.
WHAT? I DON'T KNOW WHAT SHE'S TALKING ABOUT.
SHE MUST HAVE MISTAKEN SOMEONE ELSE FOR ME.
MISTAKEN SOMEONE ELSE...?
カタ
TMP
...
SHATTER
!

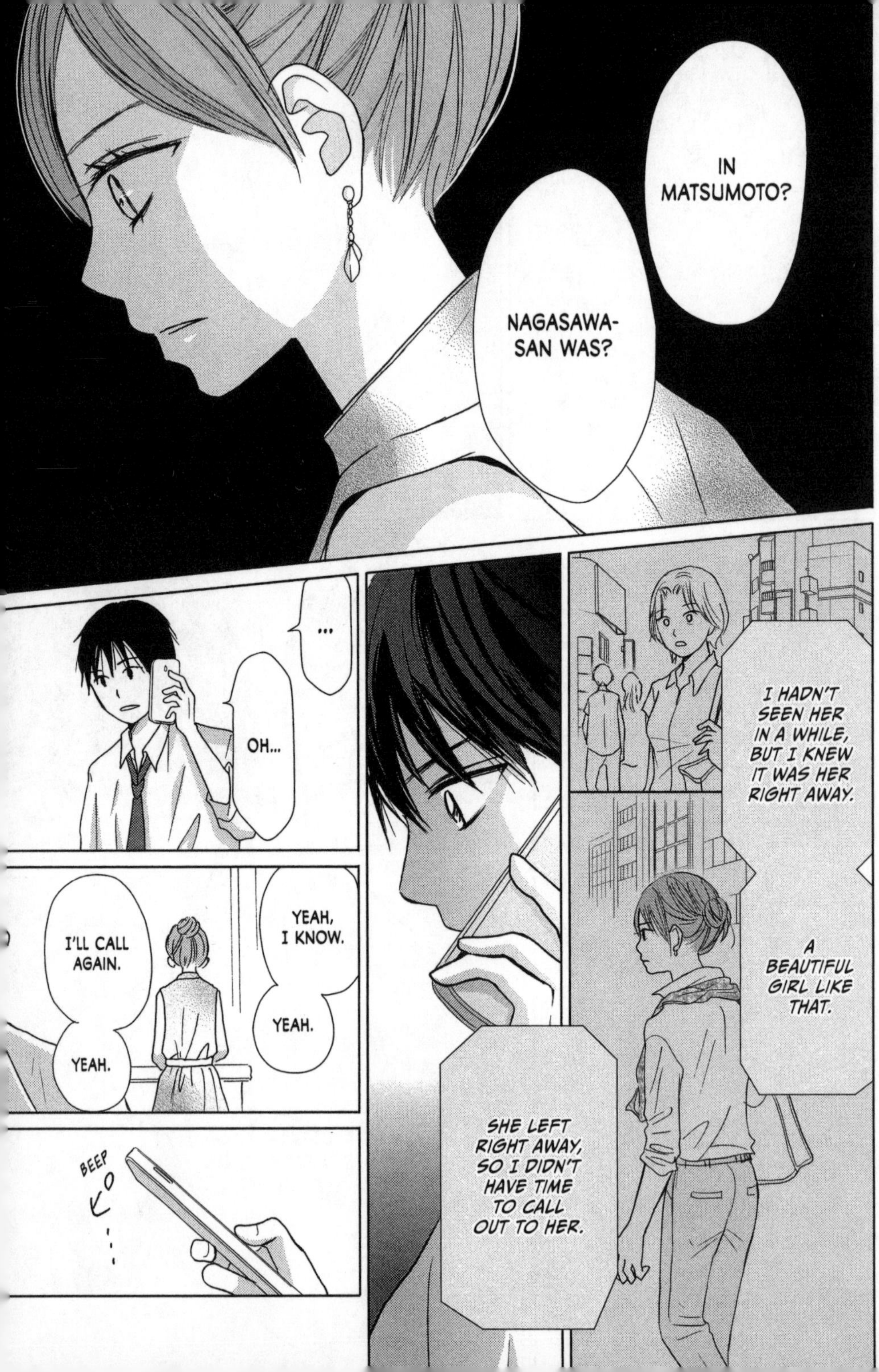
IN MATSUMOTO?
NAGASAWA-SAN WAS?
I HADN'T SEEN HER IN A WHILE, BUT I KNEW IT WAS HER RIGHT AWAY.
A BEAUTIFUL GIRL LIKE THAT.
SHE LEFT RIGHT AWAY, SO I DIDN'T HAVE TIME TO CALL OUT TO HER.
...
OH...
YEAH, I KNOW.
YEAH.
I'LL CALL AGAIN.
YEAH.
BEEP

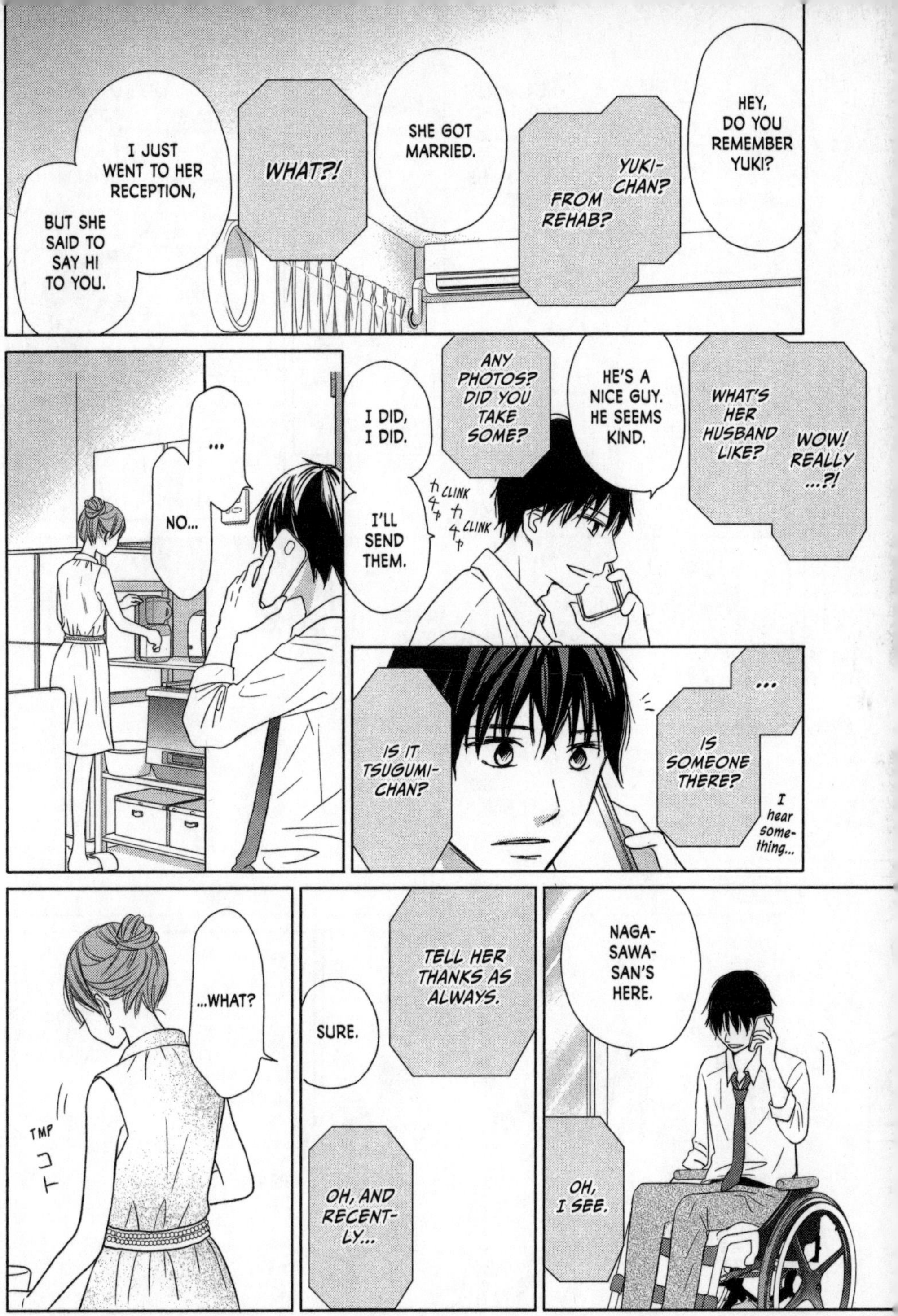
HEY, DO YOU REMEMBER YUKI?
YUKI-CHAN? FROM REHAB?
SHE GOT MARRIED.
WHAT?!
I JUST WENT TO HER RECEPTION,
BUT SHE SAID TO SAY HI TO YOU.
WHAT'S HER HUSBAND LIKE?
WOW! REALLY ...?!
HE'S A NICE GUY. HE SEEMS KIND.
ANY PHOTOS? DID YOU TAKE SOME?
I DID, I DID.
I'LL SEND THEM.
CLINK
CLINK
...
IS SOMEONE THERE?
I hear something...
IS IT TSUGUMI-CHAN?
...
NO...
NAGASAWA-SAN'S HERE.
OH, I SEE.
TELL HER THANKS AS ALWAYS.
SURE.
OH, AND RECENTLY...
...WHAT?
TMP

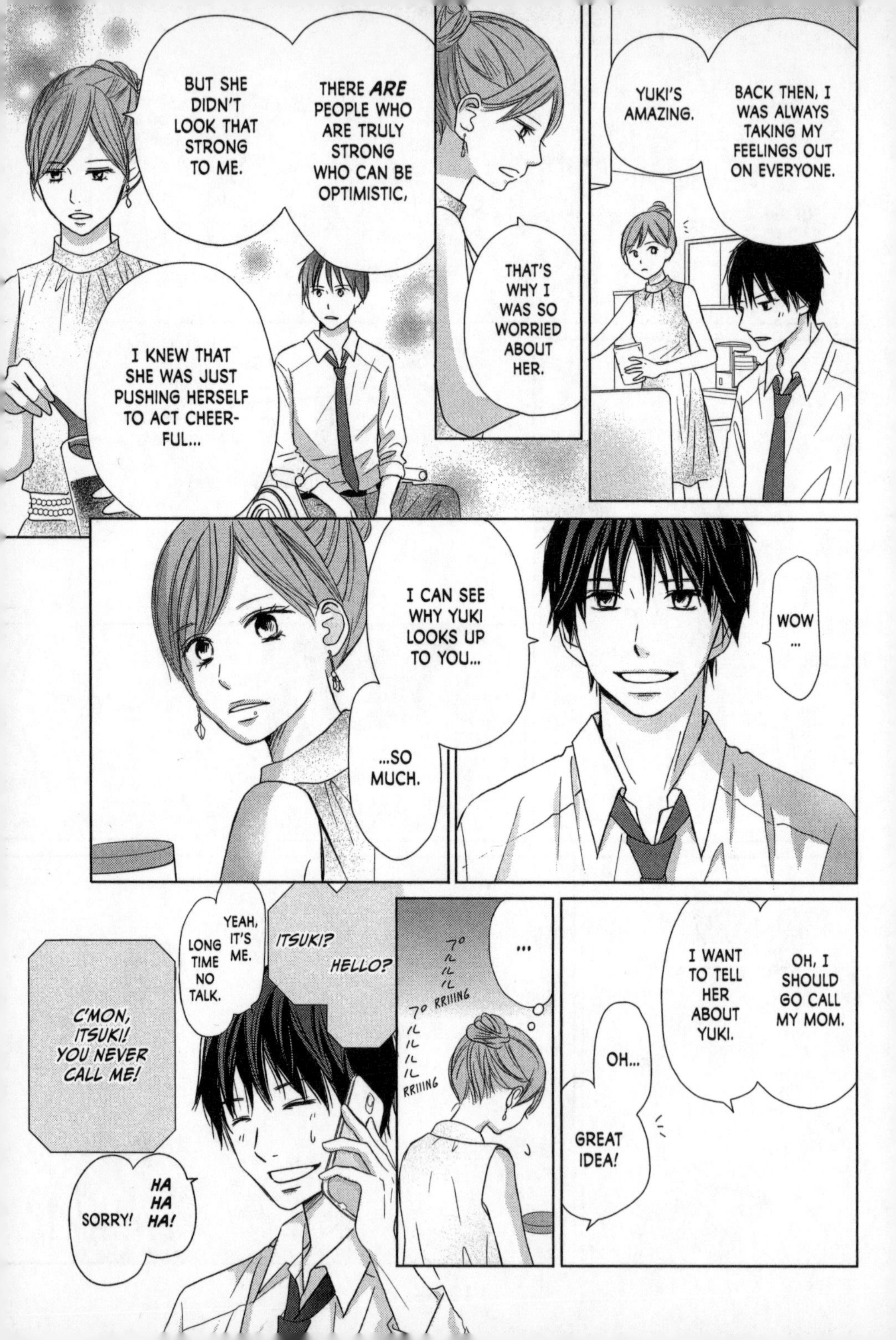
BACK THEN, I WAS ALWAYS TAKING MY FEELINGS OUT ON EVERYONE.
YUKI'S AMAZING.
THAT'S WHY I WAS SO WORRIED ABOUT HER.
THERE *ARE* PEOPLE WHO ARE TRULY STRONG WHO CAN BE OPTIMISTIC,
BUT SHE DIDN'T LOOK THAT STRONG TO ME.
I KNEW THAT SHE WAS JUST PUSHING HERSELF TO ACT CHEER-FUL...
WOW ...
I CAN SEE WHY YUKI LOOKS UP TO YOU...
...SO MUCH.
OH, I SHOULD GO CALL MY MOM.
I WANT TO TELL HER ABOUT YUKI.
OH...
GREAT IDEA!
...
プルルル RRIIING
プルルル RRIIING
HELLO?
ITSUKI?
YEAH, IT'S ME.
LONG TIME NO TALK.
C'MON, ITSUKI! YOU NEVER CALL ME!
HA HA HA!
SORRY!

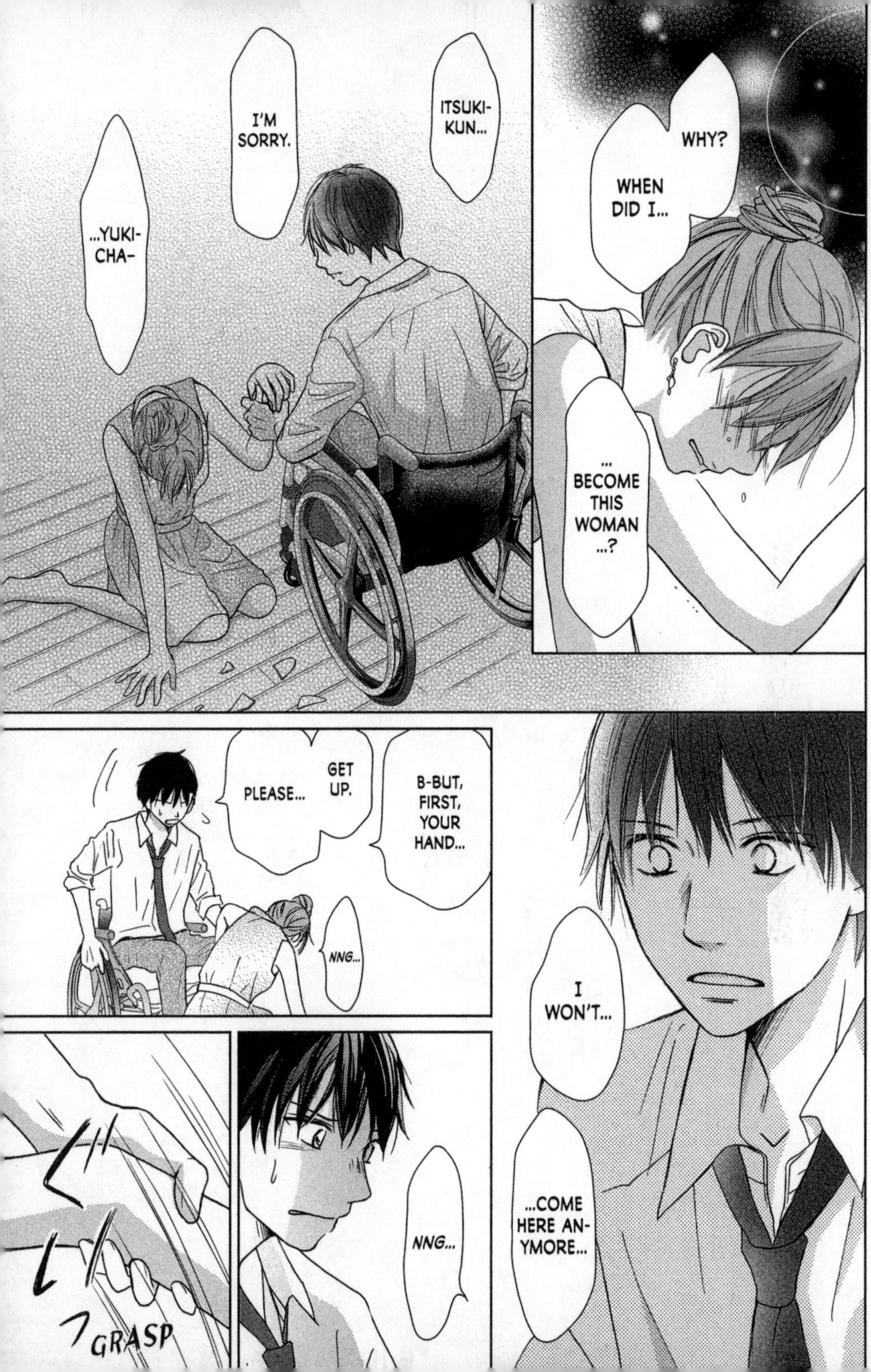
WHY?
WHEN DID I...
...BECOME THIS WOMAN ...?
ITSUKI-KUN...
I'M SORRY.
...YUKI-CHA-
I WON'T...
...COME HERE AN-YMORE...
B-BUT, FIRST, YOUR HAND...
PLEASE... GET UP.
NNG...
NNG...
GRASP

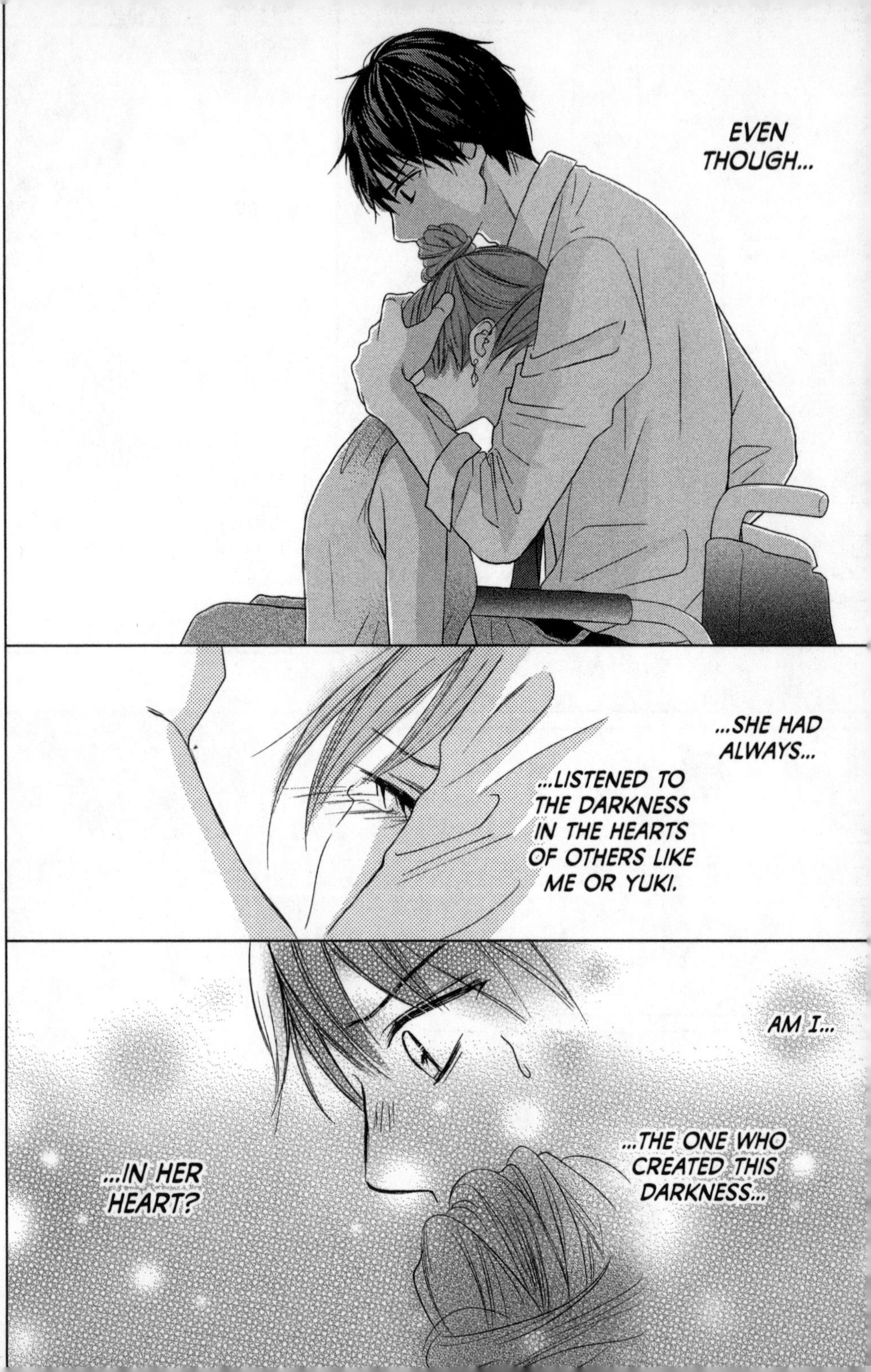
EVEN THOUGH...
...SHE HAD ALWAYS...
...LISTENED TO THE DARKNESS IN THE HEARTS OF OTHERS LIKE ME OR YUKI.
AM I...
...THE ONE WHO CREATED THIS DARKNESS...
...IN HER HEART?

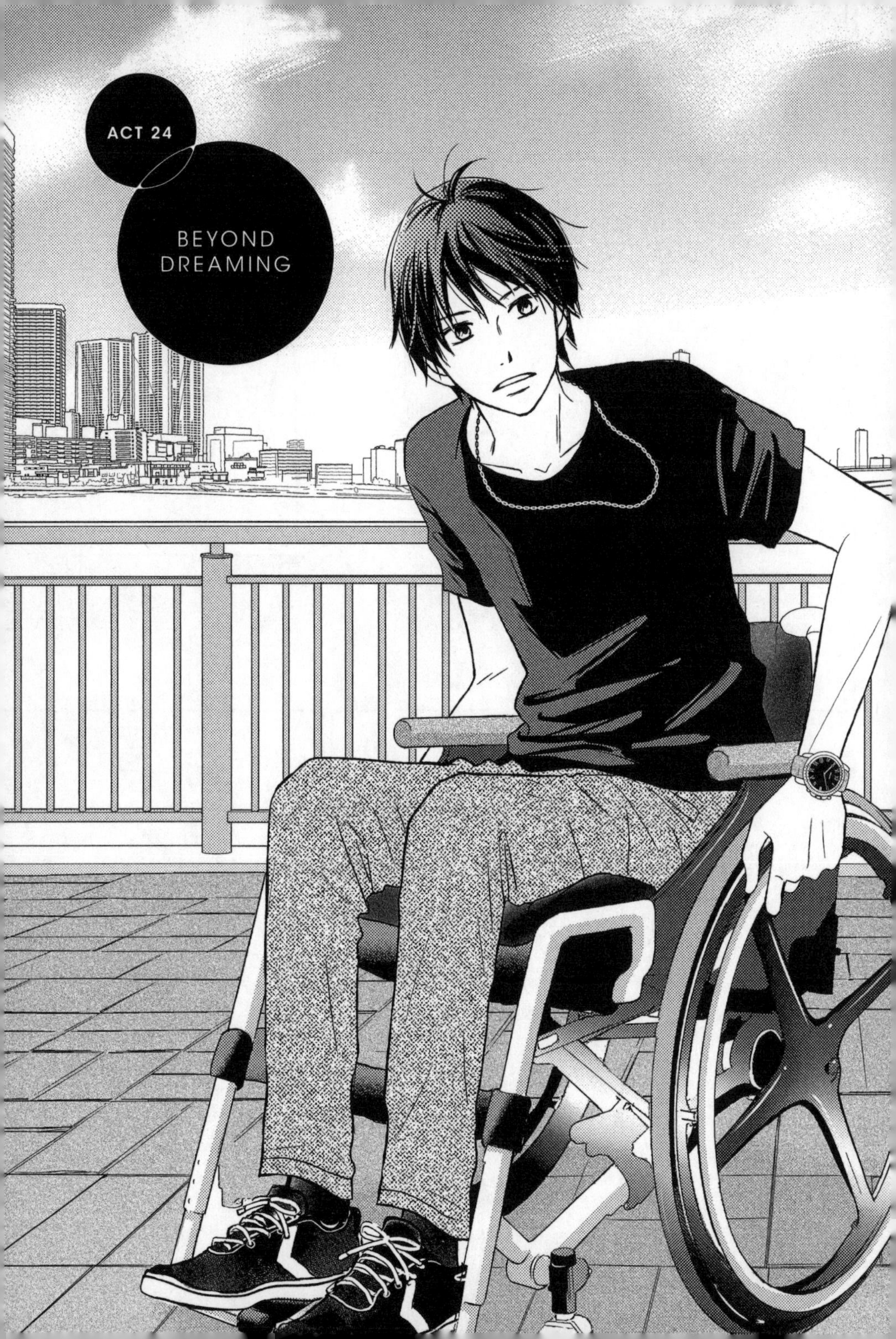
ACT 24
BEYOND DREAMING

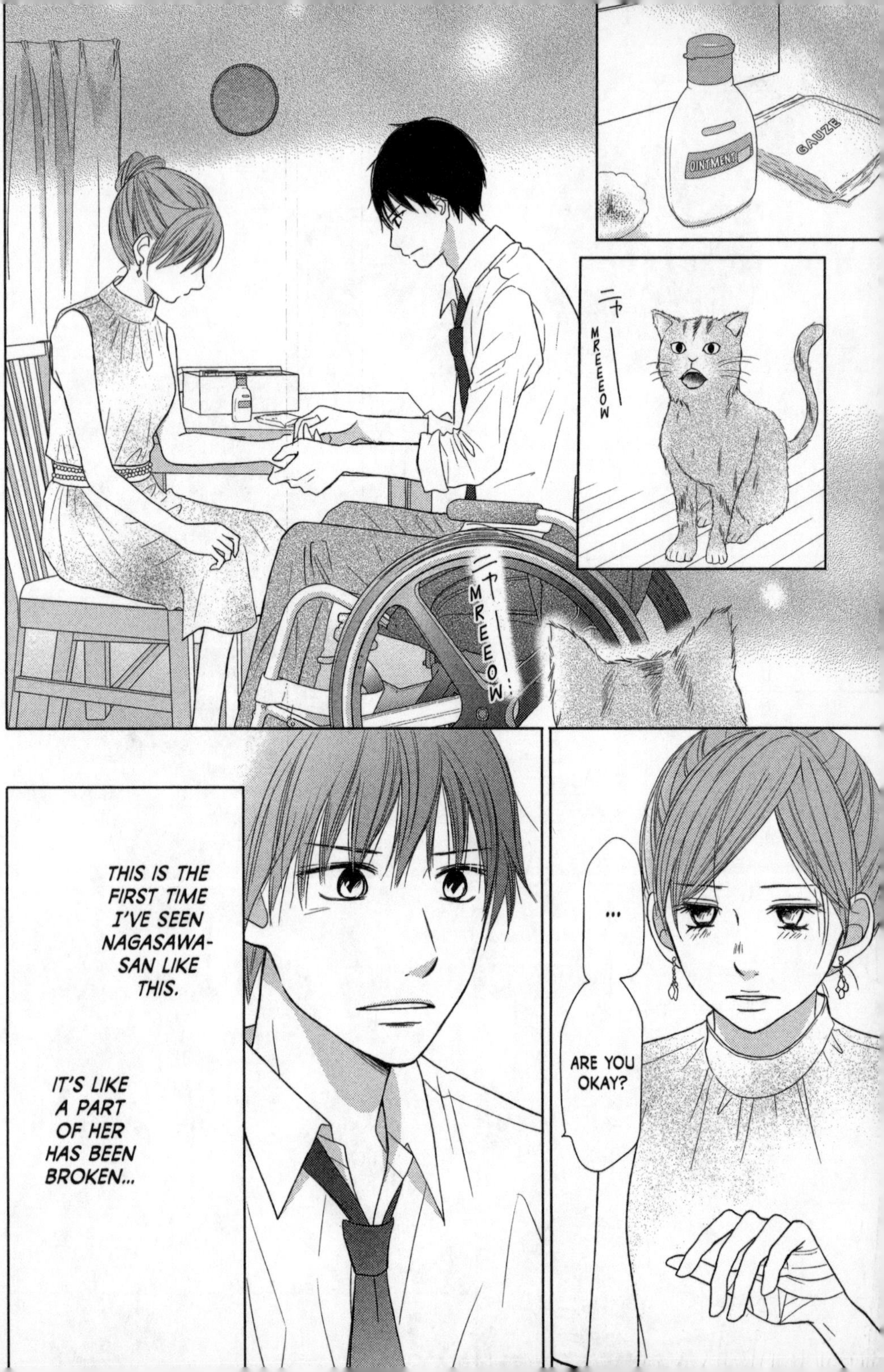

OINTMENT
GAUZE
ニャ
MREEEOW
ニャ
MREEOW...
...
ARE YOU OKAY?
THIS IS THE FIRST TIME I'VE SEEN NAGASAWA-SAN LIKE THIS.
IT'S LIKE A PART OF HER HAS BEEN BROKEN...

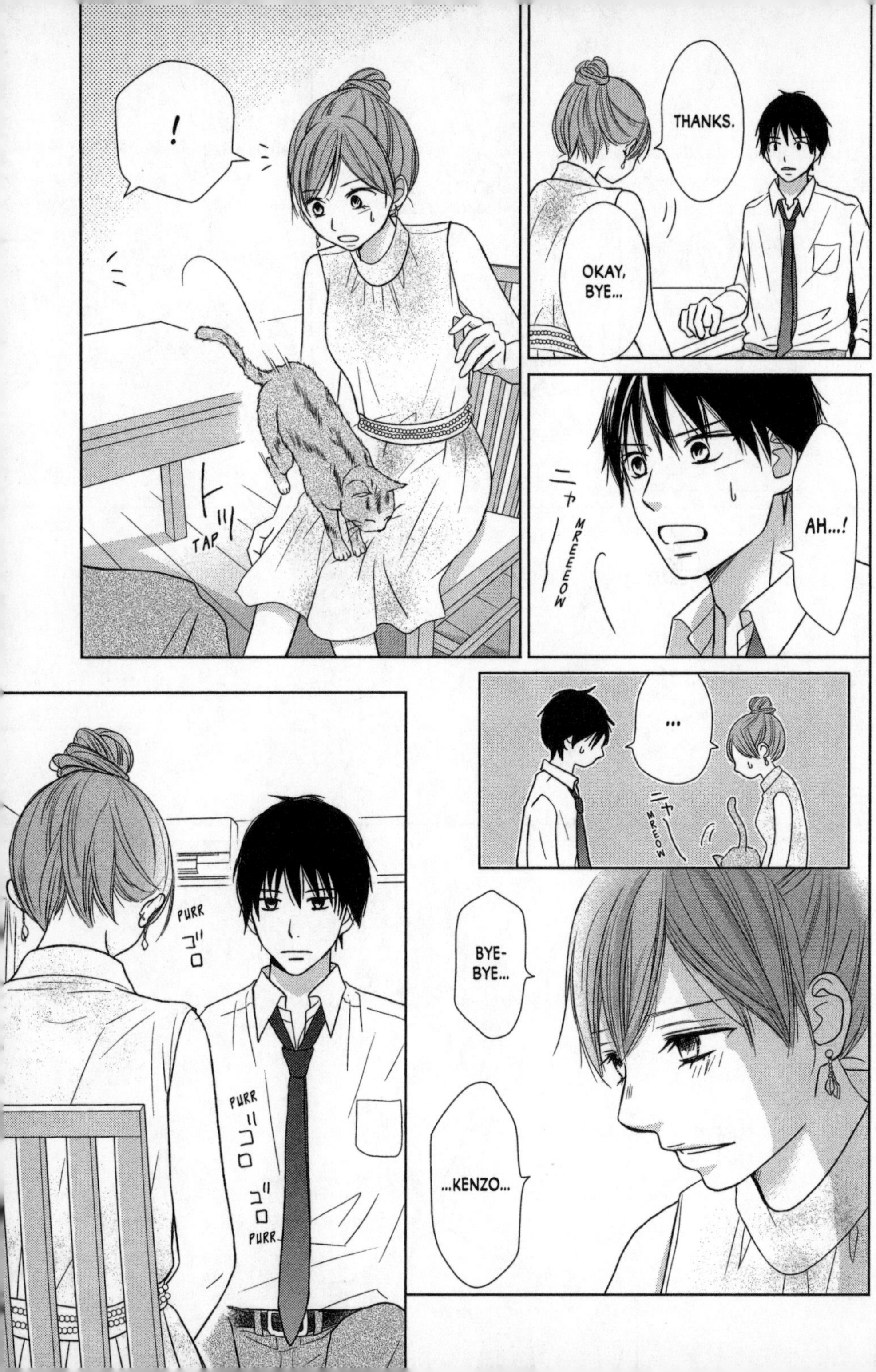

THANKS.
OKAY, BYE...
ニャー
MREEEOW
AH...!
!
TAP
...
ニャー
MREOW
BYE-BYE...
...KENZO...
PURR
ゴロ
PURR
ゴロ
ゴロ
PURR

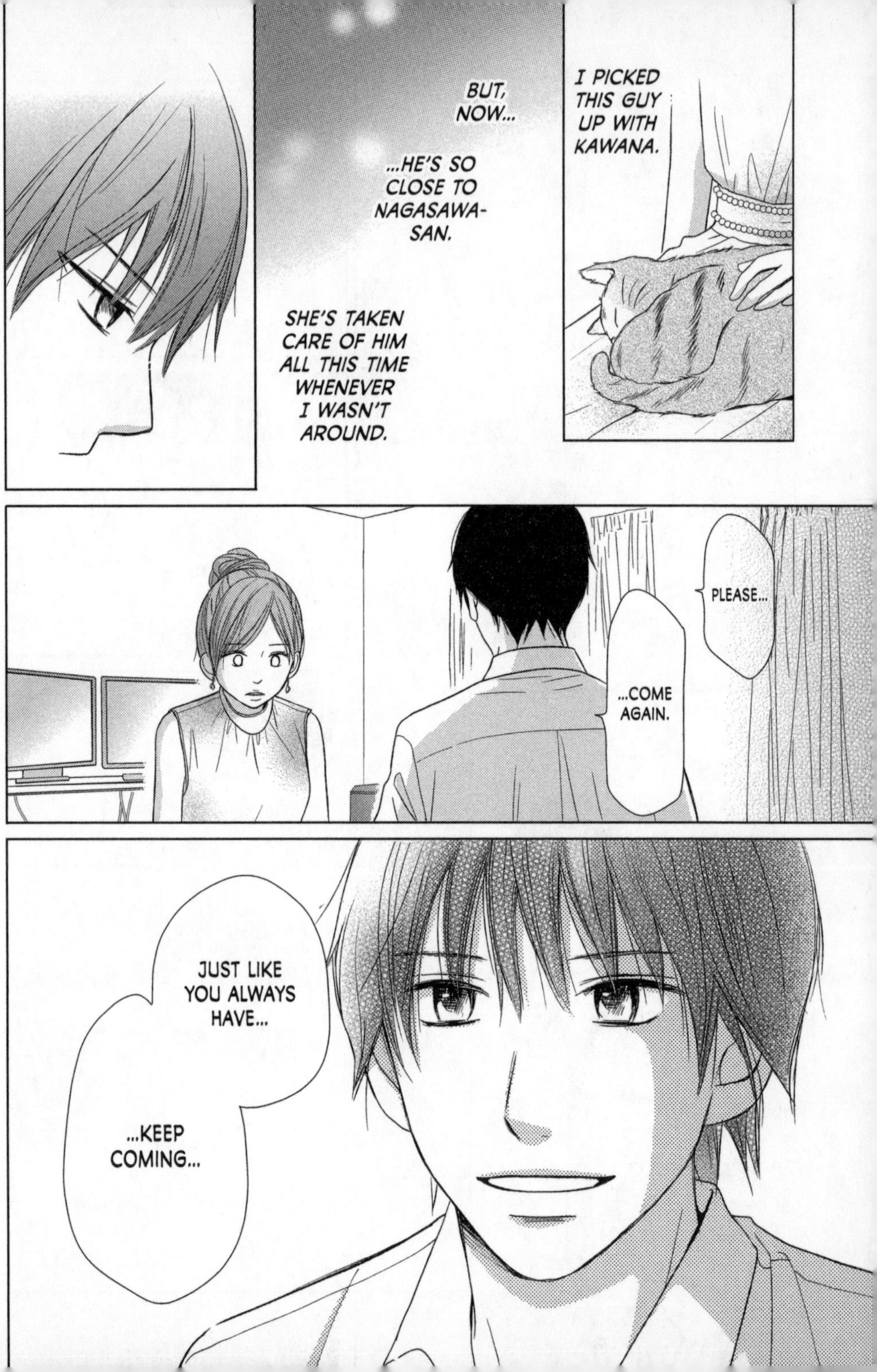
I PICKED THIS GUY UP WITH KAWANA.
BUT, NOW...
...HE'S SO CLOSE TO NAGASAWA-SAN.
SHE'S TAKEN CARE OF HIM ALL THIS TIME WHENEVER I WASN'T AROUND.
PLEASE...
...COME AGAIN.
JUST LIKE YOU ALWAYS HAVE...
...KEEP COMING...

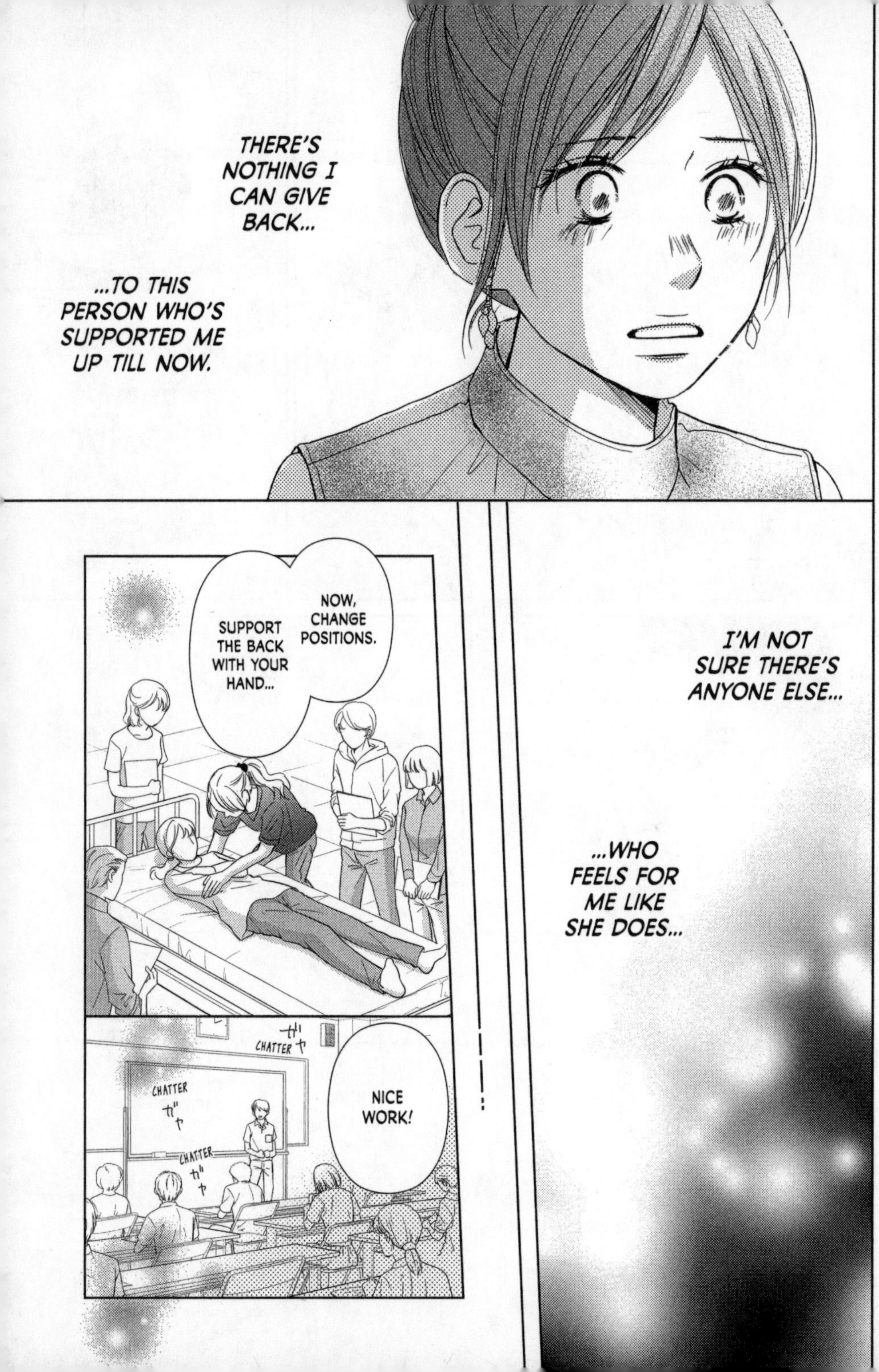
THERE'S NOTHING I CAN GIVE BACK...
...TO THIS PERSON WHO'S SUPPORTED ME UP TILL NOW.
I'M NOT SURE THERE'S ANYONE ELSE...
...WHO FEELS FOR ME LIKE SHE DOES...
NOW, CHANGE POSITIONS.
SUPPORT THE BACK WITH YOUR HAND...
ガヤ CHATTER
NICE WORK!
CHATTER ガヤ
CHATTER ガヤ

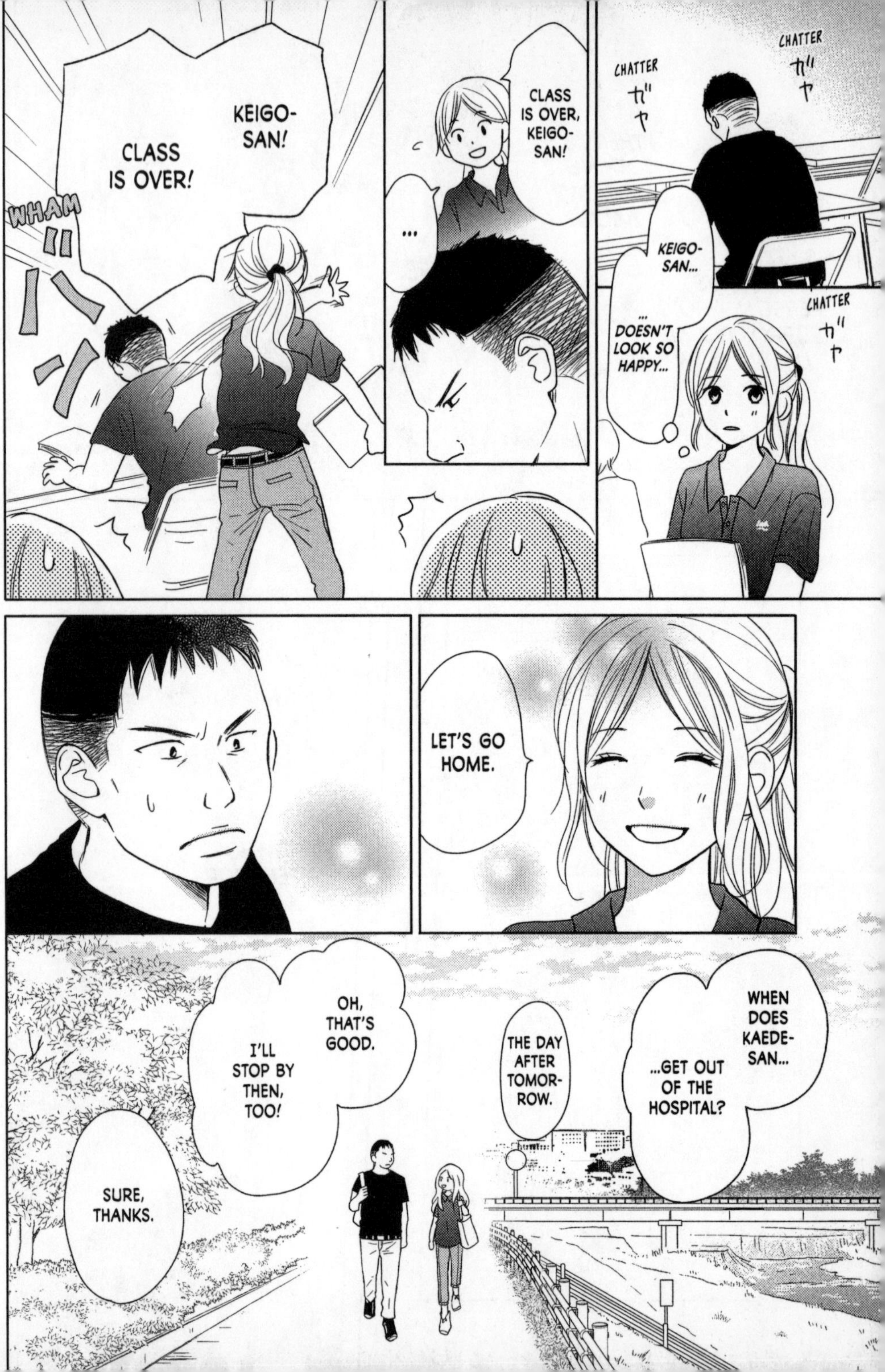
CHATTER
ガヤ
CHATTER
ガヤ
KEIGO-SAN...
...DOESN'T LOOK SO HAPPY...
CHATTER
ガヤ
CLASS IS OVER, KEIGO-SAN!
...
WHAM
KEIGO-SAN!
CLASS IS OVER!
LET'S GO HOME.
WHEN DOES KAEDE-SAN...
...GET OUT OF THE HOSPITAL?
THE DAY AFTER TOMORROW.
OH, THAT'S GOOD.
I'LL STOP BY THEN, TOO!
SURE, THANKS.

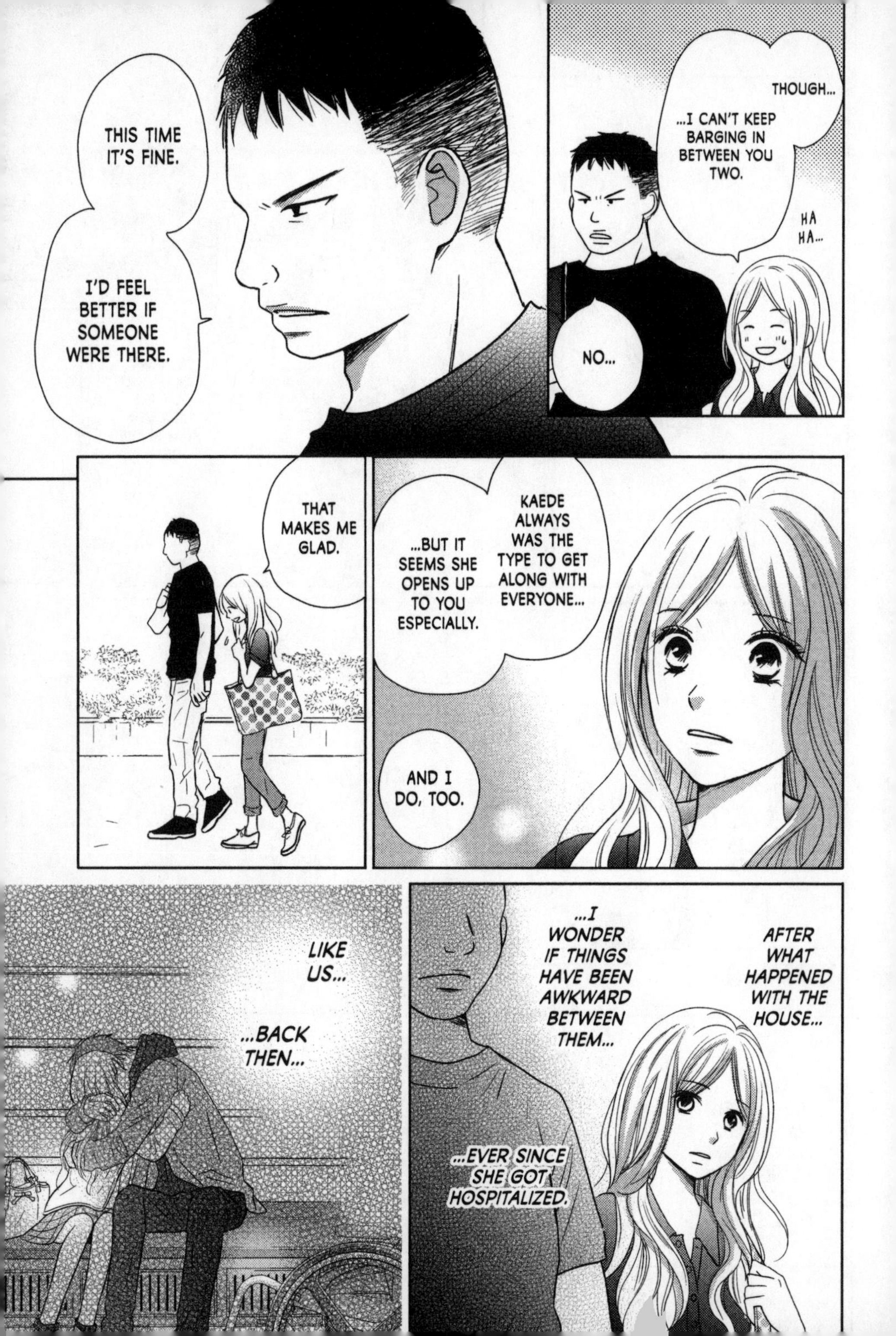
THOUGH...
...I CAN'T KEEP BARGING IN BETWEEN YOU TWO.
HA HA...
NO...
THIS TIME IT'S FINE.
I'D FEEL BETTER IF SOMEONE WERE THERE.
KAEDE ALWAYS WAS THE TYPE TO GET ALONG WITH EVERYONE...
...BUT IT SEEMS SHE OPENS UP TO YOU ESPECIALLY.
AND I DO, TOO.
THAT MAKES ME GLAD.
AFTER WHAT HAPPENED WITH THE HOUSE...
...I WONDER IF THINGS HAVE BEEN AWKWARD BETWEEN THEM...
...EVER SINCE SHE GOT HOSPITALIZED.
LIKE US...
...BACK THEN...

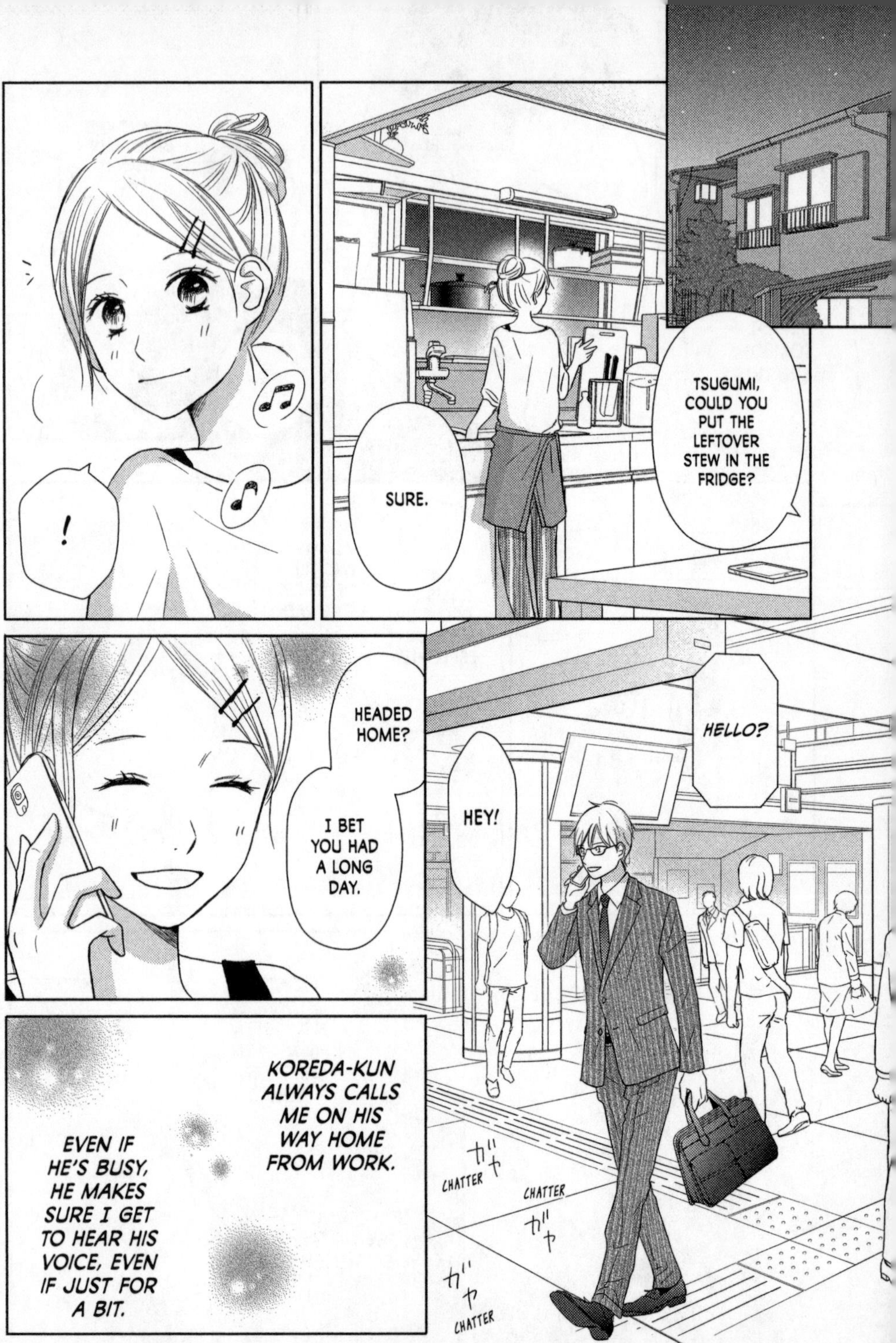
TSUGUMI, COULD YOU PUT THE LEFTOVER STEW IN THE FRIDGE?
SURE.
!
HELLO?
HEY!
ガヤ CHATTER
ガヤ CHATTER
ガヤ CHATTER
HEADED HOME?
I BET YOU HAD A LONG DAY.
KOREDA-KUN ALWAYS CALLS ME ON HIS WAY HOME FROM WORK.
EVEN IF HE'S BUSY, HE MAKES SURE I GET TO HEAR HIS VOICE, EVEN IF JUST FOR A BIT.

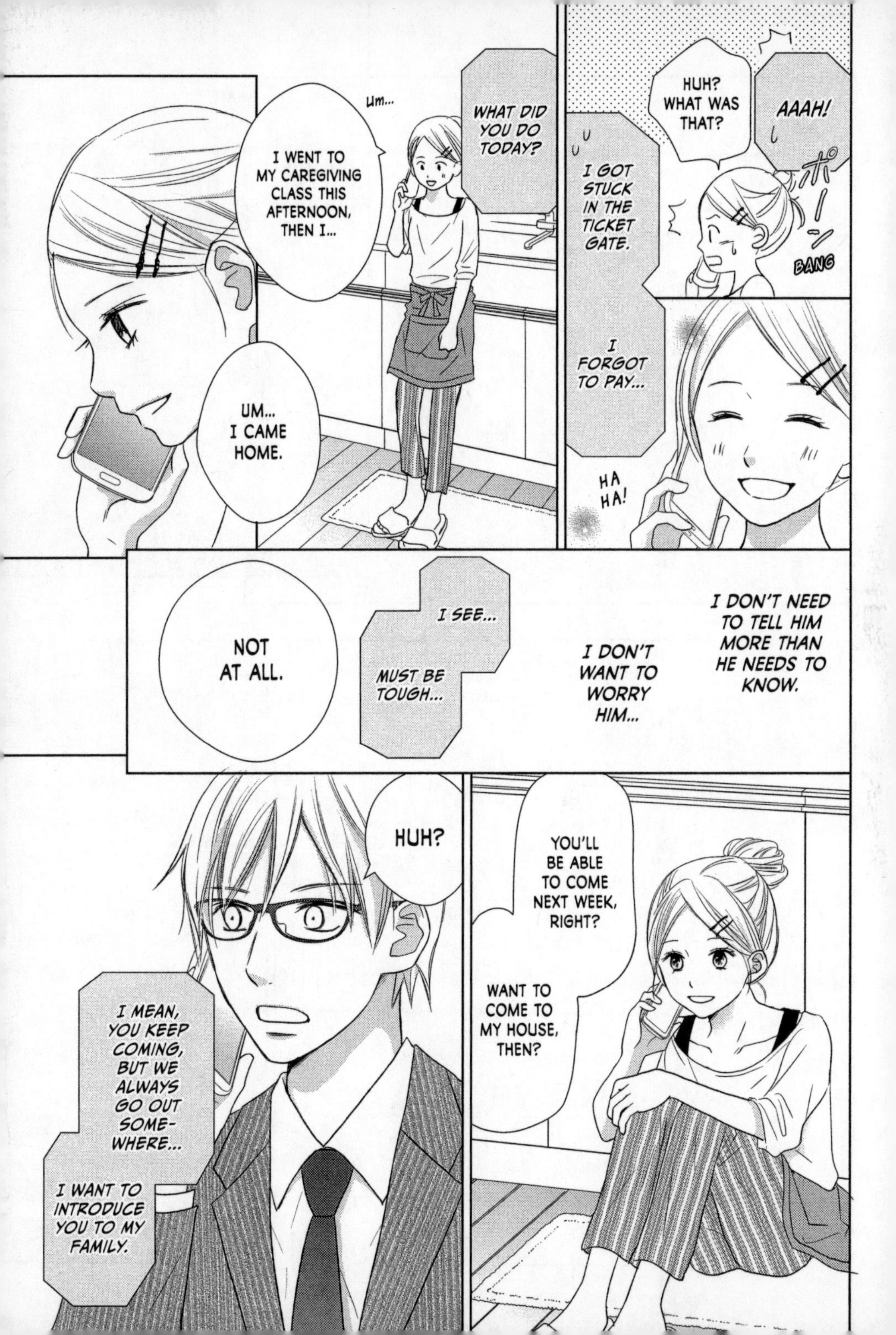
AAAH!
HUH? WHAT WAS THAT?
ポン
BANG
I GOT STUCK IN THE TICKET GATE.
I FORGOT TO PAY...
HA HA!
WHAT DID YOU DO TODAY?
Um...
I WENT TO MY CAREGIVING CLASS THIS AFTERNOON, THEN I...
UM... I CAME HOME.
I DON'T NEED TO TELL HIM MORE THAN HE NEEDS TO KNOW.
I DON'T WANT TO WORRY HIM...
I SEE...
MUST BE TOUGH...
NOT AT ALL.
YOU'LL BE ABLE TO COME NEXT WEEK, RIGHT?
WANT TO COME TO MY HOUSE, THEN?
HUH?
I MEAN, YOU KEEP COMING, BUT WE ALWAYS GO OUT SOME-WHERE...
I WANT TO INTRODUCE YOU TO MY FAMILY.

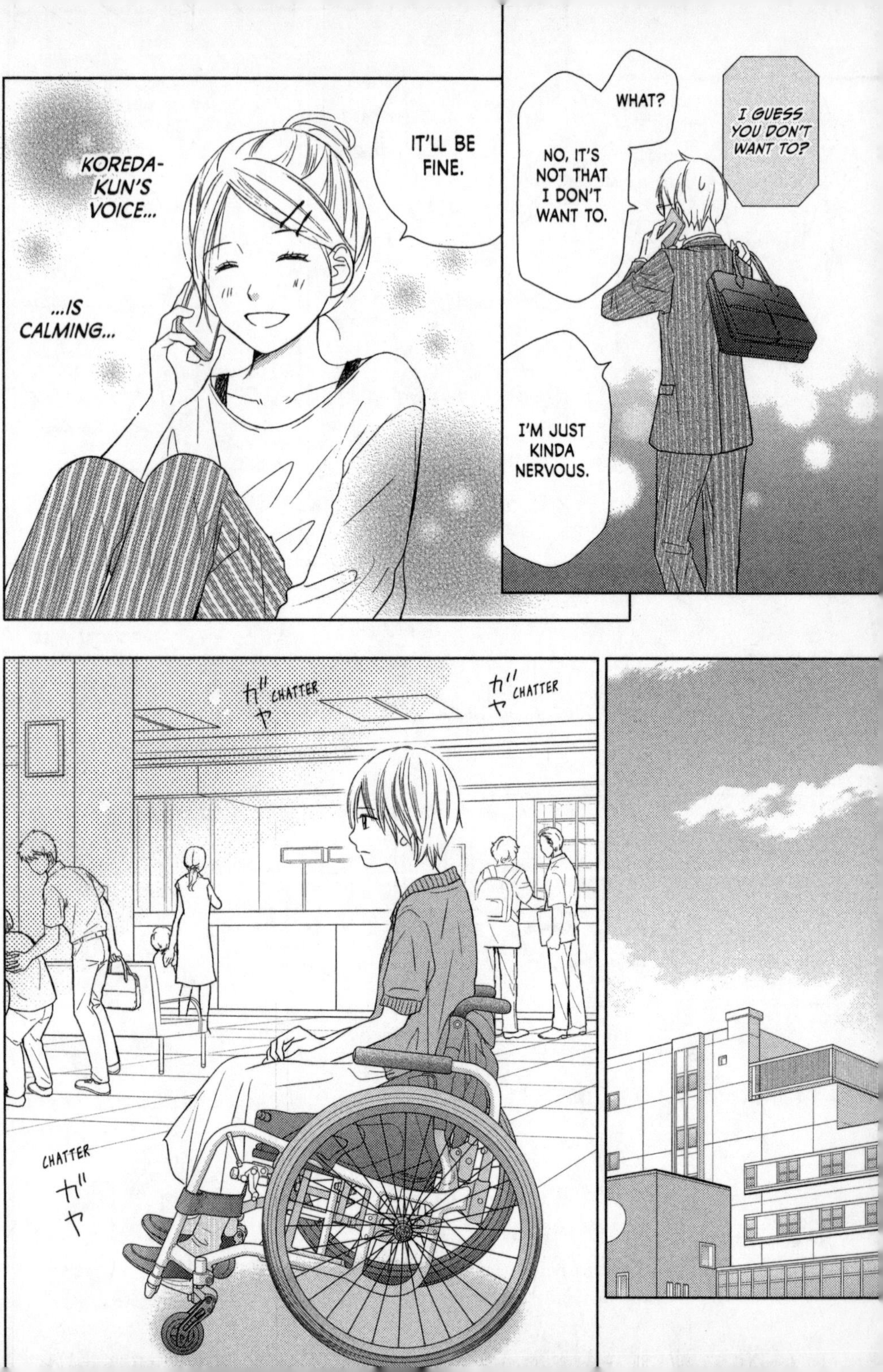
I GUESS YOU DON'T WANT TO?
WHAT?
NO, IT'S NOT THAT I DON'T WANT TO.
I'M JUST KINDA NERVOUS.
IT'LL BE FINE.
KOREDA-KUN'S VOICE...
...IS CALMING...
ガヤ CHATTER
ガヤ CHATTER
CHATTER ガヤ

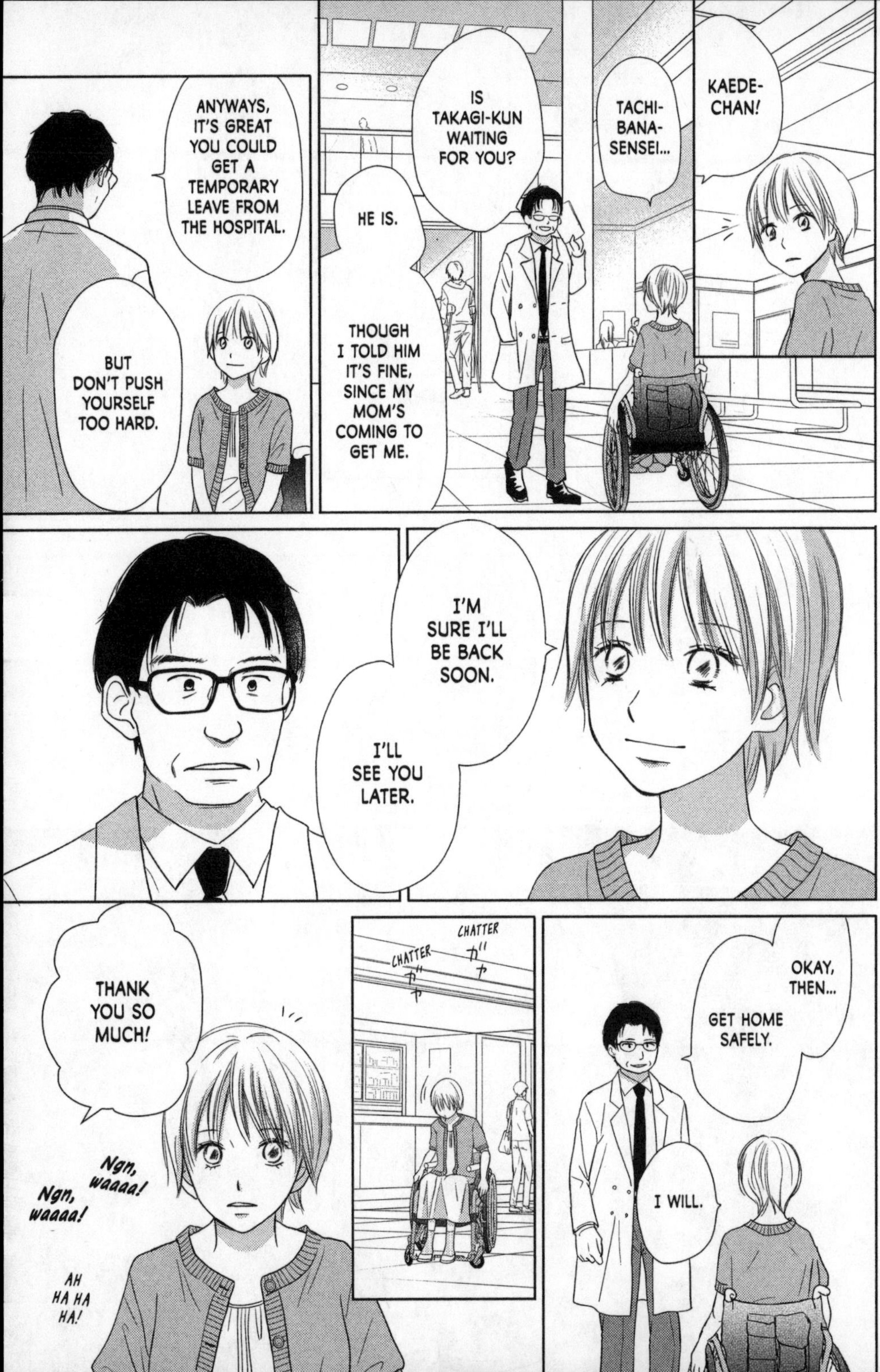
KAEDE-CHAN!
TACHI-BANA-SENSEI...
IS TAKAGI-KUN WAITING FOR YOU?
HE IS.
THOUGH I TOLD HIM IT'S FINE, SINCE MY MOM'S COMING TO GET ME.
ANYWAYS, IT'S GREAT YOU COULD GET A TEMPORARY LEAVE FROM THE HOSPITAL.
BUT DON'T PUSH YOURSELF TOO HARD.
I'M SURE I'LL BE BACK SOON.
I'LL SEE YOU LATER.
OKAY, THEN...
GET HOME SAFELY.
I WILL.
CHATTER
CHATTER
THANK YOU SO MUCH!
Ngn, waaaa!
Ngn, waaaa!
AH HA HA HA!

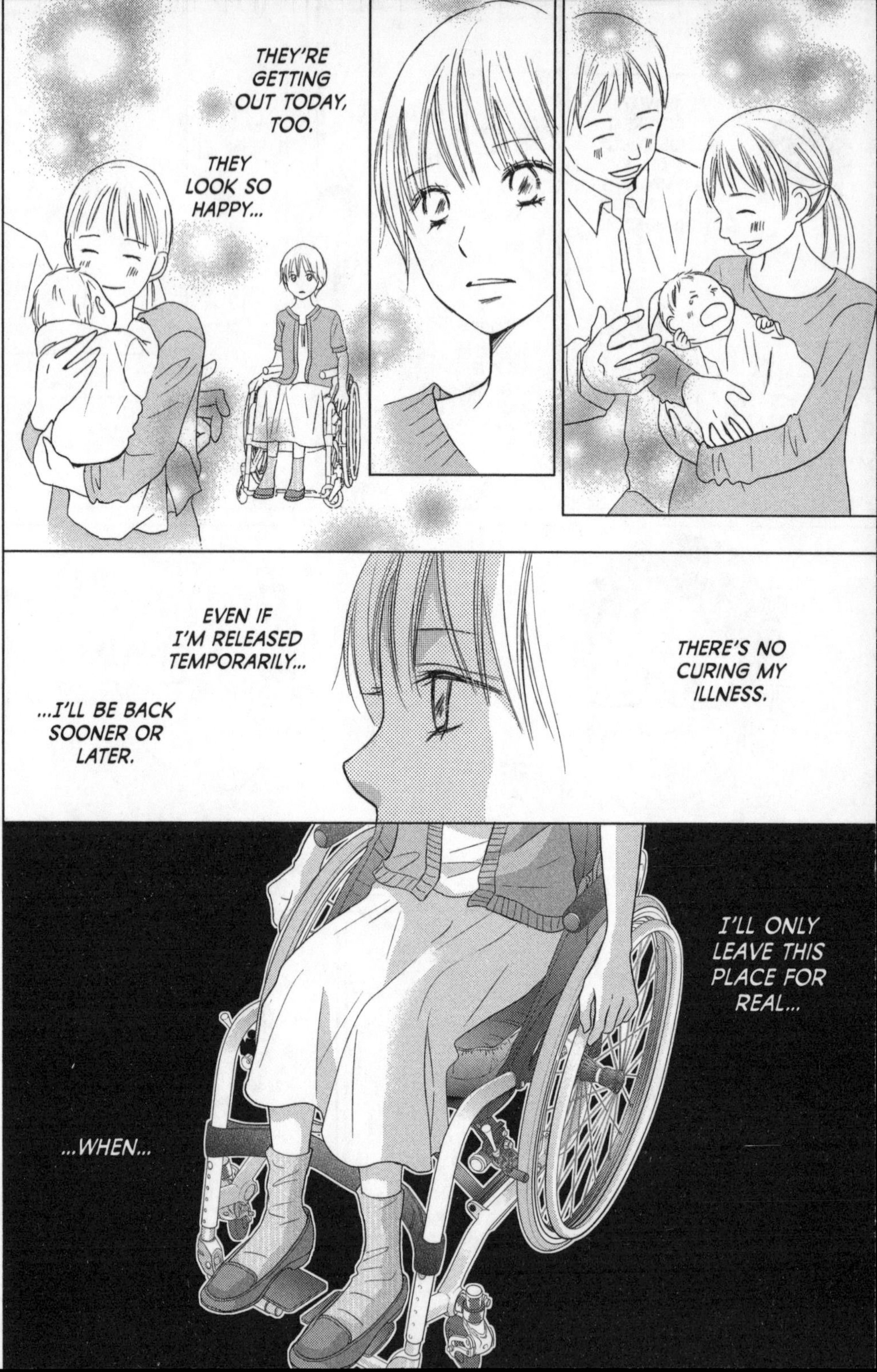
THEY'RE GETTING OUT TODAY, TOO.
THEY LOOK SO HAPPY...
THERE'S NO CURING MY ILLNESS.
EVEN IF I'M RELEASED TEMPORARILY...
...I'LL BE BACK SOONER OR LATER.
I'LL ONLY LEAVE THIS PLACE FOR REAL...
...WHEN...

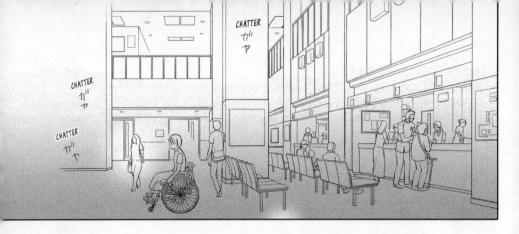

CHATTER ガヤ
CHATTER ガヤ
CHATTER ガヤ
WHAT?
SHE'S NOT HERE?
I THOUGHT SHE HAD ALREADY GONE HOME.
WASN'T HER MOTHER HERE TO PICK HER UP?
SHE NEVER TOLD ME ABOUT THAT.
WHY DON'T YOU CALL KAEDE-SAN?
プルルル RRIIING
プルルルル RRIIING
...
SHE'S NOT ANSWERING...

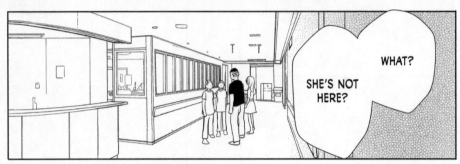

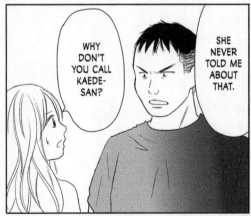

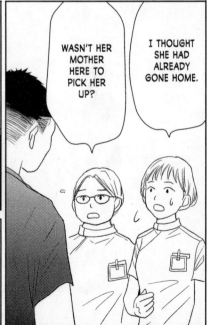

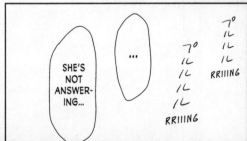

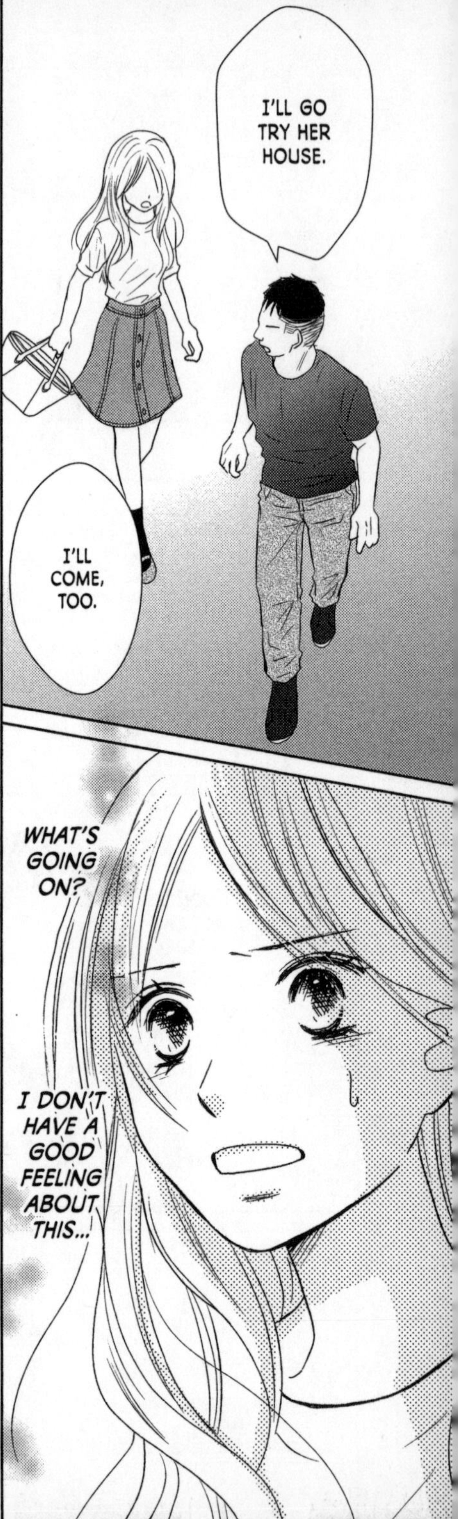
I'LL GO TRY HER HOUSE.
I'LL COME, TOO.
WHAT'S GOING ON?
I DON'T HAVE A GOOD FEELING ABOUT THIS...
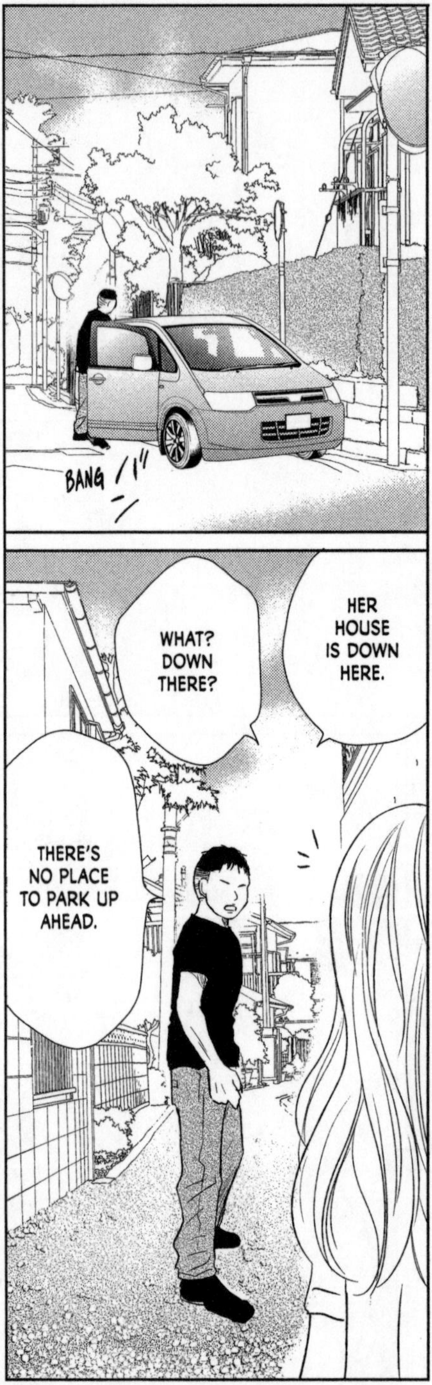
BANG
HER HOUSE IS DOWN HERE.
WHAT? DOWN THERE?
THERE'S NO PLACE TO PARK UP AHEAD.

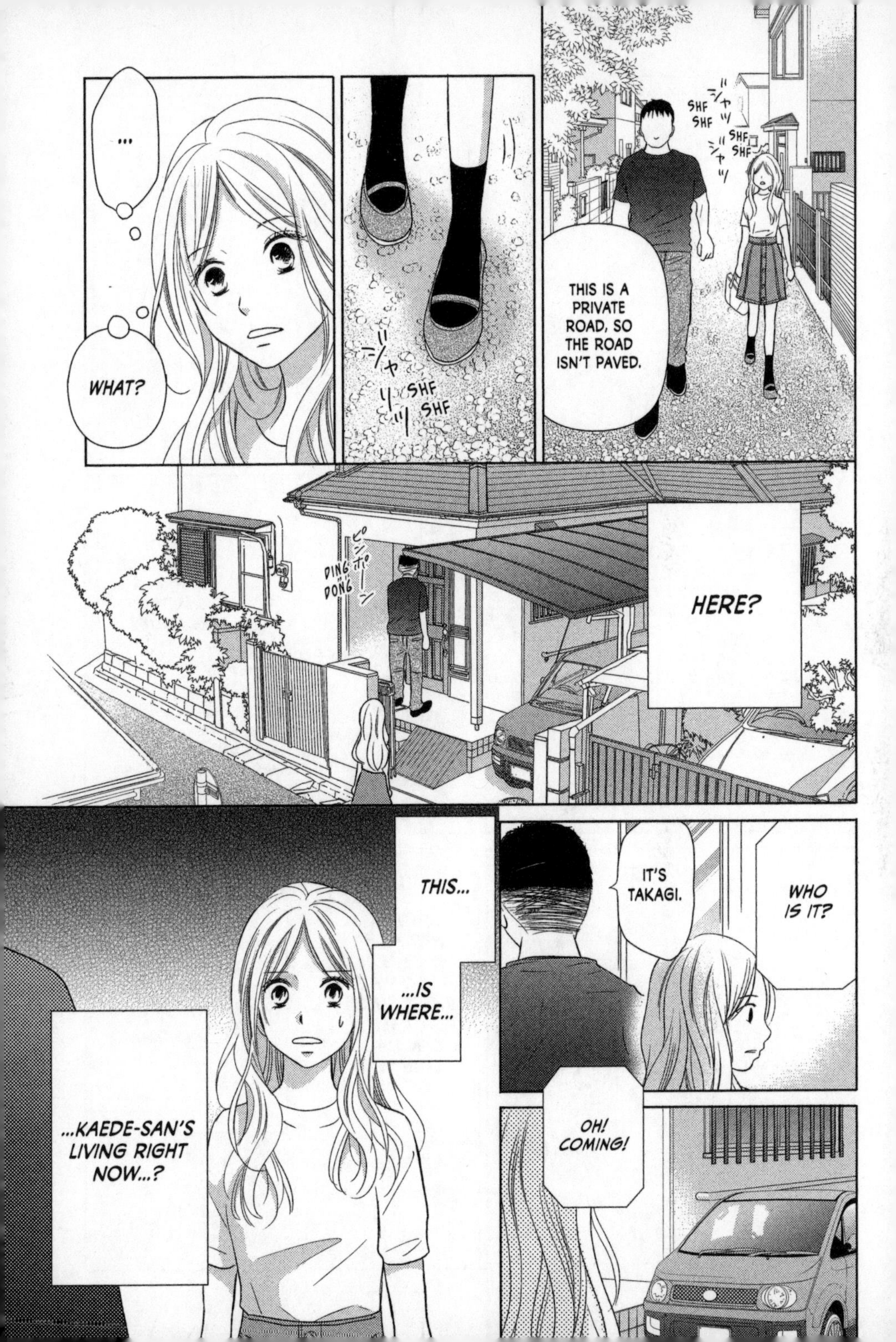
SHF SHF
SHF SHF
THIS IS A PRIVATE ROAD, SO THE ROAD ISN'T PAVED.
SHF SHF
...
WHAT?
DING DONG
HERE?
WHO IS IT?
IT'S TAKAGI.
OH! COMING!
THIS...
...IS WHERE...
...KAEDE-SAN'S LIVING RIGHT NOW...?

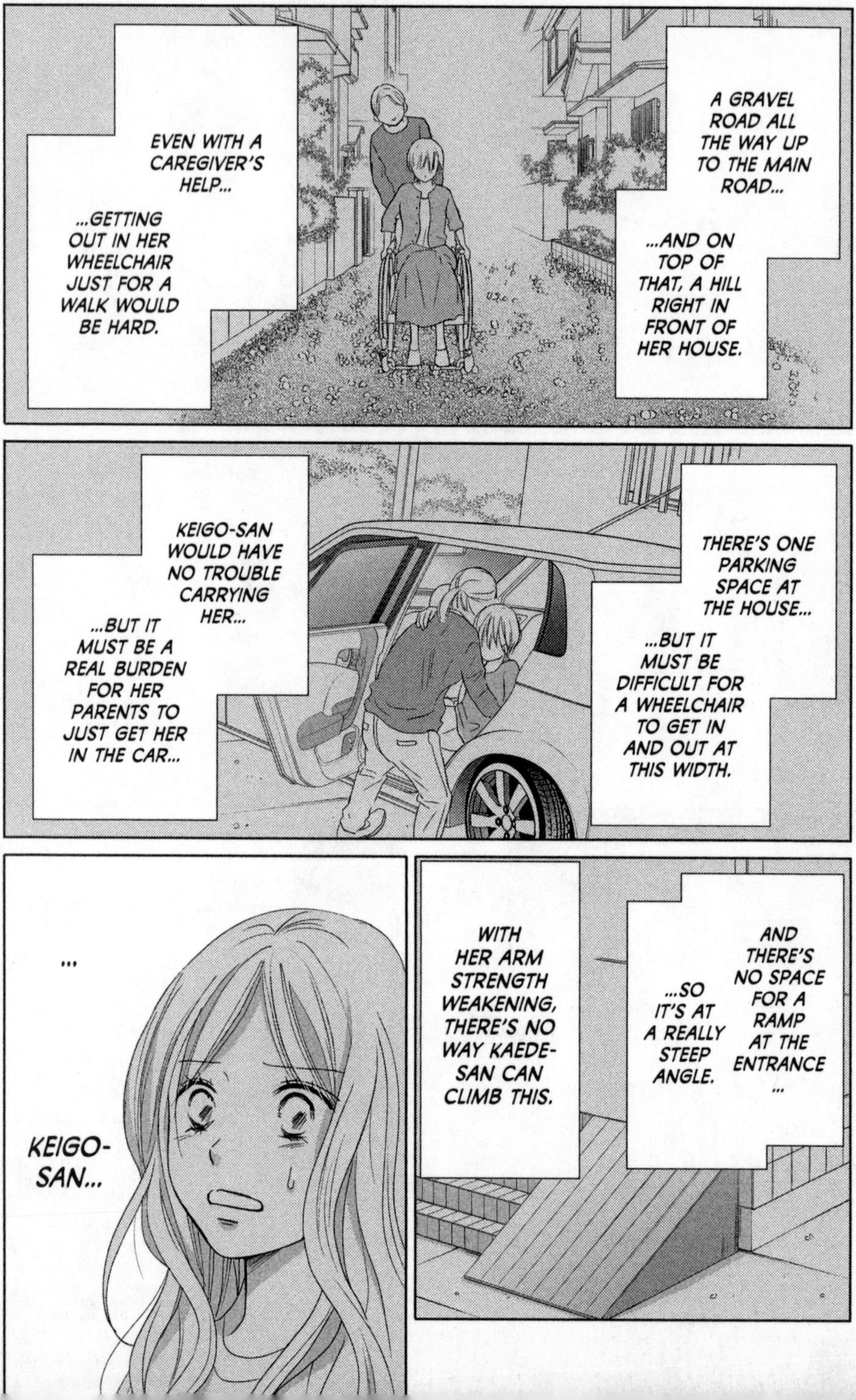
A GRAVEL ROAD ALL THE WAY UP TO THE MAIN ROAD...
...AND ON TOP OF THAT, A HILL RIGHT IN FRONT OF HER HOUSE.
EVEN WITH A CAREGIVER'S HELP...
...GETTING OUT IN HER WHEELCHAIR JUST FOR A WALK WOULD BE HARD.
THERE'S ONE PARKING SPACE AT THE HOUSE...
...BUT IT MUST BE DIFFICULT FOR A WHEELCHAIR TO GET IN AND OUT AT THIS WIDTH.
KEIGO-SAN WOULD HAVE NO TROUBLE CARRYING HER...
...BUT IT MUST BE A REAL BURDEN FOR HER PARENTS TO JUST GET HER IN THE CAR...
AND THERE'S NO SPACE FOR A RAMP AT THE ENTRANCE...
...SO IT'S AT A REALLY STEEP ANGLE.
WITH HER ARM STRENGTH WEAKENING, THERE'S NO WAY KAEDE-SAN CAN CLIMB THIS.
...
KEIGO-SAN...

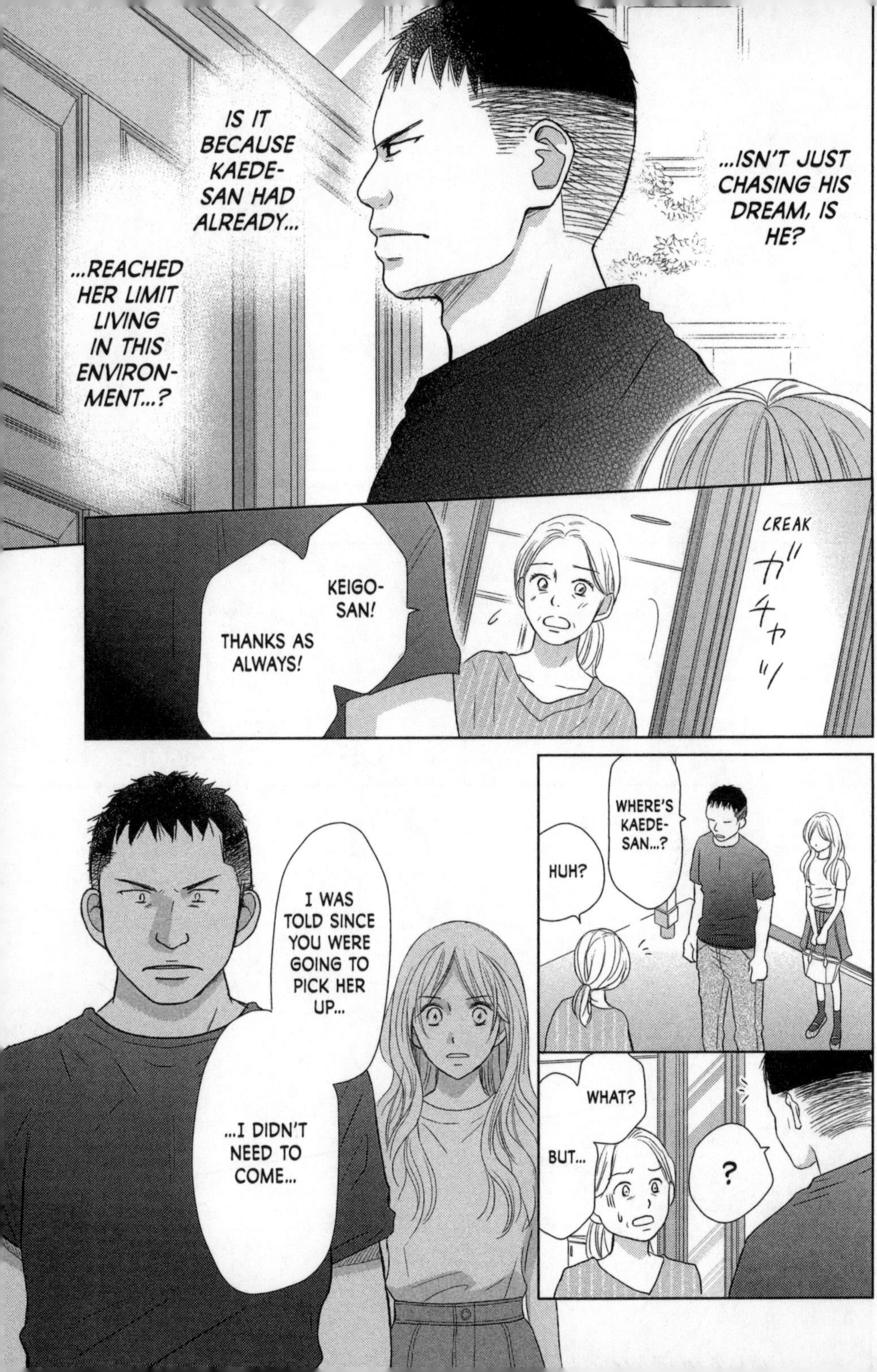
...ISN'T JUST CHASING HIS DREAM, IS HE?
IS IT BECAUSE KAEDE-SAN HAD ALREADY...
...REACHED HER LIMIT LIVING IN THIS ENVIRONMENT...?
CREAK
ガチャッ
KEIGO-SAN!
THANKS AS ALWAYS!
WHERE'S KAEDE-SAN...?
HUH?
?
WHAT?
BUT...
I WAS TOLD SINCE YOU WERE GOING TO PICK HER UP...
...I DIDN'T NEED TO COME...

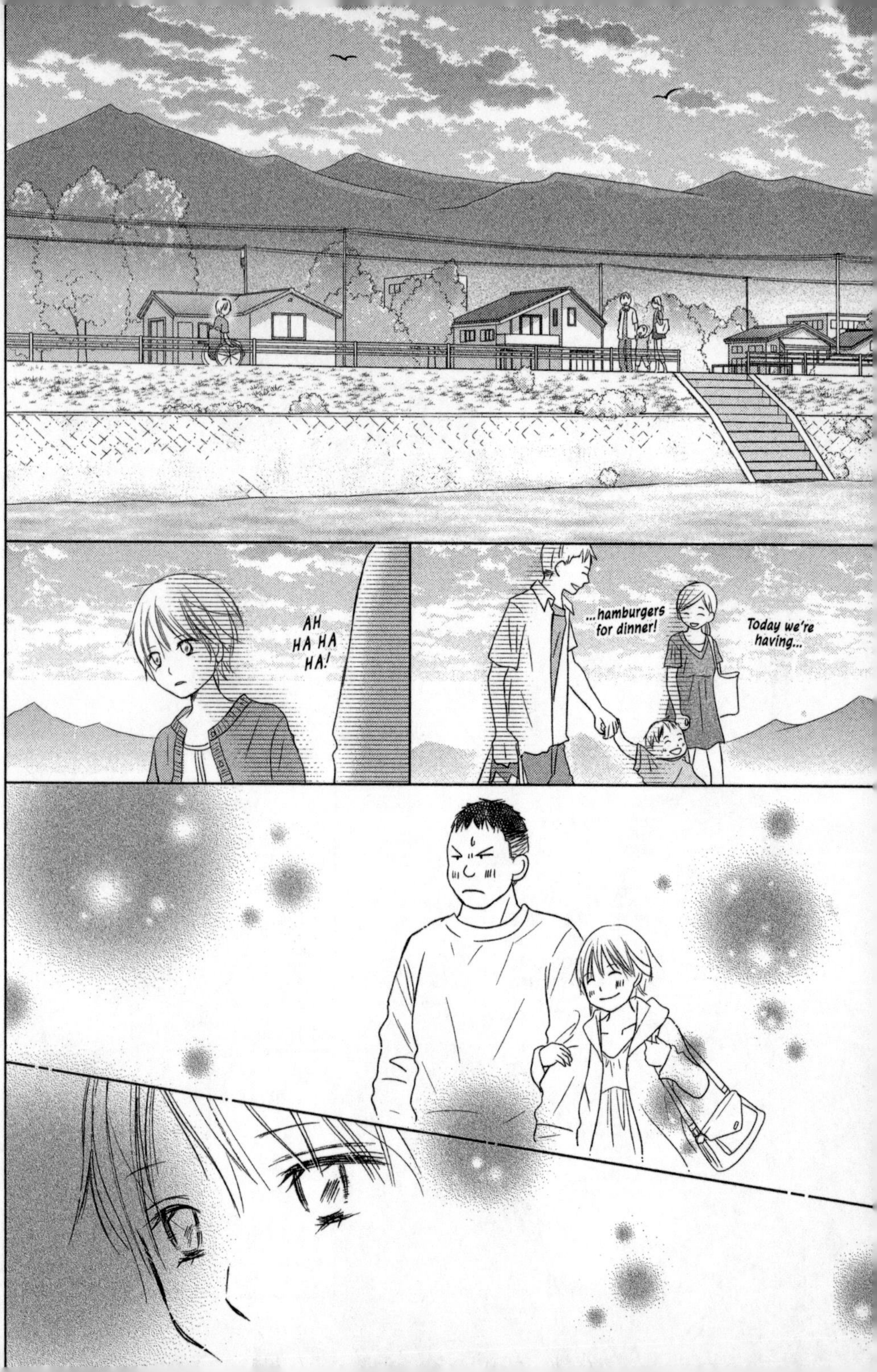
Today we're having...
...hamburgers for dinner!
AH HA HA HA!

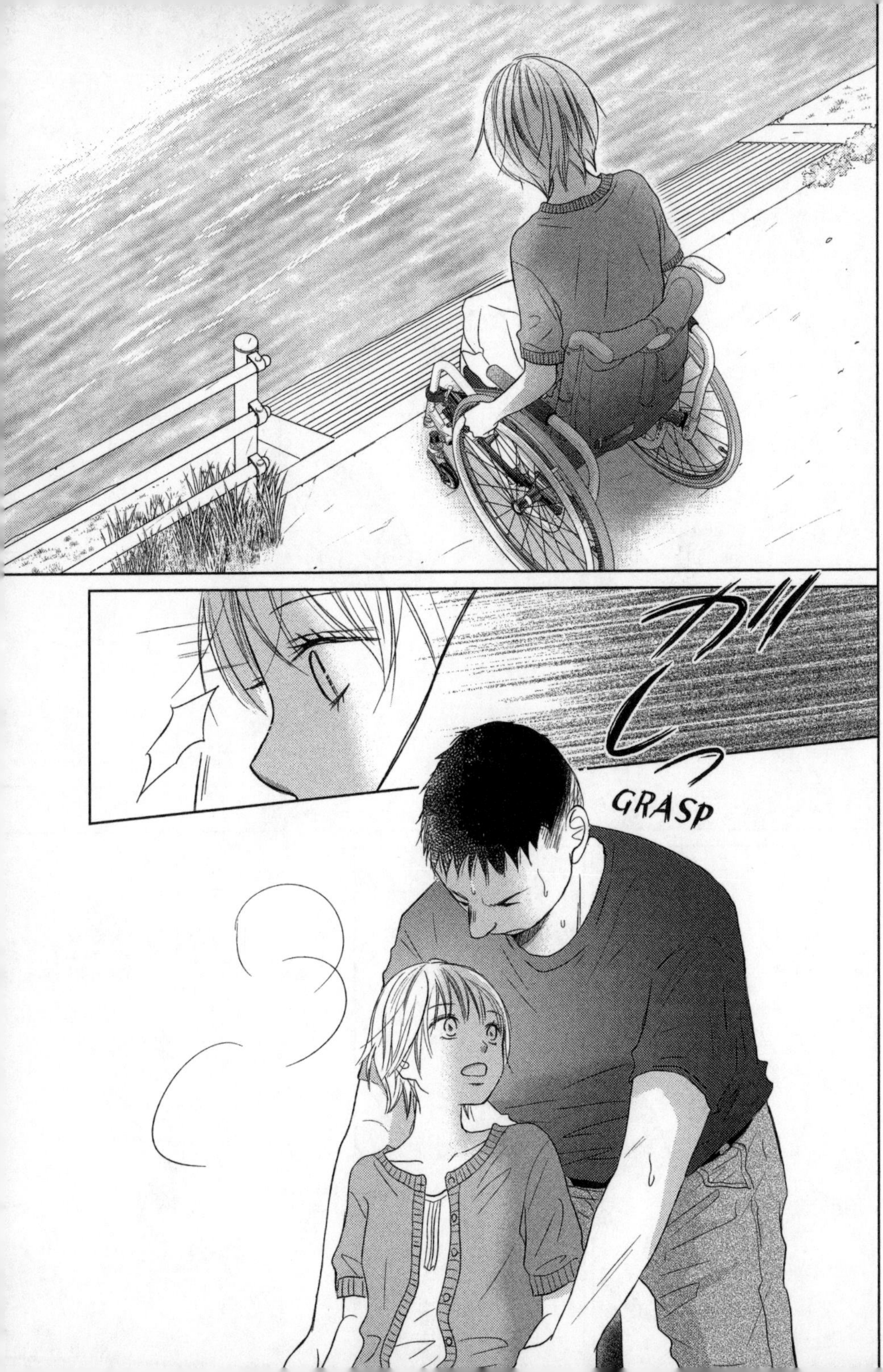
ガシッ
GRASP

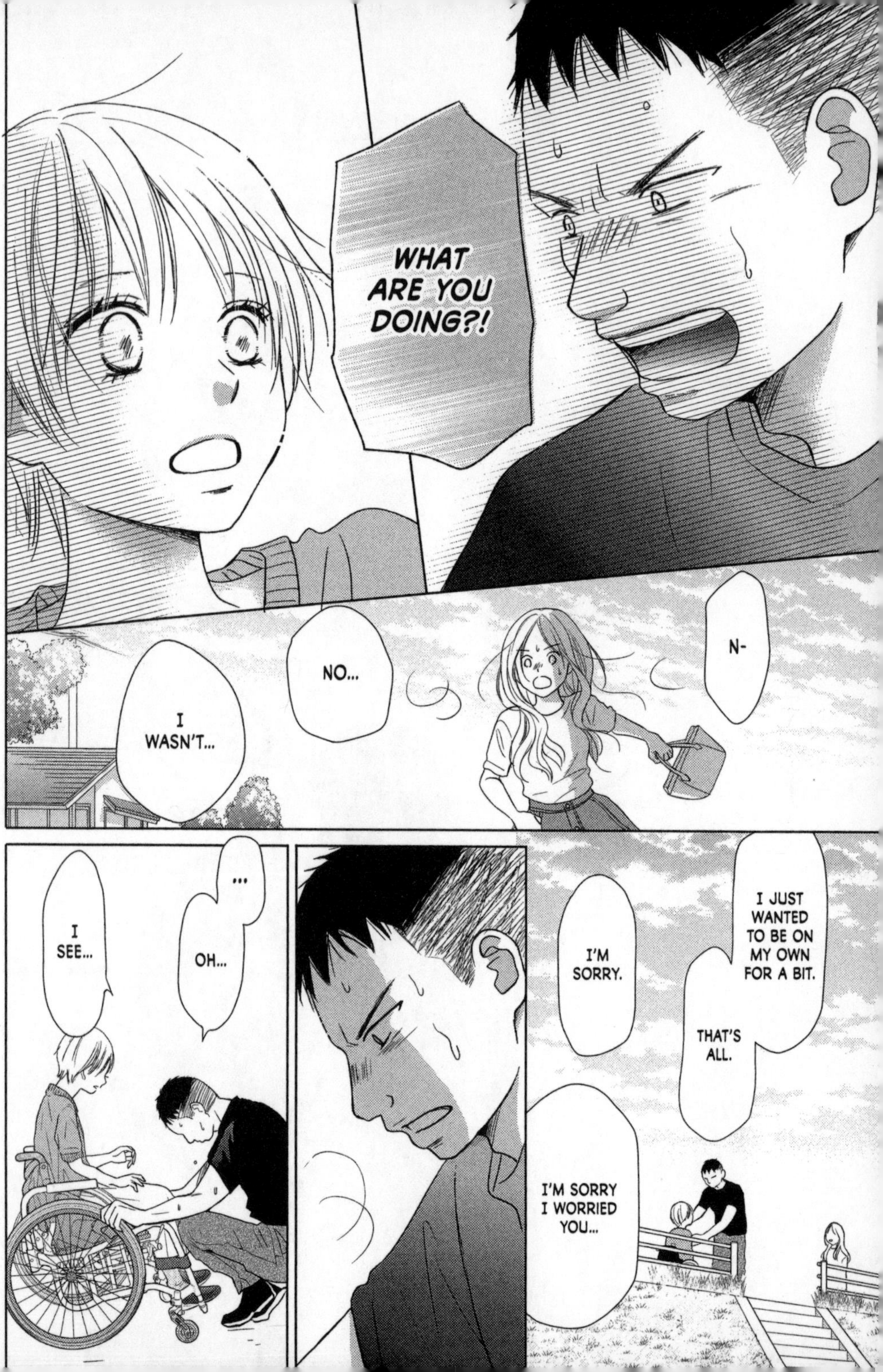
WHAT ARE YOU DOING?!
N-
NO...
I WASN'T...
I JUST WANTED TO BE ON MY OWN FOR A BIT.
THAT'S ALL.
I'M SORRY.
I'M SORRY I WORRIED YOU...
...
OH...
I SEE...

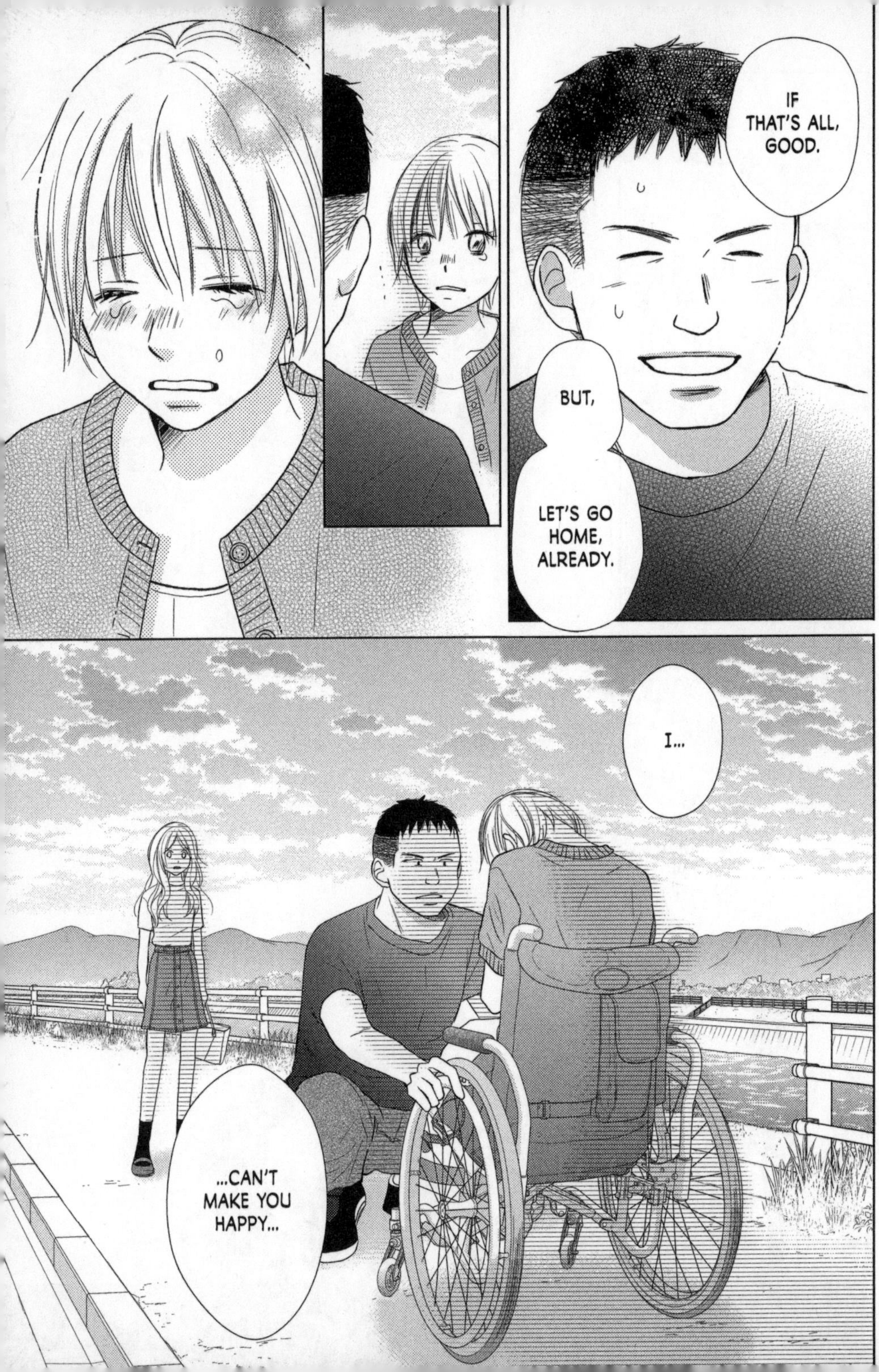
IF THAT'S ALL, GOOD.
BUT,
LET'S GO HOME, ALREADY.
I...
...CAN'T MAKE YOU HAPPY...

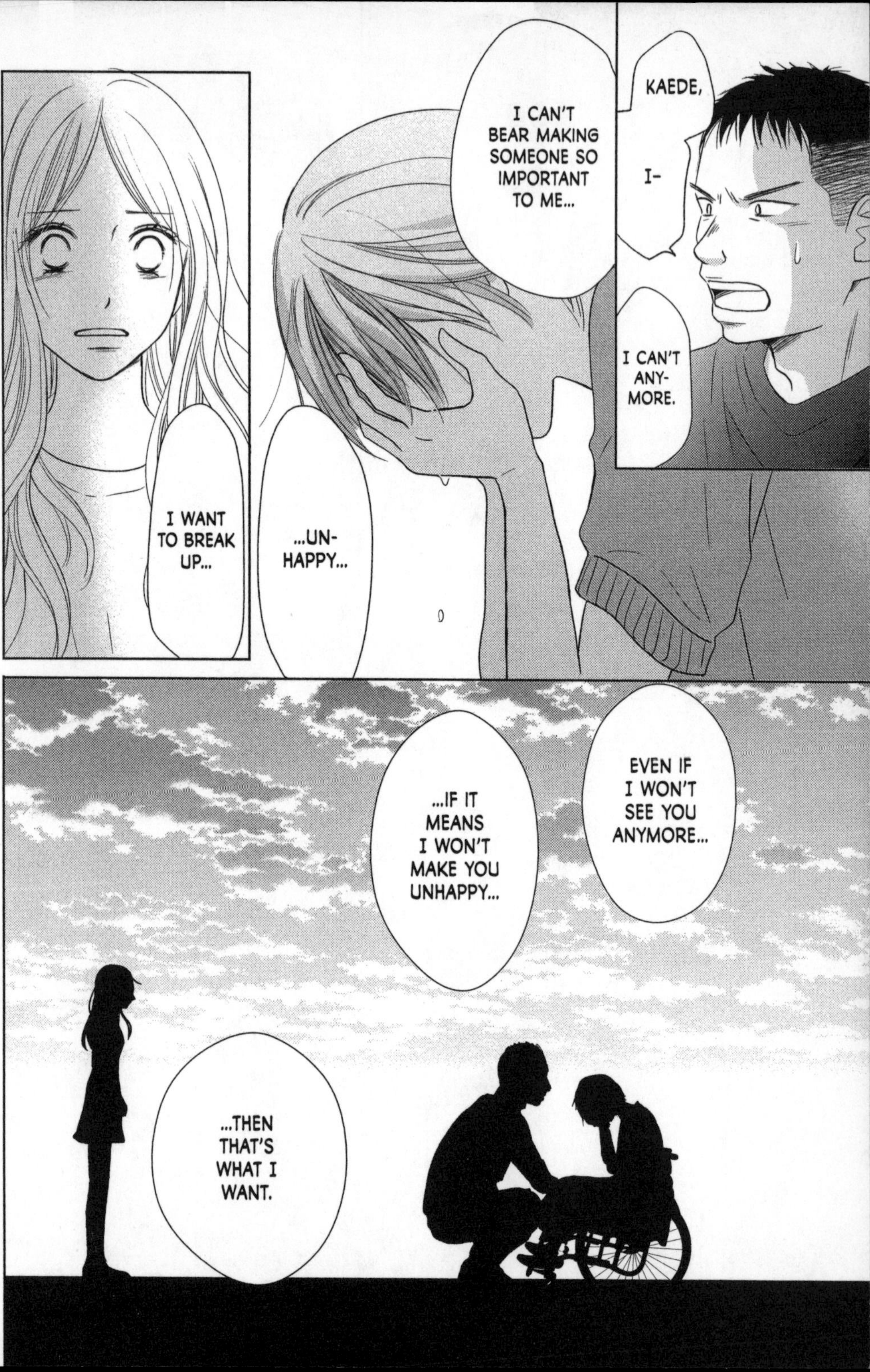
KAEDE,
I-
I CAN'T ANYMORE.
I CAN'T BEAR MAKING SOMEONE SO IMPORTANT TO ME...
...UN-HAPPY...
I WANT TO BREAK UP...
EVEN IF I WON'T SEE YOU ANYMORE...
...IF IT MEANS I WON'T MAKE YOU UNHAPPY...
...THEN THAT'S WHAT I WANT.

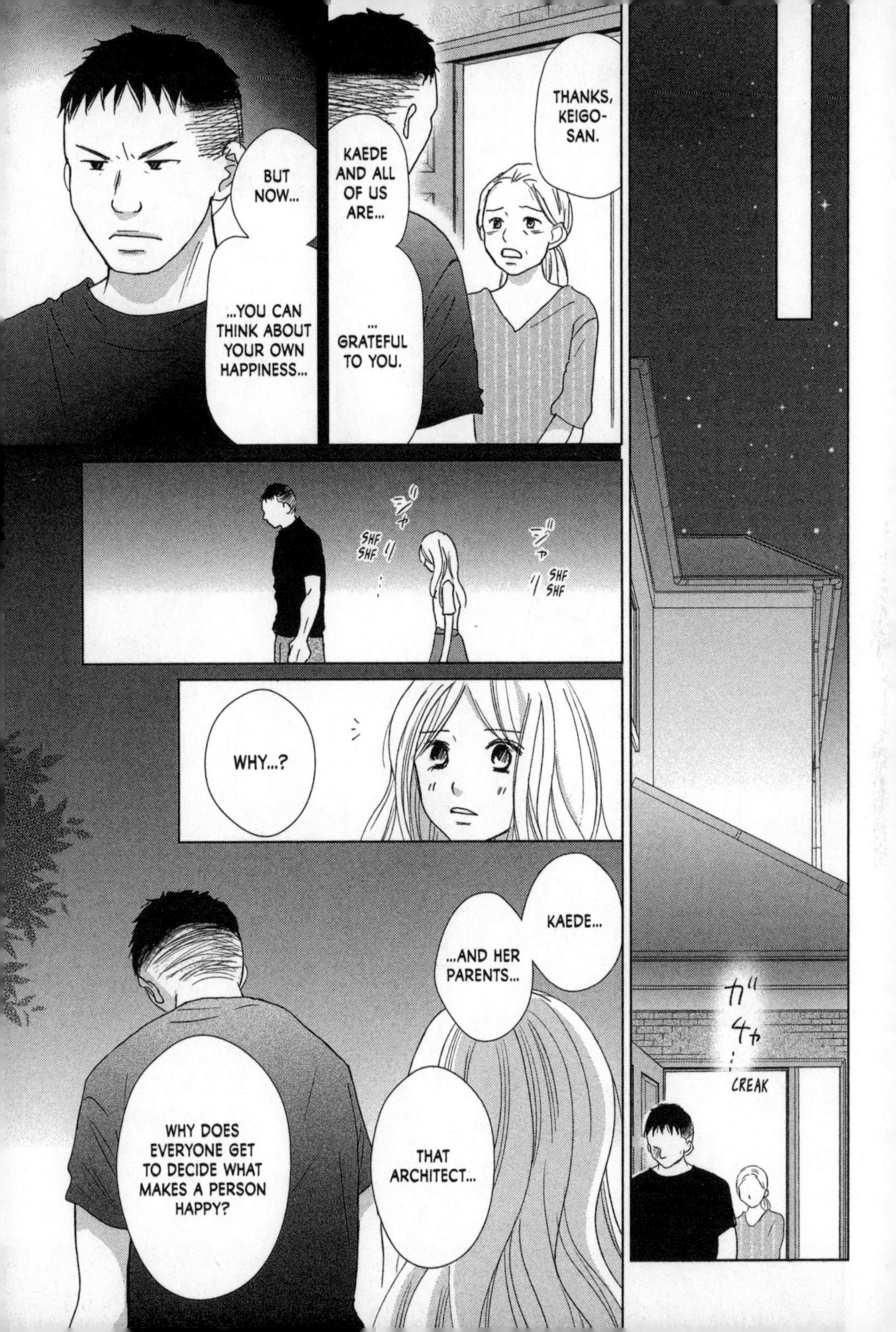
CREAK
THANKS, KEIGO-SAN.
KAEDE AND ALL OF US ARE...
... GRATEFUL TO YOU.
BUT NOW...
...YOU CAN THINK ABOUT YOUR OWN HAPPINESS...
SHF SHF
SHF SHF
WHY...?
KAEDE...
...AND HER PARENTS...
THAT ARCHITECT...
WHY DOES EVERYONE GET TO DECIDE WHAT MAKES A PERSON HAPPY?

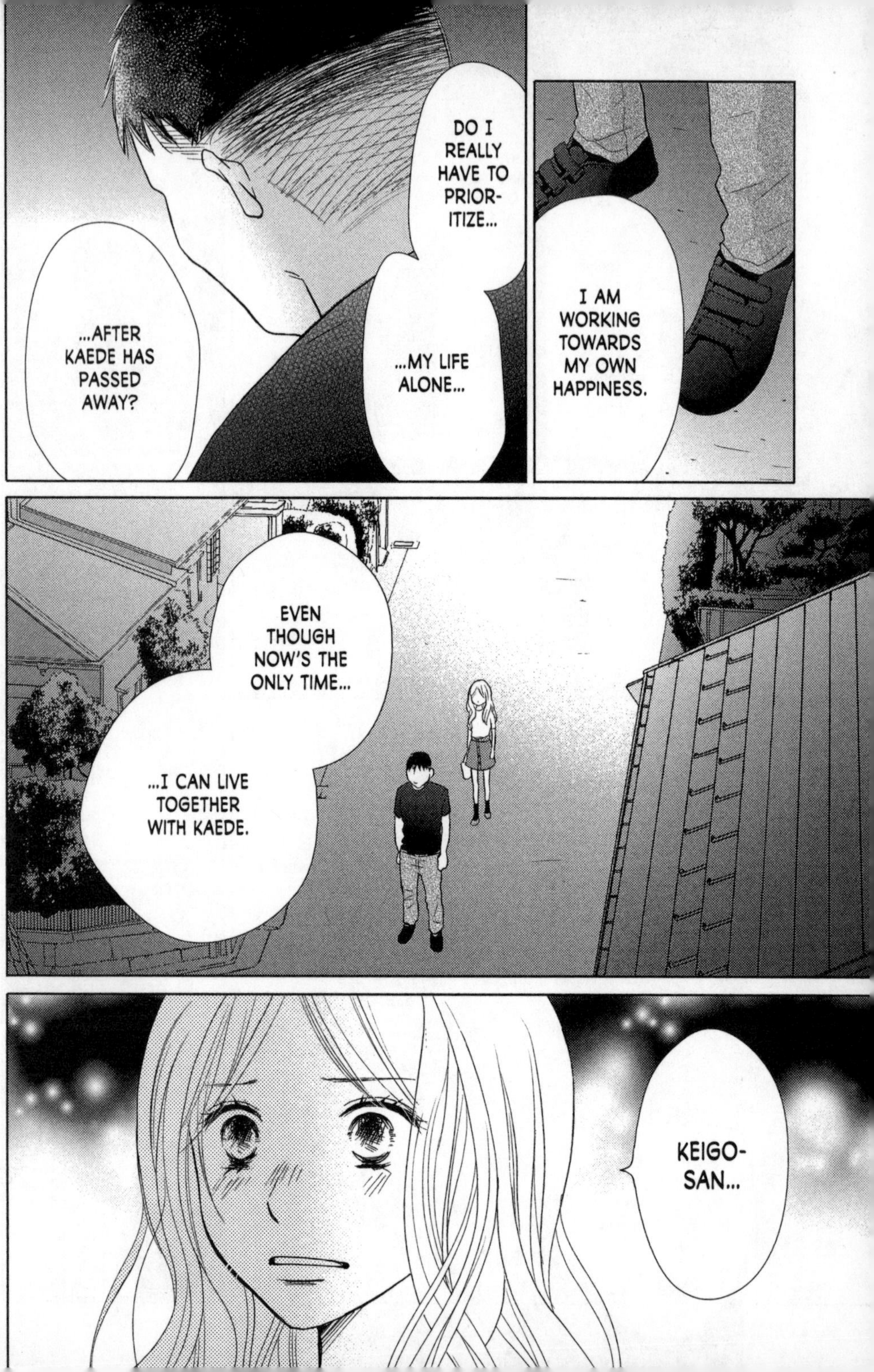
I AM WORKING TOWARDS MY OWN HAPPINESS.
DO I REALLY HAVE TO PRIOR-ITIZE...
...MY LIFE ALONE...
...AFTER KAEDE HAS PASSED AWAY?
EVEN THOUGH NOW'S THE ONLY TIME...
...I CAN LIVE TOGETHER WITH KAEDE.
KEIGO-SAN...

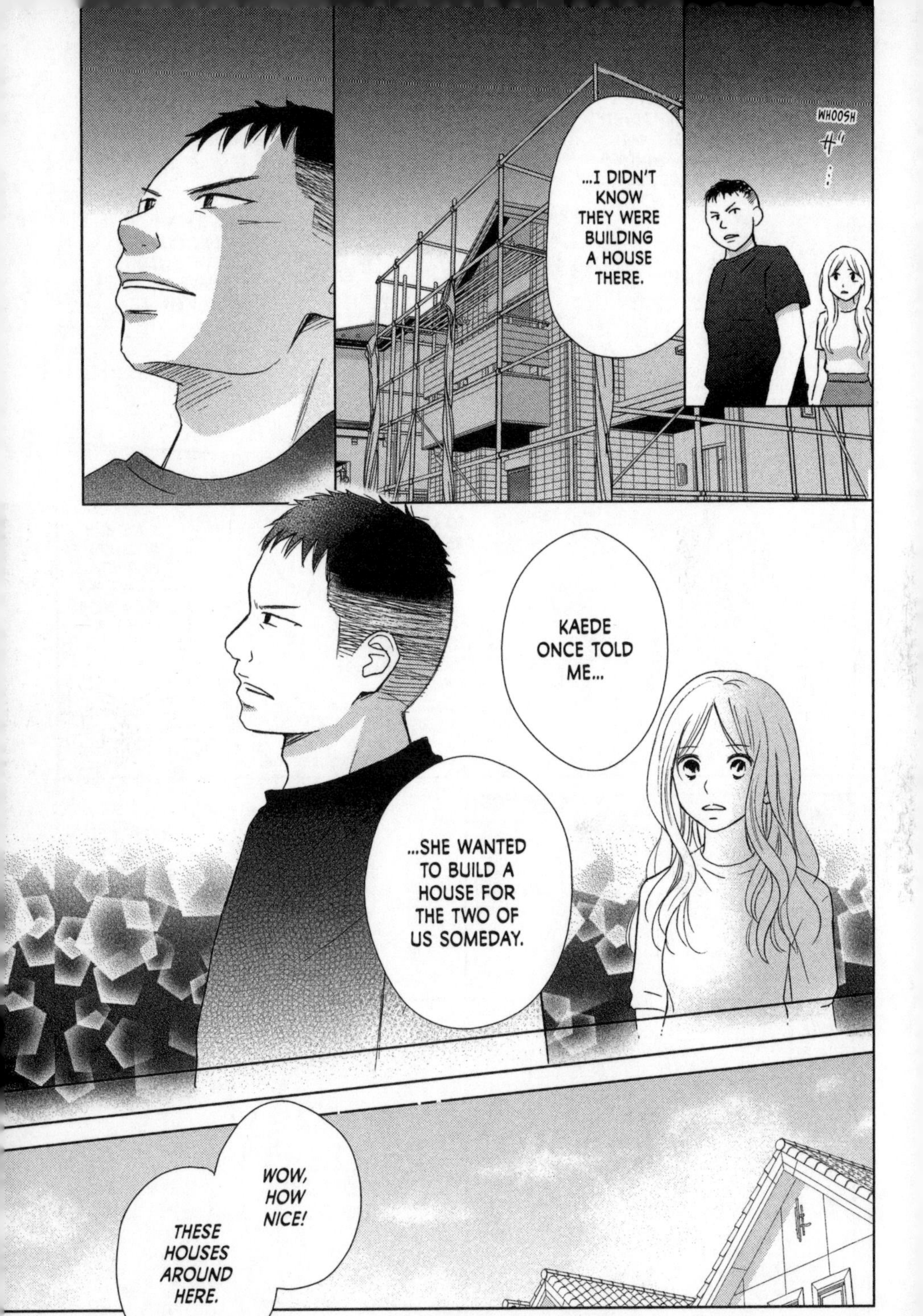
WHOOSH
...I DIDN'T KNOW THEY WERE BUILDING A HOUSE THERE.
KAEDE ONCE TOLD ME...
...SHE WANTED TO BUILD A HOUSE FOR THE TWO OF US SOMEDAY.
WOW, HOW NICE!
THESE HOUSES AROUND HERE.

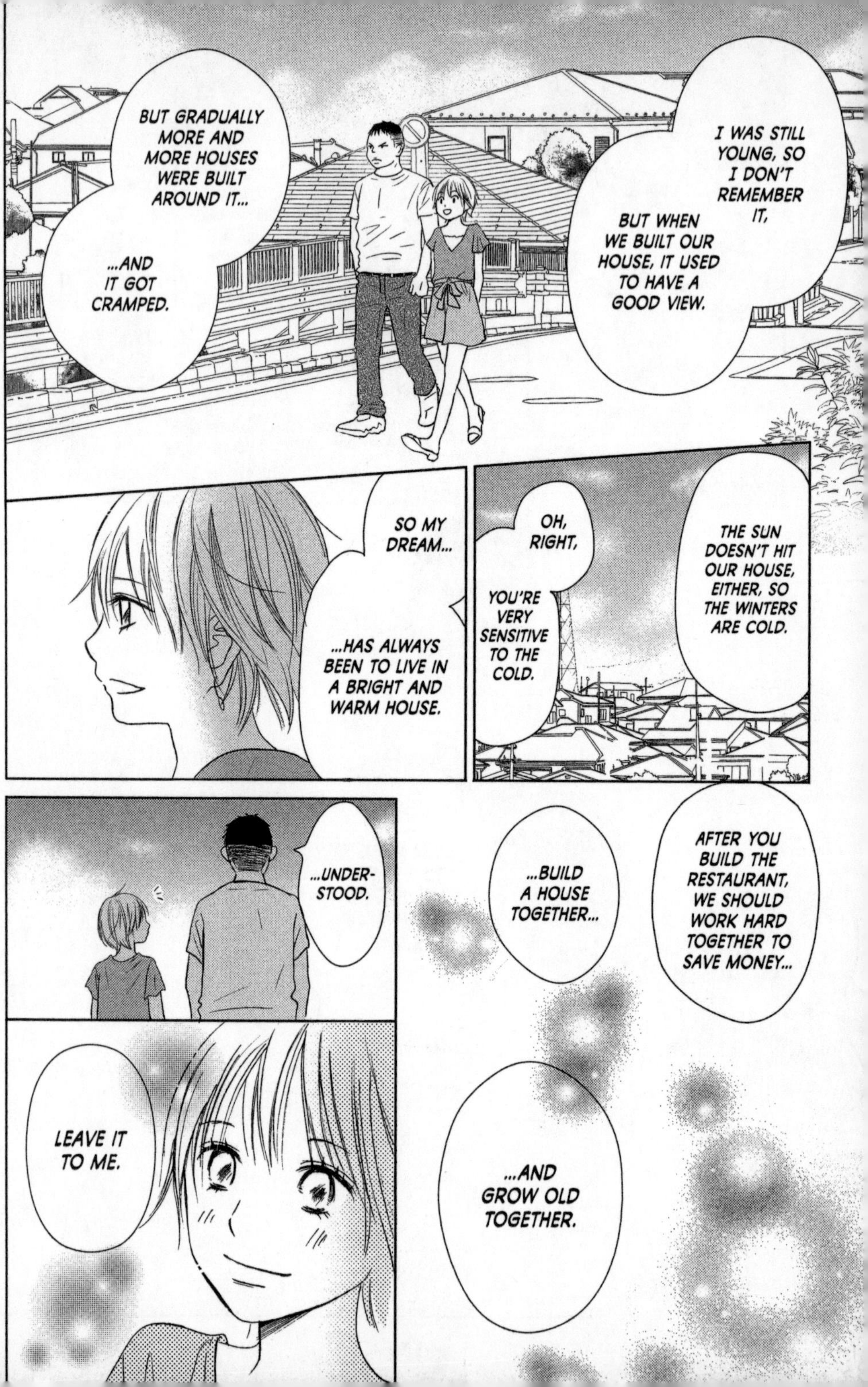
I WAS STILL YOUNG, SO I DON'T REMEMBER IT,
BUT WHEN WE BUILT OUR HOUSE, IT USED TO HAVE A GOOD VIEW.
BUT GRADUALLY MORE AND MORE HOUSES WERE BUILT AROUND IT...
...AND IT GOT CRAMPED.
THE SUN DOESN'T HIT OUR HOUSE, EITHER, SO THE WINTERS ARE COLD.
OH, RIGHT,
YOU'RE VERY SENSITIVE TO THE COLD.
SO MY DREAM...
...HAS ALWAYS BEEN TO LIVE IN A BRIGHT AND WARM HOUSE.
AFTER YOU BUILD THE RESTAURANT, WE SHOULD WORK HARD TOGETHER TO SAVE MONEY...
...BUILD A HOUSE TOGETHER...
...AND GROW OLD TOGETHER.
...UNDER-STOOD.
LEAVE IT TO ME.

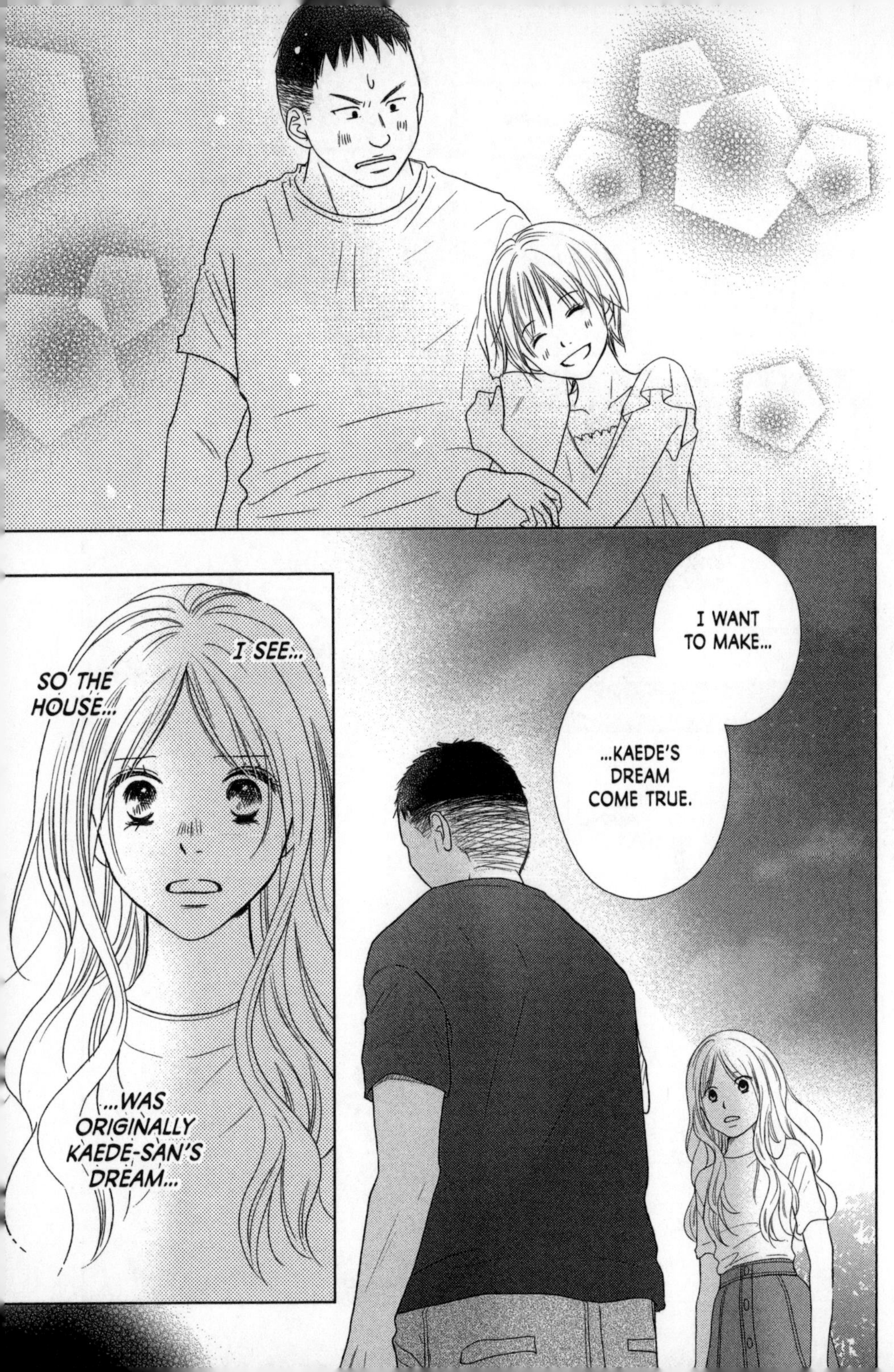
I WANT TO MAKE...
...KAEDE'S DREAM COME TRUE.
I SEE...
SO THE HOUSE...
...WAS ORIGINALLY KAEDE-SAN'S DREAM...

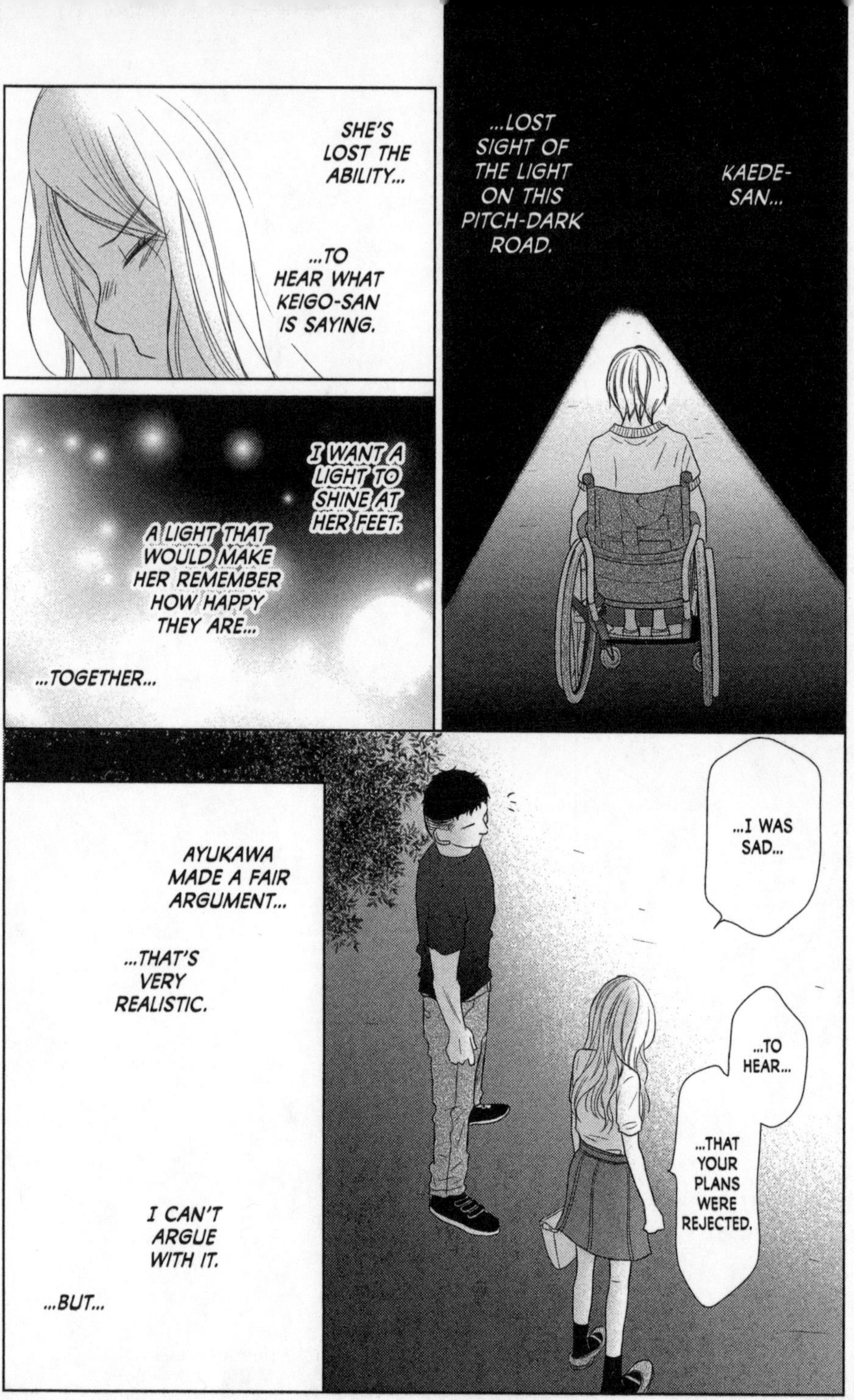
KAEDE-SAN...
...LOST SIGHT OF THE LIGHT ON THIS PITCH-DARK ROAD.
SHE'S LOST THE ABILITY...
...TO HEAR WHAT KEIGO-SAN IS SAYING.
I WANT A LIGHT TO SHINE AT HER FEET.
A LIGHT THAT WOULD MAKE HER REMEMBER HOW HAPPY THEY ARE...
...TOGETHER...
...I WAS SAD...
...TO HEAR...
...THAT YOUR PLANS WERE REJECTED.
AYUKAWA MADE A FAIR ARGUMENT...
...THAT'S VERY REALISTIC.
I CAN'T ARGUE WITH IT.
...BUT...

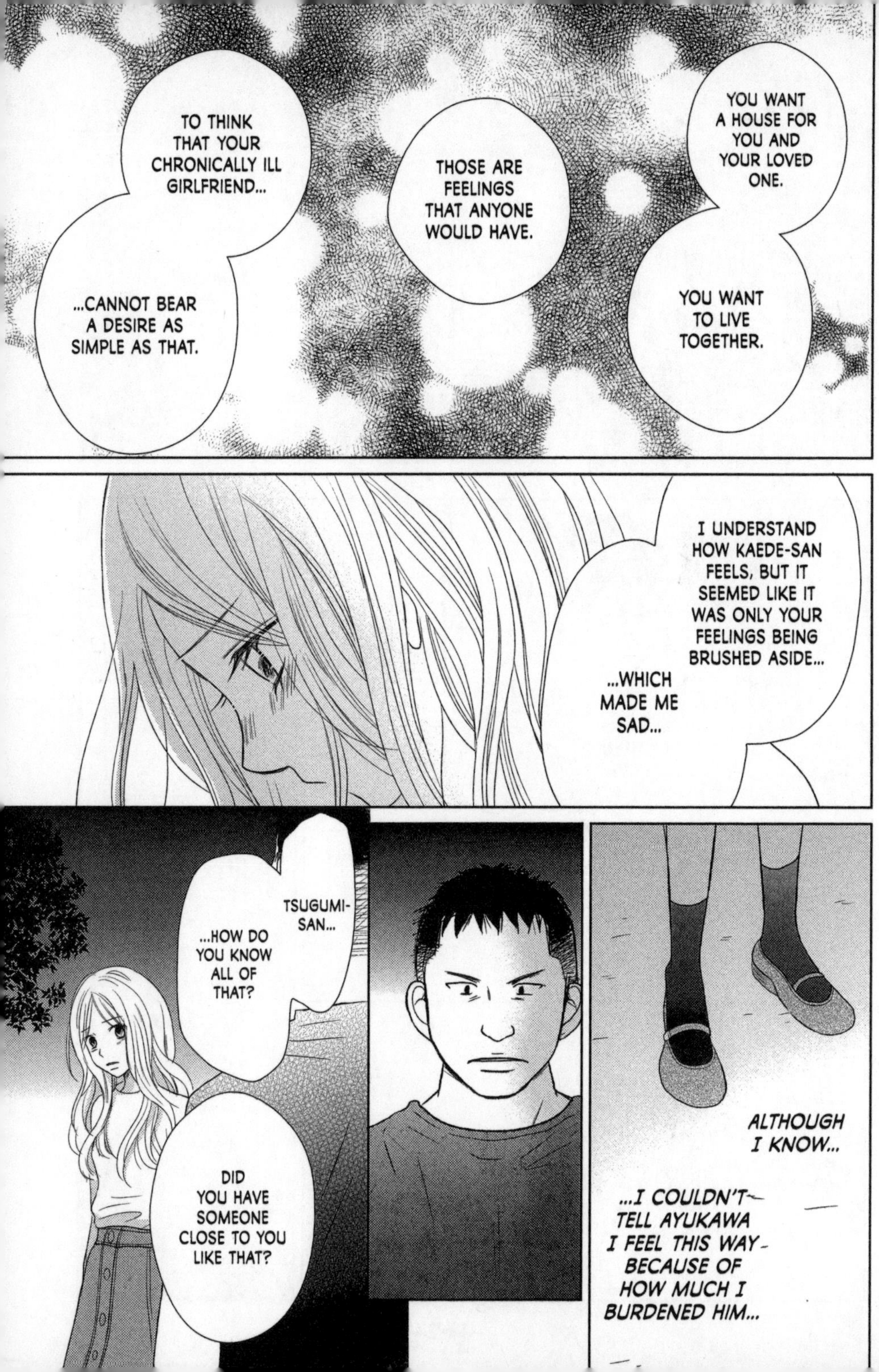
YOU WANT A HOUSE FOR YOU AND YOUR LOVED ONE.
YOU WANT TO LIVE TOGETHER.
THOSE ARE FEELINGS THAT ANYONE WOULD HAVE.
TO THINK THAT YOUR CHRONICALLY ILL GIRLFRIEND...
...CANNOT BEAR A DESIRE AS SIMPLE AS THAT.
I UNDERSTAND HOW KAEDE-SAN FEELS, BUT IT SEEMED LIKE IT WAS ONLY YOUR FEELINGS BEING BRUSHED ASIDE...
...WHICH MADE ME SAD...
ALTHOUGH I KNOW...
...I COULDN'T TELL AYUKAWA I FEEL THIS WAY BECAUSE OF HOW MUCH I BURDENED HIM...
TSUGUMI-SAN...
...HOW DO YOU KNOW ALL OF THAT?
DID YOU HAVE SOMEONE CLOSE TO YOU LIKE THAT?

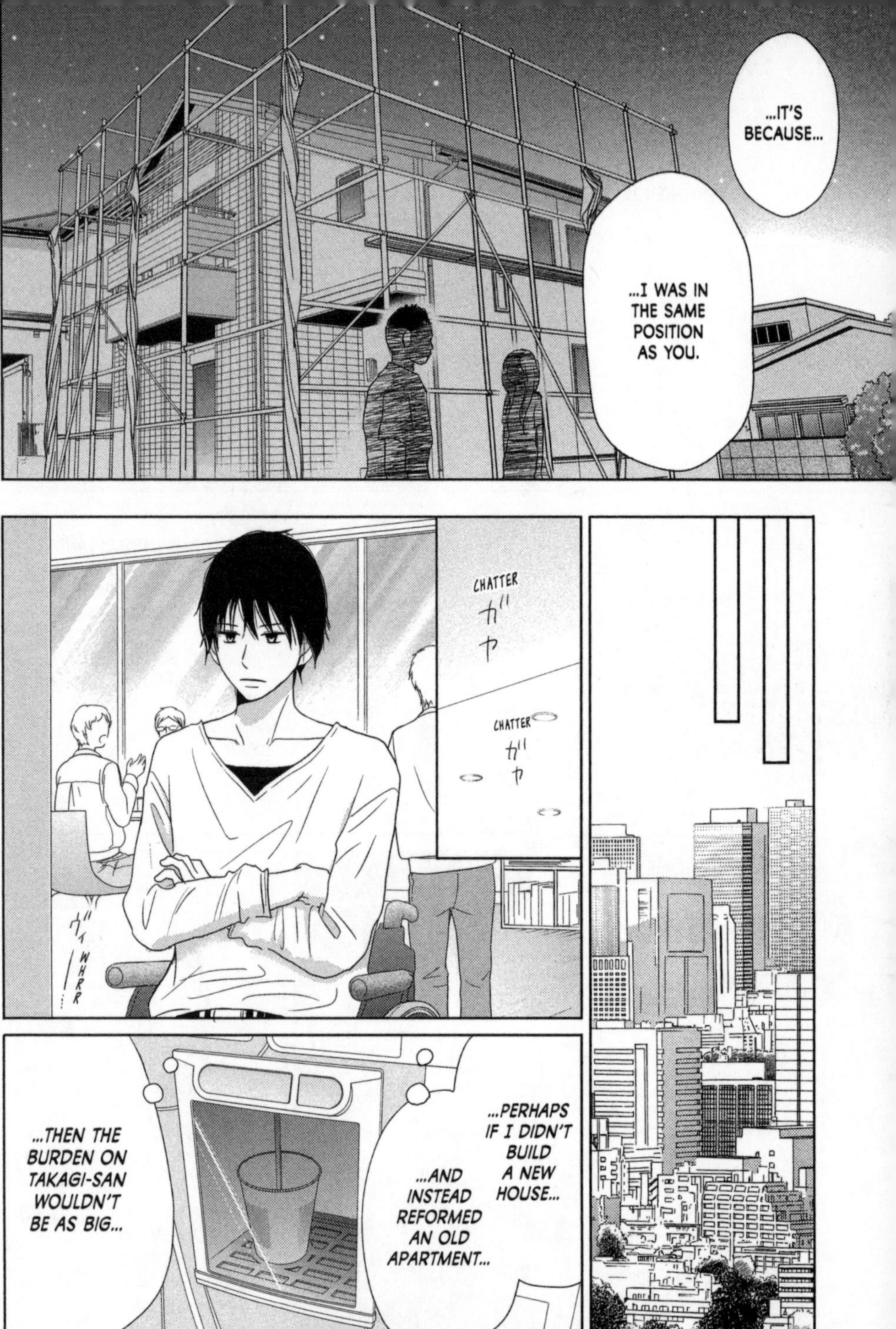
...IT'S BECAUSE...
...I WAS IN THE SAME POSITION AS YOU.
CHATTER ガヤ
CHATTER ガヤ
WHRR ヴィー...
...PERHAPS IF I DIDN'T BUILD A NEW HOUSE...
...AND INSTEAD REFORMED AN OLD APARTMENT...
...THEN THE BURDEN ON TAKAGI-SAN WOULDN'T BE AS BIG...

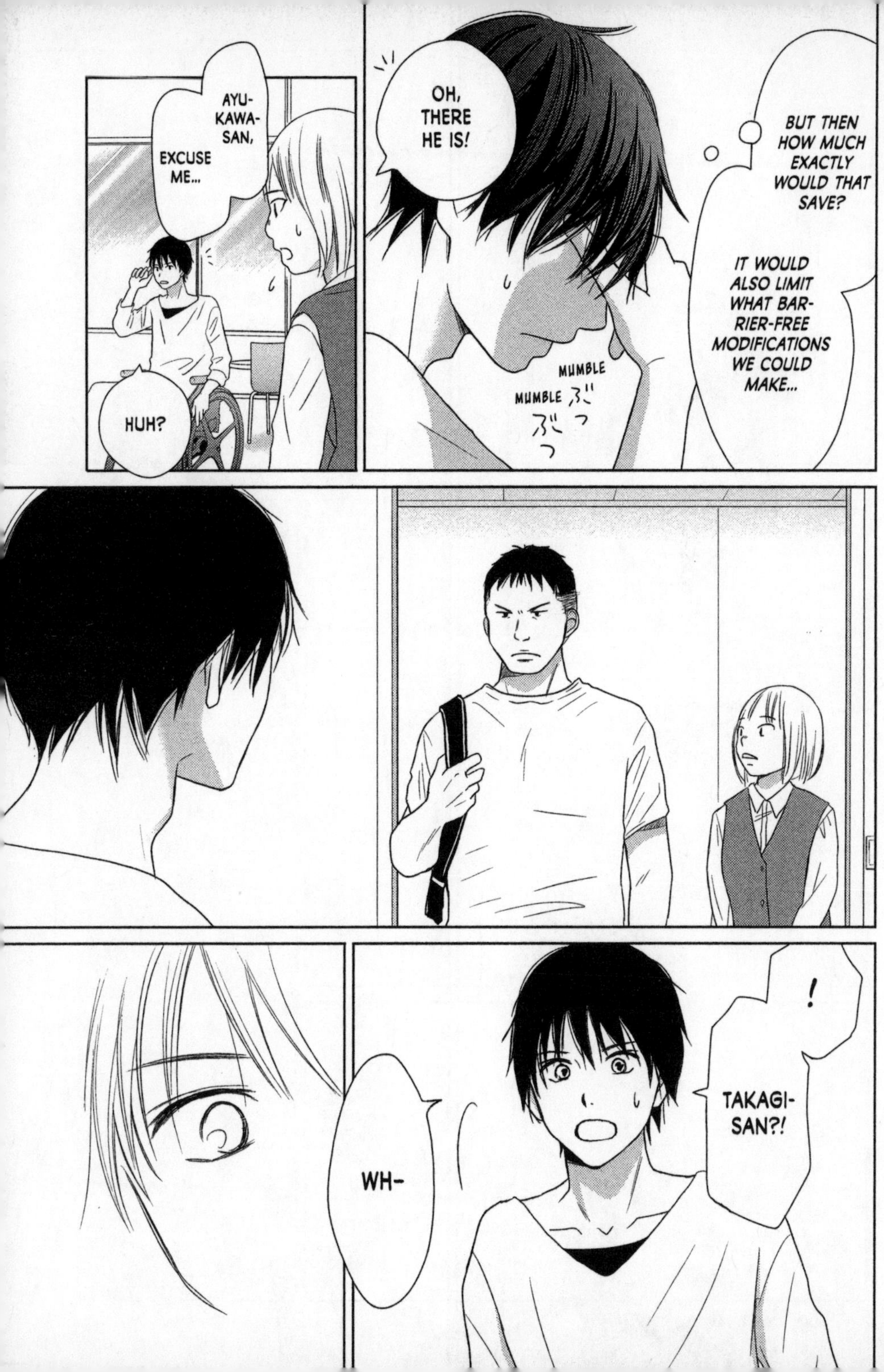
BUT THEN HOW MUCH EXACTLY WOULD THAT SAVE?
IT WOULD ALSO LIMIT WHAT BAR-RIER-FREE MODIFICATIONS WE COULD MAKE...
MUMBLE MUMBLE ぶつぶつ
OH, THERE HE IS!
AYU-KAWA-SAN, EXCUSE ME...
HUH?
!
TAKAGI-SAN?!
WH-

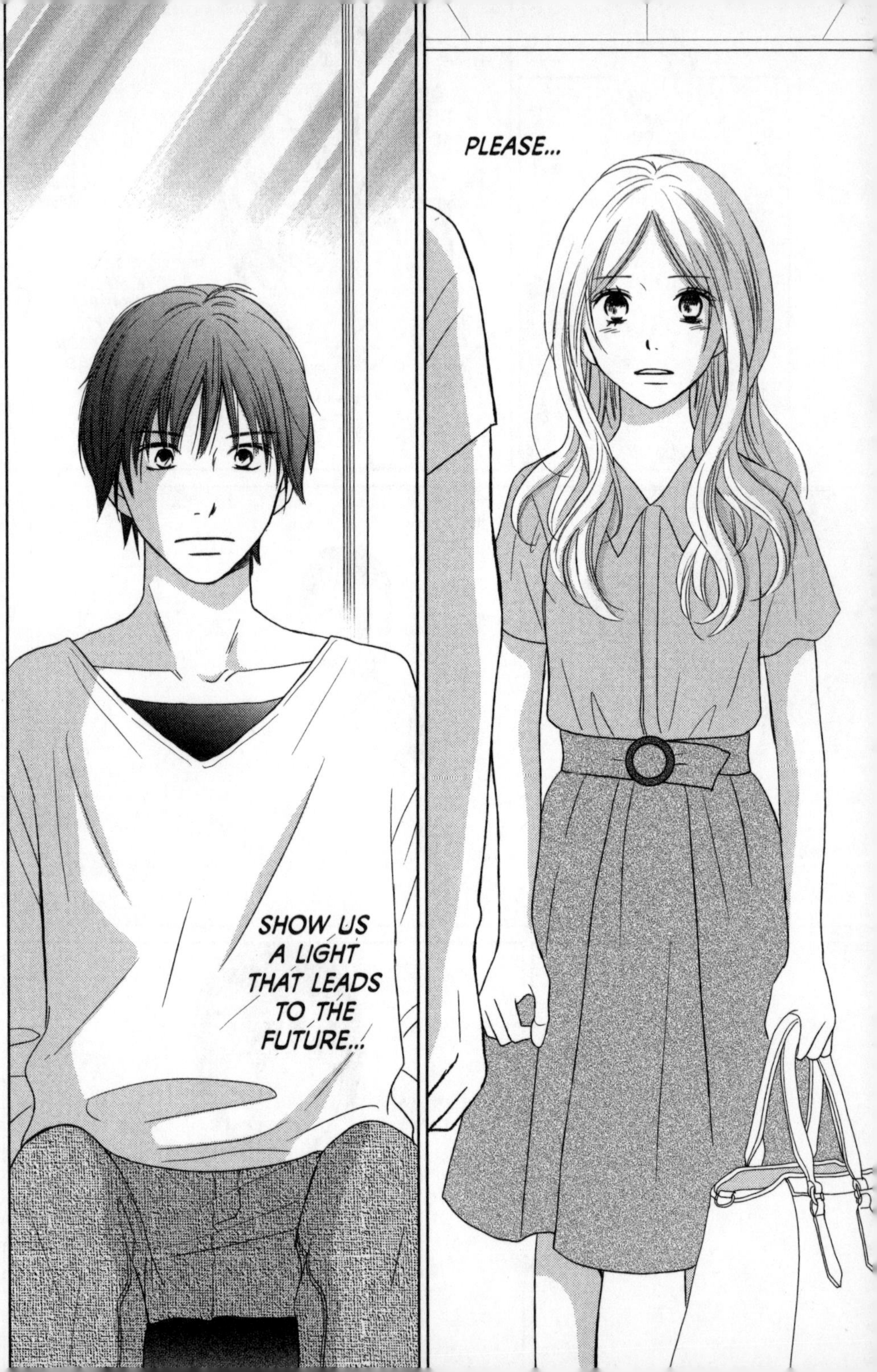
PLEASE...
SHOW US A LIGHT THAT LEADS TO THE FUTURE...

PERFECT WORLD

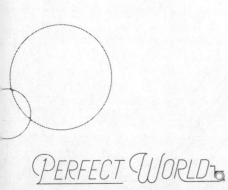

— Thank you for reading *Perfect World* volume five! —

I'm always so encouraged by the warm support from everyone.
Things have passed by so quickly, as we're already on volume five.

Lately, I've been getting a lot of feedback that the turns of events are always
so sad that people want to drop the story. Aaah…⸜⸜ I'm so sorry. To both my
readers, and to my protagonists. Even so, there are those who are hanging in
there and continuing this story. I'm really just so thankful. I will keep trying my
best so that all of you, even if it's really just one person, can keep reading this
story. Hope to see you in the next volume!

I really got a lot of help with this volume. I have to go to Nagoya a lot for
research, but the other day I also went to Nakatsugawa and Kyoto.

At the research site in Nakatsugawa, I ate mashed sweet potato and chestnuts.
I will never forget how delicious it was…

And in Kyoto there was an unprecedented blizzard.
That was tough! But snow-blanketed Tokyo was
very beautiful! ₍ᵒ̴̶̷̤̀ω ᵒ̴̶̷̤́₎

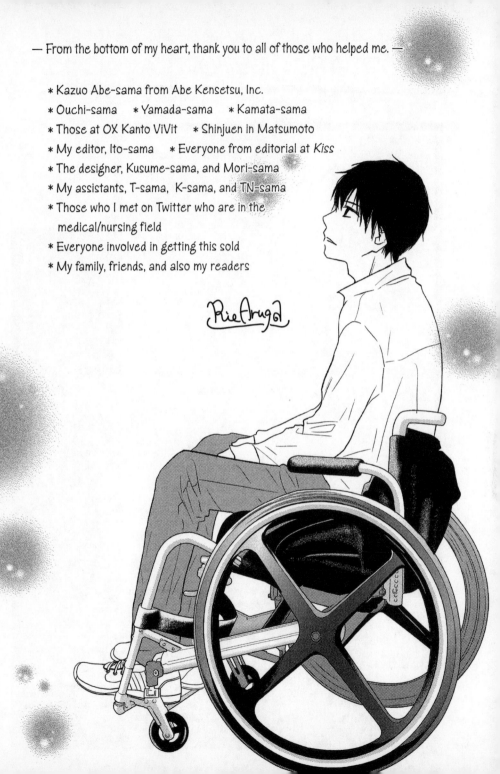

— From the bottom of my heart, thank you to all of those who helped me. —

* Kazuo Abe-sama from Abe Kensetsu, Inc.
* Ouchi-sama   * Yamada-sama   * Kamata-sama
* Those at OX Kanto ViVit   * Shinjuen in Matsumoto
* My editor, Ito-sama   * Everyone from editorial at *Kiss*
* The designer, Kusume-sama, and Mori-sama
* My assistants, T-sama, K-sama, and TN-sama
* Those who I met on Twitter who are in the
  medical/nursing field
* Everyone involved in getting this sold
* My family, friends, and also my readers

Rie Aruga

A SMART, NEW ROMANTIC COMEDY FOR FANS OF *SHORTCAKE CAKE* AND *TERRACE HOUSE*!

Living-Room Matsunaga-san © Keiko Iwashita / Kodansha Ltd.

A romance manga starring high school girl Meeko, who learns to live on her own in a boarding house whose living room is home to the odd (but handsome) Matsunaga-san. She begins to adjust to her new life away from her parents, but Meeko soon learns that no matter how far away from home she is, she's still a young girl at heart — especially when she finds herself falling for Matsunaga-san.

Knight of the Ice ©Yayoi Ogawa/Kodansha Ltd.

SKATING THRILLS AND ICY CHILLS WITH THIS NEW TINGLY ROMANCE SERIES!

Yayoi Ogawa

A rom-com on ice, perfect for fans of *Princess Jellyfish* and *Wotakoi*. Kokoro is the talk of the figure-skating world, winning trophies and hearts. But little do they know... he's actually a huge nerd! From the beloved creator of *You're My Pet* (*Tramps Like Us*).

Chitose is a serious young woman, working for the health magazine *SASSO*. Or at least, she would be, if she wasn't constantly getting distracted by her childhood friend, international figure skating star Kokoro Kijinami! In the public eye and on the ice, Kokoro is a gallant, flawless knight, but behind his glittery costumes and breathtaking spins lies a secret: He's actually a hopelessly romantic otaku, who can only land his quad jumps when Chitose is on hand to recite a spell from his favorite magical girl anime!

THE SWEET SCENT OF LOVE IS IN THE AIR! FOR FANS OF OFFBEAT ROMANCES LIKE *WOTAKOI*

Sweat and Soap © Kintetsu Yamada / Kodansha Ltd.

In an office romance, there's a fine line between sexy and awkward... and that line is where Asako — a woman who sweats copiously — meets Koutarou — a perfume developer who can't get enough of Asako's, er, scent. Don't miss a romcom manga like no other!

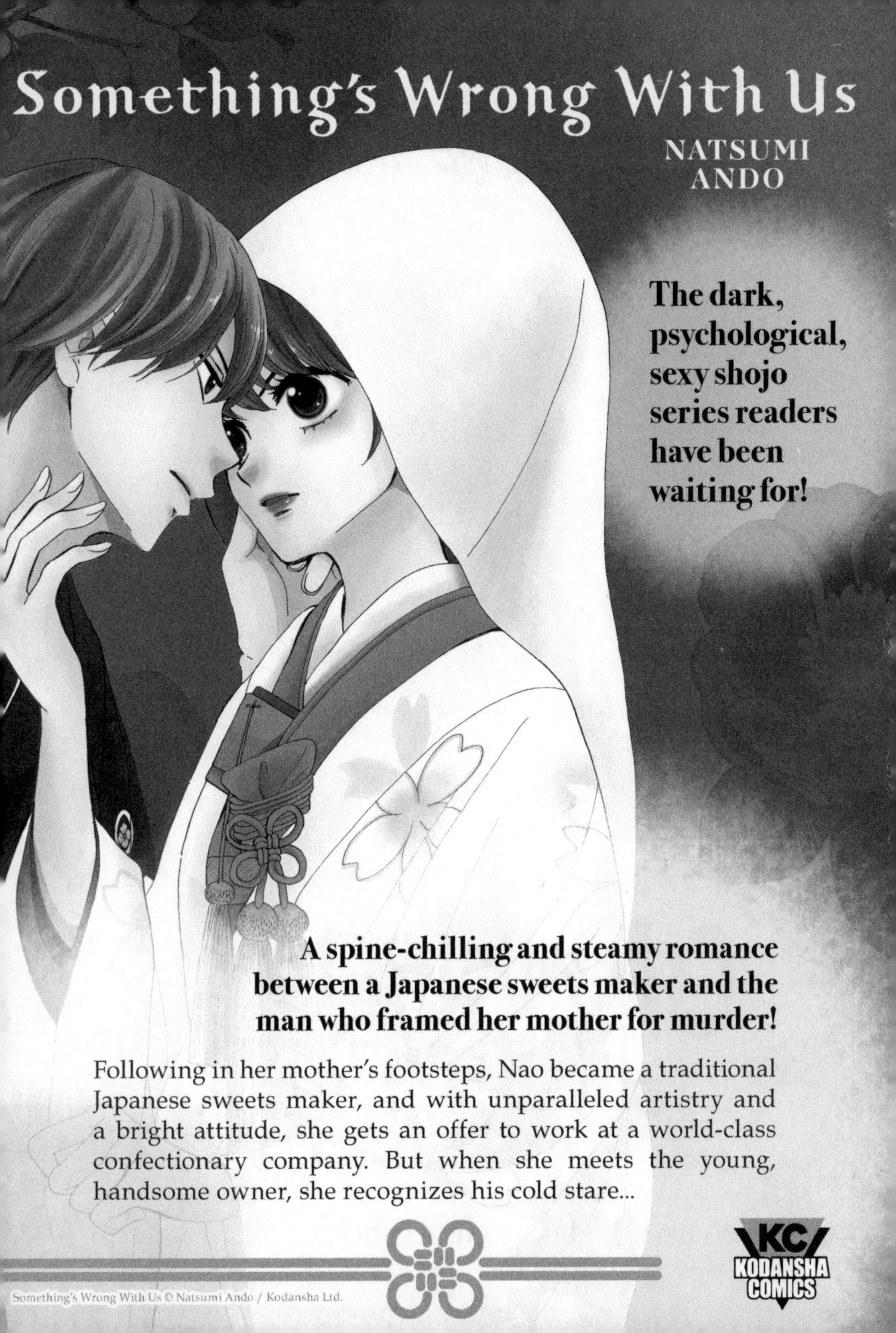
Something's Wrong With Us
NATSUMI ANDO
The dark, psychological, sexy shojo series readers have been waiting for!
A spine-chilling and steamy romance between a Japanese sweets maker and the man who framed her mother for murder!
Following in her mother's footsteps, Nao became a traditional Japanese sweets maker, and with unparalleled artistry and a bright attitude, she gets an offer to work at a world-class confectionary company. But when she meets the young, handsome owner, she recognizes his cold stare...
KC KODANSHA COMICS
Something's Wrong With Us © Natsumi Ando / Kodansha Ltd.

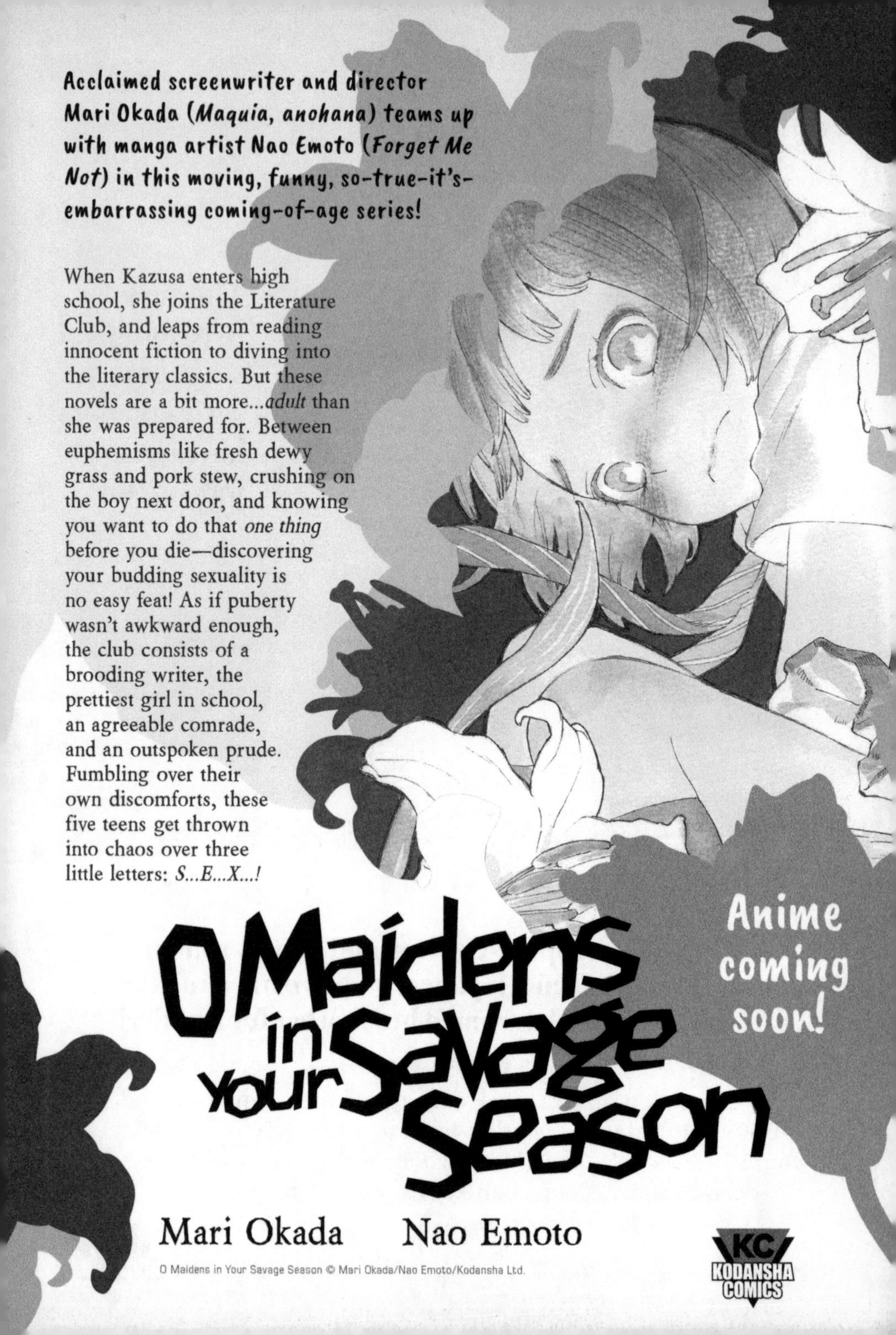

Acclaimed screenwriter and director Mari Okada (*Maquia, anohana*) teams up with manga artist Nao Emoto (*Forget Me Not*) in this moving, funny, so-true-it's-embarrassing coming-of-age series!
When Kazusa enters high school, she joins the Literature Club, and leaps from reading innocent fiction to diving into the literary classics. But these novels are a bit more...*adult* than she was prepared for. Between euphemisms like fresh dewy grass and pork stew, crushing on the boy next door, and knowing you want to do that *one thing* before you die—discovering your budding sexuality is no easy feat! As if puberty wasn't awkward enough, the club consists of a brooding writer, the prettiest girl in school, an agreeable comrade, and an outspoken prude. Fumbling over their own discomforts, these five teens get thrown into chaos over three little letters: *S...E...X...!*
Anime coming soon!
O Maidens in Your Savage Season
Mari Okada
Nao Emoto
O Maidens in Your Savage Season © Mari Okada/Nao Emoto/Kodansha Ltd.
KC KODANSHA COMICS

MAGIC KNIGHT RAYEARTH
25TH ANNIVERSARY EDITION
CLAMP

A BELOVED CLASSIC MAKES ITS STUNNING RETURN IN THIS GORGEOUS, LIMITED EDITION BOX SET!

This tale of three Tokyo teenagers who cross through a magical portal and become the champions of another world is a modern manga classic. The box set includes three volumes of manga covering the entire first series of *Magic Knight Rayearth*, plus the series's super-rare full-color art book companion, all printed at a larger size than ever before on premium paper, featuring a newly-revised translation and lettering, and exquisite foil-stamped covers.

A strictly limited edition, this will be gone in a flash!

KC/
KODANSHA
COMICS

Perfect World 5 is a work of fiction. Names, characters, places, and incidents are the products of or are used fictitiously. Any resemblance persons, living or dead, is ent

A Kodansha Comics Trade Paperback Original
Perfect World 5 copyright © 2017 Rie Aruga
English translation copyright © 2020 Rie Aruga

All rights reserved.

Published in the United States by Kodansha Comics, an imprint of Kodansha USA Publishing, LLC, New York.

Publication rights for this English edition arranged through Kodansha Ltd., Tokyo.

First published in Japan in 2017 by Kodansha Ltd., Tokyo as *Perfect World*, volume 5.

ISBN 978-1-64651-059-7

Original cover design by Tomohiro Kusume and Maiko Mori (arcoinc)

Printed in the United States of America.

www.kodanshacomics.com

9 8 7 6 5 4 3 2 1
Translation: Rachel Murakawa
Lettering: Thea Willis
Additional lettering: Sara Linsley
Editing: Jesika Brooks and Tiff Ferentini
Kodansha Comics edition cover design by Phil Balsman

Publisher: Kiichiro Sugawara

Director of publishing services: Ben Applegate
Associate director of operations: Stephen Pakula
Publishing services managing editor: Noelle Webster
Assistant production manager: Emi Lotto, Angela Zurlo